# Globalization and Social Policy in Africa

# GLOBALIZATION AND SOCIAL POLICY IN AFRICA

Edited by

Tade Akin Aina,
Chachage Seithy L. Chachage
& Elisabeth Annan-Yao

CODESRIA

COUNCIL FOR THE DEVELOPMENT OF
SOCIAL SCIENCE RESEARCH IN AFRICA

**Globalization and Social Policy in Africa**


Avenue Cheikh Anta Diop Angle Canal IV, B.P. 3304 Dakar, 18524, Senegal
Web site: www.codesria.org


ISBN: 2-86978-130-X

Typeset by Sériane Ajavon. Printed by Lightning Source.

First printed in South Africa by UNISA Press

Distributed in Africa by CODESRIA

Distributed elsewhere by
African Books Collective, Unit 13 Kings Meadow, Ferry Hinksey Rd.,
Oxford, OX2, 0DP UK
Website: www.africanbookscollective.com

CODESRIA would like to express its gratitude to the Swedish International Development Cooperation Agency (SIDA/SAREC), the International Development Research Centre (IDRC), Ford Foundation, Mac Arthur Foundation, Carnegie Corporation, the Norwegian Ministry of Foreign Affairs, the Danish Agency for International Development (DANIDA), the French Ministry of Cooperation, the United Nations Programme for Development (UNDP), the Netherlands Ministry of Foreign Affairs, Rockefeller Foundation, FINIDA, NORAD, CIDA, IIEP/ADEA, OECD, IFS, OXFAM America, UN/UNICEF and the Government of Senegal for supporting its research, training and publication programmes.

# Contents

## Part III: Globalization, Women's Work and Citizenship



## Part IV: Higher Education and Globalization

# List of Tables

# 1

# Introduction: How Do We Understand Globalization and Social Policy in Africa?

**Tade Akin Aina***

How do we understand globalization and social policy in Africa today? Can globalization bring Africa significant social and economic benefits? Can it in any positive manner, transform the lives and livelihoods of its peoples? Can it provide a solution to the poverty and underdevelopment that overwhelm the continent or does it aggravate these problems? These are questions evoking many answers, all of which are vigorously contested and forcefully held.

Although it is better understood now than it was in the 1980s, globalization as a process and phenomenon remains an issue whose discussion is embroiled in its own complexity and in the controversy generated by the widely polarized positions held in regard to it. Globalization in Africa, at the turn of the twenty-first Century, has come to mean many things to a wide range of actors and vested interests. Each of these possesses an understanding and viewpoint depending on the vantage point from which the world is seen and what kind of politics and belief system defines its location. However, it cannot be denied that the dominant position defining the understanding of globalization in the world today is taken from a perspective that sees the world from the so-called 'Eurocentric' or 'Economic North' position portraying the world from the perspectives of the dominant political and economic interests prevalent in Europe, Japan and North America (Slater 1995: 367; Aina 1997: 18-20; Nabudere 2000).

Beyond the realm of ideas, and in its unfolding, globalization not only has real meaning but also touches the lives, livelihoods and life chances of many ordinary peoples in Africa. That point of contact, at which globalization, irrespective of how it is defined and perceived, an exercise which, in itself is riddled with contradictions and ambiguities (Aina 1997; Nabudere 2000; Helleiner 2000), intersects with real peoples' lives, is what has rarely been examined in any serious way in recent works on the subject, particularly in Africa.

By focusing on the relationships between globalization and social policy, the contributions in this book attempt an examination of the different areas of significant contacts between globalization and ordinary peoples' lives. This is done through the entry point of that broad area of practice and thought known as social policy. In doing this, the work here posed some challenges that the contributors tackled in different ways. The first, which has remained the perennial character of this terrain of practice and reflection, is the definitional approach, or the specification and clarification of the scope of thought and action covered by the notions of globalization and social policy. As we shall see in this volume, although the usage has not only been contested and contradictory but also confused, according to Helleiner (2000: 2), many of the contributors are clearly unambiguous in their understanding of the notion. A second set, closely related to the first, has to do with the focus of analysis, that is, how do we study a phenomenon and process such as globalization? Is it through an emphasis on a set of abstractions and reflections, or through grappling with existing processes, events and struggles with which people are engaged? Or, is it done through a subtle combination of all these elements? Again, most of the contributors of this volume seem tired of the pretentious, vacuous post-modernist self-flagellation that has been substituted for recent reflections on the subject and prefer the route of more systematic empirical studies.

On the other hand, social policy in Africa is under attack by an array of forces located in the recent history of the continent. The forces include perceptions and realities of the inadequacies and mismanagement of colonial and post-colonial elite rule, the experiences of crisis and adjustment of the 1980s and 1990s, and more significantly, the forces of globalization which were more fully unleashed during the decades of crisis and adjustment in Africa.

This book also constitutes an attempt to document certain aspects of this challenge to social policy in different contexts and parts of Africa. It is, however, more than a set of studies on individual countries, regions and sectors documenting the impact of globalization on social policy. It is part of long drawn-out debate and discussion of the 1980s and 1990s in Africa on how we understand the era of crisis and adjustment, and the related globalization process. It is about how these affected institutions, policies and peoples in contemporary Africa. It is also about the transformation of the roles of the state and other social and economic sectors in social provisioning and human development, in an increasingly transnational world.

However, any meaningful and relevant analysis of globalization and social policy in Africa must start with an understanding of the twin processes of poverty and development. It must investigate both process and context as they relate to the recent history and experiences of the different countries. Such an analysis must revisit the 'development process', its promises and failures, and, in particular, the recent epoch of persistent crisis and adjustment. It must also recognize the significance of the era of crisis, not only for the development process, but also for overall policy-making. An important further component of such an analysis is the understanding of what can be called development 'consciousness'. This refers to the ways people perceive, think, and are conscious of development as a process intended to transform their lives, and improve their material and other well-being in a positive and beneficial direction.

These elements of the analysis are important because one of the major consequences of Africa's prolonged crisis (and her encounter with globalization), has been not only the delegitimization and undermining of the African state and the erosion of its capacity to provide basic and other forms of services, but also the emergence of a form of social consciousness that denies the validity and relevance of both social policy in the development process and the development process itself as a key element of social transformation. Quite often, this denial is couched in the technocratic language of public sector and social policy reform (involving rationalization, privatization, deregulation and liberalization) that challenges the basis and practice of what used to be conventional social and basic services provisioning.

As the various contributions in this book demonstrate, this systematic denial and reorientation of the nature and role of social policy are the result of Africa's encounter with the current era of globalization. This encounter has been facilitated and accompanied by the appropriation of the responsibility for economic and social development management in several African countries by International Financial Institutions (IFIs) in the 1980s and 1990s. This appropriation has been defined mainly in terms of the dominance of a neo-liberal market fundamentalist doctrine emphasizing unrestrained and often partially considered deregulation, liberalization and privatization of social and basic services (Mkandawire and Olukoshi 1995; Mkandawire and Soludo 1999). The contributions in this book question both the process and the outcomes of this imposition and facilitation of the globalization process in Africa today. They point out that rather than improving the quality of life for Africa's peoples, the approach has only worsened it. In other words, globalization has attacked the development process as it relates to ordinary poor peoples. It is the development process seen not as mere economic growth, but as a holistic process of systematic transformation of citizens' livelihood in a beneficial manner. The development process is also expected to enhance the attainment of individual and collective well-being, eliminate poverty and advance emancipation from domination, socio-economic injustice and inequality. In short, in the words of Armatya Sen (1999), it is 'development as freedom'. More than ever, Africa's encounter with globalization has revealed that Africa needs not only to reclaim this kind of meaningful development, but also to face the challenges of social and economic reconstruction. This is with particular reference to the rebuilding of social institutions and support systems eroded by years of neglect, war, mismanagement and crisis, and the efforts made by both internal and external forces to undermine them.

This book argues in many subtle ways that reclaiming meaningful development and reconstructing African societies in the era of their encounter with globalization can be tackled effectively only through systematic and sustained social, economic and political initiatives. These involve the struggle for good governance and basic rights, and the establishment of sustainable and relevant economic development strategies that include frameworks for coherent and appropriate social policies geared towards building and rebuilding institutions, recovering peoples' self-confidence and renewing social integration and social justice.

However, as many of the contributors noted, systematic state-led social provisioning was one of the earliest victims of the International Financial Institutions' solutions to the economic crisis that ravaged the nations of Africa. Conventional social policy, in terms of provision of basic services by the state, was generally seen as wasteful and negative, contributing little or nothing to economic growth and national revenues. This book challenges the undifferentiated negative view of social policy. It attempts to show that social policy is an intrinsic aspect of a meaningful development process, especially during stages of transition and reconstruction such as we have in most of Africa today. It further challenges the undemocratic and non-participatory manner in which IFIs, policy experts and African governments reviewed and eliminated these policies. They particularly failed to consult or provide for the participation of the supposed beneficiaries and stakeholders, especially the marginalized and excluded sectors such as the urban poor, peasants, poor women, children, the youth and the elderly.

This technocratic and managerial insensitivity and arrogance bring up a point that requires endless reiteration. It is the fact that concern with social policy and social development is not a mere 'technocratic' and at times 'sectoralist' concern with 'welfare' or policy-making as a means to some distant acknowledgement of the need for 'poverty alleviation'. Concern with social policy and social development is at the heart of a deep preoccupation with human development and its objectives of transforming the human condition. In other words, it is primarily a concern with human well-being, how it is conceived, organized and institutionalized, and how the burdens and benefits of achieving it are distributed across various classes and sectors of society. This concern, of course, is not new and can be traced back to earlier debates on the nature of social inequality and justice and how this should be tackled. These issues are still on the theoretical and policy agenda, as evidenced by the concern with the social policy debate expressed by politicians and intellectuals worldwide (Torres 1995).

## Lessons learned from the studies

The studies in this volume present a set of lessons for understanding the relationship between globalization and social policy. Rather than returning to the extensive discussions of the definitional questions, I shall attempt to use the examination of the key lessons learned here to discuss how the key issues and the contributors handle other methodological questions.

### * That globalization has not been necessarily benign, as far as Africa and Africans are concerned

This position runs through the contributions in this volume. Although primarily related to the definitional question, this position is not completely determined by that question; and in many ways it is no longer a new story told by African researchers alone. The United Nations Development Programme (UNDP), in its 1999 Human Development Report, comes to the same conclusion about the different elements of globalization, namely the economic, political, technological and cultural, for vast areas of the developing world. Africa and South Asia constituted the least advantaged regions of the world in this report. The United Nations Research Institute for Social Development (UNRISD) does the same in some of its publications such as 'State of Disarray' (UNRISD 1995). It is this position that made authors like Jan Pieterse note that '...globalization generates so much anxiety, insecurity and resistance' (Pieterse 2000: xxi). In Africa, globalization has not only generated so much anxiety, insecurity and resistance; it has generated an almost unanimous perception of polarization, pain and greater inequality along with a feeling of almost insurmountable threat to ordinary peoples' livelihoods and cultures.

The authors in this volume however seem to focus on economic globalization, a more specific aspect of globalization. Apart from Ibeano, whose study is on refugees and humanitarianism, the other African authors consider globalization mainly from the point of view of economic liberalization, privatization, market and state deregulation and the roles played by the International Monetary Fund (IMF) and the World Bank in imposing this process through economic reform packages and structural adjustment programmes (SAPS). In fact, many of the authors citing Ghai (1992) and Samir Amin (1992, 1998) were explicit in seeing globalization and structural adjustment programmes as identical twins, if not one and the same. It was pointed out that the economic reform policies neither recognized nor respected the complexity and diversity of the political economies of the African countries and therefore imposed homogenous neo-liberal market fundamentalist solutions to their economic crises. Thus, the pervasive poverty, multiplicity of crises and the need for a comprehensive process of social reconstruction and institution building were not central to the adjustment packages. Of course, poverty worsened, with per capita incomes in Africa in 1999 lower than they were in 1970 (UNDP 1999: 36).

As far as Africa is concerned, one related aspect of the malignant nature of globalization was that, as in many other places like Indonesia and parts of Eastern Europe and the old Soviet Union, globalization was imposed through adjustment programmes, regardless of the social integration-oriented political systems and institutions. The much-touted goals of political liberalization supposedly advanced in most of the African countries paid only lip service to genuine participatory democracy and the social integration of the marginalized and excluded poor peoples of these countries. Thus, economic liberalization was often accompanied by increased repression and oppression (Mkandawire and Olukoshi 1995), mass violation of human rights and increased personal and collective insecurity through insurrections, civil wars, banditry, organized crime and the collapse of state-provided social support systems. Finally, the deliberate neglect of history and issues of social justice and democratic governance led to attacks on existing policies and efforts meant to redress historical wrongs such as the massive programmes to combat the effects of apartheid in South Africa and other social programmes in education and health initiated for the poor and other groups. These programmes were seen in different parts of Africa as populist and lacking sound economic sense. As Adejumobi, Magubane, Ben Hammouda, Alubo and other authors in this volume have shown, such social policy efforts are not only an integral part of an effective economic development strategy, as they built human resources and social capital, but they are also central to the political legitimization of regimes and indispensable for cementing social integration.

*** That social policy is inseparable from an economic and human development strategy**

Like globalization, the definition of what constitutes social policy is complicated by history, ideological and political differences and the dominant orientations of the communities of practice (Townsend 1975; Bramley 1986; MacPherson and Midgley 1987; Aina 1997, 1999; Deacon 1997). These points above have led to a wide range of different definitions linked to specific welfare and social security traditions. However, they have in common varying degrees of understanding of the roles and use of social provisioning, social regulation and social distribution in 'fighting, alleviating, reducing or eliminating' poverty. Social policy is, therefore, often viewed from either a narrow, sectoralist and often 'managerialist' perspective focussed on the administration of social welfare and social security, or from a more holistic and transformational perspective of social development.

The contributors in this volume preferred to work with the latter, broader definition of social policy, even when they seem to focus on social services and social welfare delivery, as Adejumobi does in his chapter. Hence, there is a linking of social policy with the colonial experience, the history of underdevelopment, the pervasiveness of poverty and the political projects of ruling elite and regimes. Social policy is thus seen as 'the set of systematic and deliberate interventions in social life..., to ensure the satisfaction of basic needs and the well-being of citizens. It is an expression of socially desirable goals through legislation, institutions and administrative programs and practices in accordance with specific development objectives'(Aina 1999:73). The contributions in this book ranged from a focus on the use of social policy to eliminate poverty, as an aspect of the more visionary positions within the nationalist project of the independence movements, to the post-colonial perversion and instrumentalization of 'neo-traditional' social policy efforts, such as the 'Harambee', for gaining electoral support. These trends appear with more or less clarity in the contributions of Adejumobi, Ben Hammouda, C. U. Okoye and U. O. Okoye, and Pius Kakai Wanyonyi. Ben Hammouda also explores the question of social policy as central to the legitimization of regimes. They further show how when such legitimization is eroded, alternative and anti-state forces like the Islamic fundamentalist groups in the Maghreb can undermine state legitimacy through their own mechanisms of social provisioning. Gimode, in his study of Islam and social policy in Kenya, examined the spaces provided by political neglect and the exclusion of specific ethnic and religious groups. While discussing the role of Islamic philanthropy in filling these social and political spaces, he did not explicitly pursue the implications of these activities for the political de-legitimization of the state and the possible growth of political Islam.

Poverty trends and reduction, protection of the vulnerable, and enhancement of individual and social capabilities as the responsibility of the state and society, are related themes of social policy delivery that Aredo, Alubo, Chachage, Mohammed Yunusa, Ndiaye, Anugwom and Anugwom, Ibeano, and Okoye and Okoye examined in their wide-ranging interpretation of social policy, which encompassed the provision of urban services, the reform of higher education and the status of refugees, income, pension, employment and social security policies. The transformations that globalization has occasioned through public policy reforms and adjustment policies were the focus of analysis of these studies. From the rich array of the materials, we learn from these studies that the making of social or any other policy for that matter, is not always an innocent and neutral act resulting mainly from a balanced, objective analysis of reality or sheer altruism. Social policies in Africa are often the subject of manipulation and influence by diverse interests and are riddled with inequalities of gender, race, class, region and age. Certain inequalities such as those of gender, for example, despite being highly negative and visible, are rarely perceived as reproducing systematic social and economic inequities in the predominantly patriarchal societies and sexist states. Gender blindness and discrimination still constitute the predominant characteristics of the economic and social policies formulated and implemented in most of Africa. This is without any consideration of the unequal relations between the sexes either in the households, or in terms of access to strategic resources, such as land and credit (Sow 1993), or in key areas such as education, health, employment and politics. Gender inequality is therefore a persistent aspect of conventional social policy, with the result that, rather than empowering women, social policies contribute to reinforcing and expanding inequitable relations and structures (Williams 1989; Etta 1994).

Another important lesson from this volume is that the years of crisis and adjustment have fundamentally transformed social policy as we know it in Africa, from its colonial and post-colonial forms. As the contributions show, social policy in Africa is being reworked through economic reforms and the forces of globalization. A lot of the changes have negative forms as they further strip already vulnerable groups of their traditional protection. But there is also a significant amount of transnational effort that is positive transformation and in favour of poor people (Fowler 1992, 1995; Deacon 2000). Unfortunately, apart from Ibeano and Alfred Inis Ndiaye, no other contributors devoted much attention to a detailed analysis of social policies as carried out by international civil society organizations, multilateral and bilateral aid agencies and development institutions. These efforts that Deacon (2000) has characterized as 'global social policy', are more complex and diverse than is generally assumed. Although still subject to the dominant pressure of neo-liberal thinking and ideas, there are strong currents of dissent based on the ideology and social foundations of some of these organizations, and more recently, their encounter with the transitions in post-communist societies of Eastern Europe (Deacon 2000).

Currents of transnational and global social policies are therefore emerging and contributing to reshape the terrain of social policy formulation and implementation in the Third World in general and Africa in particular. These policies are carried out by a wide range of institutions and organizations such as the multilateral and bilateral donor agencies, the social justice international NGOs such as Oxfam, Christian Aid, Action Aid and their allies. The different approaches compete with the dominant positions of the World Bank and the International Monetary Fund, and while they possess less influence with national governments, they are beginning to constitute a basis for pluralism and alternatives in policies.

### * That the state remains the dominant arena of social policy-making and implementation in transitional and fragmented societies

A recurrent element in the contributions to this book is the impact that the dominant neo-liberal policies that have constituted a key element of adjustment led globalization, have had on state power and role in African countries.

The authors treading the well-worn paths of studies on the politics of structural adjustment in Africa (Mkandawire and Olukoshi 1995), show how the emphasis on the reduction of the role of the state, on privatization and the retrenchment of public sector workers has contributed to weakening state capacities not only for the delivery of social and basic services, but also for organizing and managing public safety and security and guaranteeing an optimal environment for private investment and enterprises.

The argument for reconsidering the role of the state in Africa is not one that is unaware of the misuse and mismanagement of resources that have been a feature of the post-colonial state in Africa. It is an argument that recognizes these limitations but at the same time situates them in the context of African nations as transitional societies emerging from decades of crises and adjustments, and in which several key social and public institutions have either been damaged and perverted, or allowed to decay. The challenge is therefore not an undifferentiated attack on the state as a key public institution, but rather, that of a process of reconstructing and reconfiguring the state to ensure greater responsiveness and relevance and increased accountability and effectiveness. Macro-economic policies that do not include carefully considered processes of political changes, that do not emphasize inclusion, decentralization, devolution, participation, and consultation of national and local stakeholders and sectors, cannot lead to a legitimate and meaningful reconstruction of the state and the establishment of acceptable national agendas and projects. As repeatedly pointed out by authors such as Adejumobi, Ben Hammouda and Magubane, several features of the globalization process have only complicated the legitimization strategy of African politics, even for regimes that set out to effect social justice agendas such as the African National Congress government of the post-apartheid South Africa. A central element of the legitimization strategy has been the provision of basic social services such as education, primary health care, water and sanitation, and in some cases, employment, at affordable costs to marginalized and excluded groups. It is the state and governmental institutions that have been the key providers of these services in Africa. The non-state actors, irrespective of their localized efficiency and effectiveness, have not yet attained the coverage and presence of state and state-related institutions.

*** That Africa's solutions to the social policy and development crisis must come from within in order to be sustainable and legitimate**

Although the authors in this volume do not spend much time on solutions to the social policy crisis, they recognize that it is a political crisis. And therefore, its solution must start from the political domain rather than that of macroeconomics. The experience with the failure of the structural adjustment programmes to obtain internal legitimacy and create any meaningful and substantial local constituencies over the past two decades shows that externally-imposed solutions will only fail, even after extensive investments. Thus, the politics of structural adjustment in Africa has not been a transformational and participatory politics. This, unfortunately, is the lesson that the World Bank is assumed to have learnt with the Poverty Reduction Strategy Process (PRSP), its new social policy agenda. However, formal participation without recognition of the material and social interests of the largest sectors of the population and a process of consensus–building and inclusion will not build the legitimacy and the necessary constituencies that the nationalist and liberation struggles in Africa once won for the nationalist politicians. Again, the importance of the role of the state and public institutions, political parties, business, labour and civil society and cultural institutions is central here. The point at this juncture is that post-crisis and post-adjustment transformation strategies and processes, while recognizing past errors of post-colonial politics in Africa, cannot obtain the legitimate mandate for any meaningful movement forward without reclaiming the fundamentals of human development.

However, apart from these lessons, this introduction will not be complete if we do not point out an omission of the examination of the trends in the evolution of social policy in Africa. While some of the contributors work with some mode of periodizing the specific countries or regions of their concern, there is an absence of explicitly stated trends that map the way social policy has developed across the continent and how encountering globalization has affected it.

## Broad trends in social policy

Given the importance of the need to situate the context, I will attempt a brief and broad summary of these trends. Before going any further, we need to remind ourselves that social policy in Africa has not been static. It has evolved in response to the major events in the history of the national formations and changes in international and global dynamics. Broadly speaking, Africa's relevant history can be divided into the colonial and post-colonial periods. This applies to most of the continent's countries, except for a few ones that were either subjected to attempts at conquest or were parts of the sphere of influence of the colonial powers, even though they never experienced formal colonial domination. However, this characterization does not represent an undifferentiated development, and within each period, there are distinct phases with specific trends often shaped by particular national experiences, as the contributions by Ben Hammouda, Magubane and Aredo show.

## The colonial period

The colonial period was very complex, with great variations across and within regions and countries. These variations resulted both from the ways societies were differentially incorporated into the global capitalist system and from the functions they fulfilled within it (Amin 1976). The cultural and political peculiarities of the colonial power or source of influence—be it Belgian, British,

French, Portuguese or Italian (to a lesser extent)—also affected how specific states and political economies emerged.

Formal social policy in Africa during the colonial period emerged from these complex and often contradictory influences shaped by 'the ideologies and structures of state provision', which 'reflected a very narrow interpretation of social welfare' (Boyden 1990: 200). As a result, colonial social policy was largely determined by the colonial mission, and it took a residualist approach. In different parts of Africa, the colonial mission was shaped and interpreted through the pressures of dominant interest groups such as missionaries, settlers, traders, mining groups, colonial officials (military and administrative) and privileged local groups such as kings and chiefs and some ethnic and racial intermediaries such as 'mulattos', 'assimilados', Asian and Levantine business men.

Colonial social policy was also restrictive both socially and spatially. In many cases, across Africa, social services were located only in urban areas or neighbourhoods where colonizers were found in large numbers. According to Boyden, 'the type of welfare services provided... reflected the concerns of the rulers rather than the needs of the ruled' (1990: 180).

One of the explicit priorities of colonial governments was to provide protection for the expatriate community against a hostile physical environment. The Nigerian health service, for example, was established in the areas where expatriates lived primarily as a result of the great fire that consumed Lagos in 1877 and the outbreak of bubonic plague in 1924. The expatriate settlers and colonial administrators were also worried about the threat to themselves of youth crime, and made begging, vagrancy and public order concerns predominant.

One outcome of the concentration of social services and other forms of amenities in these colonial centres was the emergence of cities with origins in colonization and the growth of uneven and unequal spatial and socio-economic development. Social policy was thus selective, discriminatory and exclusionary, geared towards protecting and advancing colonial interests and those of white settlers (Patel 1992). Social policy benefited the local population only if it played an important role in the colonial structure or if continuous exclusion could fundamentally threaten colonial interests. For example, colonial powers only introduced environmental health services in coastal West Africa once malaria had become rampant in the region.

### The Post-colonial period

With the transition from colonial to post-colonial administration, social policy took on completely different functions and objectives. It became a means of legitimizing the new regimes constructed by the African post-colonial states. The era that can be described as the post-colonial period included two distinct overlapping phases. The first is the early post-independence or nationalist phase. The second is the crisis and adjustment phase that ushered in the period marked by the dominance of neo-liberal market fundamentalist ideology and the approach to global capitalism. This latter phase had its clearest manifestation in the economic crisis of the 1970s, which expressed the process of global restructuring of capitalism.

### The early post-independence or nationalist phase

This phase roughly refers to the first 10 to 15 years of independence for most countries of Africa, ranging from the late 1950s to the mid-1970s. It coincides not only with the attainment of independence by most states in Africa but also with a surge of nation-building and development projects, heady optimism, collective self-confidence, and some economic growth, albeit over a short period. This 'happy' period ended with the first global economic crisis, attributed to the increase in petroleum prices endorsed by the Organization of Petroleum Exporting Countries (OPEC). Along with the oil crisis, and its associated economic downturn, other phenomena began to take shape. These included drought and famine resulting from the Sahelian ecological disasters, and a wave of persistent political problems. These political problems included the spread of authoritarian and undemocratic regimes, the rise of insurrections and civil wars, and the consequent near collapse of the state and legitimate political order in places like Burundi, Liberia, Rwanda and Congo Kinshasa.

This phase was one of consolidation and expansion of the neo-colonial accumulation model that characterized the development paths of much of Africa's political economy. Central to this model was the legitimization strategy of the populist, and in some cases, socialist programmes of the nationalist movements and parties that came to power after independence. A key element of the legitimization strategy was a strong social policy initiative tied to a 'constructionist' approach to economic development, that is, the building of physical and social as well as human infrastructures. This was the period of 'constructing' elaborate social subsidies and major social programmes in education, housing, health, urban planning. These were matched by the construction of new physical signs of nationhood, such as airports, military bases, skyscrapers, five-star hotels, elite residential estates, parliamentary and office complexes, and the sites of the early import-substitution and export-processing industries. It was an era that also witnessed some affluence for the more privileged strata and classes of most African nations. At the same time, it was an era that witnessed the demand for greater space in the political and economic spheres by vocal social groups such as the growing urban workers and the emerging middle classes. As captured in Ben Hammouda's contribution, this phase was predominantly geared towards expanding social and economic structures to incorporate rising indigenous interests and groups barred from the colonial systems. Addressing these demands was central to the nationalist legitimization model and constituted perhaps the core of an attempt to 'spread the fruits of independence' to those groups with greater clout. A social policy framework directed at social provisioning rather than distribution or social regulation was key to this model.

However, the accumulation and legitimization models ran into trouble and soon reached the real limits of their capacity to incorporate more and more new elements both socially and economically, given finite resources, unfavorable global economic trends, increasing corruption and rapidly growing populations. From the late 1960s to the early 1970s, the core elements of the 'nationalist project' began to disintegrate politically. The struggle for legitimization and incorporation gave way to increasing authoritarianism and monolithic politics. The emergence and consolidation of one-party states became a common feature, as identified with military regimes run increasingly through clientelist and personal rule mechanisms. With this decline of popular democratic politics and the collapse of the economies, the social policy frameworks became equally eroded and downplayed. Social services and social infrastructures decayed, from sheer neglect and mismanagement or, where they existed in rudimentary forms, were appropriated by local barons and misused for political patronage.

### The crisis and adjustment era

This is the era that we recognize as containing that constellation of forces in the contemporary spread of global capitalism now known as globalization. It expressed the social and economic forces and dynamics now at play in the context of globalization and that have produced changes in political and economic regimes in addition to redefining patterns of social relations between economic and social groups and ethnic and gender relations. Ibeano, Anugwom and Anugwom, Magubane, Wanyonyi, Gimode and Ben Hammouda, all in their various chapters in this book, have attempted to deal with different aspects of these changes. In fact, such changes have reorganized the social and class structures of the colonial and nationalist era, creating new sets of winners and losers, of which the vast majority of the population are the latter. In this phase, economic crisis expressed in persistent economic decline, 'the debt crisis', and the resultant attempts to implement externally-imposed economic recovery programmes were the dominant features of most African countries.

As many of the authors in this book have pointed out, the World Bank and the International Monetary Fund designed a set of policies and strategies to respond to this crisis. These policies, if not directly designed by them, were implemented with their assistance and oriented by their philosophy and their perception of the correct economic strategy. These globalized responses to national problems, often aimed at 'stabilizing' or 'adjusting' the economies, were formulated in market fundamentalist terms and conceived as palliatives for economies maladjusted by excessive state intervention, price distortions and excessive subsidization of urban sectors. At the beginning, these predominantly macro-economic strategies neither considered local nor national politics, nor showed concern for the 'softer' human dimensions of social equity and justice. As the authors in this volume demonstrate, structural adjustment policies greatly affected social policies, social provisioning and the overall well-being of the populations. Privatization, commercialization and reduction in neglect or complete government withdrawal directly affected social policies and social provisioning. With the above changes, ordinary peoples and communities had little or no option but to resort to autonomous and creative means of ensuring the satisfaction of basic needs. Although suffering from intense deprivations, they took steps to avail themselves of those services the state neglected or had no capacity to provide. There was also the response from organized philanthropy and the emerging global civil society in the form of international, regional and national Non-Governmental Organizations and some international agencies and groups including members of the United Nations family such as UNICEF and the UNDP. The impact of these pressures and criticisms was the emergence of Adjustment-related social policy responses, again designed principally by the World Bank and meant to mitigate or reduce the 'social costs of adjustment'. These, and the efforts of ordinary citizens' groups, communities and the non-governmental sector, constituted what one can call the social policy efforts of the adjustment and crisis era—the era of contemporary globalization. These have three major features in terms of both their agents and implementation.

First, there is the new type of local, small-scale provider of social services. These differ from the conventional indigenous sources of social provisioning based on the social solidarity systems of families, lineages and kinship (Aina 1997). These providers are often private initiatives operating along the lines of the informal sector, mainly for a fee. They involve a wide range of service provision, such as waste disposal, sale of water, education, and road construction and repairs, among others. These are actually locally-based, rudimentary, often crude and informal modes of social provisioning that emerged in response to the failure or withdrawal of state provisioning.

A second feature is the expansion of the role of the communities, individual volunteers and philanthropy in service provision. This response covers a wide range of institutional forms and traditions, including those based on indigenous cultures, religious concepts and beliefs and imported forms of organized philanthropy. Their roles include provision of both voluntary and compulsory services such as road building, drainage clearing, environmental sanitation, social defense, neighbourhood watches and vigilante groups. As Gimode and Wanyonyi show in their chapters, they also carry out relief and emergency functions. The institutionalization of these services takes on different forms.

The volunteer sector has also witnessed the growth of both local and international non-governmental organizations (NGOs), often initiated, encouraged and funded by both private foundations and other multilateral and bilateral donors (Aina 1993). These agents have come to play a major role in redefining social policy priorities and formalizing and diffusing the application of institutional and managerial approaches to their implementation. They are spreading the use of accounting systems and modes of financial reporting, management and governance structures, and even ideological and value systems for 'NGO service culture, lifestyle and language' (Aina 1993: 140). In other words, in addition to carrying out what Fowler described as the 'internationalization of welfare' (Fowler 1992, 1995) NGOs are also internationalizing institutional structures, approaches and ideologies.

A third feature—perhaps the most significant, because it implies an extensive investment in resources—is the emergence of a generation of neo-liberal social policies or adjustment-driven social policies. These involve responses of the International Financial Institutions, principally the World Bank and The International Monetary Fund, to the criticisms leveled by scholars, NGOs, communities and some UN institutions at the different phases of the adjustment programmes in Africa. These attempts at providing a 'human face' to adjustment involved the design of what was initially described as the 'social dimensions of adjustment' (SDAs), carried out in Africa as 'Programmes to Mitigate the Social Costs of Adjustment' (PAMSCADs). More recently, we have the 'rediscovery' and 'rehabilitation' of poverty and participation in the Poverty Reduction Strategy Process (PRSP). This is a very important characteristic of current social policy and its globalized dimension, not only because the main agents are the IFIs, particularly the World Bank, and governments of the region, but also because this is beginning to lay the basis for social policy in the age of globalization. Although Inis Ndiaye and Ibeano address this trend peripherally in this volume, it is an important issue in many ways. The first is that efforts to design neo-liberal social policies are being harmonized and replicated across countries and are affecting the lives of millions of peoples. Initially, these new policies operating as SDAs were designed and implemented with little or no debate in the countries affected and with little or no real participation of the recipients in identifying their needs. As Ndiaye has shown in this volume, despite the lack of regard for basic democratic and participatory principles, some of these projects are presented at the micro-level as participatory interventions. In practice, however, they are often designed by foreign specialists and usually managed and evaluated, using indicators and benchmarks about which the subjects are never consulted. The SDAs were therefore alienating, top-down interventions. Scholars such as Hutchful (1994), Gayi (1995), Mhone (1995) and Vivian (1995) have offered effective criticisms of these neo-liberal social policy initiatives.

These authors stress the fact that:

> SDAs tend to be short- to medium-term; they focus mainly on public works and infrastructure-rehabilitation and employment-generation programs; they concentrate on building specific skills, particularly those at inferior artisanal levels; they tend to put emphasis on private-sector inputs, namely, through small-scale contractors and entrepreneurs, micro-enterprises, and the informal sector; and they favor the creation of alternative structures for social service provision, either through the recruitment of personnel, boards or other similar arrangements. Also, the projects are often demand-driven, whereas clients are often self-selecting: the projects attempt to promote specific institutional, management, and operational approaches based on a belief in efficiency and the superiority of private enterprise; and these projects are often donor-funded from external sources (Aina 1999: 84).

In more recent times, we no longer hear about SDAs but more about PRSPs. The emphasis is on the form and process, stressing participation and local ownership. One is not sure of the extent to which the neo-liberal aspects of the social policies have been revised. For the moment, one gets the impression of 'smoke and mirrors' (Hutchful 1994), and conceptual manipulations that appropriate popular and progressive notions such as participation, empowerment, community and equity. These are then repackaged as significant strategies for social transformation. By adopting popular and social justice-related notions, these initiatives are made more acceptable. However, questions related to how the new policies contribute to the reconstruction of African societies and economies, and to authentic human development, are never directly addressed. This is where Vivian's call (1995: 23) becomes imperative:

> Social sector reform models must be assessed in terms of their overall social efficiency and effectiveness as well as their impact on social development. Social policies have long-term effects on social divisions and social structures, and if safety nets become institutionalized as an alternative model of social provisioning, a long-term question is raised. What will be the legacy of the neo-liberal approach to social services provisioning? Will it promote or retard progress toward social development and positive forms of social integration?

It is questions like these that politics and policies in Africa must address, if social policy is to be linked to the development process and the real needs of the ordinary poor peoples of the continent. It is only by doing so that social policy can become a means of supporting not only authentic human development but also the reconstruction and transformation needed to overcome Africa's legacy of colonial misrule as well as the pains and suffering of the post-colonial era of crisis and adjustment.

It is hoped that the chapters in this book have contributed to drawing attention to these issues, thereby creating not only awareness but also the need for more research and thinking on social policy in the era of globalization in Africa.

## Organization of the book

The rest of this book is organized around five main themes. The first theme deals with 'Economic and Regional Trends'. The three chapters by Said Adejumobi, Zine Magubane and Hakim Ben Hammouda deal with socio-economic and regional trends, particularly in the era of crisis and adjustment. The authors show how similar global trends of economic liberalization have affected different regions of Africa, such as West Africa, the Maghreb and South Africa, and how these affect social policy. Even though the studies cover regions with different history, cultures and contemporary political development, they agree on the impact of globalization not only on policies but also on the very structure and role of the state. The second theme consisting of three chapters by Aredo, Ndiaye and Mohammed–Bello Yunusa continues the issue of 'linkages between poverty and the reduction and deterioration of social services provision through globalization'. The contributors, particularly Aredo, recognize that poverty is not new to Africa, but that it has been complicated in recent times by both global and local factors. Three chapters by Okoye and Okoye, Anugwom and Anugwom, and Ibeano, deal with the third theme of 'Globalization, Women and Citizenship'. Examining the relationship between adjustment-led globalization and women's work intensity, household well-being, the lives of wage-earners and conditions of refugees, the authors move beyond the discussions of social provisioning to the interface between the realm of basic needs and basic rights. Ibeano, in focussing on refugees, introduces a dimension that questions the impact of global policy-making, as defined by international institutions, on a vulnerable, yet growing group of actors that are an outcome of Africa's endless crises—refugees. Two chapters by Chachage and Alubo deal with the theme of 'Higher Education and Globalization'. The authors examine the relationship between the market-led reforms in higher education and the management and delivery of the services in one university in South Africa and across the system in Nigeria. Both authors show how the reforms have affected the fulfillment of the relevance, mission and the nature of management and learning in the universities. The two contributions by Gimode and Wanyonyi that deal with religious and cultural institutions, examine non-conventional mechanisms of social provisioning that have emerged in some African countries either as a result of the failure or of dwindling capacity of the state to provide basic services. They focus on how alternative bases of solidarity constitute the platforms for social interventions either in providing emergency relief or other basic services. Wanyonyi shows how 'Harambee', a form of pre-colonial mobilization of community self-help, has been transformed and modernized to become an asset mobilization strategy that includes fund-raising and voluntary labour. Gimode's chapter on Islam and social policy also discusses the transformation and modernization of non-Western 'cultures of giving'

— such as that of Islam — into organized modern philanthropy that occupies the space neglected by the modern Kenya State.

In the concluding chapter, Chachage and Annan-Yao review the 'passages in the life' of the notion and phenomenon of globalization in Africa. The authors link the understanding of the notion with what they described as '...attempts at the moral rehabilitation of what was being contested by critics of SAPs'. In pointing out the way forward beyond globalization, the authors call for a reconstruction of the state in Africa, a re-examination of citizenship and a re-conceptualization of both elements within a pan–territorial and pan-African context. Appropriating the dynamic of de-territorialization in the globalization process, Chachage and Annan-Yao advocate a re-territorialization that extend the borders of emancipatory politics and social justice issues across current national political boundaries, through the formation of counter-movements, alliances and coalitions that fight social injustice, exclusion and inequality. It is on this basis of extra and pan-territorial organization and action that they posit the reclamation of genuine and people-centred social policy and human development as a counter-factor to the negative features of contemporary globalization.

## Note

* Tade Akin Aina is currently the Regional Representative, the Ford Foundation, Office for Eastern Africa.

## References

Aina, T. A., 1993, 'Empowering Environmental NGOs: The Experience of the Nigeria Environmental Study Action Team', in R. Sandbrook and M. Halfani eds., *Empowering People: Building Community, Civil Associations and Legality in Africa*, Centre for Urban and Community Studies/University of Toronto.

Aina, T.A., 1997a, 'Globalization and Social Policy in Africa, Issues and Research Directions', Working Paper No. 6/96, Dakar: CODESRIA.

Aina, T.A., 1997b, 'The State and Civil Society: Politics, Government and Social Organization in African Cities', in C. Rakodi ed., *The Urban Challenge In Africa*, Tokyo: United Nations University.

Aina, T.A., 1999, 'West and Central Africa: Social Policy for Reconstruction and Development', in D. Morales-Gomez, ed., *Transnational Social Policies: The New Development Challenges of Globalization*, London: Earthscan Publications.

Amin, S., 1972, 'Underdevelopment and Dependence in Black Africa: Origins and Contemporary Forms', *The Journal of Modern African Studies*, vol. 10, No. 4, pp. 503-24.

Amin, S., 1992, *The Empire of Chaos*, New York, Monthly Review Press.

Amin, S., 1998, *Capitalism in the Age of Globalization*, London: Zed Books.

Bakker, I., 1994, 'Introduction; Engendering Macro-economic Policy Reform in the Era of Global Restructuring and Adjustment', in I. Bakker ed., *The Strategic Silence: Gender and Economic Policy*, London: Zed Books, in association with the North-South Institute.

Bangura, Y., 1995, 'Perspectives on the Politics of Structural Adjustment, Informalisation and Political Change in Africa', in T. Mkandawire and A. Olukoshi eds., *Between Liberalization and Oppression: The Politics of Structural Adjustment in Africa*, Dakar: CODESRIA Book Series.

Boyden, J., 1990, 'Childhood and the Policy-Makers: A Comparative Perspective on the Globalization of Childhood', in A. James and A. Prout eds., *Constructing and Reconstructing Childhood: Contemporary Issues in the Sociological Study of Childhood*, London: The Falmer Press.

Brodie, J., 1994, 'Childhood and the Boundaries: Gender and the Politics of Restructuring', in I., Bakker, ed., *The Strategic Silence*, London: Zed Books.

Cornea, G. A., Jolly, R. and Stewart, F. eds., 1987, *Adjustment with a Human Face*, Vols. I and II, Oxford: Clarendon Press.

Deacon, B. with Hulse M. and Stubbs P., 1997, *Global Social Policy: International Organizations and the Future of Welfare*, Thousand Oaks, I.A.: Sage Publications.

Espring-Andersen, G., 1990, *The Three Worlds of Welfare Capitalism*, Cambridge: Polity Press.

Etta, F.E., 1994, 'Gender Issues in Contemporary African Education', *Africa Development*, Vol. XIX No. 4, pp. 57-84.

Fowler, A., 1992, 'Distant Obligations: Speculations on NGO Funding and the Global Market', *Review of African Political Economy*, No. 5, pp. 9-29.

Fowler, A., 1995, 'NGOs and the Globalization of Social Welfare: Perspectives from East Africa', in J. Semboja and Ole Therkildsen eds., *Service Provision under Stress in East Africa*, Copenhagen: Centre for Development Research,/ Nairobi: East African Education Publishers.

Gayi, S.K., 1995, 'Adjusting to the Social Costs of Adjustment in Ghana'. Problems and Prospects', *The European Journal of Development Research*, Vol. 7, No. I, pp. 77-99.

Ghai, D., 1992, Structural Adjustment, Global Integration and Social Democracy, Geneva, United Nations Research Institute for Social Development (UNRISD), Discussion Papers No. 37.

Hardoy, J. E., Cairncross, S. and Sattherthwaite, D., eds. 1990, *The Poor Die Young: Housing and Health in Third World Cities*, London: Earthscan.

Hill, M. and Bramely, E., 1986, *Analysing Social Policy*, Oxford: Blackwell.

Hutchful, E., 1994, 'Smoke and Mirrors: The World Ban's Social Dimensions of Adjustment (SDA) Programme', *Review of African Political Economy*, No. 21, pp. 569-584.

Jamal, Vali and Weeks, J., 1993, *Africa Misunderstood or Whatever Happened to the Rural-Urban Gap*, ILO, London: Macmillan.

Jones, H., 1990, *Social Welfare in Third World Development*, London: Macmillan.

Laakso, L. and Olukoshi, A. O., 1996, 'The Crisis of the Post-Colonial Nation-States Project in Africa', in A. O. Olukoshi and L. Laakso, eds., *Challenges to the Nation-States in Africa*, Uppsala: Nordiska Afrikainstutet, Institute of Development Studies, University of Helsinki, Finland.

Maclean, M. and Dulcie Groves eds., 1991, *Women's Issues in Social Policy*, London: Routledge.

MacPherson, S. and Midgley, J., 1987, *Comparative Social Policy and the Third World*, Sussex: Wheatsheaf Books.

Marshall, T. H., 1950, 'Citizenship and Social Class', in T.H. Marshall and T. Bottomore, 1992, *Citizenship and Social Class*, London: Pluto Press.

Mhone, G. C. Z., 1995, 'The Social Dimensions of Adjustment (SDA) Programme in Zimbabwe; A Critical Review and Assessment', in *The European Journal of Development Research*, Vol. 7, No. 1, pp.101-123.

Midgley, J. *et al.*, 1986, *Community Participation, Social Development and the State*, London: Methuen.

Mkandawire, T and Soludo, C.C., 1999, *Our Continent, Our Future: African Perspectives on Structural Adjustment*, CODESRIA/IDRC/African World Press.

Mkandawire, T., and Olukoshi, B., eds., 1995, *Between Liberalisation and Oppression: The Politics of Structural Adjustment in Africa*, Dakar: CODESRIA.

Morales-Gomez, D., A., 1995, 'Introduction: Development and Social Reform in the Context of Globalization, in D. Morales-Gomez and M. Torres, eds., *Social Policy in a Global Society: Parallels and Lessons from the Canada-Latin American Experience*, Canada: IDRC.

Nabudere, D, W, ed., 2000, *Globalisation and the Post-Colonial African State*, Harare: AAPS Books.

Oxfam, 1993, 'Africa: Make or Break: Action for Recovery', Oxfam Report, Oxford, England.

Patel, L., 1992, '*Restructuring Social Welfare': Options for South Africa*, Johannesburg: Raven Press.

Pieterse, Jan Nederveen, ed., 2000, Global Futures: Shaping Globalization, London and New York: Zed Books.

Sen, Armatya, 1999, *Development As Freedom*, New York: Alfred A. Knopf.

Slater, D, 1995, 'Challenging Western Visions of the Global: the Geopolitics of Theory and North-South Relations,' The European Journal of Development Research, Vol.7, No.2., pp.366-388.

Torres, M. A., 1995, 'Conclusion: Social Policy in a Time of Uncertainty', in D. Morales-Gomez and M. Torres, eds., *Social Policy in a Global Society*.

Townsend, P., 1975, *Sociology and Social Policy*, NTC: Penguin Books.

United Nations Development Programme, 1999, 'Human Development Report', 1999, Oxford: Oxford University Press.

United Nations Research Institute for Social Development, 1995, *States of Disarray: The Social Effects of Globalization*, Geneva: UNRISD.

Vivian, J., 1995, 'How Safe Are Social Safety Nets? Adjustment and Social Sector Restructuring in Developing Countries', *The European Journal of Development Research*, Vol. 7, No. 1, pp. 1-25.

Williams, F., 1989, Social Policy: A Critical Introduction, Cambridge: Polity Press.

# Part I

# Economic and Regional Trends

# 2

# Economic Globalization, Market Reforms and Social Welfare Services in West Africa

**Said Adejumobi***

Globalization is creating new threats to human security in rich and poor countries.

—UNDP (1999: 3)

## Introduction

More than ever, the global economy in the last two decades has witnessed an unprecedented integration process marked by the attenuation of national boundaries in economic transactions and a steady decline in state domestic economic powers. Kenichi Ohmae (1990) aptly described this development as the emergence of a 'borderless World'.

Economic globalization seeks expression in a transnationalised context of capital goods, services, information technology, production and policy focus. This phenomenon has serious implications for and reconstitutes not only the economic and political arena but also the social sphere in terms of social services production and delivery. The concept of the welfare state that philosophically and ideologically underpinned the notions of social protection, welfare and security is under siege in many countries. Everywhere, as Dharam Ghai (1996: vii) rightly noted, the welfare state is being recast in new directions.

The process of economic globalization has been facilitated by four main factors. First, the collapse of socialist regimes in most parts of the world meant the hegemony of the liberal capitalist ideology with far-reaching implications for economic outlook and orientations. Secondly, the unprecedented activities of multinational corporations (MNCS), with the phenomena of mergers, acquisitions and interlocking relationships on a global scale led to a gradual transformation of the global economy. Thirdly, the revolution in information technology has transformed the world into a 'global living room and common market-place' where ideas, goods and services are freely traded. The fourth element is the rise of market reforms as a global economic creed, a phenomenon partly engendered by the global economic crisis, which prompted a search for alternative economic and policy paradigms, and more importantly, by the rise of the neo-liberal orthodoxy, with its emphasis on market rules and their infallibility. Market reforms couched in the policy of the structural adjustment programmes (SAP) for the Third World countries, with its emphasis on state decontrol of the economy and the social policy space and economic liberalisation and deregulation, constitute a major instrument of economic integration and globalization in the 1990s. The policy assumes a standard framework and economic philosophy, which not only link most economies together but also define the configuration of domestic policies. Indeed, to use the words of Dharam Ghai (1992), 'economic globalization and market reforms are interdependent and mutually reinforcing'.

How does the process of economic globalization and market reforms affect the provision and delivery of social welfare services in West Africa, particularly for education and health? How is social policy being reconstituted and what are the changing nature and the context of the ground rules of production, exchange, delivery and consumption of those services? What effects do these have on the majority of the people and the society in general? This paper draws largely on examples from Nigeria, Ghana and Cote d'Ivoire.

This chapter focuses in part one on a conceptual and theoretical discourse on economic globalization and market reforms. Part two dwells on the genealogy of social welfare service provision in relation to the state and the ensuing crisis in this regard. Part three is on the reconstitution of the basis of social welfare services provision in Africa based on the market orthodoxy, its underlying theoretical logic and policy conception, and its effects. Part four is a critique of the market logic in the provision of social welfare services.

## Economic Globalization and Market Reforms: Conceptual and Theoretical Issues

The concept of globalization ordinarily suggests a shift in the spatial form and extent of human organization and interaction to a transnational or inter-regional level. It is conceived as a compression of time-space relations in which transnational networks involving world factories, labour flows, lending facilities, communications, new knowledge, information technologies and cultural norms are bridging the boundedness of the territorial state with increasing rapidity (Goldhalt *et al.* 1997; Mittleman 1993). Economic globalization therefore denotes the widening and intensification of international linkages and interactions in trade, investments and economic policy orientation in the world (World Bank 1996; Rosenau 1997). It connotes the internationalisation of production, capital, and marketing, in which the world is integrated into a 'global factory, global money market and global shopping centre' (Adejumobi 1993).

A major issue in the discourse on globalization is whether there is anything new in the process, or whether it is possibly a new euphemism for an older and continuous process, which has been variously described and analysed. In other words, is globalization a new euphemism for 'universalism', 'internationalisation' or 'worldisation', which depicts the trajectory in the historical development of capitalism? Meiken Woods, for instance, argues that the concept of globalization is one of an 'ideological mystification' of capitalism which tends to create, quite fraudulently, an intellectual convergence between neo-liberal thought and radical persuasions on the benign nature of the global economy (Wood 1997).

However, scholars like Sivanandan (1997), Petrella (1997), Rosenau (1996) and Giddens (1997) hold a contrary view. According to them, there is something new about the phenomenon of globalization which marks it out differently and therefore requires that it be studied as such. As Sivanandan argues, globalization constitutes an epochal shift in capitalism because it has brought about qualitative changes in the development of the forces and mode of production, which have in turn induced significant changes in the social relations of production.

In Richardo Petrella's view, globalization constitutes a new phenomenon because it suggests a diminished role for national governments in the design of the rules for global governance, where financial markets, corporate strategies and consumption patterns have taken a global dimension at an unprecedented level (Petrella 1996). For Anthony Giddens, globalization is something relatively new in history, as the concept describes an increasing inter-penetration between individual life and the global future, a phenomenon which transcends the economic arena and encapsulates the development of the world system or large-scale global institutions (Giddens 1997: 4-5). However, globalization, as Rosenau (1997: 36) rightly points out, is a concept that implies change; it is a phenomenon to be conceived as a process, rather than a prevailing condition or a desirable end state, which differentiates it from the concept of 'globalism'.

The historical and contemporary dimensions of economic globalization have been changing over time, in relation to the configuration of power and interests and the nature of the dominant social forces in the international arena. These are manifested in four areas: trade, finance, foreign direct investments and market reforms. In the 1950s and 1960s, the rapid expansion of trade was the driving force behind economic globalization. In the 1970s, the lead role was played by the capital flows financed by Western commercial banks. In the 1980s, foreign direct investment and technological flows were the dominant element of economic globalization, while in the present conjuncture, market reforms, as established in Structural Adjustment Programmes (SAPs), represent the latest instrument of economic globalization. SAPs, as Mohammed Ould Mey (1994) argues, constitute the latest globalist policy advocating the attenuation of all borders, barriers and policies which might interfere with capital accumulation on a global scale.

Two major theoretical issues have arisen in the discourse on economic globalization. The first centres on the role of the state in the economy and policy-making and the second, on the effect or impact of economic globalization on economic progress, and social welfare, especially in its spatial dimension. In both contexts, two divergent positions are discernible. The first concerns the impact of the growing transnationality and 'borderlessness' of economic transactions and activities on the authority and economic powers of the nation-state, especially as market reforms and economic liberalization policies foisted by the World Bank and the I.M.F. on developing countries vitiate the capacity of domestic economic policy-making. At one level, some argue that economic globalization erodes the national market—one of the basic foundations of the nation-state—and that the nascent global economic space is replacing the national space as the most relevant and strategic space (Heredia 1997). On the other hand, some scholars insist that despite the challenges posed by globalization, the state will remain the site of political authority, economic regulations and decisions, although there will be alterations in the nature of state power in this regard. At any rate, even though globalization may have strong economic logic, it is essentially a political phenomenon so the state as a political formation, as Linda Weiss (1997) argues, will remain a major political actor in its configurations and activities. What may simply take place under globalization is not the diminution of state power, but its reconstitution in a rapidly changing world economy.

Two major positions are also discernible in the discourse on the possible effects of economic globalization on economic progress and social welfare. On the one hand, the liberal perspective contends that there is a correlation between economic globalization and economic progress, which in turn engenders better living standards and social welfare for people. Globalization through open economies and the promotion of neo-liberal economic policies tends to promote higher growth rates by stimulating better resource allocation, greater competition, transfer of technology and access to savings (Fitzgerald 1997; Petrella 1996; World Bank 1996; Henderson 1992). As Ricardo Petrella notes, economic globalization initiates the movement from an era of the 'wealth of nations' to the era of the 'wealth of the world' (Petrella 1996: 68). Put differently, economic globalization promotes not only the transnationalisation of wealth creation but also of human development and relative equity in access to resources (Abedian 1998: 24). Whatever disintegrative effects economic globalization may have, they could be regarded as mere transitory problems, which would be levelled up as the process matures and radiates a multiplier effect in the global economy. The general position seems to be that 'economic globalization has no alternative and is irreversible' (Albo 1996).

On the other hand, a more radical perspective argues that economic globalization accentuates class, regional, national and local inequalities. It increases disparities in wealth, resources and power, and also reflects the increasing contradictions between capital and labour, and the logic of accumulation between the local and international levels (Beberoglu 1997; Heredia 1997; Callaghy 1997; Amin 1994, 1987; Ould Mey 1994; Arrighi 1982). Economic globalization has produced a marked deterioration in the capacity of most Third World countries to influence events in the international arena. Conditions in the domestic economies of those states have rapidly declined. Globalization has imposed immense pressure in the transformation of local communities in the Third World, a situation resulting in the rapid commodification of production, urbanisation, exploitation of wage labour, growth of poverty, environmental degradation and class polarisation in those communities (Beberoglu, 1997: 33). Economic globalization has deepened social inequalities and poverty such that, since the 1980s, poverty has grown in absolute terms throughout the developing countries and has increased in both absolute and relative terms in much of Africa and Latin America (Heredia 1997: 386).

The skewed and grossly uneven nature of spatial economic development, resource and income distribution accentuated by economic globalization is well captured by the UNDP. According to its 1999 report, the OECD countries, with 19 per cent of the global population, have 71 per cent of the global trade in goods and services, 58 per cent of the foreign direct investment and 91 per cent of all Internet users. The assets of the top three billionaires in the West are more than the GNP of all least developed countries and their 600 million people (UNDP 1999: 3). The share of trade, economic activities and investment for Third World countries, especially Africa, continues to decline. For example, in its 1997 *World Investment Report,* UNCTAD noted that Africa's share of foreign direct investment flows in 1996 was the lowest since the early 1980s, while official aid flows also fell by 48 per cent in 1996, the lowest in 10 years. Thus, rather than promoting sanguine global economic integration, co-operation and harmony, economic globalization, with its inherent contradictions perpetuates polarization and inequalities. In the view of Samir Amin (1994) 'Globalization via the market' is a reactionary utopia.

In addition, economic globalization also evokes contradictions in other important respects. First, while the process tends toward economic integration on a global scale, the phenomenon of economic differentiation and discrimination among nations, based on regional economic groupings, is intensifying. Secondly, restrictions on labour mobility, especially those from the Third World, increase as economic globalization proceeds. This suggests that economic globalization is about capital and not labour, and about accumulation on a global scale, and not income redistribution. In a significant sense, therefore, it is essentially a class project, which has national and international dimensions. Thirdly, while through its network of information revolution economic globalization increases the demand for equity in terms of income and standard of living on a global scale, the same contradictory process also seeks to reduce state capacity in terms of economic and social policy options, especially in the provision of social welfare services. Thus, what it creates in most Third World countries is a revolution of rising expectations, which remain largely unfulfilled.

The extent to which economic globalization and market reforms therefore improve the provision and delivery of social welfare services in Africa remains quite contentious. Perhaps what should be emphasised at this point is that the underlying philosophy and mode of the provision of those services are being reconstituted from the state to the market process, with the emphasis on rationality, efficiency and effectiveness. The extent to which these goals are achievable in the new process remains highly problematic and suspect.

## The State and Social Welfare Services: Genealogy and Dimensions

Historically, in most parts of the world, the provision of social welfare services has been mostly a state project. As long as there have been rulers, there have been state-owned lands, buildings and state-run services (Letwin 1988: 1). With specific regard to social welfare services like education, health care and water supply, although private provision of those services, especially in the case of the former two, is not unknown, the state is often responsible for their provision to the majority of people. Various state departments or tiers of government are created to handle those tasks.

Globally, two issues have been germane to the involvement of the state in the provision of social welfare services. First, and quite important, is the philosophical and ideological conception of the state and its role in society. Although the theoretical discourse on the state in terms of its origin and essence is diverse, there seems to be a consensus on the need for state involvement in social welfare services. Classical discourse on the state, such as the social contract theory, viewed the state as the product of a 'social pact' by the people. They chose to give up some of their individual rights and powers to a sovereign, in return for the guarantee of law and order, human dignity and social welfare. Indeed, in Jean Jacques Rousseau's conception, the basic values that the state must try to protect are life, liberty and social welfare (Rousseau 1913).

The issue of social welfare features quite prominently in both liberal and Marxist theories of the state. In the liberal theory, although the private sector is seen as the engine of development, the state, according to Adam Smith, is required to perform three functions. These are, the guarantee of law and order, the administration of justice, and the erection and the maintenance of public works, which may be beneficial to society, but which the private sector finds uneconomical or unattractive (Smith 1936: 650-651). Essentially, Smith used the term 'public works' broadly, to refer to those activities in the infrastructural and social sector like education, health care provision, road construction and the like which may be instrumental to the process of capital accumulation, but are less open to capitalist investment. Also, from the liberal tradition, the Keynesian theory adopts an innovative approach in explaining state involvement in the social sector. In this regard, although the private sector and a free market are necessary and desirable for capitalist development, the internal mechanisms of these processes are faulty, thereby requiring the state to constantly intervene to maintain them in equilibrium. Hence, to achieve full employment, a reduction in inflation and growth stimulation, public expenditure, especially on public works and social services, must be kept at a significant level (Keynes 1936).

In the Marxist theory, although the state is viewed as an instrument of dominant class rule, the whole essence of the working class struggle to capture state power is to use it in serving the interest of the majority of people, by ensuring access, equity and uniform provision of social welfare services. Thus, it is not by coincidence that most socialist states, especially before the fall of the Socialist Bloc, placed a high premium on state provision of social welfare services, including education and health. This explains why a country like Cuba has one of the highest literacy rates in the world, despite its low resource base and the excruciating economic blockade by the United States.

The second issue germane to state involvement in the social sector has been of a class nature. It is the struggle between labour and capital often mediated by the state through legal codes and constitutional norms, in which the state seeks to negotiate social cohesion in society. It is through this process, from a historical viewpoint, that labour or the working class has been able to wrest concessions from capital and the state for the dominated groups in society. This process largely characterised the evolution of the social welfare system in most of the developed countries. The demand by labour for full employment, fair working conditions, reasonable standard of living and protection of their social and economic rights, including the right of all citizens to education and good health services, has characterised this historical class struggle. In an important sense therefore, the struggle between classes and social forces within national contexts has been relevant to the state concern for and investment in the social sector.

In Africa, the state has been the main provider of social welfare services. Four reasons account for this. The first is the historical antecedents of colonial rule. Under colonial rule, the responsibility for providing both infrastructural facilities and social services like roads, railways, education and modern health care services rested principally with the colonial regime. Although missionary groups also supplemented the efforts of the colonial state, especially with regard to education and health care, colonial social services were very restricted, as the objective was not to promote development in those countries but to facilitate the process of colonial exploitation. Thus, at independence in the 1960s, Africa ranked as the poorest continent in terms of the provision of social services. For instance, Africa's educational structure was the worst in all the regions of the world (Lall 1992). A major challenge to the post-colonial regimes therefore consisted of bridging the gap in the provision of social welfare services. Secondly, one of the aspirations of the anti-colonial struggle by the African people was to achieve better living standards. Fulfilling this aspiration required huge state investments in the social sector. These included extending the educational base, health care services, employment and water supply. The third element was the imperative of national development. It was considered that, for national development to be stimulated, it was necessary to invest in the social sector as a basis for creating sound minds that could promote development and also engineer a very conducive social environment for the development process. Thus, various national development plans formulated by most African countries after independence highly prioritized the issue of social welfare services. Finally, African culture and societal values tend to place a great deal of emphasis on the human element in society, a phenomenon which partly defines the social welfare approach to development adopted by several post-independent African leaders. Their political philosophies were therefore largely human-centred and couched in the ideology of welfarism. These include Julius Nyerere's philosophy of Ujamaa, Kenneth Kaunda's'Humanism', Kwame Nkrumah's 'Conscientism', Leopold Senghor's 'Negritude', and Obafemi Awolowo's philosophy of 'Democratic Socialism'. The common denominator of all these political philosophies was the overriding concern with the human element, social existence and well-being in the state (Adejumobi 1999: 87-108).

A combination of all the above factors engendered huge state investments in the social sector in the post-colonial era in Africa. For example, in Nigeria's first National Development Plan (1962-1968), a sum of 667.9 million Naira was allocated to the social sector; this increased to 16,572.9 million Naira in the second National Development Plan (1970–1974) (Onokerhraye 1984: 5), and the figures increased substantially under successive development plans. In Côte d'Ivoire, while the social sectors of education and health were allocated 28.4 per cent of the state's current expenditure in 1965, this increased to 30.2 per cent in 1970, and to 33.4 per cent in 1975 (Tuinder 1978). The expansion in those countries' educational base was also phenomenal. For instance, in

Nigeria, while primary school enrolment was 2,849,500 and the number of primary schools was 15,703 in 1960—when the country attained independence—by 1980, primary school enrolment had increased to 15,607,505 (Sambo 1998). In 1976, the state introduced a policy known as the Universal Primary Education scheme (UPE), with a view to creating better access and opportunities for all Nigerian children to primary education. At the tertiary level, while Nigeria had only one University in the colonial era, at independence in 1960, this increased to 6, and then to 17 in 1980, and around 30 in 1983. Student enrolment rose sharply from 1,000 in 1959, to 113,158 in 1983, and then to 250, 000 in 1994. In Côte d'Ivoire, while only 33 per cent of the primary school age group were enrolled in school at independence, by 1975, about 55 per cent of this age group were already enrolled. For secondary education, enrolment grew from 15,000 at independence in 1960 to nearly 90,000 in 1975, while the University of Abidjan, which was established in 1959 with less than 1,000 students, had an enrolment of 6,000 by 1975 (Tuinder 1978: 74-75).

In Ghana, the Pan African philosophy adopted by Kwame Nkrumah at independence in 1957 generated a serious concern about the social welfare condition of not only Ghanaians, but also the whole of African peoples.

Apart from significantly expanding the pre-tertiary education sectors, state investment in tertiary education was also prominent. Between 1962 and 1965, two universities were established in Ghana—University of Ghana—in 1962, and Kwame Nkrumah University of Science and Technology, later renamed University of Science and Technology, after the overthrow of Nkrumah. Student enrolment in these institutions rose sharply. At University of Ghana, Legon, student enrolment rose from 5,380 in 1970 to 8,500 in 1985. At Kumasi, this increased from 1,394 to 3,600 at the same period (Ade Ajayi et al. 1994). With regard to health care services, the first decade of independence in most African countries saw considerable improvement in health care provision (World Bank 1981). This development spanned also the second decade in many of those countries. For example, in Nigeria, the public health care sector continued to expand tremendously between 1975 and 1986. The number of doctors increased fourfold, that of hospital beds doubled, and the population of nurses and midwives tripled (Odumosu 1996: 128). Indeed, public hospitals in Nigeria, like the Island Maternity in Lagos, had the best reputation for maternal care, child delivery and child health services, which all strata of society patronized.

In all these cases, the delivery of social services was largely undertaken by the state as part of socio-economic development projects financed by the state.

## Charting New Course: Market Fundamentalism and the Delivery of Social Welfare Services

By the early 1990s, there was a gradual shift in the concept and logic of the provision of social welfare services in Africa towards the market logic. Two major factors accounted for this: the festering economic crisis that devastated the continent from the 1980s, and the adoption of the Structural Adjustment Programme (SAP)—an economic policy foisted by the World Bank and I.M.F on developing countries. The economic crisis in Africa was reflected in the deepening fiscal crisis of the state, declining foreign exchange receipts, balance of payment and the debt profile of most African countries. Estimated at US$10.8 billion in 1970, Africa's debt rose to $113 billion in 1980, to $278 billion in 1990, and further to $300 billion in 1994. This debt is almost equal to the region's Gross National Product (GNP) and three and a half times its export earnings package. Growth in GDP in Africa fell from 5.9 per cent in 1965–1973 to 0.5 per cent in 1980–1987. By the end of the 1980s, about thirty-four out of nearly forty-two poorest countries in the world were in Africa. Indeed, Africa was a major recipient of the global economic recession, given the dependent nature of most African economies (Adejumobi 1993, 1995).

In the context of declining financial resources, one of the areas of state expenditure badly affected by this development was the social services sector. Between 1980 and 1985, social spending in Sub-Saharan Africa dropped by 26 per cent as compared to 18 per cent in Latin America, in real terms (Weiss 1995: 121). Although the reality of fiscal stringency imposed some constraints on state expenditure, in Africa in general, the introduction of the Structural Adjustment Programme (SAP) was the most decisive factor in the reconstitution and decline of state spending in the social sector. The SAP, which John Mihevc (1995) described as the fundamentalist economic doctrine emerging under the spell of globalization, was a phenomenon analogous only to theological fundamentalism. Under this policy, Africa's economic crisis was construed as a state crisis deriving, among others, from the inefficiency, irrationality and wastefulness of the state, especially in its spending pattern. As the World Bank put it, 'the state is at the heart of Africa's economic stagnation and decline' (World Bank 1994). A major component of the state spending, which is generally viewed as bloated and wasteful, is that of the social welfare sector. In making for economic recovery therefore, the state must be made to retreat, in terms of its expenditure, especially in the area of social welfare services, while state investment in infrastructural services must be withdrawn and such enterprises privatised. Generally, the SAP policy emphasises cuts in state expenditure, the withdrawal of state subsidy on social welfare services, adjustment of exchange and interest rates, commercialisation and privatisation of public enterprises, liberalization of trade and deregulation of the economy.

It would be necessary to unravel the underlying theoretical arguments of the neo-liberal orthodoxy, which informs the logic of SAP, holding sway in the globalization period, with particular regard to the reconstitution of the basis and logic of providing social welfare services. Here, the new emphasis is on markets rather than the state. With specific reference to social welfare services, especially education and health, the arguments of the neo-liberal school revolve around three major theses. These arguments are neither coherently articulated, nor organically inter-linked in their discourse, but they constitute the major theoretical planks of the neo-liberal position, which we seek to put together and later deconstruct. These are the *private good* theory, the *efficiency and resource allocation* argument, and the urban coalition thesis (Adejumobi 2000b). We shall discuss these issues in sequential order.

The first theory holds that social welfare services are essentially private goods, to which the principle of exclusion could be applied and on which users' charges should be imposed. Education and health services are considered to be private goods, for which the beneficiaries could be made to pay, since the benefits of such services accrue more to the individual rather than to the society, although in varying degrees. For example, in all sectors of education in Sub-Saharan Africa, the World Bank argues that the private rate of return is far higher than the social rate of return. For primary education, while the social rate of return is 24.3 per cent, the private rate of return is 41.3 per cent. For secondary education, the social rate of return is 18.2 per cent, while the private rate of return is 26.6 per cent. For tertiary education, the social rate of return is the lowest, at 11.2 per cent, while the private rate of return is 27.8 per cent (World Bank 1995: 22). The implications of this are twofold. First, all layers of education are essentially private goods which yield more benefits for the individual or the consumer, rather than the society; as such, beneficiaries must be made to contribute to, if not bear, the full financial burden of those services. Secondly, since the social rate of return is very low in tertiary education, the state should divest itself from financing and provisioning it. Beneficiaries of higher education must be made to pay for it. With regard to health care, although the World Bank did not produce data on its social and private return rates, the argument still stands that it is a private good, for which users or beneficiaries must be made to pay user fees or charges, although in varying degrees. The user fee in the health sector is meant to achieve cost recovery and promote genuine needs.

The *efficiency and resource allocation* argument holds that there has been a tremendous misallocation of resources by the state in the social services sector mainly because of the 'free' nature of those services being provided by the state. The point is that demand has often swelled up to outstrip the supply of those services, simply because those services are provided free of charge by the state. What then occurs is the creation of 'artificial excess demand' which unduly gulps state resources. In the case of Côte d'Ivoire, a World Bank researcher, Batiaan A. den Tuinder, puts it poignantly:

> The rapid increases in enrolment and costs at all levels of the educational system can be largely attributed to an excessive demand for education, a consequence of the fact that education is essentially free for private individuals and that sizeable increases in incomes are associated with additional years of schooling. In short, the private benefit of education is far in excess of the private cost (Tuinder 1978: 286).

By the 1990s, this argument had come full circle for the World Bank and became a basis of policy design in the social sector for African countries. In addition to the 'artificial excess demand' argument for resource misallocation, other two arguments were forwarded in this regard. The first one is that since those services are free, corruption and wastage are the norm. The case of the pilfering of drugs by medical personnel in public hospitals is often cited as an example. Hence, the state keeps on spending money, which may not necessarily deliver the service for which it was meant, but provides an easy and illegal source of additional income for some people. In order to curb this gross resource misallocation by the state, the basis and the rules for the provision of such services must change. The second argument concerns resource misallocation within the social welfare sector itself. Since the state funds everything, it seldom prioritises very well. Rather than concentrating on basic health care services, the state emphasises grandiose medical projects, and rather than focusing on primary education, which yields more social benefits to society, the state spends colossal funds on tertiary education which, according to the World Bank, is of less societal value in Africa. The net effect is that resources are grossly wasted and misallocated, contributing tremendously to the financial stress on the state. Even within the sub-sectors of education, the World Bank insists that there is resource misallocation, arising from misplaced priorities. For instance, with regard to higher education, the World Bank argues that there has been an overtly undue emphasis on 'less productive' courses in the Arts, Humanities, and Social Sciences in the planning and funding of university education to the detriment of professional programmes like medicine, engineering, and accounting. These latter courses, the World Bank continues, are what a dynamic economy requires, and which in the first instance justify higher education programmes in Africa. The Arts and Humanities programmes are essentially of less utility to the market and not readily convertible into profit or employment. This is the basis of massive graduate unemployment in Africa (Adejumobi 2000b). Thus, in order to correct this inefficiency and resource misallocation in tertiary education, there must be the rationalisation of programmes and courses in the universities, while a downsizing of the staff strength of those institutions should be encouraged as a cost-saving measure.

The final theoretical plank of the neo-liberal argument is the *urban coalition thesis*. Although this argument was originally advanced by Robert Bates (1981) and Michael Lipton (1982) to explain the crisis in the agricultural sector in Africa, it has since become a standard theoretical premise in justifying the SAP. The gist of the theory is that, because of their capacity to organise and control state machinery, urban interests and elites often succeed in cornering most of state expenditure for their constituency, to the detriment of the rural dwellers who are largely dispersed and poorly organised (Adesina 1994: 4-11). In addition, there is a net transfer of subsidy from the rural farmers to the urban population who often insist on low food prices and price control by the state. In other words, the state is usually held hostage by urban interests and forces, who sway public policies in their own favour, not because of their economic role, but due to their organised power and proximity to the state power control systems. As such, public infrastructure, social services, education and health care facilities, employment opportunities and industrial development projects are usually concentrated in urban areas. SAP is meant to correct this anomaly by encouraging public investment in the rural areas and instituting a regime of incentives encouraging agricultural production with favourable terms of trade for peasants and the rural population.

Specifically adapted to the social welfare services sector, the urban coalition thesis holds that there has been spatial disparity in the provision of social welfare services, which is biased against the rural population. A rural-urban dichotomy arises in the explanation of state investment in the social sector. This is at two levels. At the first level, there is a mass concentration of state resources on layers of education and health services desired by urban dwellers. These include secondary and tertiary education, as opposed to the primary education needed by the rural folks, and modern/urban-based clinical services, as opposed to primary health care needs, which are likely to benefit the rural folks. Secondly, the siting of most educational and health services, from primary to tertiary education and from primary health care (PHC) to modern clinical services, is largely skewed in favour of the urban areas, whose population constitutes the minority in most of the countries studied. Thus, the minority benefits more from state investment in education and health services. In a World Bank study on Ghana, it was discovered that there was a marked disparity in the subsidy granted by the state to the rural and the urban dwellers in the provision of health services. On average, urban dwellers received a subsidy of 2,223 Cedis (Ghanaian currency) while for rural dwellers the amount was 1,459 Cedis in 1989. By 1992, the urban population received a subsidy of 5,808 Cedis, while the rural population had 3,039 Cedis (World Bank 1995b). Also, in Ghana, only 3 per cent of the rural population lived in a community with a doctor and only half in communities with health facilities (Brown and Kerr 1997: 73). The state's financial commitment to the primary health care programme (PHC) in Ghana is only about 20 per cent of the health budget, while the urban-based health care system gulps about 59 per cent of the health budget (Okyere, Asante and Gyekye 1993: 17). The emphasis of the Ghanaian health system is on curative urban-based high-technology medical services, rather than the preventive community-based health care services (Brown and Kerr 1997: 73). Also, in Côte d'Ivoire, about 54 per cent of total recurrent expenditure and 61 per cent of capital expenditure on health in 1990 were earmarked for the tertiary health sector, mostly concentrated in the urban areas (Sahn 1994: 278).

Hence, the argument of the neo-liberal orthodoxy, with respect to the *urban coalition thesis,* is that resources must move away from urban-based social services of health and education provision by the state, to the rural needs. These are primary health care, which should be further decentralised, and an emphasis on primary education that benefits the majority of the rural population. Even here, cost recovery should be emphasised, through graded formats that are largely favourable to the rural dwellers. John Weiss captures the argument well:

> Currently, much emphasis is given to reallocation of expenditure under education and health budgets to ensure that the services more significant to the poor are protected. In education, this involves a focus on primary rather than higher education (rural schools, rather than urban colleges or universities) and in health, a focus on basic preventive, rather than more elaborate curative treatment (rural clinics and water and sanitation facilities, rather than urban hospitals). In addition, it is argued that if the poor are to be provided with free or close to free health and education facilities, the non-poor should meet some or all of the cost of the service they receive. This can involve charges for state schools and hospital attendance or the encouragement of private education and medical services (Weiss 1997: 120).

In summary, the position of the neo-liberal orthodoxy, which constitutes the major premise of market reforms in the provision and delivery of social welfare services, suggests the following. First, a general reduction in the state financial commitment to the provision and delivery of social welfare services and the encouragement of private initiative, finance and delivery of social welfare services. Second, a disaggregation of social welfare services, between that of primary and secondary concerns (namely primary health care and primary education on the one hand, and secondary/university education and modern medical clinical services, on the other). On the basis of this disaggregation, the state must undertake the partial or full commercialisation of those services. This should be done by charging user fees or tuition fees, as the case may be, for those services. It is through this process that cost recovery, efficiency, effectiveness, equity and relevance could be promoted in the provision of those services. In other words, the neo-liberal orthodoxy advocates deregulation, commercialisation and privatization of social welfare services.

In most of the African countries where state policy on the social sector is being reconstituted to fit the neo-liberal recommendations, state expenditure on the social sector of education and health has gone down remarkably. In Nigeria for example, the SAP era marked a sharp deterioration in the state budgetary allocation to the health and education sectors. While in 1981, the health sector was allocated 3.1 per cent of the Federal Government expenditure, by 1986, when SAP began, this fell to 1.9 per cent, to 0.6 per cent in 1987, and then to 1.1 per cent in 1991. The same trend is recorded for the education sector. Whereas the share of the total Federal Government expenditure for Education was 8.2 per cent in 1983 (before SAP, but in the throes of economic crisis), this dropped to 2.0 per cent in 1987 (after the commencement of the SAP), although it increased slightly to 2.3 per cent in 1991.

Between 1994 and 1998, there was a dramatic increase in the allocation to the education sector due to domestic pressures for investment in human capital. The share for education in the Federal budget at this period was 7.8, 12.9, 12.3, 11.5, and 10.2 per cent for 1994, 1995, 1996, 1997 and 1998; respectively (ASUU 1998). On average, between 1994 and 1998, the allocation to the education sector represented 10.9 per cent of the total Federal Government expenditure. Although this figure appears high, it falls far short of the allocation to a sector like defence. Between 1994 and 1998, Federal Government allocation to the defence sector was 15.7 per cent of the total budget on average (ASUU 1998). When an appreciable increase in allocation to the education sector occurred by 1994, the World Bank had already classified Nigeria as a case of 'adjustment gone wrong'.

The deprioritization of education on the state agenda in the adjustment era produced a negative effect on school enrolment. For example, while the level of primary school enrolment was 15,607,505 in 1980, by 1994/95 the figure had dropped to 12,977,225. In a localised study of primary education in five states — Oyo, Ogun, Osun, Ondo and Lagos — it was discovered that market reforms had a deleterious impact on this sub-sector of education as it increased the private cost of schooling beyond the affordable rate for the average Nigerian parent. Although the governments in those states claimed to be offering free primary education, many hidden costs were borne by the parents. In fact, parents had to purchase school uniforms, provide for midday meals, textbooks, exercise books, footwear, school bags, etc., in addition to paying for or procuring items such as chairs and desks, sports and games materials, development levies, and examination fees, which were hitherto financed or provided by the government (Gboyega et al. 1998). This situation led to a decline in the rate of primary school enrolment ratios, high drop-out rates, and a high level of poor performance among primary school pupils in those states. Neither secondary or tertiary education fared better either (Adejumobi 2000a; Chukwuezi et. al. 1998; Albert 1995).

The health sector also recorded a drastic decline in performance. The Nigerian Demographic and Health Survey (NDHS), which offers perhaps one of the best information sources on health status in Nigeria, reported in its 1990 survey that 'the health status of the Nigerian population is generally poor and there are remarkable differences among the socio-economic groups' (Odumosu 1996: 131). In a more detailed study of five local government areas in Southern Nigeria, it was revealed that market reform policies occasioned a drastic deceleration in access, quality and public provision of primary health care services (Okafor et. al. 1998). There was a sharp decline in primary health care components like antenatal clinical services. As a result of the increasing cost of primary health care services, alternative therapies including traditional medicine and self-medication, which are cheaper than modern medical services, became the norm among the majority of people in both the urban and rural areas.

In Ghana, apart from the early stages of the Economic Reform Programme (ERP), state spending on the social services sector has been on the increase, compared to the situation in the 1970s and 1980s (Anyemedu 1993: 30; Brown and Kerr 1997: 73). In the education sector for instance, state spending on the sector as percentage of total Government expenditure rose from 14 per cent in 1984 to 25 per cent between 1986 and 1991. The reason for this was that Ghana's education and health care services were already in a very deplorable state (due to the virtual collapse of the Ghanaian economy) before the introduction of the ERP, which required urgent attention. However, overall, the allocation to this sector under the ERP remained very low. For example, between 1990 and 1994, health expenditure averaged just 1.2 per cent of the GDP (World Bank 1995b). In both the education and health sectors, the agenda of market logic is being imposed in Ghana. The Hospital Fees Policy was introduced in 1985 to reinforce users' contribution towards the cost of medical services rendered by state hospitals. These include cost of consultations and treatment, as well as full cost of drugs, with the exception of some immunisations. The system came to be known in Ghana as the 'cash-and-carry' health system. A discriminatory fee system was instituted, in which the fee schedule varied according to the age of the user (child versus adult), the service level, treatment location (urban versus rural), nationality (Ghanaian versus non-Ghanaian), and nature of the service (curative versus preventive) (Brown and Kerr 1997: 73-74). However, certain categories of health services such as antenatal and postnatal immunisation were exempted from fee payment (Okyere Asante and Gyekye 1993: 16-17).

With regard to education, the Ghanaian Government introduced an Educational Reform Programme that was supported by the World Bank in 1987. Apart from the structural component of the reform, it introduced a new logic into the financing of education in Ghana. From primary to tertiary level, different ranges of user fees were introduced. Low user fees were charged in primary and junior secondary levels, textbook fees were introduced for grades 3 - 10, and non-instructional services, like feeding, were completely privatised at the secondary level (World Bank 1995). At the tertiary level, cost recovery measures were introduced in 1989. Student services like accommodation, feeding and housing were completely de-subsidised by the state. Moreover, tuition fees were to be paid by students. However, large-scale student protests and resistance forced the state to reconsider some level of subsidy on accommodation and tuition.

The implications of the introduction of a market logic in the provision of health and education services by the state in Ghana have been quite devastating. Neither the rural nor the urban population seems to have fared any better through the policy. In a field study of seven rural communities in the Volta Region of Eastern Ghana, which Brown and Kerr conducted in 1995 on access of the rural population to health care and education services, the findings were very revealing. These include: first, that there was a shrinking access of the rural people to primary health care services due to the introduction of user fees. These fees, even if meagre, are highly prohibitive for the people, most of whom lived below the poverty line. The consequence was that the people left the domain of modern or Western health care services and retreated into local or traditional herbal medicare, which they considered accessible, cheap and convenient. For others who preferred Western medical services, the option was simply not to seek medical services, at all, in view of the fact that they could not afford what they preferred. It was discovered, for example, that 72 per cent of mothers in those rural communities did not seek medical care for their pre-school children due to the cost (Brown and Kerr 1997: 75). On the whole, the health condition of those communities declined substantially with the prevalence of common diseases like malaria. In the case of two communities, Brown and Kerr had this to say:

> Villagers in Gbefi and Wli-Afegame felt that their health status had improved over the past twenty years, but believed it had suffered a setback since the most recent introduction of users' fees. Villagers are afflicted by common seasonal complaints, including malaria, 'waist pains' (chronic backache), knee pain, dizziness, high blood pressure, headache, cough, colds, snakebites (the second cause of death in adults after malaria), stiff necks and asthma (Brown and Kerr 1997: 76).

In the education sector too, the impact of user fees was no less damaging to those rural communities. Most parents complained about the increasing cost of sending their children to school. Not only did they pay fees; they also bought uniforms and textbooks, contributed to the Parent-Teacher Association (PTA) fund, procured furniture for their children to use in school, etc. The result was a decline in primary school enrolment, estimated at 60 per cent for all children, with girls' enrolment being worse off (Offei-Aboagye 1994: 13-16).

## Deconstructing the Myth of the Market in Social Welfare Services

Although economic globalization may appear to be a purely economic project, the reality is that it is largely a political exercise serving ideological and political functions in the global arena. It is an element of social control and political and ideological hegemony for the dominant forces in the international arena. As Ray Bush and Morris Szeftel (1998: 176) argue, it is a powerful political force used in legitimating the international pressure put on states in the South to accept the hegemony of international capital within their borders, and to foist on them economic and social policies that serve the interests of international capital and its ideology.

I will focus on deconstructing the myth of the market with regard to the provision of social welfare services, at two levels. The first dimension is what I refer to as the contradictory processes and policy advocacy of the neo-liberal orthodoxy in a global context. In this regard, it is first observed that while the World Bank and the Western nations insist on reduced state spending for the education and health sectors in Africa, in contrast, those sectors constitute major areas where countries like the United States and Britain are investing more public resources. Indeed, education and health are major political issues on the agenda of the ruling parties in those countries, yet Africa does not deserve the same. Secondly, while the state is being pressurized into withdrawing from the health and education sectors, the same multilateral institutions (especially the World Bank) and Western countries advocating this are also insisting that African countries should secure more external loans to support and restructure those social welfare services. The contradiction is that as the state withdraws from the social welfare sector it is being made to incur more external loans (funds which in some cases, like that of Nigeria, could be raised locally in the first instance) to service those sectors. The consequence, in terms of the escalating debt crisis, could be appalling. Thirdly, while there is an insistence on a withdrawal or reduction of state spending on social sectors like education and health care services, nothing worthwhile is being mentioned by the World Bank on arms and the defence sector in Africa. Indeed, countries like Britain and France have shown a great deal of ambivalence towards the issue of arms reduction and defence budget cuts in Africa, even when this issue was raised at the World Bank forum (*Africa Confidential* 1995). The truth is that, given the internecine conflicts in Africa, this continent is a major buyer of arms from those countries. With an apparent lull in the arms industry, Africa is needed to keep up sales. The preference of the World Bank and the Western countries therefore appears to be for 'guns', not health or education for African people.

The second dimension of the myth of market logic in the provision of social welfare services is what I refer to as the three fallacies of the market. These are the fallacy of *private good*, the fallacy of cost recovery and the fallacy of *rural support.* With regard to the first, although social welfare services may be construed as a *private good*, since the principle of exclusion could be applied and users' charges imposed, this is not a sufficient basis for classifying those services as such. The social and national dimensions and consequences of those services make them essentially public goods. For example, while health care or pipe-borne water may be considered as private goods, for which people could be charged, their importance to and consequences for the social well-being and development of society and the nation are enormous, and this essentially qualifies them as public goods. The problems of disease, growing poverty and illiteracy that may result from lack of access to those services can be detrimental to the nation.

On the second fallacy, the notion of cost recovery brandished by the neo-liberal orthodoxy obscures the reality of who pays for the public provision of social services. Since it is the citizens who pay either directly or indirectly for services provided by the state through the various forms of taxes paid, those services could not be considered free in the first instance; neither can imposing users' fees on those services be regarded as cost recovery. Imposing users' fees on either education or health care services therefore simply means imposing additional costs on the recipients of those services. In addition, why is the social sector the target of financial adjustment and 'cost recovery'? Why not a sector like defence that is considered largely unproductive and resource-consuming? Furthermore, why can a class approach not be adopted towards cost recovery in those sectors? In other words, why should the corporate sector not be made to share the burden of financing certain services since it benefits more through the state and uses the products of services like those of the education sector? The reality is that the idea of cost recovery is more of a political than an economic issue.

The last element is the concept of rural support that characterizes the neo-liberals' discourse on social welfare services. Here, the essence of the reforms is to create better access and equity in the provision of those services to the rural areas. The rigid dichotomy between the urban and the rural, as upheld by the neo-liberal orthodoxy, is fallacious. There is a social mix and, of course, a network of interactions and migration between the rural and the urban areas. Most urban dwellers in Africa usually relate with, and maintain their rural identity. Likewise, many rural dwellers have social networks and relations with the urban areas, such that they also mostly frequent urban areas and get their support base from migrant urban labour. In addition, available data do not suggest that the rural communities have benefited any better from the policy of the commodification of social welfare services.

## Conclusion: A Future in the Past?

Africa is the most beleaguered continent in the world. The rates of economic, social and political decline are quite alarming. Africa is the only region where, for some three decades, economic growth barely kept ahead of population growth, where the debt burden estimated at US$227 billion in 1999 is greater than the total economic output, with the aggregate debt-export ratio estimated at 239.9 per cent in 1996 (Sparks, 2000: 13). GDP per capita fell from $661 in 1980 to $518 in 1997, while life expectancy at birth and the adult literacy ratio stood at 48.9 years and 58.5 per cent in 1997, respectively (UNDP 1999). Indeed, a large chunk of the African population is still caught in the poverty trap, surviving on less than $1 per day. Yet, Africa remains the laboratory of questionable economic and social policies, which continue to reverse the gains of post-colonial development especially in the area of social welfare services.

Although the problem of shrinking financial resources is real for most African countries, the social sector need not be the major victim of adjustment in state spending. Other sectors like defence, and internal security, require close scrutiny by the advocates of market reforms. In addition, there are other ways of meeting the shortfall in state finances to the sector, rather than commoditizing those services.

Neither the experience of the West, both in its historical and contemporary manifestations, nor that of the so-called newly industrializing countries, suggests a state retreat from social investment. State investment in the social sector constitutes the background on which economic development can be constructed. The imperative of technological revolution in the twentieth century placed knowledge at the heart of global economic competition. Intellectual property rights are increasingly assuming a sacred and competitive character in the global economy. The application of market rules to the provision of social welfare services might push Africa into the past, rather than supporting her march into the future. As Frances Stewart (1994: 112) rightly submits, a resumed and accelerated progress in developing human resources must be placed at the forefront for sustainable development in African countries.

Two options are plain on the changing role of the state in the social sector in Africa. The first consists of the state giving the private sector a lead role in the provision of those services and subsidizing it heavily, in order to make those services accessible and affordable for the public. The second option requires that the state overhaul its service delivery machinery to make it more efficient and responsive to public needs. In either case, the state will continue to be a key and relevant actor in the provision of social welfare services, especially in the areas of education and health in Africa.

## Note

* Department of Political Science, Lagos State University, Lagos, Nigeria.

## References

Abedian I, 1998, 'Economic Globalisation; The Consequences for Fiscal Management', in I. Abedian and M. Biggs, eds., *Economic Globalisation and Fiscal Policy,* Oxford: Oxford University Press.

Academic Staff Union of Universities (ASUU), 1998, 'The 1998 Budget and Education in Nigeria', mimeo, Ibadan: ASUU.

Ade Ajayi J.F, Goma L K.H. and Ampah Johnson G., 1994, *The African Experience with Higher Education*, Accra: Association of African Universities.

Adejumobi S., 2000a, 'Structural Adjustment, Students' Movement and Popular Struggle in Nigeria: 1986–1996', in Attahiru Jega, ed., *Identity Transformation and Identity Politics under Structural Adjustment in Nigeria,* Uppsala: Nordic Africa Institute, pp. 204-234.

Adejumobi S., 2000b, 'Knowledge for Sale: The Politics of University Education Reform in Africa: A Nigerian Example'; in B. Berner and P. Trulsson, eds., *Manoeuvring in an Environment of Uncertainty: Economic and Political Change in Africa,* London: Ashgate, (forthcoming).

Adejumobi S., 1999, 'Privatisation Policy and the Delivery of Social Welfare Services in Africa: A Nigerian Example', *Journal of Social Development in Africa,* Vol. 14, No.2, pp. 87-108.

Adejumobi S., 1997, 'Marketising Public Welfare? A theoretical critique of the Logic of Privatisation in the Social Sector', *Journal of Economics and Allied Studies,* Vol.1, No.1.

Adejumobi S., 1996, 'Structural Adjustment, Privatisation Policy and Infrastructural Services in Africa: With examples from Nigeria and Ghana', Research Report submitted to CODESRIA project on African Perspectives on Structural Adjustment in Africa, Dakar: CODESRIA.

Adejumobi S., 1995, 'Adjustment Reforms and its Impact on the Economy and Society in Nigeria', in Said A. and Momoh A., eds., *The Political Economy of Nigeria Under Military Rule: 1984–1993,* Harare: SAPES.

Adejumobi S., 1995, 'Structural Adjustment and Multinational Corporations in Nigeria: Impact and Implications', *Development and Socio-Economic Progress,* No. 64, October - December.

Adejumobi S., 1993, 'Nigeria and Multinational Corporations: An Appraisal of First and Union Bank Plc', in J. Owoeye, ed., *Nigeria in International Institutions,* Ibadan: College Press.

Adekanye, B., 1993, 'Military Occupation and Social Stratification', Inaugural Lecture, University of Ibadan.

Adesina, J., 1994, *Labour in the Explanation of an African Crisis.* Dakar: CODESRIA.

*Africa Confidential,* October 20, 1995, Vol.36. No.21, pp.1.

Aina, T., 1994, 'Quality and Relevance: African Universities in the 21st Century', Research Report submitted to Donors by the African Education Working Group on Higher Education, Accra: Association of African Universities.

Albo, G., 1996, 'The World Economy, Market Imperatives and Alternatives', *Monthly Review,* December.

Amin, S., 1994, 'The Future of Global Polarisation', Review, Fernand Braudel Centre, Binghamton University,Vol. XVII, No. 3, Summer.

Amin, S., 1993, 'The Post-War Cycle (1945–1992)', *Review of African Political Economy.*

Amin, S., 1987, 'The Crisis: the Third World, North-South, and East-West', in E. Hansen (ed.) *African Perspectives on Peace and Development,* London: Zed Books.

Anenso Okyere W, Asante F. and Gyekye L. O. , 1993, *Policies and Strategies for Poverty Alleviation in Ghana, Technical Publication*, Legon: University of Ghana, ISSER.

Anyemadu, K., 1993, 'The Economic Policies of the PNDC', in E. Gyimah-Boadi, ed., *Ghana under PNDC Rule,* Dakar: CODESRIA.

Assie-Lumumba N., and Lumumba-Kasongo, 1996, 'The Impact of Structural Adjustment on Higher Education in Africa', Research Report submitted to the CODESRIA Research Project on African Perspectives on the Structural Adjustment Programme in Africa, Dakar: CODESRIA.

Arrighi, G., 1982, 'Economic Crisis and Crisis of Hegemony', *Political Internationale,* Vol. 11, No.2, Spring.

Bate, R., 1981, *Markets and States in Tropical Africa: The Political Basis of Agricultural Politics,* Berkeley: University of California Press.

Berbeoglu, B., 1997, 'Globalisation and its Impact on the Third World: A Comparative Historical Analysis', *Development and Socio- Economic Progress*, No. 69.

Boyer, R., and Drache D., eds., 1997, *State Against Market: The Limits of Globalisation,* London: Routledge.

Brendan, M., 1993, *In the Public Interest? Privatisation and Public Sector Reform*, London: Zed Books.

Brown, L. R., and Kerr J., 1997, 'Ghana: Structural Adjustment Star Pupil?', in L. Brown and J. Kerr, eds., *The Gender Dimensions of Economic Reforms in Ghana, Mali and Zambia*, Ottawa: North-South Institute.

Bush, R, and Szeftel M., 1998, 'Commentary: "Globalisation" and the Regulation of Africa', *Review of African Political Economy,* No.76.

Callaghy, T.M., 1997, 'Globalisation and Marginalisation; Debt and International Underclass', *Current History,* Vol. 96, No. 613.

Ghai, D., 1996, 'Forward to the Book', in *Welfare States in Transition: National Adaptations in Global Economies*, Gosta Esping-Anderson, ed., London: Sage Publications.

Ghai, D., 1992, 'Structural Adjustment, Global Integration, and Social Democracy', UNRISD Discussion Paper.

Giddens, A., 1997, 'Anthony Giddens on Globalisation', *UNRISD News*, No. 15.

Goldhalt, D. et al., 1997, 'Economic Globalisation and the Nation-State: Shifting Balances of Power', *Alternatives*, No. 22.

Griffin, K. and Khan A.R. , 1992, *Globalisation and the Developing World: An Essay on the International Dimension of Development in the Post-Cold War Era*, Geneva: UNRISD.

Haffajee, F., 1998, 'The African Debt Cow is Milked Dry', *Mail and Guardian*, October 30 to November 5.

Keller, W. W. and Pauly L., 1997, 'Globalisation at Bay', *Current History,* Vol. 96, No. 613.

Keynes, J. M., 1936, *The General Theory of Employment, Interest and Money,* London: Macmillan.

Killicken T, 1995, 'Structural Adjustment and Poverty Alleviation: An Interpretative Survey', *Development and Change*, Vol. 26, No. 2.

Lall, S., 1992, 'Structural Problems of African Industry', in F. Stewart and S. Wangwe, eds., *Alternative Development Strategies for Sub-Saharan Africa*, London: Macmillan.

Letwin, O., 1988, 'Privatising the World: A Study of International Privatisation', in *Theory and Practice*, London: Lassell.

Lipton, M., 1982, 'Rural Development and the Retention of the Rural Population of Developing Countries', *Canadian Journal of Development Studies,* Vol. III, No. 1.

Logan and Mengisteab, 1989, 'The Potential Impact of Privatisation in Health Care Delivery in Sub-Saharan Africa', *Scandinavian Journal of Development Alternatives,* Vol. 8, No. 1, March.

Mihevc, J., 1995, *The Market Tells Them So: The World Bank and Economic Fundamentalism in Africa*, London and New Jersey, Zed Books.

Mittleman, J., 1993, 'Global Restructuring of Production and Migration', *African Journal of Political Economy.*

Mittleman, J., 1996, 'Rethinking Regionalism in the Context of Globalisation', *Global Governance,* No. 2.

Odumosu, O., 1996, 'Structural Adjustment, and its Impact on Social Services', in Fadahunsi A. and Babawale T., eds., *Nigeria: Beyond Structural Adjustment: Towards A Popular Democratic Alternative*, Lagos: Fredrich Ebert Foundation.

Offei-Oboagye, E., 1994, 'The Effects of Structural Adjustment on Opportunities in the Education of Women - What are the Issues?' paper presented to the Workshop on Structural Adjustment and Women: What are the Issues?, Accra, August.

Onokarhoraye, A.G., 1984, *Social Services in Nigeria: An Introduction,* London: Kegan Paul.

Ould-Mey, M., 1994, 'Global Adjustment: Implications for Peripheral States', *Third World Quarterly,* Vol. 15, No. 2.

Rosenau, J. N., 1997, 'The Complexities and Contradictions of Globalisation', *Current History,* Vol. 96, No. 613.

Rousseau, J. J., 1913, *The Social Contract and Discourses.* (translated with an Introduction by G. D. H. Cole) London: Everyman's Library.

Sambo, A. A., 1998, interview conducted by M. Aluko on the 'State of Primary Education in Nigeria' with Sambo A. A., Executive Secretary, National Primary Education Commission, Nigeria, Internet information by M. Aluko on October 12.

Sahn, D. E., 1994, 'The Impact of Macroeconomic Adjustment on Incomes, Health and Nutrition: Sub-Saharan Africa in the 1980s', in Cornia G. A. and Helliner G. K., eds., *From Adjustment to Development in Africa: Conflict, Controversy, Convergence and Consensus?* London: St. Martins Press.

Samolf, J., Metzler J., and Sail T., 1992, 'Education and Development; Deconstructing a Myth to Reconstruct Reality', in A. Seidman and F. Anang, eds., *21st Century Africa; Towards A New Vision of Self-Sustainable Development,* Trenton and Atlanta: Africa World Press and African Studies Association Press.

Sleeman, J. F., 1979, *Resources for the Welfare State: An Introduction*, London: Longman.

Sparks, D., 2000, 'Economic Trends in Africa South of the Sahara', in *Europa, Regional Survey of the World: Africa South of the Sahara*, London: Europa Publications.

Sivanandan, A., 1997, 'Capitalism, Globalisation and Epochal Shifts; An Exchange', *Monthly Review*, February.

Smith, A., 1936, *An Inquiry into the Nature and Causes of the Wealth of Nations*, New York: Modern Library.

Stein, H., 1991, 'Structural Adjustment, Human Needs and the World Bank Agenda', *Journal of Modern African Studies*, Vol. 29, No. 1.

Strange, S., 1997, 'The Erosion of the State', *Current History*, Vol. 97, No. 613.

Stewart, F., 1994, 'Are Short-term Policies Consistent With Long-term Needs in Africa?', in G. A. Cornia and G. K. Helleiner, eds., *From Adjustment to Development in Africa; Conflict, Controversy, Convergence and Consensus?* New York: St Martins Press.

Sweezy, A.M., 1997, 'More (or Less) on Globalisation', *Monthly Review*, Vol. 49, No. 4.

Tuinder, B. A., 1978, *Ivory Coast: The Challenge of Success*, Washington: World Bank.

United Nations Development Programme, 1999, *Human Development Report 1999*, New York: UNDP.

Wallerstein, I., 1997, 'Integration to What? Marginalisation from What?', *Scandinavian Political Studies*, Vol. 20, No. 4.

Weiss, L., 1997, 'Globalisation and the Myth of the Powerless State', *New Left Review*, No. 225, September-October.

Wisner, B., 1992, 'Health of the Future/the Future of Health', in A. Seidman and F. Anang, *21st Century Africa: Towards a New Vision of Self-Sustainable Development*, Trenton and Atlanta: Africa World Press and Africa Studies Association.

Wood, E.M., 1997, 'A Reply to A. Sivanadan', *Monthly Review*, September.

World Bank, 1996, *Global Economic Prospects and Developing Countries*, Washington: World Bank.

World Bank, 1995, *Priorities and Strategies for Education: A World Bank Review*, Washington, World Bank.

World Bank, 1995b, 'Ghana; Growth, Private Sector and Poverty Reduction', A Country Economic Memorandum, Country Operations Division, West and Central Africa Department, World Bank.

World Bank, 1994, *Adjustment in Africa: Reforms, Results and the Road Ahead*, Washington, World Bank.

World Bank, 1989, *Sub-Saharan Africa: From Crisis to Sustainable Growth*, Washington, World Bank.

World Bank, 1988, *Education in Sub-Saharan Africa*, Washington, World Bank.

# 3

## Globalization and the South African Transformation: The Impact on Social Policy

**Zine Magubane***

### Introduction

There has been much talk in recent years about globalization and the new trend towards an increasingly globalized economy. Although globalization has arguably been occurring in one form or another since at least the eighteenth century, the last ten years have borne witness to some of the most tumultuous activities the global economy has ever known. The collapse of the East Asian 'miracle' and the financial difficulties faced by Mexico, Brazil, and Russia, alongside renewed attempts by multilateral institutions and transnational capital to institutionalize their global power via the Multilateral Agreement on Investment (MAI) and GATT/WTO, are but a few examples of what some regard as a 'sea-change' in the world economy. The fact that this global economic turbulence coincides with the heady years of South Africa's transition makes the analysis of the impact of globalization on post-apartheid social policy both pressing and interesting. There is no doubt that South Africa will, without a doubt, influence and be influenced by global economic processes. Indeed, when President Clinton spoke in front of the South African Parliament on March 26 1998, he remarked that America had a 'profound and pragmatic' stake in South Africa's success. Two days laterlater, he used the dedication of the Ron Brown Centre in Johannesburg as a second opportunity to promote the African Growth and Opportunity Act (AGOA), which, in his words, would help American business to help itself while spurring 'growth and opportunity and freedom in the rest of the world'. The ostensible aim of the Act was to liberalize trade between the United States and Africa. However, it makes extremely onerous demands. Participating countries have to adhere to IMF structural adjustment policies, which include reductions in government spending, a cut in corporate taxes, and the privatization of state assets. The Act also requires participating countries to join the World Trade Organization, something that many African countries have resisted doing because of its bias against developing countries. The Act, which requires African countries to provide 'favorable' conditions for foreign investment, basically amounts to an effort to attempt to force states to adopt policies that are at variance with the needs of their constituents. Despite continued talk of 'free markets' and 'non-interventionist states', what is really being suggested is that the state intervenes so as to create a hospitable environment for corporate and finance capital. Thus Bob Herbert, in a New York Times editorial, describes the proposed measure as creating 'a situation ripe for wholesale exploitation' (June 7, 1998).

Both Nelson Mandela and Thabo Mbeki pronounced the AGOA Bill 'unacceptable' and the South African business magazine *Finance Week* declared the major beneficiaries of the Clinton's African plan to be American corporations. However, the debates that have been waged over post-apartheid macro-economic policy demonstrate that, with or without the 'Growth and Opportunity Act', global economic processes and conditions will profoundly impact South Africa's domestic policies. As Philip Nel (1999) discovered about globalization in his survey of the attitudes of governing elites vis-à-vis globalization, 'globalization has become not only become a salient issue, but also a highly contested one in current public debates in South Africa' (22).

When the African National Congress (ANC) inherited the mantle of power in 1994, it also inherited a long legacy of structural inequality. The major focus of social policy has so far been and continues to be the elimination of centuries of apartheid and its racially based development and underdevelopment. The state quickly decided that the only way out of this quagmire comprized measures such as the following:

(a) an effective employment strategy to expand the formal sector of the economy;
(b) a planned and coordinated investment and industrialization strategy that would include the targeting and promotion of sectors and areas of economic activity that would have the most potential for the creating jobs with the highest of sustainable employment;
(c) a plan for the expansion of the public sector expansion in areas of service areas delivery such as the mass delivery of public infrastructure, public works, and the promotion expansion of low-cost affordable housing; and
(d) fiscal and monetary policies that would encourage productive and employment creating investment while penalizing speculative or employment-shedding investment.

This process of restructuring production and the economy would, naturally, require the participation of the state and the investment of international capital.

As was noted in the Tripartite Alliance Discussion Document on 'Assessment of the Current Phase of Transformation':

> The realities of our global and national situation are such that big capital controls substantial resources without which we cannot carry forward our own national democratic transformation. The power of big capital, while not unchallengeable, is substantial and, particularly on the financial markets, is able to manipulate and destabilize (1997a).

The need to engage with global capital in order to realize the goals of transformation has introduced a profound contradiction whereby the demands of the former strongly impact on and delimit the scope of the latter. As Ngwenda (1997) explained:

> it is ironic that just as the long struggle for majority rule in our country has finally come to fruition, it appears that, at the same time, a process called 'globalization' has come to limit the capacity of democratically elected government to represent the people who elected it (25).

The great challenge facing the ANC, therefore, is how to maintain the momentum of socio-economic transformation in the era of capitalist globalization wherein the state is rapidly losing its room for manoeuvre.

The decline of national economies and state sovereignty in the era of capitalist globalization is generally attributed to the highly mobile character of finance capital, which is widely held to have the freedom to enter and leave markets and national economies at will. When people in business and government circles speak of globalization or South Africa's 're-emergence' into the global economy, they are referring to this phenomenon of 'emerging markets' whereby portfolio investors purchase equity and bonds in developing economies whose stock exchanges and financial markets, although risky, offer potential high returns. The image of South Africa as a 'hot' spot for international investment increased tenfold after U.S. policy makers listed it as one among ten 'Big Emerging Markets' (BEMs). The BEMs are expected to produce up to 75 per cent of real world economic growth and, as such, the management of their economies moved rapidly to the forefront of US policy considerations.

Given the relatively recent nature of the political transition and the legacy of underdevelopment, the African National Congress-led government inherited, it is important, therefore, to assess the extent to which global economic pressures and the desire to capitalize on global economic opportunities are impacting efforts at transformation. To this end, this essay will examine the ways in which the new government is reconciling the demands of globalization with the desire to transform South Africa into a more equitable society. It will focus primarily on the government's macroeconomic strategy for 'Growth, Employment and Redistribution' (GEAR) and the proposed industrial policy because these two policies were the key means by which the government hoped to create growth in their economy and thereby create jobs, redistribute income, and provide funds for social expenditure and welfare programmes. Indeed, the success of post-apartheid social policies hinges critically on the success of the macroeconomic and industrial policies. These policies, in turn, are profoundly influenced by and have sought to engage with the challenges of globalization.

## State Sovereignty in the Era of Globalization

Many (although by no means all) theorists describe globalization as a process by which geographic distance becomes less of a factor in economic, political, and socio-cultural relations due to the existence of new technologies, new business formations, and the existence of supra-national political and economic institutions. There is general agreement that the last few decades have witnessed a shift in the regime of accumulation from one with rigid labour processes, labour markets, methods of production and patterns of consumption, to one where these processes are marked by much greater fluidity. This new era is also characterized by the emergence of new sectors of production, new means of providing financial services, new markets, and greatly intensified rates of commercial, technological and organizational innovation. In particular, the 'newness' of globalization is typified by the increasing significance of financial markets, which is both the most major driving force behind the pressure for globalization and the lead cause of instability in national economies, particularly in the developing world. As Giddens (1990) indicates:

> globalization can thus be defined as the intensification of world-wide social relationships which link distant localities in such a way that local happenings are shaped by events occurring many miles away and vice versa (64).

These changes are thus giving rise to what Harvey (1989) termed as 'time-space compression' wherein the time horizons of private and public decision-making have shrunk while satellite communication and declining transport costs have made it increasingly possible to spread these decisions immediately over an ever wider and more variegated space.

Their concern with the opening of the economy and the increasingly prominent role played by the financial markets have naturally caused current theorists of globalization to rethink what the status and role of the state might be within a rapidly changing international economy. The new global economic relations are widely believed to pressurize the abilities of nation-states to managing domestic social relations, particularly class relations. Indeed, one of the most heated debates within the larger globalization literature has centered on the impact of the transnationalization of capital on state autonomy. There is a general consensus that the existence of mobile investment capital has inaugurated a process whereby states' powers over their national economies are severely curtailed. As Arrighi (1998) explains,

> the idea of globalization was from the start intertwined with the idea of intense interstate competition for increasingly volatile capital and a consequent tighter subordination of most states to the dictates of capitalist agencies (1).

The notion that supranational capital, labour and information flows have the potential to undermine the sovereignty of individual nation-states is, according to many theorists, not only the most unique aspect of globalization but also the most worrisome. The basic contention is that in light of the existence of a globalized financial system, states are not free to exercise power over their national economies because those states whose policies are deemed unwise by private financial traders will be punished as the value of their currency declines and their access to capital diminishes (Evans 1997). As Mittleman argues (1997):

> the scope for state autonomy... is reduced in the context of economic globalization... In a globalized division of labor, the state no longer primarily initiates the action in, but rather reacts to, world-wide economic forces (7).

Although the extent to which state sovereignty is threatened under globalization continues to be debated (Weiss 1998; Panitch 1997) the one point on which all theorists, without regard to ideological orientation, seem to agree is that states on the 'periphery' of the global capitalist economy, variously referred to as 'third world', 'underdeveloped' or 'developing' states are going to be faced with newer and even more profound challenges to their economic sovereignty and efficacy. Mittleman (1997), who argues that 'truncated globalization debars the bulk of Africa from gaining access to the world's productive processes' sums up the prevailing attitude (18). He argues that for the countries of Africa, the greatest challenge is to demarginalize when national options are severely constrained by the forces of globalization.

It is important to situate the recent talk about the collapse of state efficacy and sovereignty in Africa within the context of the Bretton Woods Institutions and their vested interest in reducing the role of the developmentalist state in Ssub-Saharan Africa. As Mkandawire (1998) notes 'the state is today the most demonized institution in Africa' (1). Thus, the reduction of its role in the economy is one of the key goals of the IMF and the World Bank.

The rhetoric of 'good governance' has recently come to dominate discussions about the African state, and multilateral lending institutions have taken it upon themselves to use 'good governance' as the fundamental criteria guiding their lending policies. Although a variety of issues are grouped under the heading of 'good governance'—-including efficient public service, an independent judicial system, a legal framework to enforce contracts, an accountable administration, pluralism, a free press, and respect for law and human rights—the overwhelming emphasis has been on encouraging a minimalist state that throws its support behind neo-liberal economic policies. Thus, the the IMF and the World Bank have insisted on a package of reforms that have severely and purposefully weakened African states. As Mkandawire (1998) goes on to note:

> the significance of the view that African states never played a developmental role lies in the fact that it has led to a set of measures by the Bretton Woods Institutions that have maladjusted African states. To avoid clientaelism and rent-seeking, the state is squeezed fiscally and even politically. This weakened state then exhibits the incapacity to carry out its basic functions. This is then used to arguinge that the state in Africa is not capable of being developmental (2).

In recent years, the IMF and World Bank have become even more aggressive in their efforts to transform African states into what Robinson termed 'transmission belts and filtering devices for the imposition of the transnational agenda' (1996: 19). The publication of the 1997 World Bank Report, 'The State in a Changing World', thus marked a significant shift—not so much in the Bank's attitude towards the object of the state, but rather, in its candour. In the 1997 Report, the Bank speaks of the need for a strong state to protect and correct markets and thus provide a nurturing environment for globalization, which, in their words, 'begins at home' (12). The Report then goes on to advocate a range of actions that should be taken by states to facilitate their integration into capitalist globalization such as reducing corporate taxes, opening markets, reducing social spending, raising interest rates and reducing inflation. The Report also recommends that states play an active role in discouraging politically influential groups that might advocate 'levying unexpected taxes on the private sector, or of redistributing economic benefits' or putting 'restrictions on the operation of markets' while encouraging the appointment of a 'conservative central bank governor who is more opposed to inflation than society in general' (51). In essence, the Bank is arguing for the state to play a critical role in shifting the balance of class forces within states so as to silence those that would attempt to stand in the way of particular kinds of initiatives on the part of Western-based transnational and multinational capital. The importance of the 1997 World Bank Report lies, therefore, not in its policy prescriptions, which remain as uninspiring as they ever were. Rather, the report demonstrates very clearly the extent to which globalization, in the words of Leo Panitch (1997), is being 'socially democratized' with the international institutions that sponsor globalization, instead of by-passing or displacing the state, in operating to guarantee a certain type of state restructuring.

## The Impact of Globalization on South Africa's Macroeconomic Policy

As was mentioned above, South Africa soon came to be considered one of the 'hottest' emerging markets and was able to attract a great deal of investor interest after the 1994 political transition. In the wake of the 1994 elections, there was a net increase of R92 billion (about R651 US$) in non-resident holdings of South African equities and bonds. More than one- third of all trades on the Johannesburg Stock Eexchange in 1997 were transactions by foreigners. Gross daily turnover on the South African foreign exchange market increased from under $6 billion in 1993 to over $12 billion in 1998. However, in May and June of 1998, capital flows to South African financial markets suddenly reversed from an inflow of R16 billion to an outflow of R7 billion. The Rand also dropped by an average of 16 per cent against major currencies between May and August, and average share prices on the Johannesburg Stock Exchange fell by 33 per cent from its all-time high in May of 1998 (Gelb 1999). The vulnerability of South Africa's economy in the face of capital mobility quickly became the focus of debate in business and government circles. Business leaders warned that South Africa needed to 'get its fundamentals right' if it wanted to attract and retain foreign investment. At the same time, the loss of state sovereignty became an issue of increasing concern to South Africa's governing elite. As Nels (1999) explaines:

> South African decision-makers are deeply concerned about what they perceive to be a significant loss of sovereignty…[which] became a major theme in the speeches of President Mandela's speeches a during 1997 and 1998…Mandela identified not only identified financial markets as the beneficiaries in this struggle for sovereignty, but he also claimed that state sovereignty of the state had been transferred, in crucial respects, to institutions of international governance (22).

The new government was particularly anxious about the impact that globalization would have on the Reconstruction and Development Plan (RDP), which was aimed at redistributing wealth and overcoming the structural legacy of apartheid. Unveiled in late 1994, the RDP was developed within the ANC as an economic alternative for South Africa. As an economic policy framework, it placed the challenge of meeting basic needs at the center of economic growth and development. The RDP argued for the integration of five basic policy programmes: meeting basic needs, developing human resources, rebuilding and restructuring the economy, building democracy, increasing participation and maintaining macroeconomic balance. The government created an RDP Office in the Office of the President, which was equipped with an RDP fund to supplement departmental budgets and entice line departments towards RDP objectives. The expressed goal of the RDP office was to support and assist departments in implementing the RDP as well as encourage-synergy between the various departments by means of strategic task teams, policy work and developmental planning (Goldin and Heymans 1999).

Shortly after the policy was unveiled, the ANC found itself facing extremely vocal criticism. Representatives from the business and financial sectors immediately criticized the RDP as a 'socialist' measure that was incompatible with the realities and demands of globalization. Shortly after the appearance of the original RDP base document, the Development Bank of South Africa began circulating the RDP Green Paper, which was the first unambiguous attempt by their economists to encase the RDP within a neo-liberal macro-economic framework. The RDP White Paper soon followed. Although less neo-liberal, the White Paper still maintained a commitment to free markets as the engine of economic growth.

The lack of clarity around macro-economic issues was one of the major vulnerabilities of the RDP. One of the major (and most valid) criticisms put forth by the Opposition was that the RDP lacked a workable and coherent macro-economic framework. Indeed, the parts of the proposal that dealt with macro-economic issues were ambiguous. Thus, when the Rand depreciated rapidly between January and February of 1996, the South Africa Foundation—a conglomerate of the fifty largest business interests in South Africa—seized the opportunity to cite the 'socialist' slant of the RDP and its contradictory macro-economic framework as the proximate cause. It was, of course, the generally volatile nature of financial markets at that time, much more than ANC policy, that was responsible for the fluctuations in the Rand. Nevertheless, the ANC was under considerable pressure to 'deliver' a macroeconomic policy when it hastily unveiled its macro-economic framework, 'Growth, Employment and Redistribution (GEAR), in May of 1996.

GEAR departed significantly from the RDP in that it stressed the need for growth first, to be followed by distribution. As a package of reforms, it also conformed much more closely to neo-liberal prescriptions. GEAR is premised on the idea that creating an 'investor friendly' environment will provide a basis for economic growth, job creation, and wealth redistribution. As such, it represents the marriage of neoclassical economic growth theory to Keynesian notions about investor confidence. Under the GEAR mandate, the state introduced outward-oriented, 'investor friendly' measures such as keeping interest rates high, making the labour market more flexible, privatization of select state assets, lifting of exchange controls and cutting government consumption spending. The model predicted that this economic framework would create 400,000 new jobs by the turn of the century and boost the annual growth rate to 6 per cent. GEAR explicitly ruled out expansionary fiscal policy as a means of lifting the economy onto a higher growth path.

At the heart of GEAR is a deep concern over the government's budget deficit, the argument being that:

> Deficits lead to higher inflation and interest rates, exacerbating the burden of interest payments on the fiscus. More importantly, in the present climate of instability, a fiscal expansion would precipitate a balance of payments crisis. Without attention to more deep-rooted reforms, there is no possibility of sustained accelerated growth (1996: 3).

The concern over the budget deficit arose from the onerous nature of repaying the state's inherited debt, given South Africa's extremely high interest rates. When the interest rate is combined with inflation (which is just under 10 per cent) 20 cents out of every Rand collected in revenue is earmarked for servicing the accrued interest. There has, however, been some talk of renouncing and re-negotiating the debt, which was largely inherited from the previous regime. Indeed, the cruel irony of the debt is that it was the result of spending undertaken by the previous regime to 'buy' itself more time by means of increased expenditure on security and patronage politics. In effect, the apartheid regime attempted to buy allies in the form of corrupt Bantustan regimes and slight increases in salaries and personal benefits for select elements of the African majority. The extent to which renouncing or cancelling this debt is feasible is severely constrained by the fact that much of the debt is internal debt, owed to the pension funds. Therefore, any renunciation has the potential of depriving many working people in South Africa of their pensions[1].

The way in which GEAR was implemented cannot be understood outside of the phenomenon of globalization. Globalization both precipitated GEAR and provided its epistemological framework. On the former point, GEAR was hastily drawn up in the midst of a financial crisis that was precipitated by international portfolio investors that rushed to sell Rand assets in favour of safer currencies. It was, in the words of a COSATU discussion paper, 'a clear case of policy driven by panic' (1997: 15). On the latter issue, GEAR was profoundly influenced by neo-liberal prescriptions about growth and investment. GEAR was intended to raise fixed investment in South Africa by providing a welcoming and stable environment for global financial investors. The assumption was that growth in the South African economy was constrained by a lack of investment and the low level of domestic savings in the country meant that the investment needed for economic development and reconstruction would have to come from outside.

Furthermore, GEAR was designed to increase aggregate demand by encouraging exports. In order to maintain export competitiveness, GEAR attempted to halve the deficit by reducing expenditure on wages, while cutting corporate tax rates. Select state assets were privatized in order to increase efficiency and attract new investment. At the same time, exchange controls were liberalized for both foreign investors and South Africans. Foreign companies were thus able to borrow locally with increased ease, and local investors were able to expand their international portfolios by exporting funds to foreign stock markets. Finally, tax incentives were also established to encourage manufacturing investment.

Because GEAR was designed to encourage foreign investment, it was quickly beset by one of the principle contradictions of globalization, mainly that maintaining stable capital inflows often has contradictory effects on domestic growth. So-called 'credible' policies for global financial investors often have negative effects on growth because speculative and short-term investors dominate the globalized world economy. This was precisely the dilemma encountered in South Africa. The long-term goal of both GEAR and the RDP was to encourage long-term productive investment. However, the overwhelming focus of GEAR had to be on short-term sustainability concerns—hence, the tight monetary and fiscal policies. In the end, however, this policy primarily attracted 'hot money' or portfolio investors who purchased investments in liquid assets that were easily reversible and quickly moved out of the country when other opportunities arose. GEAR, in the words of one South African economist, 'manifestly failed to provide a credible framework for productive investors' (Gelb 1999: 155).

Although the policies pursued under GEAR were extremely 'investor friendly', they did little to encourage investors other than portfolio investors, and these only part of the time. Thus, virtually all of GEAR's targets were missed. The anticipated increase in Foreign Direct Investment (FDI) was not realized. Rather than new plants and equipment, the bulk of the FDI was related to the purchase of existing assets through privatization and merger/acquisition deals. Outflows of foreign investment in 1997 far outstripped what came in ($2.3 billion as opposed to $1.7 billion). Annual growth also fell from 3.2 to 1.7 to 0.1 per cent in 1996, 1997 and 1998, respectively. Unemployment worsened considerably, with job losses totalling more than half a million during the ANC's first term. The real value of the Rand fell by 16 per cent in 1996 alone. The Reserve Bank's main interest rate was pushed up to 17 per cent, which was far higher than GEAR's prediction (Bond 2000).

The spectacular failure of GEAR led to a fierce debate within business and government circles. Representatives of big business concerns such as the South Africa Foundation tended to view the failure as a consequence of the government's refusal to go far enough with neo-liberal reforms, due to pressures from 'left wing' elements—meaning the South African Communist Party (SACP) and the Congress of South African Trade Unions (COSATU). On the other hand, the SACP and COSATU criticized the assumptions about the state, the market, labour, and capital that were embedded within GEAR—a perspective shared by this author. GEAR's major shortcoming was that it accepted the neo-liberal assumption that market mechanisms allocate resources efficiently and that government actions should be limited to correcting market failures and thus enabling markets to work more efficiently. This represents a major theoretical shortcoming, as market prices in South Africa do not reflect a neutral, natural, or efficient distribution of resources. Rather, they reflect the industrial structure and allocation of resources bequeathed by apartheid.

The South African economy is comprised of a highly developed 'mineral-energy complex', (Fire and Rustonjee 1996) which encompasses gold, coal, petrochemicals, electricity generation, processed metal products and mining machinery and an underdeveloped capital goods sector. Basic needs industries have been persistently and purposefully underdeveloped. Social services and wages are also very low. At the same time, the luxury manufactured goods sector (targeted largely at the white minority) is both uncompetitive and over-productive (Bond 2000). Since the late 1960s, the South African economy has been in the midst of a long-term structural crisis, the result of what Robert Brenner (1999) has termed an 'over-accumulation' of capital. Brenner defines over-accumulation as a situation wherein capital cannot be put back into productive investment. It is typically characterized by an oversupply of unsold commodities, large numbers of unemployed workers, and unused capital goods in the form of plants and equipment. Brenner identifies the over-accumulation of capital as stemming from the general tendency for competition and technological innovation within capitalism to produce an increased capital-labour ratio in production. In simpler terms, competition and technological innovation increasingly tend to result in more machines than workers. This in turn leads to a growth in productive capacity beyond what consumer markets can bear. Capital tends to respond by either pushing over-accumulated capital into commercial real estate and infrastructure or into speculative financial assets.

Both processes have been at work in South Africa since the first massive glut in the inventory of consumer goods that occurred in 1967, which forced capital out of production and into the money and capital markets and ended in the 1969-1971 stock market crash. From the late 1970s onwards, over-accumulation encouraged the shift of productive resources into speculative overseas investment as well as the speculative construction of commercial property, the massive build-up of luxury housing and the total neglect of low-cost housing. Banks also went 'offshore', opening up branches in 'hot money' centres like the Cayman Islands and Zurich, while ignoring South Africa's black townships. Likewise, mining houses searched out new overseas acquisitions while ignoring the possibility of investing locally. There was also a massive drop in private sector investment in plant and equipment. At the same time, parastatals expanded and the state increased expenditure on infrastructure, transport, and investment in export processing zones (EPZs) where cheap manufactured goods were assembled at much lower wages and under increasingly onerous working conditions.

As a result of South Africa's crisis of over-accumulation the ANC inherited a state that was shedding employment in the manufacturing sectors, and the majority of Africans were either unemployed or underemployed. Affordable housing was virtually non-existent, while over-building and speculative construction of commercial property generated artificially high land prices in central business districts. At the same time, basic needs goods at affordable prices were not produced, while luxury goods were overproduced. Although the economy desperately needed productive investment to create jobs, capital was flowing out of the country into speculative foreign investment.

GEAR had the effect of worsening this inherited structural crisis by exacerbating the problems caused by the crisis of over-accumulation. The attempt to raise fixed investment and create employment by providing an 'investor friendly' environment did exactly the opposite, encouraging even more of the speculative portfolio investment and capital flight which helped to precipitate even more widespread job losses. GEAR reinforced and enhanced a structure of incentives faced by business that discouraged both the development of small and medium micro-enterprise and the widening and deepening of productive investment. Because the Reserve Bank focused almost exclusively on stabilizing macro-economic variables and lowering inflation, interest rates remained high. These high interest rates had an extremely deleterious impact on new investment. The government's fiscal policy further exacerbated matters with its relentless pursuit of the goal of reducing the deficit without regard to the impact of government spending on education, infrastructure, or other areas that could have potentially facilitated future growth.

In summary, GEAR represents one aspect of the ANC's multi-pronged approach to reconciling their goals of transformation with the demands of capitalist globalization. As a macro-economic framework, it encompassed such broad areas as exchange rate policy, budget deficit reduction, job creation and investment strategy. It was also the arm of policy most vulnerable to the influence of the globalization orthodoxy. Although intended as a way to realize the goal of growth with redistribution, it fell prey to the twin evils of turbulent financial markets and globalization. As a result, the economy continued to experience stagnation in the productive sector and financial speculation while growth was slow and the economy shed jobs.

### The Impact of Globalization on South Africa's Industrial Policy

The second key area into which globalization has introduced major policy shifts has been that of industrial policy. The government has attempted to achieve increased economic growth and thereby facilitate redistribution by providing a 'stable' economic environment to stimulate industry in the direction of export-led growth. The strong emphasis on industrial policy stems from the fact that without an industrial strategy, South Africa will not be able to generate development in either the industrial or the agricultural realm. Industrial processes, including agro-industry, lie at the center of rebuilding the economy as envisaged in the RDP.

There are two major assumptions that guide the current mix of industrial policies in South Africa. The first is that South Africa has an inefficient manufacturing sector which is the result of the import substitution policies pursued in the past. The second is that the mining sector is in decline due to the inefficiencies of apartheid state-led development. Ameliorative efforts are thus directed towards promoting increased openness to world markets in order to achieve export-led growth and a reduction in government intervention. The assumption is that a broad-based trade liberalization programme that includes removing import surcharges, reducing tariff levels in accordance with GATT/WTO prescriptions and exchange rate reforms, will have the effect of making it easier for firms to import machinery and intermediate goods at world prices thus expanding the number of firms producing for export.

However, this conception of industrial policy reflects a distorted understanding of South Africa's industrial structure. It assumes a false dichotomy between the mining sector and the manufacturing sector and the related assumption that the manufacturing sector in South Africa is inefficient and uncompetitive (having been built-up behind unsustainable tariff barriers) and that the mining sector is in decline. This distorted analysis gives rise to the policy prescription that, in order to become competitive and sustain export-led growth, South Africa must liberalize in order to sort out competitive from un-competitive sectors. However, this analysis does not examine the complex linkages that exist between mining and manufacturing, particularly in the 'mineral-energy complex' (Fine and Rustomjee 1996). In actuality, those sectors of manufacturing sectors that are linked to mining and energy are relatively strong and vice versa. Thus, while the share of mining in total production has been declining, its significance, when the industries to which it is linked are taken into account, has not. For example, were it not for the sectors of manufacturing related to mining and energy, the manufacturing share of GDP would not have risen above the level of 18 per cent between 1980 and 1989. However, when the sectors related to mining are included, the share of manufacturing in GDP increased steadily over this nine-year period, peaking at 26 per cent of GDP in 1989 (SACP 1997b).

This understanding of South Africa's industrial structure throws the current stress on liberalization and the scaling back of state involvement in industry into serious question. The sectors in which South Africa has world class technological and export capabilities (such as industrial chemicals, basic iron and steel, and non-ferrous metals) are those in which state intervention has been greatest. For example, large-scale mining capital worked with and through the state to develop a subsidized transport infrastructure which served the production needs of the conglomerates. Through ownership and control of Eskom, the state intervened to supply cheap electricity as which was a major subsidy to mining and large-scale industry (Christie 1984). Thus, the current emphasis on openness to world markets to achieve export led-growth, as opposed to re-orienting government intervention, flies in the face of South Africa's industrial history.

The emphasis on export orientation and competitiveness also underplays the importance of the domestic market and domestic demand as an engine for economic growth. The lack of attention to the domestic market also tends to put policies of redistribution (which would enhance the purchasing power of the majority) on the back burner and therefore priviledges a 'growth first, redistribution second' approach over the 'growth through redistribution' approach originally promulgated through the RDP.

The industrial policy, much like GEAR, exacerbates the structural inequalities and economic crises that were the inherited from legacies of apartheid. Measures to promote the restructuring of companies into internationally competitive exporters incorrectly assumed (largely on the advice of World Bank consultants) that the underdevelopment of the manufacturing sector was due to the high level of protection from imports. Thus, trade was liberalized and even more machinery and intermediate goods were imported, thereby further exacerbating existing tendencies towards an under-developed capital goods sector and a bias against the production of affordable consumer durables for the domestic market. Virtually no attention was paid to the possibility that growth could be driven by an increase in demand for domestic consumption demand, rather than by exports. Likewise, no attention was given to the possibility that the income redistribution of income and the promotion of higher wages (both components of an 'inward' rather than 'outward' investment strategy) could provide the engine for economic growth, development, and redistribution.

## Ideology, Policy, and the Role of the Welfare State: The Impact of Globalization

In his survey of elite conceptions about globalization in South Africa, Philip Nel (1999) found that:

> Sixty percent of the respondents, including many in the business community, agreed that whatever re-distributive intentions the government may have had, these have been curtailed by financial markets. A large majority of the opinion elite therefore believes that the government has lost a degree of policy autonomy to the markets (23).

Globalization has, thus, had a significant impact on the stance the ANC has taken towards state-sponsored social welfare initiatives. This impact has occurred chiefly in the ways in which the state and its functions are being conceptualized and re-conceptualized in light of the demands placed on them by globalization. Typically, developmental, welfare states are characterized as large, interventionist, and oftentimes socialist. This image stands in marked contrast to the 'lean and mean' state under neo-liberal capitalist globalization.

When the ANC assumed the mantle of power in 1994, it launched the RDP under the guise of what they termed a 'national-democratic developmental state,' which attempted to break away from the simplistic dichotomy of either a minimalist state (as defined by neo-liberal globalization) or a maximalist state (as typified by Soviet centrally-planned economy). As was explained in paragraph 1.3.6 of the RDP base document, the RDP 'broke decisively' with the view that development is a marginal effort of redistribution to areas of urban and rural poverty and favoured the idea that growth should be accomplished through development. The guiding premise of the RDP was that national oppression could only be successfully addressed in the context of socio-economic transformation. As was explained in the discussion document paper entitled 'All Power to the People: Draft Strategy and Tactics of the African National Congress':

> South African capitalism gave birth to a collective of black workers whose class position and social existence placed it at the head of the struggle for freedom. By dint of its activism and organization, this class won the respect of all the other motive forces as the leader of the National Democratic Revolution. Along with the poor rural masses, the working class stands to gain most from the success of transformation. Because of its organization and role, and objectively because of its numbers and position in the production process, the working class is critical to this process (ANC 1997b: 9).

This vision of transformation was not limited to the domestic realm but rather aimed to contribute to the restructuring of international relations in the interest of the poor.

'We are moved in this regard', the document continues,

> by the conviction that as long as injustice, poverty and conflict exist anywhere on the globe, so long will humanity find within itself the individuals, movements and governments to co-operate in their eradication. The ANC is a proud part of these international forces (15).

The national democratic developmental state as the ANC envisioned it had a critical role in coordinating various aspects of society, including but not limited to the economy. It was hoped that the state would carry out this role not through a monopoly of ownership or detailed central planning. Rather, the state would unlock and lead various factions of the economy and society, channelling their efforts and energies towards developmentalist goals. There would be a concurrent shift from government to governance and from state-centeredness to partnerships and from planning to process. Accordingly, this developmental state would not be a class neutral entity. Rather, it would be aligned with to a progressive/worker dominated movement. In other words, it would operate under the hegemony of the African working class, which is not only the majority but is also the class that was most abused under apartheid and continues to suffer the most today (SACP 1997a).

The conceptions about the state and its role in the redistribution of wealth that are expressed through GEAR and the export-oriented industrial strategy indicate a significant shift in the ideology around the appropriate role of the state in the transformation process. This ideological shift has been the most significant source of tension within the ANC/ COSATU/ SACP Alliance. The ANC's 1997 discussion document paper, The State and Social Transformation, which was intended in some ways as a defence of the government's new attitude toward global capital, was heavily criticized by both COSATU and the SACP. Critics noted that The State and Social Transformation, alongside GEAR, represented a capitulation to the neo-liberal conceptualization of the state that has become such a key aspect of the 'globalization orthodoxy'. Under this formulation, the state is viewed as no more than a technicist and 'class-neutral' entity, mediating between capital and labour. As stated in paragraph 4.10 of 'The State and Social Transformation':

> The democratic state must also seek to forge a democratic and equitable partnership as well as a working relationship between capital and labour in the interest of social stability, economic progress, reconstruction, and development. In the context of the South African situation, the tension between labour and capital demands special attention by the democratic state because it can easily be confused with or can help to exacerbate the problems associated with the national question.

Both COSATU and the SACP were immensely critical of the document's portrayal of the state as a mediator, equidistant from both capital and labour. Jeremey Cronin and Blade Nzimande (SACP Deputy General Secretary and SACP Deputy Chairperson) noted in their critique of the ANC discussion document paper that the state, as represented in the document, represents what they term as a 'radical and curious shift' from previous ANC position papers, which stressed that the state was the leader of the democratic revolution and a representative of the working class.

The discussion paper perspective begs the very important question of how one reconciles the notion of a golden triangle, of both labour and capital standing equally at the centre of improving the conditions of life of the people with the leadership of the working class and its allies over the national democratic revolution (1997c: 44).

They go on to note that:

> ...there is a great deal that is profoundly troubling about this new way of approaching our new democratic state... The idea of harnessing the combined force of state power and mobilized mass formations is completely foreign to the ANC document (1997c:44).

Cronin and Nzimande also criticize the way in which 'The State and Social Transformation' characterizes class relations in the new South Africa, noting that the document evinces no interest in problematizing the capitalist class or its historic origins in the super-exploitation of black workers. As a result,

> the paper polemically exhorts workers not to be 'economistic', not to be 'infantile' or 'subjectivist'. But it hardly prescribes to capitalists at all. The so-called golden triangle turns out to be worse than an illusion about class neutrality. No expectations, no pressures are placed on capital (1997c: 46).

They conclude that,

> the kind of passive, regulatory pragmatism advocated by the ANC discussion paper, especially in a society beset by huge inequalities, can only serve to legitimize and entrench those inequalities. The ANC discussion paper has the title, 'The State and Social Transformation'. Its true title should have been: 'The State and Social Accommodation' (1997c: 47).

Cronin and Nzimande correctly identify the key problem with the social policies adopted by the ANC (and the perspectives advanced in The State and Social Transformation) with respect to the demands of neo-liberal globalization. The problem lies not so much in the ANC's attempt to productively engage with the pressures of globalization. Rather, the problem lies in the fact that they accepted the assumptions about states and markets that were part and parcel of the globalization orthodoxy. GEAR, in particular, unquestioningly adopted the neo-liberal, false dichotomy between the state and the market. GEAR conceptualizes the state as either replacing the market or standing wholly outside it. In assuming that the government must either directly control resource allocation or leave allocation solely to market forces, GEAR limits the role of government to implementing social expenditure programmes. It misses the fact that the state can play an important role in changing the incentives for agents in the economy. At the heart of neo-liberal economic thinking (which GEAR unhesitatingly accepted) is the idea that market forces are dominant and the only role of the state is to either facilitate their operation or, alternatively, to step aside and let them do their work. This scenario leaves no room for thinking about the state as a vehicle for shaping market forces.

A more productive and critical conception of the state and the market is to view market forces not as a system of immutable laws, but rather as a system of transaction and resource allocation that interacts dialectically with productive forces and relations. Thus, the state has the power to intervene and alter the features of market forces. Indeed, when all is said and done, most of the new government's policies of 'non-intervention' (from tariff liberalization to 'free market' reforms and the privatization of state assets) were actually forms of active intervention that shifted market forces in such a way as to further entrench historical patterns of inequality.

One of the biggest tragedies of globalization in South Africa, aside from the havoc it wreaked on the currency and the immense job losses that occurred in its wake, is the impact it has had on elite conceptions of what states can and cannot do in the name of social welfare expenditure. One of the more unfortunate legacies of globalization has been the institutionalization of the idea that the state is simply a consumer of wealth and that it creates no new wealth. From this assumption came strident attacks on the state's role in the economy through privatization, liberalization, and deregulation, all in the name of attracting investment and enhancing the prospects for economic growth. Beginning in 1996, the government has embarked on a number of privatization and joint ventures in telecommunications, mineralsing and energy, agriculture, forestry, leisure, and transport sectors. These privatization schemes have resulted in the marketizing and bureaucratizing of governance. Communities have become 'consumers' of services, which has had the effect of fragmenting them into individual households, thereby making poverty an issue of individualized household responsibility, rather than one of collective concern and rendering. This neo-liberal conception of the capacities and responsibilities of the state in terms of implementing policies that benefit the populace thus threatens to seriously undermine the new government's commitment to mass empowerment and transformation. The struggle continues to be waged in South Africa between those forces that see 1994 as having opened the possibility for a thoroughgoing revolutionary transformation, and those who merely view it as an opportunity to return South African capitalism to profitability by more thoroughly integrating the economy into imperialist-dominated global capital accumulation. As the African Communist editorialized:,

> These concerns must be the yardstick against which we measure many realities…We are justly proud of our achievements in terms of electricity, water, housing, and the beginnings of transformation in health and education. But to what extent are these being undermined, or constrained by the capacity of big capital to relativise and peripheralize our achievements? (1999: 3-4).

## Conclusion

In analyzing the ANC's post-apartheid macro-economic and industrial policies alongside ideologies about the role of states and markets in fostering developmental goals, this paper has demonstrated that globalization has had a profound impact on the social policies adopted by the post-apartheid state. The impact of globalization has not occurred simply at the level of macro-economic policy, but also at the level of ideology. When the post-apartheid state introduced a range of industrial and macro-economic reforms designed to attract investment from outside of South Africa's borders, they unwittingly adopted a way of conceptualizing the relationship between the state, the market and the global economy that reinforced both the hegemony of capitalist globalization and, in so doing, threatened to further entrench apartheid's bitter economic legacy of White development and Black underdevelopment.

## Notes

* Department of Sociology, University of Illinois, Urbana-Champaign.

1. A number of NGOs are in the process of doing further research on this question. While the results of their research are not complete, they have started to point out that there may yet be more room for manoeuvring. For example, the debt of the parastatals, which is substantial, is much more external than internal.

## References

African National Congress, 1997a, 'Assessment of the Current Phase of Transformation', *African Communist*, vol. 148, pp. 3-9.

African National Congress, 1997b, 'All Power to the People: Draft Strategy and Tactics of the African National Congress', Pretoria.

African National Congress, 1997c, 'The State and Social Transformation', *African Communist*, Vol. 146; pp. 24-42.

Arrighi, G., 1998, 'Globalization, State Sovereignty, and the Endless Accumulation of Capital', Unpublished Seminar Paper.

Bond, P., 2000, *Elite Transition: From Apartheid to Neoliberalism in South Africa*, London: Pluto.

Brenner R., 1999, *Turbulence in the World Economy*, London: Verso.

Christie, R., 1984, *Electricity, Industry, and Class in South Africa*, Albany, SUNY Press, COSATU.

Christie, R., 1997, 'A Programme for the Alliance', *African Communist*, Vol. 146; pp. 14-24, Cronin,

Cronin, J. and Blade N., 1996, 'We Need Transformation Not a Balancing Act', *African Communist*, Vol. 146, pp. 42-48.

Department of Finance, Cronin, J. and Nzimade B., 1996, *Growth, Employment, and Redistribution: A Macro-economic Strategy*, Pretoria.

Evans, Peter, 'The Eclipse of the State? Reflections on Stateness in an Era of Globalization', *World Politics*, Vol. 50, pp. 62-87.

Fine, B. and Z. Rustomjee, 1996, The Political Economy of South Africa, London: Wits University Press.

Gelb, S., 1997, 'Economic Growth, People, and the Environment', in *Between Unity and Diversity*, Gitanjali Maharaj ed., pp. 147-167, Cape Town: David Philip.

Giddens, A., 1990, *The Consequences of Modernity*, Cambridge: Polity Press.

Goldin, I. and Heymans C., 1999, 'Moulding a New Society: The RDP in Perspective', in *Between Unity and Diversity: Essays on Nation-Building in Post-Apartheid South Africa*, Cape Town: David Philip.

Harvey, D., *The Condition of Postmodernity*, London: Blackwell.

Mittleman, James, *Globalization: Critical Reflections*, Boulder: Lynne Rienner.

Mkandawire, T., 1998, 'Encouraging Developmental States in Africa', *The Daily Yomiuri*, October 16.

Ngwenda, M., 1997, 'Globalization: A Requiem for Socialism'? African Communist, Vol. 148, pp. 25-26.

Nel, P., 1998, 'Conceptions of Globalization Among the South African Elite', *Global Dialogue*, Vol. 4, No. 1, pp. 22-53.

Panitch, L., 1997, 'The Role of the State', in J. Mittleman ed., *Globalization: Critical Reflections*, Boulder: Lynne Rienner.

Robinson, W.I., 1996, 'Globalization: Nine Theses on Our Epoch', *Race and Class*, Vol. 32, pp. 13-31.

SACP, 1997a, 'Let's Not Lose Sight of Our Strategic Priorities', *African Communist*, Vol. 146, pp. 3-14.

SACP, 1997b, 'Some Reflections on Industrial Policy in South Africa', *African Communist*, Vol. 147, pp. 26-36.

SACP, 1999, 'June 2 Elections: A Platform to Accelerate Transformation', *African Communist*, Vol. 151, pp. 1-6.

Weiss, L., 1996, *The Myth of the Powerless State*, Ithaca: Cornell University Press.

World Bank, 1997, *The State in a Changing World*, New York: Oxford University Press.

# 4

# Globalization and Social Ambivalence in the Maghreb

**Hakim Ben Hammouda***

## Introduction

This chapter attempts to examine the social consequences of globalization in the Maghreb. The study is limited to the Central Maghreb states of Morocco, Tunisia and Algeria.

To this end, the analysis of the recent developments in North Africa allows for the delineation of two major periods. The first period that began from independence to the early 1980s was characterized by strong economic growth processes that made it possible to modernize the economic structures of Morocco, Tunisia and Algeria. The independent states also played an important role in modernizing political structures through the development of the modern state and the downgrading of archaic power management structures.

The state based its legitimacy on its modernist commitment and its capacity to involve large sectors of the population in the modernization project. During the first three decades after independence, the Maghreb states disposed of their own private resources which increased with the rise in the price of raw materials in the 1970s. These resources enabled the states to make important social investments. Thus, the education sector developed very rapidly with the increase in the number of schools and universities. Also, investments in the health sector enabled the states to improve the population's access to health care for their people and led to an increase in life expectancy. The economic growth process enabled the states to integrate the population emerging from the educational systems into the jobs they created.

These economic, political and social processes were at the source of the legitimization of the nationalist project and of its capacity to mobilise the population. And yet, this project started losing its impetus by the end of the 1970s. First of all, the state's political monopoly was being questioned. In fact, the three Maghreb states experienced the emergence of a dynamic civil society that demanded a greater opening of the public space.

At the same time that the political monopoly of these states were being disputed, the debt crisis led to a halt in the rapid economic growth process and further compromised the nationalist project based on the development of an internal market through import substitution. In this regard, the opening of these economies to the global economy did not result in the revival of the economic growth process. Rather, the growing economic crisis resulted in a rapid rise in unemployment and a reduction in the states' integrating capacities. Thus, unemployment and exclusion which were limited in the era of the 1960s and 1970s began to affect graduates among the population.

The economic crisis further led to a significant state withdrawal from the social sectors. In fact, structural adjustment programmes compelled the state to reduce their deficit by cutting down their welfare expenditure.

All these changes and decisions accounted for the delegitimization of these states. This challenge was further intensified when the state was stripped of a number of prerogatives under the pressure for economic globalization. Thus, the structural adjustment programmes obliged the state to drastically reduce its deficit and, subsequently, its intervention in the investment and growth processes. The state changed from a major political and economic actor to a simple manager of a social order in crisis.

The social crisis in the Maghreb was at the root of the development of an intense social protest. In fact, in most of these countries, one observed the development of critical reactions to the state's political monopoly and the demand for a greater opening of the public space. But this protest together with the democratic movement contributed to the emergence of the Islamic movement that challenged the will of the modern state to ensure a separation between the religious and the secular in political life.

This paper features a comparative analysis between the above-mentioned three Maghreb countries. This comparison throws light on the general context of experiences in modernization and of the resultant crises. However, beyond these convergences, the paper will further clarify the specific and different trajectories adopted by each of these countries. It will explain, for example, the fervour of Islamic dissension in Algeria which appears less remarkable in Tunisia and Morocco. The hypothesis being tested here revolves around convergence and divergence vis-à-vis social policies and the expression of anti-authority sentiments in a context of globalization. Thus, it seems that if the crisis of social policies and of projects structured around the nation-state in the Maghreb is due to globalization, the diversity of expressions and manifestations of these crises are caused by the paths through which the state developed and the symbolic universe it has created.

## Development, Social Policy and National Development in the Maghreb

### *Growth and Economic Development in the Maghreb*

Two modes of economic development can be distinguished in the Maghreb. The first concerns the growth processes initiated in the 1970s by countries like Tunisia[1] and Morocco,[2] on the basis of international integration. In Tunisia, the structuring of this new method of development occurred within a historical context characterized by the crisis that raged in the centre and affected the stability of the accumulation process. At the international level, this crisis led to the disintegration of the old agro-exporting 'peripheries' in the productive systems centred around developed countries, and paved the way for research into the institution of a new international division of labour (IDL). This development resulted in a new distribution of industrial activities at the international level through the relocation of high-performance industries in the peripheries in order to face up to the profitability crisis besetting these industries. Thus, the low labour costs in the South constituted a response to the lowering of productivity gains in the North, following the exhaustion of the prevailing technical standards. Tunisia, like several Third World economies, fitted into this accumulation scheme and it tried, through several measures, to encourage the relocation of high-performance industries from the North.

However, the institution of the new growth process and the direction of industrial development towards the export of industrial products with a high labour content did not mean that industrial activities directed towards the internal market would disappear. In fact, what characterized the industrial structures of the Tunisian economy during the 1970 decade was the coexistence of an export sector with a sector for the internal market. Thus, if the chemical and textile industries devoted a growing portion of their production to exports and were increasingly directed towards the international market, other industrial sectors confirmed their internal intent. In this regard, the mechanical and electrical industries (M.E.I.), the food processing industries (F.P.I.) and the building material industries devoted nearly 90 per cent of their production to the internal market. Besides, less than a third of the entire manufactured products was exported. Thus, the development process within the Tunisian economy was based on the constant search for coexistence and a certain balance between the export sectors and those meant for the internal market.

However, despite its spectacular quantitative results, which led to references made to the Tunisian miracle, this new process was characterized by new forms of dependence and increased extroversion of the productive capacity. This dislocation manifested itself through the sectoral evolution of the Tunisian economy and, more particularly, in the marginalization of agriculture, the increased dependence of industry on imports and the poor agriculture/ industry ratio.

Even though Morocco gave priority to integration into the international economy, it differed from Tunisia, in that it used agriculture as the driving force behind its integration. Thus, the Moroccan development strategy, initiated as from the 1960s, is structured around the promotion of export crops like citrus fruits and greengroceries. The state played a central role in instituting this policy known as 'the dam policy', intended to irrigate a million hectares by 2000, through the construction of a number of dams. In fact, according to Akesbi, 'the State will itself invest massively but will also establish a whole set of economic, financial and social policy mechanisms in the hope of creating certain carry-along effects within the private sector, and as a result, consolidate the agricultural model being offered' (1995).

The priority given to agriculture and to hydro-agricultural projects more particularly is illustrated by the scope of the investments. Between 1965 and 1985, 25 per cent to 30 per cent of public investments on average were devoted to this sector. This investment effort resulted in the construction of 35 major water works and the irrigation of nearly 500,000 hectares. Moreover, the state granted a set of benefits in the form of subsidies, premium or low-interest loans for farming activities. Furthermore, the state tried to intervene in the area of agricultural prices by fixing the prices of products meant for the internal market in order to limit the rise in labour costs in the industrial sector. However, the Moroccan state did not regulate the prices of agricultural products meant for export.

Morocco thus sought to create a development process based on expanding an export-oriented agriculture. This development option was to have tremendous consequences not only on economic development but also on the social order as a whole, by ensuring continuity of the pre-colonial Moroccan method of traditional political domination. In Tunisia, on the other hand, industrial development occurred in a context marked by a new urban and modernist elite in the national movement that dominated the post-colonial State.

The new development process based on integration into the international economy was also illustrated, in both Tunisia and Morocco, by a progressive loss of control over social reproductive norms. Thus, at the level of development funding, just like in that of foreign direct investments, a net increase of external debts was observed during the 1970s.

The same trend was found in the evolution of technical standards. Actually, the institution of this new development process found expression in an increased use of technological imports, essentially in the form of capital and intermediate goods, purchase of licences and the conclusion of technical assistance agreements.

The increasing extroversion of production capacity, the progressive loss of national control over reproduction standards, as well as the state's growing intervention, necessitated the establishment of regulatory mechanisms to maintain the balance. In this perspective, internal regulation was based on effective intervention by the central state, which has become the main actor in the resolution of contradictory social interests and in maintaining a minimal coherence and cohesion required for social reproduction. But the main characteristics of the increase in state revenue resided in the substantially increasing contribution of the various cash commodities (petrol in Tunisia, phosphates in Morocco, etc.). Actually, the intervention of the state to regulate the replication of this development process was closely linked with the growth of these cash commodities.

The regulation of this development process was not limited to the management of the internal balance; it also involved directing the external balance. Thus, the new development process instituted in the 1970s was illustrated by a greater opening of these economies to the outside world. This led to a high dependence of these economies on global trade and a change in the structure of external trade. The result was a net increase in manufactured products to the detriment of primary products. However, as we will see later on, these exports remained fragile. All these mechanisms provided the regimes with a relatively stable period from the early 1970s to the early 1980s.

In Algeria, the industrialization process was centred around the development of the internal market, and it promoted the emergence and structuring of the capital goods and intermediate goods sectors. These development processes rejected international specialization, and tried to support their political independence through the construction of an autonomous and self-centred national economy. Foreign direct investment was very limited and foreign interests, essentially in the hydrocarbon sectors, were nationalised. Besides, the development of private capital was supervised and directed mainly towards non-strategic structures like consumer goods, the building material sector or certain service activities like catering and hotel business.

In this development process, the state played a central role with regard to industrialization through the establishment of an important sector of government-owned firms. In fact, as pointed out by Jaidi:

> the State appears as the impelling force of an in-depth industrialization aimed at establishing an integrated field of activity. The extension of the public industrial sector should provide the objective bases for an increased autonomization of the development process (1987).

Furthermore, the state created a monopoly in other strategic sectors such as external trade, the monetary and financial system and the key social sectors like education and health. Controlling these services should have enabled the society to build a dynamic and autonomous economy easily.

During the 1970s decade, the rapid increase in oil prices led to an acceleration of economic growth and a rapid increase in investment in Algeria. This resulted in the development of an industrial core representing the first elements of coherence. The industrial process thus initiated and funded with oil earnings was geared towards structuring an autonomous industrial base and reducing dependence on the outside world. Thus, in place of a development logic dominated by and completely integrated into the world market, the economy tried to develop internal processes with a view to providing the development system with an autonomous base through a significant industrialization effort.

However, while industry received considerable financial resource provisions, agriculture was marginalized. This led to a serious crisis within the farming community and significant rural depopulation aggravated by the action of the colonial administration in its massive displacement of people, with a view to thwarting the political and military action of the anti-colonialist movement. Furthermore, the agricultural difficulties made these economies rely heavily on the outside world for essential commodities.

In spite of these difficulties, Algeria's substantial oil revenue in the 1970s made the development process relatively stable and it ensured the functioning of the principles of regulation. Thus, externally, the increase in oil prices encouraged the development of import capacity and enabled the economy to acquire the capital goods and technological assets necessary for industrialization, as well as final consumer goods. Internally, the oil revenue also enabled the state to accelerate industrial development and, particularly, to ensure the population's free access to all the basic social services. It was from this capacity to integrate that the state drew its legitimacy in these countries, in the 1970s.

This brief outline of the historical context has allowed us to enumerate the main characteristics of the models of growth in the Maghreb. However, despite the specificities of these systems, it is possible to bring out the characteristics common to capital growth in the post-national period. The first characteristic lies in a tendency to marginalize agriculture, especially in Algeria and Tunisia. This led to the countries' heavy dependence on the rest of the world for food.

Parallel to the marginalization of the agricultural sector, the growth process in the Maghreb economies was characterized by a severe dislocation of productive structures. Thus, industry was not linked with agriculture, and industrial activities presented a relatively low degree of integration, leading to the heavy dependence of Maghreb economies for their technological inputs, particularly, their capital goods. Furthermore, this constant recourse to outsiders to satisfy the needs of the local economy and the population intensified the financial constraints, which were absorbed by the repeated calls for payment of foreign debts.

These elements glaringly point to the contradictions arising from the various models of development used in the Maghreb. However, these difficulties were contained, thanks to the amount of cash commodity money in this region, which gave the illusion of smooth growth in the 1970s.

## *National Construction, Social Policy and Legitimization*

In most North African countries, the anti-colonial struggle was the primary source of legitimization for the post-colonial powers. However, this first source was soon overtaken by the promotion of the social integration capacity of the economic growth processes initiated in the 1970s. It will be recalled at this point that the social regulation in the Maghreb is characterised by an active state intervention in income redistribution and, particularly, in taking care of part of the costs of labour production, by subsidising consumer prices for certain essential commodities and subsidising—through public firms—certain strategic goods and services such as water, electricity, public transport and health.

Furthermore, the economic growth process initiated in the 1970s was able to absorb the new elite that graduated from the modern education system and assure them of rapid social mobility. It was thanks to this social integration capacity that the state was able to build its legitimacy and ensure that the population supported its logic despite the contradictory projects based on a tradition or membership of a trans-state community. As Camau explained in respect of the Maghreb,

> the allegiance to its authority (the state) found compensation in statements likely to guarantee improved living standards. This 'State clientelism', a form of compromise between those who governed and those who were governed, determined the support of the peoples and their action solely based on their distributive capacities' (1990:421).

But more than the civil society's support of the logic of political modernity, it is a division of roles in which the society leaves politics to the state in exchange for economic and social mobility. In fact, commenting on the Algerian society, A. El-Kenz indicated that even though individual and social rights were recognized in theory, the people could aspire to only social rights. On the one hand, the state promoted the right to work, to education, to health, and to housing; on the other hand, the state controlled opinion, social organization, expression, etc. Hence, a form of implicit 'social pact' was established between the civil society that seemed to abdicate its political rights in favour of the state which, in exchange, guaranteed their social rights. Security against freedom seemed to be the terms of this social contract (El-Kenz 1990:11). Hence, the State-Society relations in the Arab world in the 1970s were marked by this social consensus based on the division of roles: the state as a political space and the civil society as a universe for the satisfaction of needs.

Concurrent with these common legitimization values, each national social order had specific forms of legitimization. Thus, in Morocco, the origin of the royal family and its descent from Medina was often used to explain the longevity of the Alaoui reign. In Tunisia, the post-colonial state project aimed at constructing a modern society capable of reconciling the specific and the universal, and neutralising old political allegiances. In this case, the state would find the sources of its legitimization in the ideology of modernity and, more particularly, in the notions of critical reasoning and separation of political power from religious influence. Finally, in Algeria, parallel to the anti-colonial struggle, the post-colonial state found a new source of legitimacy in the Ulemas'[3] participation in power as well as in their religious reference. Thus, the theme of specific socialism, based on a reconciliation between the ideals of equality, economic independence and traditional Islamic values, dominated the public debate. In fact, L. Addi wrote that

> since it did not have an ideology of its own, the FLN borrowed that of the Ulemas', which is at odds with political modernity, whose two constitutive principles are the autonomy of the individual, a subject of law, and the critical conscience with regard to social practices'.

As from then on, and every time the historical legitimacy weakened, the state appealed increasingly to religion, and this led to the emergence of state fundamentalism, which paved the way for a fundamentalism based on protests, following the economic development crisis in the 1980s.

Beyond the convergences, particularly in terms of relations between state and societies, this presentation has enabled us to grasp the differences between the three mechanisms of state construction in the Maghreb.

However, the post-colonial order in the Maghreb, with its territorial entities, and its management of politics, was unable indefinitely to resist the contradictions that it was confronted with. Thus, as from the early 1980s, the outbreak of the crisis of nation-state in the Maghreb was evident.

## Globalization and Failure of Social Policies in the Maghreb: Crisis of the Growth Processes

The models of national construction, the main characteristics of which we have tried to identify, reached their limits in the early 1980s. In fact, it appeared that from the point of view of both the economic balances and the productive process, the development model instituted in the 1960s and 1970s underwent a crisis. This crisis found expression essentially in the debt situation, external imbalances, budget deficit and inflationist tensions.

In Algeria, the deepening of the agricultural crisis led to a sharp decline in agricultural productivity and created the need to resort to the outside to satisfy the food needs of the population. On the other hand, the industrialization effort initiated in the 1970s called for high imports in technology, which, in the absence of a local technical capacity, was translated into a technological dependence on the outside world.

All these constraints led to a malfunctioning of the external balance of payments and resulted in the widespread recourse to international debts to cope with imbalances in external payments. Moreover, these constraints were more important as they coincided with a drop in oil prices from the early 1980s resulting in a net decrease in oil earnings. This reduction led to a decrease in investments and the collapse of economic growth in Algeria.

In Tunisia and Morocco, the growth process was blocked by the non-existence of an imported technology control strategy and the abandoning of all national productive integration efforts manifested by the negative progress of capital returns. In order to control and maintain the conditions of a rise in capital, and subsequently, the profit rate, two mechanisms were applied:

(a) an increased recourse to the importation of new technology as a result of the dislocation of the productive structures and in order to maintain high levels of labour productivity; and
(b) a double action in distribution in order to maintain real salaries at a low level and to give productivity gains to non- wage-earner revenues.

Thus, these procedures aimed at maintaining the profit rate penalised the internal market-related sectors since they did not promote the development of demand. In this sense, the search for a connection, at the production level, between internal and external sectors, came up against the appropriateness of production to the social needs, when it came to realisation. If for sectors connected to the internal market, the national space constituted the natural outlet, for export-related sectors, integration to the international market was the major concern. This contradiction at the centre of growth models established in these economies from the 1970s was not formal, since it presupposed the existence of different regulation procedures.

This interpretation of the source of the crisis placed emphasis on the power struggle between internal market -related enterprises and those dependent on the external market as well as the stakes of a solution to the crisis. However, despite these difficulties perceptible in the mid-1970s, the stability of the growth process was not called in question and the system continued to function. This continuity was attributed to the role played by the method of regulation method and its capacity to absorb the emerging contradictions.

The situation continued until the early 1980s, when the accumulation of contradictions started showing through the inability of the regulation method to absorb them. Thus, structural stability was disrupted and the economic growth system implemented since the early 1970s entered into a crisis.

The consequence of the economic crisis was twofold. The first was political and involved the consequences of this economic discontinuity on the project for the legitimization of the government in place. Actually, the crisis substantially decreased the government's social integration capacity. It will be recalled that the increasing ineffectiveness of the anti-colonial struggle rhetoric, with the emergence of new generations born after independence, led the authorities to consider as central to the legitimization process the capacity of the development process to integrate and promote different social sectors. In this sense, the failure of the economic growth process resulted in the crumbling of the legitimization project. The effects of this crisis were all the more important since, according to M. Camau, they affected 'the groups enjoying a rise in social status, the new middle classes, within which the most contradictory values and trends' coexist and which are therefore among the groups most exposed to the 'schizophrenic duality' (1990:439).

At the institutional level, this economic discontinuity was combined with the increase in vote-catching practices to maintain the groups that supported the government within the population. Thus, the modern state, weakened by the failure of these socialisation and integration methods, was undermined, on the one hand, by the necessary reference to the law and modern rational legality, and on the other, by the escalation of vote-catching methods. This economic, social and institutional crisis was at the root of the legitimization crisis of the modern state in the Maghreb and, more particularly, of the society's disputing the state's political monopoly. Thus, we have seen all over the Maghreb the increase in democratic demands and eruption of the civil society in politics in the 1970s and early 1980s. This crisis deepened with the increased urban marginalization in the 1980s caused by the implementation of structural adjustment programmes.

## *Structural Adjustment and Globalization in the Maghreb*

The outbreak of the debt crisis in August 1982 led donors to prepare the international debt strategy and define means and institutions to ensure that this crisis was not transformed into a real financial crisis capable of bringing about the collapse of the international finance system. Since then, the IMF became, at the institutional level, the leading organ in terms of Third World debt management. Thus, before negotiating their debt with the London Club for private creditors and the Paris Club for public creditors, developing countries had to sign a confirmation agreement with the IMF.

Even though a SAP was officially adopted in Tunisia in 1986, the government had embarked on a budget deficit reduction programme since the early 1980s. It was within this framework that the state decided in 1983 to withdraw from the reproduction of the labour force by eliminating the subsidy on basic commodities. These measures led to the bread riots of January 1984, and the government subsequently adopted a more cautious attitude when it came to introducing the SAPs.

The official analysis of the crisis in Tunisia endorsed the results of the evaluation that B. Belassa made for the World Bank. He recommended a programme of reforms aimed at re-establishing the balance of payments as well as reorganizing productive structures.

The set of actions, in the form of both prices and quantities, constituted the basics of the SAP adopted in Tunisia. This programme sought to contain the rise in the demand and the adaptation of internal economic structures to the exigencies of the world market. Thus the dynamics of this model brought about a break with the structuring of the internal and external sectors as the basis of the growth model of the 1970s, since the external sector was given priority in the allocation of resources. Thus, the Bretton Woods institutions and the public authorities, through SAP, favoured a complete reorientation of development choices and priorities by imposing an extroverted model that cancelled out all autonomous development possibilities and encouraged the process of normalizing the productive structures of the economy, and their integration into the world economy.

The Economic and Social Council of Tunisia expressed serious reservations about on these choices which also came under pressure from the industrial middle class linked to the internal market. This explains the slowdown in the implementation of certain reforms, particularly those related to import liberalisation.[4] As a result of pressure from the World Bank and IMF, these initial reservations gave way to a new certitude which led to an acceleration of the reform movement (Bessis et al. 1987).

In Morocco, the drop in the price of phosphates as from 1976 aggravated the public deficit, which increased from 9.7 per cent of the GDP in 1978 to 12.4 per cent in 1980.[5] Besides, the external deficit increased rapidly from 7.9 to 12 billion dollars between 1978 and 1983, which gave rise to a rapid debt growth, the service of which absorbed nearly 50 per cent of the export earnings in 1983.

It was in this environment of crisis that the SAP was introduced in Morocco with effect from 1981 (Abouhani 1994). The reform mainly aimed at reducing the public deficit through state disengagement from basic commodity subsidies. Thus, the government decided to increase the price of basic commodities from 14 to 77 per cent. These increases kindled a vast movement of protest within the opposition and workers' unions. To defuse the crisis, the government decided to cut these price increases by half. But the trade unions insisted on their annulment. The Democratic Labour Confederation called for a general strike on Saturday 20 June 1981, while the Moroccan Labour Union decided to organise a strike in Casablanca on 18 June. These strikes observed by the majority of workers turned into riots in the country's major cities and were severely suppressed by the authorities. Thus, both opposition and union leaders were arrested, their offices closed and newspapers proscribed. Trials were organised in major cities and harsh verdicts were pronounced against union militants and demonstrators.

However, this popular mobilisation against structural adjustment did not prevent the authorities from continuing and expanding the economic choices. Thus, various reforms were initiated to reduce the internal and external balances but especially to accelerate the international integration of the economy into the DIT through a greater opening to the world market.[6] But the social and popular mobilisation against the adjustment spread and resulted in the January 1994 riots and the December 14, 1990 strike.

In contrast to Tunisia and Morocco, Algeria succeeded in resisting SAP for a long time. In fact, according to Yachir (1993), even if the government opted for economic reforms from the early 1980s with Chadli's coming to power, 'the ruling group never once thought of giving up state regulation, or cutting out the public sector which they only thought of decentralising with regard to agriculture, industry as well as the building and services sectors'.

The fragility of the Algerian model became visible in 1985-86, with the drop in oil prices and the depreciation of the dollar, which was used to purchase-hydrocarbon exports. The drop in export earnings prompted a cessation of public investments and a collapse in growth which became negative (-1 per cent in 1987 and -2 per cent in 1988). Besides, there was an explosion in external indebtedness as the service ratio increased from 35 per cent of exports in 1985 to 54 per cent of exports in 1986.

In this context of profound crisis, the Algerian government undertook a series of reforms with effect from 1986 (F. Yachir 1993). The state-controlled agricultural sector was dissolved, and the land and farming materials were distributed to workers. The public industrial sector also experienced reform in 1988 with the creation of holding companies exercising ownership rights over public enterprises. Moreover, the banking sector was improved through reforms aimed at automating banks and substituting state financing with bank financing subjected to the rules of profitability.

However, these reforms did not have the expected effects, with debt service reaching 87 per cent of export earnings in 1988. The budget deficit reached 5 per cent of GDP, the gradual price liberalization and depreciation of the national currency accelerated inflation, while unemployment continued to increase rapidly.

The rapid deterioration of the economic situation was the root cause of the October 1987 riots. However, the new government appointed by Chadli in September 1989 with Hamrouch as Prime Minister broke with the vacillation of previous governments and openly opted for a more conventional SAP. The Hamrouch government analysed the 1985-86 crisis as resulting from the lack of eagerness shown by political authorities to implement the reform programmes decided by the same authorities. These reforms sought to extend the measures taken by the Merbah government in terms of the state's withdrawal from the operation of the economy in favour of a market regulation. This programme was approved by the IMF after intense negotiations in April 1991. This agreement was not the first to be signed between Algeria and the IMF, but it was the first, according to Yachir, to take up, in their entirety, almost all the standardised measures which usually define structural adjustment programmes implemented in the Southern countries (1993:34).

The implementation of these reforms faced strong resistance from the UGTA, the workers' union, and the association of public firm managers. Thus, there was an explosion of social conflicts in 1989-90. These conflicts enabled trade unions to impose a series of measures that went against the SAP, like the setting up of unemployment benefits, the creation of a 'social net' by the Ghozali government with a view to absorbing the effects of the suppression of subsidies on food products, the restriction of the freedom to lay off workers, etc. These demands elicited a response from the Abdessalam government which, without rejecting the agreement with the IMF, undertook to renegotiate some of its aspects. Moreover, this government defined a new development programme aimed at relaunching the industrialization programme abandoned by the various Chadli governments, through a more rigorous management of the external constraint. After Abdessalam's departure, the Malek government embarked on new negotiations with the IMF in order to sign an agreement that would enable it to reschedule the external debt. Thus, contrary to other Arab economies, the implementation of a SAP in Algeria encountered strong resistance both from workers' and employers' unions and from public authorities. But the scope of the imbalance, particularly the external debt, and the strong dependence on the outside for food and technology, made it for more difficult to define an alternative development strategy.

Nevertheless, these reform programmes could not restimulate economic growth and were no more than crisis management strategies. Actually, with its pernicious social and political effects, the deflation seemed to be a characteristic feature of the economic growth process induced by structural adjustment in the Maghreb economies. This view gained acceptance among public authorities, in the re-establishment of the internal balance which was done through a drastic reduction of state intervention with regard to development and social regulation. The same logic led to the re-establishment of the external balance, with a substantial reduction of imports, which aggravated the depressionist trends in the Maghreb. In Morocco, the improvement of the external balance was facilitated by the rescheduling of the external debt. The reduction of the external balance led to the reestablishment of the import capacity of the Maghreb economies. However, this capacity was used for final consumption, and it cost a lot more than in the past.

SAP, on the contrary, failed to usher in a new growth process based on export promotion. In fact, despite the existence of a voluntarist policy, export activities were limited to activities with a high labour content and an increase in service (essentially tourism) activities.

At the social level, the implementation of the SAP was manifested in the substantial drop in job creation which, combined with a relatively sharp demographic growth, led to a rapid increase in unemployment in the Maghreb. Urban youth unemployment in fact increased faster than the global unemployment volume. Like the rapid increase in unemployment, all the adjustment-related reforms led to a decrease in real salaries. This decrease dates as far back as the 1980s. The immediate effect of the growing precariousness of the social situation resulting from the implementation of the SAP was the deepening of poverty in the Maghreb.

## Social Policy Crisis and Protests Against the State in the Maghreb

Structural adjustment programmes did not provide the Maghreb states with the possibility to build new economic and social standards to replace those in crisis. At the social level, more than a deterioration of the population's living conditions, we were faced with a social ambivalence between two societies: on the one hand, a modern society accustomed to the styles of consumption and formal production, and, on the other, a society of marginality.

Thus exclusion, rootlessness and urban misery became the basic characteristics of the social landscape in the Maghreb countries. This situation was at the root of the radicalisation of protests against the modern state and it progressively led to its de-legitimization. The disintegration of the universe of state legitimization was accentuated in the Maghreb just like in other Third World countries, by its being divested of prerogatives in terms of economic decisions, development choices and social regulation by supra-national organs within the globalization framework. In his last book, *The Age of Extremes*, Eric Hobsbawm (1994) wrote:

> supra-national decisions will be taken by managers of major international credit agencies, which represent the resources of the oligarchy of the richest countries. As the gap between rich and poor deepens, this global power seems to increase. Since the 1970s, the World Bank and IMF, with the political backing of the United States, have followed a policy that systematically promotes the orthodoxy of the free market, free enterprise and global trade freedom, and which suits the American economy at this end of century just as it suited Great Britain during the preceding century, but which does not necessarily suit the rest of the world (580-581).

Thus the SAPs, conceived as an alternative to the blocking of national development mechanisms, resulted in the growing marginalization of Maghreb economies within the globalization movement, as well as the increased state de-legitimization.

This protest against the State followed the contours of the social ambivalence in the Maghreb. In fact, one observes the coexistence of the world of 'modernity',[7] consisting, on the one hand, of all the organisations, socio-professional associations, political parties, comprising what is referred to today as 'civil society' in the Arab world and, on the other, the world of 'marginality'.

The world of modernity expresses its protests against the State in the democratic political space. This protest is based on a specific analysis of the source of the crisis of modernity in the Maghreb. In fact, for this trend of thought, the rationalisation of economic and social structures was blocked by the neo-patrimonialism of political structures and the communal nature of social relations. On the one hand, the personalisation of political power and its non-separation from the economy reduced the efficiency of modern productive structures, and subsequently weakened the economies of the Maghreb. On the other hand, the persistence of communal social relations hampered the development of individuals and their participation in the modernisation of Maghreb societies. Thus, the crisis of modernity stemmed from its truncated nature. The modern project then had to be pursued and developed by strengthening the rationality through a return of the subject. This project placed on the intellectual scene the issue of citizenship and was supposed to depoliticize religion without denying the sacred character of the divine text. Actually, citizenship enables Muslim societies to 'embark on a secularisation process', says Addi, 'in which the sacred and the profane are distinctly separated, thus making [religion] lose its claims to worldly power. Religion therefore loses all political authority in the public space where it has so far served not as a spiritual ideal but as a temporal ideal' (Addi).

From the political viewpoint, this project was expressed in the fight for democracy and for respect for human rights. This trend was based on the calling to question of the task-sharing of the 1960s and 1970s between the state, which dominated politics, and civil society that was reduced to the satisfaction of needs. This questioning did not involve the state alone; it also attacked the state's monopoly over politics. It thus involved civil society's desire to reappear in the political field. This democratic struggle was combined with a fight for the respect of individual freedoms with a view to freeing people from the communal weight of social relations.

The modern society was faced with the world of marginality, markedly more important because of the growth of exclusion. This counter-society comprises populations excluded from modern production and consumption methods, and settled in a new urban space. This world was the object of struggles between political authorities and Islamic movements. And yet, while the states restricted themselves to a repressive control policy, the Islamist movements tried to penetrate these spaces by re-socialising them, using the mosques. Thus, they developed sports clubs, cultural associations and solidarity associations to help the needy.

This penetration was carried out through the exaltation of community values and solidarity in the face of the growing individualism in Maghreb societies. Moreover, this moralist view came with the development of an austere life which then became a norm of social behaviour. This norm was all the more important since pauperisation restricted the youths' access to modern consumption. Actually, according to Roy, the 'Islamists present an apology of chastity, virtue, far from a certain art of living peculiar to Muslim civilisation. They transform into dignity what has so far been an expression of the depreciation of the self image' (1992:79).

This marginal society generated a radical political attack against the modern state. This de-legitimization was basically due to both social exclusion and to the refusal to separate the temporal from the religious, embodied by the modern state under the influence of integrist propaganda. However, the forms of Islamic penetration in the world of urban marginality varied from one country to another. In fact, if in Algeria the Islamists were able to transform this counter-society into a real social movement against the state,[8] in Morocco and Tunisia, this penetration is still relatively insignificant and occurs in various degrees.

The extent of the Islamic protest and the identity withdrawal in Algeria and its limited nature in the other two countries can be explained by the specificities of the construction of the post-colonial state. In Algeria, the religious referent participated in the legitimization of power. Furthermore, as the historical legitimacy crumbled, the government increased its recourse to the religious leaders to fend off a secular and modernist opposition. Thus, the regime's lack of legitimacy in the late 1970s and its refusal to liberalize the political system ultimately induced it to change its 'socialising' ideology into a 'fundamentalism working not against the State', says Deheuvels, 'but within the State' (Addi). According to Addi, the aim of this state fundamentalism was to 're-islamize the society using the State', i.e. moralising social space on the basis of Islamic standards. However, the growth of the economic crisis and the incapacity of the government to provide adequate solutions to it resulted in the overtaking of state fundamentalism by a fundamentalism based on protests against the state and all forms of politics not subjected to religion.

In Tunisia, o n the contrary, the protest against the state was based on the very principles of the modernist project, and essentially concerned the state's monopolization of politics. This protest was not specific to the secular opposition, which was legally recognized in the early 1980s, but also involved the Islamic opposition. As Camau, noted, 'the upsurge of Islamists and the new institutional centrality of traditionally "reformist" intellectuals are both akin to the same phenomenon—the weakening of the vote-catching compromise—which guaranteed the monopoly of mediation for the ruling elite'. Thus, this protest against the state essentially took the form of a call for a new conversion of the political space into greater democratization and pluralism.

In Morocco, the forms of protests against the state were, in some respects, similar to those of Tunisia, in seeking to reduce the patrimonial nature of the ruling power. In fact, the opposition aimed to modernise a traditional state, and give civil society greater access to politics. In addition, the opposition regularly flirted with the idea of the conversion of the political system into a constitutional monarchy to mark its determination to reduce the King's monopoly of politics, while acknowledging, however, the historical legitimacy of the Alaouite dynasty.

These factors enable us to grasp the differences in the forms of expression of post-colonial crises in the Maghreb. The peculiarities result from the specific historical processes of the construction of the state in the three countries. Thus, neither the strong Islamic protest in Algeria nor the democratic demands in Tunisia and Morocco result from the imperviousness of the Arabo-Muslim societies to Western modernity, as claimed by neo-Orientalists. In fact, this analysis enables us to put forward the idea that the forms of protests against the state and its monopolization of politics in the Maghreb, tend to follow the contours of state construction projects and confront them with their own universe of legitimisation.

Besides, after the euphoria of the 1980s, the Islamic movements are no longer analyzed today as movements of identity carrying a 'specific' course of modernity for Maghreb countries. Actually, these movements have in varying degrees participated in the political debate and established themselves as components of the political field whose legitimacy they contested a few years ago. Thus, after the destruction of the sacred aura surrounding them, the Islamic movements have ceased to be a social force above civil society trends and organisations and have become an immanent political force. Today,

> 'Islamism is essentially political. It is not that it has a political dimension, but that it is often nothing more than a sacred status to the political rejection of the established political authority, without developing an attitude of positive assumption of an autonomous identity', according to Khosrokhavar (1994: 25).

The normalisation of Islamism in the political field induced a number of intellectuals and specialists to question, like all political forces, its programme and the capacity of its proposals to provide appropriate solutions to the crisis facing the Arab societies. In this perspective, we cannot but observe that Islamism is confronted with difficulties, with regard to at least two questions. The first is economic and concerns the inability of Islamism to define a coherent development project capable of substituting for the marginalization of Arab countries in the globalization movement. Actually, Islamism seems to hesitate between two economic projects: the first is liberal and is defended by traditional Sunnite middle class more conformist to the spirit of the Sharia, and the other, closer to the radical trends with a preference for strong state intervention in the economy. But, beyond this general orientation, and 'apart from the injunction to be virtuous, which hardly resists the opening of markets', writes Roy, 'there is no specific model of an Islamic economy, except for the determination to give to the financial practices that we are already acquainted with (taxes, loans), different names that comply more with Islamic law' (Roy 1992; Gresh 1994).

Besides, at the cultural level, the Islamist project consists merely of a criticism of Western culture and a complete return to traditional values. Because of the poverty of the cultural model and its refusal to take into consideration the plurality of expression in the Maghreb, the influence of Islamism on the societies is clear. In this perspective, the family which, by virtue of the Sharia, escapes from external views as well as from state control becomes the place for protests in the daily existence of the Islamist project. Thus, more than ever, Islamism appears like a negative protest force against globalization and its destructive consequences in the Arab world, without being able to develop new proposals and a new societal project.

The Iranian experience has shown that the radical revolutionary Islamism project changed very quickly, with its coming to power, into a repressive de-modernization programme. In fact, Islamism, according to Khosrokhavar:

> demodernises society, without being able to take it back to traditional Islam that has become irremediably disintegrated. The de-modernization is repressive because it is carried out under the aegis of an anti-democratic order that suppressed the need for freedom for a modernized youth, caught up in the Islamic movement (1994).

Confronted with this growing protest, the state sought to obtain a new legitimacy based on new values defended by the World Bank and the IMF. Actually, the defence of private enterprise and state disengagement from the economic sphere became the authorities' new key words, and the state thus became the guarantor of the accumulation of individual wealth. Moreover, one observes a new social recomposition within the state apparatus with the disappearance of former 'political' rulers and the appearance of a new generation of technocrats, whose prerogatives are limited to more economic management.[9] These developments characterize the state's response to the political crisis. In fact, through the promotion of technocrats, the governments advocate a strategy for the depreciation of politics and the reduction of its field of expression. Thus, the authorities respond to attacks against its monopoly over politics by depreciating it and refusing civil society access to its management.

The new state hegemony reconstruction strategy entails some uncertainties. In fact, it presupposes that the Maghreb countries will succeed in being integrated into the world economy, in order to back up the new ideological view. Moreover, it is becoming increasingly difficult to be opposed to democratic demands, and the liberal view, with regard to the economy, should be combined with a greater liberalization of political life. Finally, the reduction of the political field and its marginalization destroys the capacity of societies to withstand the extremist temptations of certain fundamentalist groups, and reduces the state's options with regard to the security situation.

Finally, this analysis has enabled us to understand the post-colonial state construction process in the Maghreb. In this regard, the social policies are an integral part of its discourse and its political legitimization practice. And yet, the crisis of the growth processes, as from the early 1980s, resulted in the questioning of social policies implemented by the Maghreb states and a rapid development of unemployment and social exclusion. This new context brought about state de-legitimization and the rapid development of Islamic fundamentalism. The crisis of the nationalist model in the Maghreb today calls for the reconstruction of a new development project and provision for the growing social needs of the populations.

## Notes

* Chief, Trade and Regional Integration Division, Economic Commission for Africa, Addis Ababa.

1. See Hakim Ben Hammouda, *Economie tunisienne: ajustement et crise de l'insertion internationale*, F.T.M., Dakar, 1994.
2. See A. Abouhani, *Le Maroc: crise de modèle de développement et perspective de changement*, F.T.M., Dakar, 1994.
3. The Ulemas are Islamic scribes and scholars who were responsible for the education, justice and religious affairs sectors, once Algeria achieved independence.
4. See M.H. Zaïem, 'Les forces sociales et le plan d'ajustement structurel', *Le Maghreb*, No. 187, 2 fév. 1990.
5. See Ch. Morrison, 'Adjustment, Income and Poverty in Morocco', *World Development*, vol. 19, n°, 1999.
6. For further details, see: Mr. Abdel-Fadil, Les programmes d'adjustement structurel en Egypte et au Maroc- Entre prévision et réalisations, Editions du Centre d'Etudes Stratégiques, de Recherche et de Documentation, Beyrouth/Liban, 1994.
7. This term is used by A. El-Kenz in 'Le mouvement social et les forces politiques dans l'Algérie des années 1990', *Forum du Tiers-Monde*, Dakar, 1994.
8. See A. EL-Kenz's analysis, (1994), *op. cit.*
9. These developments were analyzed by M. Diouf. For the case of Sénégal, see: M. Diouf, 'Le clientélisme, la 'technocratie' et après?' In M.C. Diop (sous la direction), *Sénégal. Trajectoire d'un Etat*, CODESRIA, Dakar 1992.

## References

Bessis, S., 1987, 'Banque Mondiale et FMI en Tunisie: 'Une évolution sur trente ans'', in *Annuaire de l'Afrique du Nord*, Tome XXVI.

Yachir, F., 1993, *Algérie: l'ajustement inachevé.*

Hobsbawm, E., 1994, *The age of extremes, the short twentieth century, 1914-1991*, M. Joseph Ltd, Penguin Group, London, pp. 580-581.

L. Addi, *op. cit.* p. 144.

O. Roy,, 1992, *L'échec de l'Islam politique*, Seuil, Paris, p. 79.

Deheuvels, L-W., 1992, *Islam et pensée contemporaine en Algérie,* Editions CNRS, Paris, p. 273.

Addi, L., *op. cit.* p. 31.

Khosrokhavar, F., 1994, Marginalisation de la jeunesse, marginalisation des élites, A. Gresh (sous la direction), *Un péril islamiste?* Editions complèxes, Bruxelles, p. 131.

Roy, O., *Un bilan d'échec,* A. Gresh (sous la direction), *Un péril islamiste?* , op. cit., p. 58.

Khosrokhavar, F. , *op. cit.,* p. 135.

Akesbi, 1995, De la 'politique des barrages' à la politique d'ajustement, quel avenir pour l'agriculture marocaine? *Mondes en développement.*

Jaidi, L.,1987, *Etat-Nation et intégration économique arabe: vers un nouvel espace régional,* Annuaire de l'Afrique du Nord, Editions du CNRS.

Addi, L., Forme néo-patrimoniale de l'État et secteur public en Algérie, p. 28.

El-Kenz, A., 1990, 'La société algérienne aujourd'hui—Esquisse d'une phénoménologie de la conscience nationale', A. El-Kenz (sous la direction), *Algérie et la modernité,* CODESRIA, Dakar/Sénégal, p.11.

Camau, M., 1990, *Le Maghreb, Collectif, Les régimes politiques arabes,* PUF, Paris, p. 421.

Camau, M., *Le Maghreb, Collectif, Les régimes politiques arabes*, p. 439.

# Part II

## Poverty and Social Services Provision

# 5

# Global and Local Factors and the Welfare of the Poor in Ethiopia: 1974–1997

**Dejene Aredo** *

## Introduction

This chapter attempts to characterize and explain temporal price behaviour in Ethiopia in general and in Addis Ababa in particular with a focus on two often neglected questions: (i) What happened to the cost of living in Ethiopia over a period of twenty-four years? and (ii) What factors can explain these changes? Explanatory variables are classified into two broad categories, namely, global or external factors and domestic or local factors. The central argument of the paper is that global factors, though important, did not play a primary role in determining household welfare positions in the context of a least developed and predominantly subsistence economy such as that of Ethiopia. In this type of economy, structural constraints, which are basically domestic and local in nature, would a play central role in influencing consumer price indices.

The data for this study come from secondary sources, mainly from the surveys and report of the Central Statistical Authority (CSA) and of the National Bank of Ethiopia (NBE).

The rest of the paper is organized as follows: The second section presents the historical background. The third section characterizes retail price behaviour in the context of changing political regimes using simple statistical techniques. The fourth section considers external developments relative to changes in domestic price changes. The fifth section presents details of changes in the cost of living in the country. The sixth section examines terms of trade between rural and urban areas. The final section summarizes the major findings of the study and provides concluding remarks.

## Background

Prices serve as a measure of value expressed in terms of other commodities in monetary units. They are the primary instruments of decision-making by both producers and consumers, thus making them one of the crucial macroeconomic variables (MEDaC 1999). Hence, changes in prices are the most important indicators of the relative scarcity of factors of production or commodities in an environment where they are market-determined. The Consumer Price Indices (CPI) are among the most widely used indicators of the general price level. The latter, which is a weighted average of all group indices, serves as measure of inflation in an economy.

An investigation of the temporal behaviour of the Addis Ababa prices pointed to the existence of strong cyclical movements, depending on weather conditions, significant long-run increases and noticeable seasonal movements (of food prices). Prices of imports, which remained almost stable during earlier years, showed strong upward trends in early 1971, following a steady but mild growth over the 1966–1970 period. The two parallel forces acting on Addis Ababa consumer prices during the 1970–1974 period can be identified as domestic food supply shortfalls arising from poor harvests and imported inflation resulting from commodity and money markets in industrialized countries. The measures taken by the imperial regime of Haile Sellasie to combat consumer price increases included increased food imports and half-hearted price control measures which were never effectively implemented. It appears that the policy-makers dealt with the symptoms and not with the causes of price escalations.

Although no attempt was made to closely investigate the socio-economic effects of the rise in Addis Ababa consumer prices, it should be noted that the noticeable fall in the purchasing power of the Birr, the Ethiopian currency, and the consequent rise in the cost of living contributed to the political uprising of early 1974.

Variations in the Addis Ababa price levels strongly manifested the operation of two types of dependence from which urban centres in Africa suffer: dependence on retarded agricultural growth and on unpredictable world commodity markets.

The steady rise in the Addis Ababa prices of consumer goods had, in different years, prompted the government to announce price control measures. However, it was in 1972 that a well-articulated basic law (Proclamation No. 31 of 1972) was promulgated. The proclamation empowered the Ministry of Commerce, Industry and Tourism to regulate trade and fix prices by public notices for any class of goods and services. However, this basic law was never effectively implemented and the declared price control mechanisms remained paper tigers. Neither the symptom nor the causes of persistent price increases in Addis Ababa were correctly identified and dealt with before things became out of hand. The monarchy was overthrown and the military junta, the Derg, assumed power in September 1974.

One of the major causes of the 1974 revolution was the unprecedented rise in retail prices of commodities in Addis Ababa. Price control was therefore among the major steps taken by the new government, the Derg, when it took over power in 1974. However, price indices in Addis Ababa still rose at fast rates. The factors responsible for the inflationary pressure could have been external, such as the prevailing international inflationary situation, or internal, such as low farm production. However, such inflationary pressure in the second half of the 1970s was not sustained and the growth rate of inflation in Addis Ababa began to decline in 1980. This decline was attributed, among other factors, to the unusually good weather conditions in 1980 and the subsequent bumper harvests in many parts of the country. However, this situation was not sustained, and the severe drought of 1984 hit the country, ushering in a nation-wide decline in food production. This pushed inflation upwards to 8.41 per cent in 1984 and the rate further rose to 19 per cent in 1985. Subsequently, inflationary pressure increased more slowly during the post-harvest period between 1986 and 1990. The government was able to control prices through the Agricultural Marketing Corporation (AMC), which imposed the quota system on farmers and purchased agricultural products at nationally uniform local prices (Dejene 1985). However, because of economic dislocations due to civil war, which brought down the Derg in May 1991, and the almost complete dismantling of price control mechanisms, both the general price and the food price levels increased dramatically, reaching 35.7 per cent in 1991.

During the post-Derg period, after 1991, that is, following the liberalization measures, the rate of inflation fluctuated from year to year owing to monetary expansion, the coffee boom and performance of the commodity producing sectors of the economy.

Price indices, as it is well known, are also important indicators of the cost of living. The general price index increased in both rural and urban areas. This is tantamount to saying that in situations of income stagnation, there is a decrease in real income, which aggravates poverty in the country. Poverty in Ethiopia is prevalent in both rural and urban areas, although more pronounced in the former.

### Price Behaviour in Addis Ababa: 1974–1997

This section attempts to achieve three objectives: (1) determine the magnitude and directions of price movements in Addis Ababa over a period of more than twenty years, (2) identify the major determinants of price behaviour and (3) indicate the major policy measures taken to protect urban consumers at the time.

Although different periods can be identified for price behaviour in Addis Ababa, attention will be given to the 1980s and 1990s. These periods can be categorized into (1) 1975–1983 (the first years of the Derg era), (2) 1984–1991 (a period characterized by central control of prices and a civil war that brought down the Derg in 1991) and (3) 1992–1996 (a period of economic adjustment).

### *1974–1983: The Early Days of the Revolution*

In this part of the paper, the behaviour of prices in the early years of the Derg regime is described in some detail. A study that covered the 1974-1980 period argued that 'during this period, there were persistent and significant increases in the prices of most goods and services' (Shiferaw 1980). Accordingly, the general and food retail prices in Addis Ababa were growing at unprecedented rates of 17.1 per cent and 20.4 per cent per year, respectively, over the 1974-1980 period. The same study identified external and internal causes of the inflationary pressure in the country in the following terms:

> The possible major factors that have contributed to the recent inflationary pressure in the country were the decrease in production, prevailing farm production and the prevailing international inflationary situation (Shiferaw 1980: 36).

In addition, Shiferaw (1980) mentioned monetary expansion, the war economy of the period, and transportation difficulties as factors contributing to inflationary pressure during the second half of the 1970s. Shiferaw also concluded that the Addis Ababa general price index was positively and closely associated with movements in the food price index. In particular, he noted that 'seasonal movement in general price index is closely associated with the seasonal variations in food items'. The general index peaked during the pre-harvest months (September-November) and dropped during the post-harvest months (January-May).

The inflationary pressure in the second half of the 1970s was not sustained. By 1980, the growth rate of inflation in Addis Ababa began to decline as the annual growth rate of the general price index dropped from 16 per cent in 1979 to 4.5 per cent in 1980. This trend persisted until 1983, when actual growth further dropped to a mere 0.80 per cent (Table 1). The behaviour of the general price index was closely associated with movements in the food price index. The latter dropped to an annual growth rate of 18 per cent in 1979 and to 5.2 per cent in 1980 and continued in this fashion until it further dropped to 0.66 per cent in 1983.

The significant decline in the inflation rate in early 1980s can be attributed to the favourable conditions that prevailed at the time. This was the time when the Derg consolidated its political power after emerging as a victorious force out of the internal and external wars of the 1970s. Above all, favourable weather conditions in 1980 contributed to bumper harvests in many parts of the country.

### *1984-1991: Price Control by the Derg*

The early years of the 1980s were encouraging. However, the encouraging development in these periods was short-lived. In 1984, a near-disastrous drought hit the country and brought about a nation-wide decline in food production. As a result, the annual growth rate of inflation rose to 8.41 per cent in 1984 and further increased to 19 per cent in 1985. The general price index reached its all-time high of 509.4 points as the food price sky-rocketed to 654.7 points (Ministry of Commerce 1963: 100).

The post-drought period (1986-1990) saw a substantial decline in the growth rate inflation. During this period, the general price index increased at the rate of 1.56 per cent and the food retail price fell by 0.34 per cent per year. However, the general price index (as well as the food price index) went on increasing over the period under study. The general price index, which dropped to 459.4 points in 1986 from 509.4 points in 1985, further increased to 544.2 points in 1990. In short, inflationary pressure increased over the 1986–1990 period. It was in 1986 that Ethiopia registered the largest fall in the rate of inflation (9.8 per cent). However, this is not surprising, as the preceding year (1985) was an abnormal year, one of unprecedented crop failure.

The relative decline in the rate of inflation during this period can be explained by three major domestic factors: (1) post-drought recovery of the agricultural sector, (2) intervention by central authorities to protect the urban poor from retail price escalations and (3) partial freeze of prices of manufactured goods. The government was able to control prices through a powerful parastatal, the Agricultural Marketing Corporation (AMC), which imposed the quota system on farmers and purchased agricultural products at uniform local prices (Dejene 1985). In addition, the socialist-oriented government subsidized food prices and introduced a rationing system in some of the urban centres. At times, the government resorted to commercial importation of food to ameliorate food shortages in urban areas. Prices of manufactured goods were determined by central authorities to the extent that state-owned enterprises were concerned. Of course, the massive inflow of food aid in the second half of the 1980s also exerted downward pressure on food prices at the country level.

Once more, the slowdown in the inflation rate was not sustained over a long period; by 1991, the Addis Ababa general price index and the food index (Ministry of Commerce 1963: 100) had jumped to an all-time high of 738.7 and 890.6 points, respectively, due to the escalation of the civil war, which brought down the Derg in May 1991. The annual rate of inflation, which stood at 35.7 per cent in 1991, surpassed even the rate experienced in 1985. In addition to the economic dislocation caused by the civil war, the almost complete dismantling of price control mechanisms had contributed to a sudden and sharp rise in food prices in Addis Ababa, as a result of which, the general price level sky-rocketed.

### *1992–1997: A Period of Market Liberalization*

During the post-Derg period, the inflation rate, as measured by changes in the Addis Ababa price index, averaged 5.84 per cent as compared to 0.34 per cent and during the 1986–90 period. However, with an index of 1000.7 points (ten times that of 1963) in 1995, this period experienced an all-time high in a span of 30 years. The yearly fluctuations in the inflation rate during this period have been attributed to three factors: (1) Monetary expansion (2) effects of the coffee boom and (3) performance of the commodity-producing sectors of the economy. For example, the rise in the inflation rate in 1994 and 1995 'was attributed to a significant increase in domestic liquidity which resulted from windfall gains from coffee exports' (NBE, 1994-95: 10) while the easing of inflationary pressure in 1996 and 1997 was attributed to what the National Bank called 'the remarkable growth in the economy (10.6 per cent in 1996) and the easing of pressure created by the coffee boom in 1994-95' (NBE 1995-96: 10).

**Table 5.1: Retail Price Index for Addis Ababa (Excluding House Rent) (1963: 100) and Inflation Rates**

| Year | General index | Food | Growth Rate | |
|---|---|---|---|---|
| | | | General index | Food |
| 1966 | 126.8 | 135.6 | | |
| 1967 | 127.8 | 133.2 | 0.79 | -1.77 |
| 1968 | 128 | 132.3 | 0.16 | -0.68 |
| 1969 | 129.8 | 135 | 1.41 | 2.04 |
| 1970 | 143 | 155.6 | 10.17 | 15.26 |
| 1971 | 143.7 | 155.4 | 0.49 | -0.13 |
| 1972 | 135 | 136.8 | -6.05 | -11.97 |
| 1973 | 147 | 154.3 | 8.89 | 12.79 |
| 1974 | 159.7 | 167.6 | 8.64 | 8.62 |
| 1975 | 170.1 | 175.1 | 6.51 | 4.47 |
| 1976 | 218.7 | 248.4 | 28.57 | 41.86 |
| 1977 | 255.1 | 290 | 16.64 | 16.75 |
| 1978 | 291.6 | 339.5 | 14.31 | 17.07 |
| 1979 | 338.4 | 400.7 | 16.05 | 18.03 |
| 1980 | 353.5 | 421.6 | 4.46 | 5.22 |
| 1981 | 375.2 | 441.2 | 6.14 | 4.65 |
| 1982 | 391.6 | 467.6 | 4.37 | 5.98 |
| 1983 | 394.6 | 470.7 | 0.77 | 0.66 |
| 1984 | 427.8 | 522.8 | 8.41 | 11.07 |
| 1985 | 509.4 | 654.7 | 19.07 | 25.23 |
| 1986 | 459.4 | 554.9 | -9.82 | -15.24 |
| 1987 | 448.3 | 521.3 | -2.42 | -6.06 |
| 1988 | 480 | 562.4 | 7.07 | 7.88 |
| 1989 | 517.6 | 599.6 | 7.83 | 6.61 |
| 1990 | 544.2 | 630.1 | 5.14 | 5.09 |
| 1991 | 738.7 | 890.6 | 35.74 | 41.34 |
| 1992 | 816.4 | 996.2 | 10.52 | 11.86 |
| 1993 | 845.3 | 1010.4 | 3.54 | 1.43 |
| 1994 | 909.5 | 1113.7 | 7.59 | 10.22 |
| 1995 | 1000.7 | 1251.1 | 10.03 | 12.34 |
| 1996 | 949.9 | 1168.2 | -5.08 | -6.63 |
| 1997 | 914.8 | 1118.6 | -0.04 | -0.04 |

**Source**: Computed from NBE, Annual Reports, various issues.

**Figure 5.1: Trends in General price and Food price indices (Index: 1963: 100)**

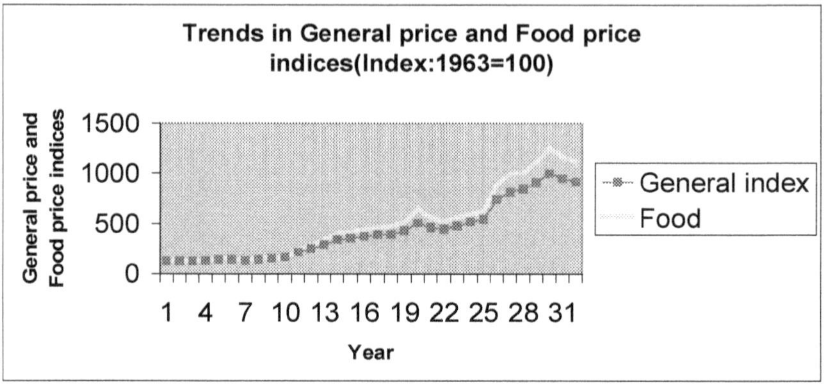


As indicated in the above figure 5.1, both the general price and the food price indices consistently increased over the whole 1966-1997 period. It is important to note that the food price index remained above the general price index during the entire period under consideration.

**Table 5.2: A Summary of Inflation Rates in Addis Ababa**

| Year | Political regime | General Index | Food |
|---|---|---|---|
| 1975 to 83 | Derg | 10.87 | 12.74 |
| 1975 to 90 | Derg | 7.54 | 8.07 |
| 1984 to 85 | Derg | 13.74 | 18.15 |
| 1986 to 90 | Derg | 1.56 | -0.34 |
| 1992 to 96 | EPDRF | 5.32 | 5.84 |

Key: IEG = Imperial Ethiopian Government
Derg = Military Council
EPDRF = Ethiopian Peoples' Democratic Revolutionary Front

## The External Sector and Prices

In this section, I will address two important external factors: foreign trade and the extent of debt burden.

### *4.1 External Trade and The Debt Burden*

External shocks can impose constraints on economic performance in Africa (Soludo 1993) and on people's welfare through unstable export earnings, changes in commodity terms of trade, changes in the cost of borrowing and through the deliberate policies of industrialized countries (e.g. agricultural and import policies of the European Union (EU).

Ethiopia's foreign trade has been characterized by a heavy dependence on primary export commodities (a sector where agricultural products account for about 90 per cent of total export earnings), low income and price elasticities, sharp swings in the demand for primary commodities and by the geographic concentration of exports (in 1992-93 as much as 77 per cent of Ethiopia's exports went to Western Europe, U.S.A. and Japan alone).

Coming back to Ethiopia's foreign trade, the visible trade deficit had been widening at an alarming rate since the mid-1970s. It was only in 1973 that Ethiopia registered a positive trade balance. The deficit increased from a mere 26 million Birr in 1960 to 2.7 billion in 1993. At the same time, the country's capacity to import (as measured by the ratio of exports to imports) plummeted from 0.9 in 1960 to 0.3 in 1993. In other words, merchandise exports covered only 30 per cent of the country's imports in 1993.

Accordingly, the ratio of the current account deficit increased from 1.7 per cent of the GDP in 1961 to 6.4 in 1980, and then to 9 per cent in 1993 (Dejene and Teferi 1995).

One factor that accounted for the country's foreign trade deficit was the unfavourable prices of Ethiopia's exports. To substantiate this, relative prices are estimated by taking coffee as a proxy for exports and crude oil for imports. These are obviously the two most important commodities in Ethiopia's foreign trade. Commodity terms of trade (1975: 100) peaked to an all-time high of 3.6 in 1977, dropped to less than one in the early 1980s and then dropped to 0.88 in 1993 after some improvements in the second half of the 1980s (Dejene and Teferi 1995). Changes in commodity terms of trade can partly be attributed to fluctuations in the world prices of coffee. It appears that there has been a more or less secular decline in the commodity terms of trade.

Ethiopia's external debt, which increased sixfold between 1980 and 1995, was estimated at more than four times the value of the country's exports of goods and services in 1995. The debt service ratio (debt as percentage goods and services) nearly doubled between 1980 (7.3 per cent) and 1995 (13.6 per cent) (*World Development Report 1997*). Table 5.3 summarizes important indicators of the debt burden in Ethiopia.

As indicated in the table, both the debt stock and the ratio of debt to GNP increased during the 1985-1997 period. The debt/GNP and debt/export ratios were 159.0 per cent and 962.9 per cent respectively, in 1997 and this made Ethiopia one of the Sub-Saharan countries with a total debt greater than its GNP, which accounted for the accumulation of arrears. The total arrears reached 83.6 per cent of the GNP and 506.2 per cent of exports in 1997 (Alemayehu 2000). The increase in arrears might be due to resource constraints that hampered the timely debt-service payments.

**Table 5.3: Some Indicators of Debt Burden**

| Year | Debt stock (in Billion USD) | Debt/GNP (%) | Debt/Exports (%) |
|---|---|---|---|
| 1985 | 5.21 | 78.1 | 932.1 |
| 1986 | 6.13 | 88 | 891 |
| 1986 | 7.36 | 99 | 1150.4 |
| 1987 | 7.70 | 100.5 | 1189 |
| 1988 | 7.84 | 98.6 | 1034.8 |
| 1989 | 8.63 | 126.6 | 1276.3 |
| 1990 | 9.12 | 171.6 | 1666.7 |
| 1991 | 9.34 | 169.2 | 2036.9 |
| 1992 | 9.7 | 157.6 | 1889.2 |
| 1993 | 10.07 | 208.5 | 1788 |
| 1994 | 10.31 | 180.3 | 1276.5 |
| 1995 | 10.08 | 168.9 | 1224.4 |
| 1997 | 10.08 | 159.0 | 962.9 |

**Source**: Alemayehu 2000

### *Exchange Rate Policy*

The exchange rate represents the major link between the national economy and the outside world, and exchange rate policies play a prominent role in most adjustment programmes. By influencing the domestic prices of tradable commodities (e.g. coffee in Ethiopia), the exchange rate directly or indirectly affects the supply and demand of almost all goods and services produced in the national economy, and also has significant effects on the overall current account and balance of payments situation.

The Ethiopian Birr has been progressively devalued since October 1992 when it dropped from U.S.$ 1=2.07 Birr to U.S. $1=5 Birr. At the time this paper was being written, the auction market price of the U.S. Dollar stood at about 7.27 Birr .

The devaluation of the Birr has impacted different sections of society differently; producers of cash crops and exporters are likely to have gained from the devaluation measure. In other words, those people who are engaged in the production and export of tradable products (e.g. coffee) were likely to gain. But, since Ethiopian farmers are mainly subsistence producers, the effect of devaluation on the rural economy may not be substantial. However, there has been a considerable rise in the prices of imported farm inputs since the devaluation of the Birr.

A significant rise in the price of fertilizers occurred in 1993 following the 140 per cent devaluation of the Ethiopian Birr. The price of DAPS rose from 107.1 Birr in 1991-92 to 176.2 Birr per quintal in 1992-93 (64.5 per cent increases). At the same time, the bank interest rate increased substantially. This resulted in a direct subsidy amounting to 15 per cent of the unit price of fertilizers. But the government removed subsidies completely by the end of 1995-96.

Adjustment policies, including the devaluation of the domestic currency, have adversely affected significant sections of rural people such as the net purchasers of food and women who head households. The net purchasers of food, who account for more than 40 per cent of the total farm householders, have experienced sharp declines in their living standard as the price of food substantially increased, following the recent market liberalization measures.

Female-headed households that account for about 18 per cent of the total farm households lack vital farm inputs including adult male labour, oxen and land. They benefit very little from the production of tradable goods (e.g. coffee) for exports. They are among the major victims of the devaluation measure.

Pastoralists, who occupy about half of Ethiopia's land area, are also among those who benefit least from the devaluation measures. Their livelihood has already been threatened by recurrent drought and animal diseases prevalent in the lowlands. The increases in the relative prices of cereals will have adverse effects on the food security status of the pastoralists.

In urban areas, the poor are among the major victims of the devaluation measure. Female-headed households who, specifically in urban areas, often derive their income from informal sector employment and not from tradable services, are likely to be adversely affected in both ways, by a decline of their nominal as well as their real income.

## The Cost of Living in Ethiopia

This section describes the patterns of household expenditure and cost of living in Ethiopia, using price indices and related variables. The nature of food prices, cost of living and structure of household expenditure/income are examined.

### *Cost of Living and Food Prices*

Price indices are standard indicators of changes in cost of living in a country over a defined period. In Ethiopia, food accounts for a major proportion of household total expenditure, as indicated in Table 4. At the country-level, food takes up the lion's share (56.78 per cent) of household total expenditure. Of this proportion, cereals account for 25 per cent, and they constitute the staple diet of the poor households. Rural people, in particular, allocate a significant portion of their budget to food. This is consistent with other studies undertaken in Ethiopia (Tadele 2000; MEDaC 1999). A CSA Survey of 1981-82 reported that this proportion was as much as 70.2 per cent.

Urbanization is often accompanied by a decline in the proportion of food in total household expenditure. In urban Ethiopia, this proportion stood at 52 per cent as compared to 58 per cent in rural areas in 1995-96. On the other hand, urban dwellers spend a substantial proportion of their incomes on house rent, utilities and transportation, as can be seen from Table 4.

It is also expected that the share of food in total expenditure should decline over a long period of time. However, in Ethiopia, this does not seem to be the case, as can be seen from the example of Addis Ababa where over a period of twenty-four years, the share of food remained at the same level, though it substantially declined in the mid-1970s: i.e. 1963: 49 per cent; 1975: 32 per cent; 1981-82: 49 per cent; and 1995-96: 49 per cent.

**Table 5.4: Household Expenditure Patterns in Rural and Urban areas: Weights Attached to Baskets of Commodities on the Basis of the HICES (1995-96)**

| No. | Expenditure Groups | Country Level | Rural | Urban | Addis Ababa |
|---|---|---|---|---|---|
| 1 | General | 100 | 100 | 100 | 100 |
| 2 | Food | 56.78 | 58.07 | 51.69 | 49.08 |
| | (of which: Cereals, Beverages) | 25 | 27.06 | 15.67 | 14.55 |
| 3 | Cigarettes & tobacco | 0.44 | 0.44 | 0.44 | 0.23 |
| 4 | Clothing &Footwear | 8.72 | 8.68 | 8.93 | 10.04 |
| 5 | House rent, construction materials, water, fuel & power | 17.19 | 16.54 | 20.06 | 12.3 |
| 6 | Furniture, h.h. equip. h.h. operation & domestic service | 5.93 | 6.02 | 5.55 | 6.78 |
| 7 | Medical care & health expenses | 1.12 | 1.02 | 1.56 | 2.12 |
| 8 | Transport & Communication | 2 | 1.23 | 5.38 | 10.2 |
| 9 | Recreation, entertainment and education | 0.6 | 0.34 | 1.72 | 3.15 |
| 10 | Personal care & effects | 1.37 | 1.3 | 1.67 | 1.94 |
| 11 | Miscellaneous goods & services | 2.06 | 2.07 | 0.98 | 3.04 |

**Source**: CSA, 1996. 'Report on the Development of Consumer Price Indices for Ethiopia', Bulletin 169.

HICES: Household Income, and Consumption, and Expenditure Survey.

The cost of living, measured by changes in price indices, has been rising in both rural and urban areas, as can be seen from Table 5.4 The general price index increased by 180 points in Addis Ababa and by 185 points in rural areas over the 1981-82 and 1994-95 periods (1981-82: 100). The relatively slower increase in the rate of inflation in Addis Ababa in the mid-1980s could be attributed to the urban-biased policy of the Derg, which established a rigid and more or less effective system of price control mechanisms resented by farmers and severely criticized by Western donors.

**Table 5.5: Urban/Rural Ratio of Price Indices, 1981-82: 100**

| Year | General Price Index | | Urban/Rural |
|---|---|---|---|
| | Rural | Addis Ababa | |
| 1981 - 1982 | 100 | 100 | 1.00 |
| 1982 - 1983 | 119.5 | 102.8 | 0.86 |
| 1983 - 1984 | 115.9 | 120.5 | 1.04 |
| 1984 - 1985 | 168.6 | 137.4 | 0.81 |
| 1985 - 1986 | 162 | 142 | 0.88 |
| 1986 - 1987 | 149.1 | 133 | 0.89 |
| 1987 - 1988 | 151.5 | 136.1 | 0.9 |
| 1988 - 1989 | 158.3 | 146.2 | 0.92 |
| 1989 - 1990 | 155.3 | 155.6 | 1.00 |
| 1990 - 1991 | 194.5 | 188 | 0.97 |
| 1991 - 1992 | 227.6 | 227.9 | 1.00 |
| 1992 - 1993 | 256.2 | 243.6 | 0.95 |
| 1993 - 1994 | 247.7 | 257.2 | 1.04 |
| 1994 – 1995 | 284.8 | 280 | 0.98 |

**Source**: Computed for CSA (1996). Report on the Development of Consumer Price Indices for Ethiopia, Bulletin 169.

In addition to the above, it should be noted that in Ethiopia, the income elasticity of demand for food is quite high, suggesting that a substantial portion of an extra income will be allocated to food. Anecdotal evidence suggests that about 80 per cent of additional household income will go to food. The marginal propensity to consume in Ethiopia could be as much as 0.7.

Besides, it should noted that as a basic necessity, food is price inelastic, meaning that households make little reductions in their purchase of food in the face of price escalations. This suggests that during times of food price escalation under conditions of income stagnation, households tend to switch their expenditures from non-food items (e.g. education and health) to food in order to make ends meet. As a result, investment in human capital can be neglected and demand for the non-food sector may be depressed. Today, no doubt, businessmen complain about limited effective demand for their non-food goods and services.

The share of food in family budgets has important implications for agricultural development. A policy that encourages the production of cash crops for exports may endanger household food security unless the country has enough foreign exchange earnings with which it can import food. The incremental income from cash crops may be directed towards food purchases, thus further escalating food prices. On the other hand, investment in new farm technologies may not receive attention from farmers, contrary to what is envisaged by structural adjustment policies.

### *The Cost of Living Relative to Income*

So far, we have been considering cost of living or rises in the price indices in isolation from the consumer's income. In this part of the chapter, we will show that increases in the retail prices in Addis Ababa indices were not offset by increases in the real wage rate or in the per capita national product. By doing so we attempt to suggest that the incidence of poverty has increased over time.

**Table 5.6: Cost of Living, Income and Labour Productivity in Medium and Large-Scale Manufacturing Industries (Index, 1981: 100)**

| Year | A.A General Price Index | Purchasing power of the Birr[1] | Av. Wage Manfg. indust. Birr/Worker | Real Wage in manfg. indust. Birr/ Worker[2] | Index of Labour Productivity | Index of wages in manfg indus | GNP per capita US.$ |
|---|---|---|---|---|---|---|---|
| 1981 | 100 | 1.00 | 2352 | 2352 | 100 | 100 | 140 |
| 1982 | 81 | 1.23 | 2540 | 3124 | 103 | 108 | 140 |
| 1983 | 105 | 0.95 | 2550 | 2423 | 108 | 108 | 120 |
| 1984 | 114 | 0.87 | 2754 | 2396 | 111 | 117 | 110 |
| 1985 | 136 | 0.73 | 2802 | 2045 | 118 | 119 | 110 |
| 1986 | 122 | 0.82 | 2998 | 2458 | 134 | 127 | 120 |
| 1987 | 119 | 0.84 | 3108 | 2611 | 84 | 132 | 130 |
| 1988 | 128 | 0.78 | 3166 | 2469 | 84 | 135 | 120 |
| 1989 | 138 | 0.72 | 3304 | 2379 | 52 | 140 | 120 |
| 1990 | 145 | 0.69 | 3172 | 2189 | 44 | 135 | 110 |
| 1991 | 197 | 0.51 | 3373 | 1720 | 33 | 143 | 100 |
| 1992 | 217 | 0.46 | 4113 | 1892 | 70 | 174 | 110 |
| 1993 | 225 | 0.44 | 4503 | 1981 | 108 | 191 | 100 |
| 1994 | 242 | 0.41 | 4726 | 1938 | 120 | 201 | 100 |
| 1995 | 267 | 0.37 | 5059 | 1872 | 142 | 215 | 100 |

**Sources:**
- CSA, 1996; 'Report on the Development of Consumer Price Indices for Ethiopia'.
- CSA, 1997; 'Report on the Large-Scale and Medium-Scale Manufacturing and Electricity Industries Survey', Bulletin 178.
- World Bank, 'World Development Report', various issues.

Changes in real income can be considered by looking at the purchasing power of the domestic currency, the Ethiopian Birr. The purchasing power of the Ethiopian Birr dropped from 1 Birr in 1981 to a mere 37 cents in 1995. This was reflected in the Addis Ababa retail price index that increased by 167 points over the 1981-1995 period (Table 5.6). As a result, real wage rate for workers in large and medium-scale manufacturing industries plummeted from Birr 2, 352 in 1981 to Birr 1, 872 (per year) in 1995. That is, a monthly wage of Birr 196 in 1981 was reduced to Birr 156 in 1995, in real terms. In other words, a pensioner who retired with 100 Birr in 1981 would get, in real terms, only Birr 37 in 1995, while a pensioner who retired in 1963 (index 1963 : 100) with Birr 100 would actually get only 10 cents in 1995!

Moreover, GNP per capita, as reported by the World Bank in current dollars, dropped from 140 in 1981 to 100 in 1995. At the same time, Ethiopia's ranking in terms of per capita GNP, dropped from sixth last to second last, only Mozambique falling behind.

Theoretically, the wage-rate is expected to be determined by labour productivity. In the Ethiopian case, the growth of the wage rate, though slower than the rise in the cost of living (the general index), has lagged behind increases in labour productivity. The labour productivity index increased by only 42 points over the period 1981–1995, while the index of the wage rate increased by 115 points.

The rise in the cost of living (or increases in poverty) can be further substantiated by other studies on poverty. The poverty situation in Ethiopia is among the worst in the world. The food poverty line, which shows the minimum daily nutritional requirement per adult per annum, is estimated at Birr 647.81 or USD 99.66 (MEDaC 1999). Based on this criterion, it is indicated that about 50 per cent of the population in the country cannot afford the minimum food requirement. It is indicated in the same document that 52 per cent and 36 per cent of the population living in the rural and urban areas cannot meet their food requirement, respectively. This shows that poverty is widespread in rural areas of the country.

Similarly, absolute poverty, which indicates insufficient access to purchasing power to cover the cost of minimum basic needs, is more pronounced in the rural than urban areas. Studies on poverty indicate that the absolute poverty line in the country was estimated at Birr 1075.03 or USD 165.4 per adult per annum (MEDaC 1999). This implies that an adult person required at least Birr 1075.03 per annum to escape absolute poverty. Table 5.7 indicates the summary of poverty situations in the country.

**Table 5.7: The Extent of Poverty in Ethiopia**

| Location | Population (per cent) | Poverty Index | Poverty Gap | Poverty severity | Contribution to poverty |
|---|---|---|---|---|---|
| National | 100.0 | 45.5 | 0.13 | 0.05 | 100.0 |
| Rural | 86.0 | 47.5 | 0.13 | 0.05 | 89.8 |
| Urban | 14.0 | 33.2 | 0.10 | 0.04 | 10.2 |

**Source**: MEDaC 1999.

It can be gleaned from the above table that, on aggregate, about 45 per cent of the population in the country are absolutely poor. This implies that a substantial proportion of the population can not attain the minimum living standard. With regard to the locational structure of poverty, it is indicated that 47 per cent and 33 per cent of the rural and urban population, respectively, live in absolute poverty. The poverty gap or intensity of poverty, which measures the extent to which the incomes of the poor lie below the poverty line, is also higher for rural dwellers than for their urban counterparts. And the severity of poverty, which is the square of the distance between the poor segment's expenditure and the poverty line, is also higher in rural than in urban areas. Since 89.6 per cent of the poor are found in the rural areas, poverty is thus highly ruralized.

The rise in the cost of living (or growing poverty) can be further investigated using data on monthly expenditure on food in Addis Ababa (see Table 5.8). In real terms, the monthly expenditure of a five-member family dropped from Birr 141 in 1990 to Birr 121 in 1991 and stood at Birr 136 in 1992. In other words, an average family in Addis Ababa consumed somewhat less food in 1991 and 1992 than it did in 1990.

**Table 5.8: Monthly Expenditure on Food for a Family of Five Persons in Addis Ababa**

| Year | Monthly expenditure in current prices (Birr/Family) | Purchasing Power of Birr (1981: 100) | Monthly expenditure in real terms (Birr/Family)[3] |
|---|---|---|---|
| 1990 | 205.4 | 0.69 | 141.45 |
| 1991 | 236.5 | 0.1 | 120.62 |
| 1992 | 295.2 | 0.46 | 135.8 |

**Source**: Goitom 1996.

**Table 5.9: Percentage of Population Affected by Poverty and Size of the Poor Communities in Addis Ababa**

| Year | Per cent of the poor | No. of poor people |
|---|---|---|
| 1990 | 45.4 | 882,335 |
| 1991 | 51.4 | 1,039,405 |
| 1992 | 63.0 | 1,330,610 |

**Source**: Goitom, 1996.

Poverty has remained widespread in other urban centres as well. According to Mekonnen (1996), 39 per cent of the population of seven major urban centres in Ethiopia lived below the poverty line in 1994. The same study estimated that, in 1994, about 44 per cent of the Addis Ababa population lived below the poverty line.

## Changes in Relative Prices in Rural Areas: Comparing the Pre-reform and Post-reform Periods

The purpose of this section is to investigate changes in relative prices in rural areas during the pre- and post-reform periods. Since it is almost impossible to consider the prices of all commodities in computing rural price indices, I have focused only on prices of likely representative goods and services in selected geographical areas in the country.

Fertilizer is the single major modern farm input used by farmers in the technology-using areas like Gojjam. Gojjam is a major teff-producing area in the country, while the Illubabor-Jimma area is well known for the production of the country's major cash crop, coffee, and for maize. Abjedid (Dire-Dawa No. 1) represents locally manufactured commodities, which are popular among rural people. The plough-tip represents locally produced farm tools, which are widely used by smallholder farmers.

The price of unskilled labour service has been taken as a proxy for the agricultural wage-rate. By considering changes in the producer prices of agricultural products relative to changes in the retail prices of non-agricultural products at the village-level, we have attempted to draw a realistic picture of commodity terms of trade prevailing during the pre- and post- reform periods.

Policy reform has registered strong impact on the producer price of coffee, a commodity that gained a lot from the liberalization measures and the progressive devaluation of the Birr since October 1992. In Illubabor-Jimma, the producer price index of coffee increased 6.5 times between the 1980–91 and 1992–96 periods, while the producer price of maize simply doubled over the same period, thus suggesting that coffee became more profitable than maize. Therefore, it is likely that farmers in the Illubabor-Jimma area tended to switch from maize to coffee.

The cost-benefit ratio of using chemical fertilizers appears to be slightly improved in areas like Gojjam, where the index for white teff increased 2.6 times, as compared to 2.3 times for fertilizers between the pre- and post-reform periods. However, farmers' decision to use fertilizers depends not only on the cost-benefit ratio (which is put at a minimum of 2:1) but also on the extent of responsiveness of output to fertilizer use.

**Table 5.10: Relative Changes in Rural Price Indices of Representative Farm Inputs, Output and Manufactured Goods in Gojjam and Illubabor-Jimma (1980: 100)**

| Goods & Services | Geographic areas | The pre-reform Period (1980-91) | Post-reform period (1992-96) | Ratio of post-reform price index to pre-reform index |
|---|---|---|---|---|
| Producer price index of white teff | Gojjam | 230.75 | 594.4 | 2.6 |
| Fertilizer price index | Gojjam | 100.08 | 225.8 | 2.3 |
| Producer price index for maize | Illubabor -Jimma | 123.5 | 241.4 | 2.0 |
| Producer price index for coffee | Illubabor -Jimma | 549.5 | 3574.6 | 6.5 |
| Rural RPI of *abujedid* (cloth) | Gojjam | 37.25 | 302.4 | 2.2 |
| Rural RPI of *abujedid* (cloth) | Illubabor -Jimma | 119.25 | 314.4 | 2.6 |
| Rural RPI of plough-tip | Gojjam | 94.08 | 101 | 1.07 |
| Rural RPI of plough-tip | Illubabor -Jimma | 82 | 111 | 1.4 |
| Rural index of wage rate | Gojjam | 124 | 230 | 1.9 |
| Rural index of wage rate | Illubabor -Jimma | 204 | 315 | 1.5 |

**Source**: Computed from various reports of CSA on rural price surveys.

The changes in terms of trade between agriculture and industry do not come out clearly. Prices of coffee increased at much faster rates than prices of *abujedid* (cloth), while prices of teff and maize increased by more or less similar rates as prices of *abujedid*. Also, prices of cereals have increased at faster rates than the wage rates. The implications of the combination of cheap labour and expensive food must be obvious. Here, it should be noted that wage earners depend on purchased food.

The smallest increases in prices between the two periods are registered by traditional farm inputs such as farm implements and labour. The price indices of both the plough-tip and the wage rate less than doubled between 1980–1991 and 1992–1996.

## Summary of the Main Findings and Conclusions

Spanning a period of twenty years, this study has attempted to investigate changes in price behaviour and cost of living in Ethiopia and to identify and explain global and domestic factors causing these changes. In the absence of price indices for the whole country, the study has focused on an analysis of inflationary pressure in Addis Ababa, the only place in Ethiopia for which retail price indices are available for quite a long period: 1974–1997.

Ethiopia has experienced substantial price escalations over the study period. But the country has never experienced hyperinflation that used to be characteristic of many Latin American countries. In fact, Ethiopia has compared favourably with other African countries in terms of increases in the general price level.

Following the upheavals of the mid-1970s and the coffee boom of 1977, the rate of inflation, which averaged only 3 per cent over the 1966–1974, jumped to 13 per cent during the early years of the Derg regime (1975–1983). On the other hand, the 1984-85 drought, which caused nation-wide food shortages, further raised the rate of inflation rate to a very high level, i.e. 18 per cent per annum. The post-drought period had been characterized by a considerable decline in the rate of inflation (1.6 per cent, the lowest ever recorded until then. But by 1991, it assumed an all-time high of 35 per cent per annum. The major contributory factors were: (i) escalation of the civil war, which brought down the Derg in the same year and (ii) and an all-out market liberalization effort by the new regime, which was spearheaded by the Ethiopian People's Revolutionary Democratic Front (EPRDF).

The reform period (1992–96) recorded an average annual growth rate of 5.3 per cent, which is much greater than the rate registered in the preceding period (1.6 per cent during 1986–1990), but much lower than the one recorded in 1991, an abnormal year. Price behaviour since 1992 has been influenced by factors such as macro-economic policies (such as progressive devaluation of the domestic currency since 1992) and recent increase in the world prices of coffee, in addition to the traditional explanatory variables like money supply and changes in weather conditions. The devaluation measure raised prices of tradable goods (coffee, in particular) and those of imported goods (including chemical fertilizers and basic necessities, such as drugs).

In Ethiopia, as in many developing countries (Ghatak 1995), the inflation rate tended to vary from one year to another. Steady rates of inflation have remained uncommon, although the long-term trend was evident. Thus, it has been difficult to predict inflationary pressure with certainty on the basis of historical trends.

An analysis of the temporal behaviour of prices relative to changes in nominal income has enabled us to investigate changes in the welfare positions of households over the period studied. This study has shown that many

Ethiopians are poorer today than some decades back. The purchasing power of the Ethiopia Birr dropped to 37 cents in 1995. Structural constraints are found to be the major determinant of changes in the rate of inflation in the country.

Structural adjustment policies have not succeeded in improving the welfare position of urban and rural households. A strategy of 'getting price right' does not necessarily mean reasonable retail prices of food for the poor. There is a need to switch emphasis from the adjustment and stabilization programme to that of poverty alleviation.

The globalization process has had a limited impact on retail price indices because the Ethiopian economy, which is dominated by subsistence agriculture, has not been sufficiently integrated into the world economy. But the big question is whether we should take the government's efforts to make the economy open to international capital as an opportunity to be exploited or as a threat to be avoided. Further research is required to investigate this issue.

## Notes

* Associate Professor of Economics, Addis Ababa University.

1. The purchasing power of the Birr (PPB) is calculated by using this formula: PPB= 100/X; where x= current year's index.
2. The real wage rate is arrived at by multiplying current nominal wage by the corresponding purchasing power of the Birr.
3. Multiplying nominal expenditure by the purchasing power of the Birr gives the Real Expenditure.

## References


Aredo, D. and Regassa, T., 1995, Ethiopia Foreign Trade (Mimeo), Department of Economics, Addis Ababa University, Addis Ababa.

Aredo, D., 1985, 'A Look into the Socialization of Distribution and Price Differentials in Selected Towns in Ethiopia', in Treuner, Taderse Kidane-Mariam and Teshome Mulat, eds., *Regional Planning and Development in Ethiopia*, IDR and IREUS, Addis Ababa.

Central Statistical Authority, 1996, 'Report on the Development of Consumer Price Indices for Ethiopia', *Bulletin 169*, Addis Ababa.

Central Statistical Authority, 1997, 'Report on the Large-Scale and Medium-Scale Manufacturing and Electricity Industries Survey', *Bulletin 178*, Addis Ababa.

Central Statistical Authority, Producer Prices in Rural Areas, Various Issues.

Central Statistical Authority, Retail Prices in Rural Areas, Various issues.

*Ethiopian Herald*, 1974b No 968, February.

*Ethiopian Herald*, 1974c No. 975, March.

*Ethiopian Herald*, 1974a, XXX, No. 959, February.

Geda, A., 2000, 'Macroeconomic Performance in Post-Reform Ethiopia', Paper presented at the Symposium organized for the Review of Ethiopia's Socio-economic performance (1991-1999).

Gemeda, G., 1995, 'Land, Agriculture and Society in the Gibie Region: Southern Ethiopia C 1850-1974', unpublished Ph.D. dissertation, Michigan State University, East Lansing, USA.

Ghatak, S., 1995, *Monetary Economics in Developing Countries*, second edition, London: St. Martin Press.

Ghirmatsion, G., 1996, 'Aspects of Poverty in the city of Addis Ababa: Profile and Policy Implications', in B. Kebede and M. Tadesse, eds., *The Ethiopian Economy: Poverty and Poverty Alleviation*, Addis Ababa.

Gurmu, S., 1980, 'An Empirical Analysis of Recent Price Trends in Ethiopia', *Ethiopian Journal of Development Research*, Vol. 4, No. 2, pp. 13-39.

Imperial Ethiopian Government, 1957, *First Five-Year Development Plan 1957-1961*, Addis Ababa.

Kirkpatrick, C.H and Nixon F.I. , 1987, 'Inflation and Stabilization Policy in LDCs', in N.Gemmel, ed., Survey in Development Economics, Oxford, Basil Blackwell.

Kirkpatrick, C.H. and Nixon F.I. , 1976, 'The Origins of Inflation in Less Developed Countries; A Selective Review', in M. Parkin and G. Zis, eds., *Inflation in Open Economies*, Manchester University Press, pp. 126-74.

Mackerth, G., 1932, *Economic Conditions in Ethiopia 1929-31*, London: His Majesty's Stationery Office.

Mahran, H.A and Gangi Y.A. , 1996, 'Causes of inflation in the Sudan 1970-1991', *Eastern Africa Social Science Research Review*, Vol. XII, No.2, pp. 13-25.

Marcus, H., 1995, *Haile-Selassie I: The Formative Years 1882-1936*, Lawrence Ville N.J.: The Red Sea Press

MEDaC, 1999a, 'Poverty Situations in Ethiopia', Addis Ababa.

MEDaC, 1999b, 'Survey of the Ethiopian Economy: Review of Post-Reform Developments, 1992/93-1997/98', Addis Ababa.

Ministry of Commerce, Industry and Planning, 1959, *Ethiopian Economic Review* No. 1, December.

Ministry of Commerce, Industry and Planning, 1960, *Ethiopian Economic Review* No.2, June.

Ministry of Commerce, Industry and Planning, 1961, *Ethiopian Economic Review* No 4, August.

Ministry of Commerce, Industry and Planning, 1963, *Ethiopian Economic Review* No. 7, September.

Ministry of Commerce, Industry and Planning, 1966, *Ethiopian Economic Review* No. 9, May.

National Bank of Ethiopia (NBE), 1966, Quarterly Bulletin, No.68.

National Bank of Ethiopia (NBE), 1972, Quarterly Bulletin, No.33.

National Bank of Ethiopia (NBE), 1974, Quarterly Bulletin, No. 101.

National Bank of Ethiopia (NBE), 1994-95, Annual Report, Addis Ababa.

National Bank of Ethiopia (NBE), 1995-96, Annual Report, Addis Ababa.

Pankhurst, R., 1968, *Economic History of Ethiopia 1800-1935*, Addis Ababa: Haile Selassie I University Press.

Sunkel, O., 1960, 'Inflation in Chile: An Orthodox Approach', International Economic Papers.

Tadele, Ferede, 2000, 'Economic Linkages and Policy Shocks in Ethiopia: Social Accounting Matrix (SAM)-based Multiplier Analysis', M.Sc. thesis, Addis Ababa University.

Tadesse, M., 1996, 'Food Consumption and Poverty in Urban Ethiopia', in Bereket Kebede Mekonne Tadesse, eds., The Ethiopian Economy: Poverty and Poverty Alleviation, proceedings of the Fifth Annual Conference on the Ethiopia Economy. Department of Economics, AAU, Addis Ababa.

Thirlwall, A.P., 1974, *Inflation, Saving and Growth in Developing Economies*, London: Macmillan.

World Bank, 1997, *World Development Report*, 1997, Washington D.C.

# 6

# Economic Reforms and Social Policies in Senegal

## Private and participatory management of social programmes: The case of the fight against malnutrition

**Alfred Inis Ndiaye***

## Introduction

Senegal is a low-income African State. Its population, estimated at close to 9 million inhabitants in 1998, grows at a rate of 2.7 per cent per annum. The country's Gross National Product (GNP) per inhabitant is 302,500 CFA F. Between 1990 and 1998, the GNP progressively increased to an average annual rate of 4.84 per cent per annum. The country is characterized by harsh economic development constraints.[1] Senegal was ranked 153rd out of 174 countries, classified on the basis of the poverty index, by UNDP in 1999. The Senegalese population is essentially rural (60 per cent still live in the rural areas), young (58 per cent of the population is under 20) and has a majority of women (58 per cent of the population).

The performance of the education and health sectors is deficient. In 1995, the percentage of children in full-time education was estimated at 55 per cent for girls and 64 per cent for boys with other huge disparities.[2] With regard to the adult illiteracy rate, it is estimated at 78 per cent for women and 63 per cent for men. Life expectancy at birth was 54 years in 1996. Malaria is the major killer in health terms with 55 per cent of notified cases. The other major killer diseases are in order of importance: skin disease, diarrhoea, respiratory diseases, anaemia, flu, oral infections, eye diseases and intestinal diseases.[3] The fact that such infections are widespread says a lot about the low standard of living that exists in Senegal, which is below that of other intermediate income countries.

At the beginning of the 1980s, Senegal signed an extended facility agreement with the International Monetary Fund (IMF) and a structural adjustment programme (SAP) with the World Bank. This initiative aimed essentially to implement policies to re-establish major macro-economic balances. The crisis that broke out at the end of the 1970s, illustrating the progressive degradation of the economic and social context during the 1960s and 1970s, made internal adjustments necessary. However, these adjustments were not enough to lead to recovery and to result in economic growth that would impact favourably on people's living conditions.

The devaluation of the CFA Franc in January 1994 opened the way to a return of the economy to a competitive situation and expansion.[4] But this relative improvement in the economic situation was not accompanied by a significant improvement in people's living conditions. Rather, we observe the persistence or reinforcement of social imbalances: unemployment and poverty advance, the level of access to basic services remains low and the decrease in salaries combined with the increase in food prices due to the devaluation of the CFA.F led to a substantial compression of household consumption.

The reform implementation process, as shown in preceding analysis, is still a cause for concern and questioning. The issue of its consequences on the roles and functions of the state, on the one hand, and on people's living conditions, on the other, has become a major concern for social scientists, the Senegalese government and its development partners.[5]

Besides, many indicators tend to show that in essence, these reforms can be perceived as having considerably weakened social policies. Implementing them will inevitably entail opening up major 'social demolition work sites'.[6] According to many analysts, the integration of certain African countries into the global market has resulted in 'reconceptualizing' the state and urging it to profoundly reform itself (Sine 1997; Diouf 1998).[7] It has been called upon to readjust its economic and social functions, in the process doing away with measures associated with the welfare state. This readjustment also means reinforcing deregulation policies which tend to 'flexibilize' and weaken the labour force.

Such perceptions of the consequences of these reforms on the functioning of the state strengthen the opinion of those who argue that the attempt to forcibly integrate African economies in the global market is effected by economic violence and at the expense of workers and the people at large. Limited state intervention in sectors such as education and health, which complies with its redefined roles and functions, has contributed in increasingly weakening and marginalizing certain social categories which, for many reasons, need its support most.

This first survey, which sheds light on certain aspects of the social and political impact of SAPs, reinforces the argument that a new social crisis has arisen in Africa (Boisset 1995). Of course, the context is different from that of Europe at the advent of industrialization. But rampant poverty in African towns and countryside has led to a social disintegration process which puts the societies to the test. It is also true that its intensity has given birth to a comprehensive social restructuring process. In fact, one can observe in African societies a vast phenomenon of economic, social and cultural resistance, the very cradle of social re-composition. In this way, the people show their refusal to passively suffer the negative consequences of the crisis and reforms. The dynamism of the so-called informal activities is generally interpreted as being the basic element of an economic and social regulation process. With regard to Senegalese society, more precisely, the contour of this popular resistance phenomenon has been clearly identified (Sow 1993; Niang 1993; Bopp 1994; Sarr 1998).

However, the existence of these forms of responses to the deepening crisis and to declining welfare state functions should not at all conceal the topicality of the social policy issue. How are social fractures tackled and managed? What are the existing mechanisms to preserve and regulate social cohesion? The various communities constantly provide answers to these questions which are at the very centre of social policy (Aina 1997). And so does the state. The latter's responses will be investigated here.

Over the past few years, intervention in the field of social policy has been very largely dominated by what can be termed the 'project approach'. One notices a lack of strategic planning, the non-existence of a coherent social policy with clearly identified objectives. On the other hand, each sector is managed through projects, if development partners accept to support them. Thus, one observes a set of social programmes jointly managed by the people and NGOs, sometimes with public bodies. Most of these social programmes are geared towards the struggle against poverty[8] and are often essentially funded by donors. The latter's role in the definition and implementation of these social programmes needs analysis. Their presence somehow shows the complexity of relations between SAPs and social policies. Consequently the 'project approach' should be closely examined. It certainly has political significance that needs to be determined.

This examination is all the more imperative since SAPs are generally perceived as a radical experiment in applied neo-liberalism. They have exerted strong pressure on the governments of developing countries 'to get them to abandon their national economic development programs and stake their people's future on an entrance, without any risks, into international markets' (UNRISD 1995: 19). From this viewpoint, in addition to stabilization, certain measures such as reducing or eliminating subsidies and local price control of goods and services and drastically reducing state intervention in the management of the economy and the supply of social services can be argued to have occurred at an exorbitant social cost. More clearly, in its ideal-type version, structural adjustment can considerably hinder the implementation of a coherent, efficient social policy. At the very least, it has to be admitted that, through the new social order it generates, the globalization process requires, on the part of the African State, another more appropriate form of social policy. In this respect, the 'project approach' can be an element of this new policy.

Moreover, in implementing social programmes, the State very often favours the participatory and community approach. It seems to have undertaken to make people more responsible through its social policies. In Senegal, since 1997, decentralization policies have been implemented in greater depth with the entry into force of the regionalization policy (Diagne 1997). Its main objective is to reinforce the capacities of the communities through their close involvement in local affairs with a view to promoting the cultural, social and economic development in their territory. The development of democracy at the local level and the transfer of certain state-retained powers to local authorities are some of the measures taken in support of local development.[9]

The centrality of the participatory approach and also the implementation of social policy should also be closely examined. What significance should it be given in a context of adjustment?

The present paper is an attempt to answer these various questions. On the basis of a case study, the fight against infant malnutrition in Senegal, it will try to understand the determinants and dynamics of the 'project approach' in the social policies adopted by the government of Senegal, to identify its political and social issues, and to understand its significance. Finally, the purpose of this study is to identify the main social policy components in a context marked by the continuing structural reforms and the constraints of globalization.

The working hypothesis is as follows: at a time of structural adjustment and structural reforms implementation, the participatory and sectoral approach to social policy is, above all in line with a strategy to reinforce these reforms. Generally, all state interventions follow the logic of adjustment: complete the reforms to facilitate the country's integration in the global market.

The results of the survey are presented as follows: in the first part, the social repercussions of reform policies in Senegal in the last twenty years or so are examined. More precisely, special attention is given to poverty, its manifestations and impact on Senegalese society. The second part attempts to analyse the social policies. To this end, after discussing the history of social policies on health and nutrition, the experience of the malnutrition eradication program in Senegal is the focus of study.[10]

## The Social Repercussions of Structural Adjustment Programmes

### *The Limits of Adjustment Programmes*

After nearly three decades of implementation, the mere mention of SAP inevitably raises one question: Has the SAP succeeded in improving Senegal's economic and social situation? For a number of reasons it is difficult to answer this question which is, however, central. First, because the stated aim of these programmes is to extricate the country from the economic crisis and to engage in a sustainable development perspective. Officially, SAP implementation is a process that demands sacrifice from the people but the limits and contours of these sacrifices have remained unclear, and this makes any attempts at assessment a tricky job. Furthermore, there is an absence of consensus on indicators for SAP assessment. Should one confine oneself to economic indicators alone or also take into account social indicators? Or, to go beyond this ambiguity, should one use a more globalizing approach?

What is the philosophy behind SAP implementation? Some economists and social scientists are quite categorical: official statements that go with SAP implementation are ideological and political legitimation. SAPs are not mainly intended for drawing the country under adjustment out of economic deadlock. Amady Aly Dieng (1997) is more precise: 'the basic objective of SAP is to put the countries under adjustment in a position to refund the external debts' (106). This, according to Dieng, explains why SAP implementation always goes with perverse social effects. These include increased social inequalities, growing poverty and unemployment through reduction in the numbers of civil servants, decreasing underprivileged classes' and wage-earners' purchasing power through the elimination of subsidies on primary foodstuffs, and cuts in health and education expenditure.

With this very critical explanation of the SAP, one can understand why, in spite of massive intervention of the Bretton Woods Institutions, Africa has still remained a developing continent—'the champion of negative indicators'. According to UNDP reports, the state of African human development remains fragile and disturbing. Since 1960, African countries have always represented over three-quarters of the countries in the so-called low 'Human Development Indicator' (HDI) group: 67.7 per cent in 1960, 86.11 per cent in 1970 and 1980, 75.60 per cent in 1995.[11] These figures express the high prevalence of unemployment, the pauperization of large sectors of the population and the deterioration of the health situation.

The continuation of SAP has other economic and political consequences such as the de-industrialization of African countries and delays in the regional integration process. So, SAPs are basically a factor of extraversion for African economies (Dieng 1997: 107). However, their implementation has in some respects favoured the emergence of democratic demands in certain countries. In this regard, they engender new hope for Africa's economic development.

Even though it takes the form of a severe indictment of the government and donors' ideological illusions, this recentring of the SAP issue can facilitate the understanding of the social repercussions of SAP in Senegal, far away from the official and unilateral perspective.

The literature on the social consequences of SAP on the living conditions of the Senegalese people has shed light on the series of economic reforms which are the very soul of SAP. The main elements of these series of reforms are, on the one hand, economic liberalization, essentially dominated by the state's effective and programmed withdrawal from the productive sector, and on the other hand, the state policy of elimination of subsidies on primary foodstuffs. Such state withdrawal gradually extends to social sectors such as education and health. Consequently, it is possible to state that Senegalese society and economy have been profoundly and negatively affected by the continued implementation of SAP, especially its structural reforms implementation component.

In this respect, certain indicators can be presented as being the most significant with regard to the impact of SAP on Senegal's social structure (Bourgoigne 1990). The most visible, and no doubt, most alarming, element is the progression of poverty in Senegalese society. This has taken place with a contrasting effect, which explains why all social categories have not felt the repercussions of SAP in the same way. Because of certain factors, women and children, on the one hand, and fixed income (salary) holders, on the other hand, seem to be the greatest victims of reforms. In addition to the progression of poverty, one observes another phenomenon, i.e. the dynamism of community life, a sign of the people's economic and social resistance (Antoine et al. 1995). Urban and rural women are identified as being at the centre of this social recomposition process.

However, these two phenomena are far from fully accounting for the impact of SAP on Senegal's social structure. They are reinforced by what is now commonly known as the redefinition of the roles and functions of the state, and which Sine (1997) terms the 'reconceptualization' of the State. According to Sine this concept accounts for the fact that

> [The State's functions], particularly the economic and social functions, must be reconsidered and readjusted…this new good governance State must 'privatize' itself to the maximum and 'de-statize' itself by giving more responsibility to private initiative while reinforcing the bases of market economy and ensuring free competition(…). The privatization process no longer spares the so-called social sectors (education, health, social affairs) up to now monopolized and essentially falling under public services (14.16).

So, this 'new' state is built on new foundations which tend to weaken its social functions. In this respect, growing unemployment, especially of the youth, and the reinforcement of poverty in Senegalese society can, in many respects, be perceived as the predictable consequences of SAP.

This statement can be considered as part of the answer to the initial question: what is the outcome of SAP implementation in Senegal?

A set of surveys conducted at the request of the government or its development partners has come out with the following findings:

(a) Adjustment programs implemented by the government of Senegal since 1980 have shown real limitations. They have not resulted in an expansion of Senegal's economy, for many reasons. These limitations partly explain the weak economic performance in the 1980s and the early 1990s.

(b) Social deficits have increased. With the strong demographic pressure, national and particularly state resources, have taken the brunt of demands with regard to food and nutrition, drinking water, health, housing and education. But, while managing various reforms, the State has not been able to adequately meet social demands. With the logic of adjustment, it was forced to favour debt servicing over investment. In this regard, adjustment served as a tool for the demolition of social policies, thus gradually and considerably increasing social deficit. Budget constraints impaired the state's ability to set up adequate and sufficient infrastructure in social sectors.

From all these facts which categorically show the failure of economic policies one gets a strong feeling that the living conditions of Senegalese people have objectively deteriorated, in other words, that poverty has intensified.

All these results give added strength to the opinion of researchers who argue that SAP should be perceived as a mechanism mainly intended to meet donor needs as a matter of priority. After showing the inability of SAP to curb the economic crisis, let us now go back to the poverty they have helped bring about, and give an account of its manifestations and impact on Senegal's social structure.

## Poverty: Its Manifestations and Impact

Official statistics fully confirm the magnitude of poverty in Senegal. Before coming back to its manifestation later, there is need for us to specify our conception and understanding of this phenomenon, so as to clarify our point of view. Who is poor? Who is not poor? It is not easy to answer these questions, one of the reasons being the absence of consensus on the definition of the concept. For this issue of definition, in reality, conceals these various problems. We shall direct our attention to two of them.[12]

The first relates to poverty assessment technique, on the basis of qualitative and quantitative criteria. How does one define the 'poverty line', i.e. the revenue level below which one is considered as poor? The poverty line we are referring to here is not identifiable because it is linked to the definition of basic needs. Should we limit ourselves to food? Or should we introduce transport, urban housing, water, even education? Depending on the case, the results obtained will be different (Lautier 1996).

The second problem, as difficult as the first, concerns taking into account the socio-economic context. Income distribution in a country has an effect on poverty levels, which explains the introduction of a dose of relativity when one refers to poverty.

Besides, this contextualization shows that the debate on poverty is first and foremost, and above all, a political debate. Poverty is at the very heart of the democratic stake.

The importance of these two problems in the definition of poverty justifies its being a privileged subject of study for economists who have insisted on the two indicators: consumption and income (Pangam 1994: 9). However, and this was shown by anthropologists and sociologists, the very idea of poverty refers also to quite specific social concerns (Blanchard et al. 1991). Where there is community solidarity, the question of individual income does not have the same meaning as in urban areas where individualism predominates. In this respect, the sociological approach to poverty offers elements which shed light on the operating mechanisms of this phenomenon, even if it has not been able to define a subject of study (Diop 1996).

Analysis of the sociological literature on poverty makes it possible to identify two types of interpretations of this phenomenon (Glazier 1981). The first is referred to as 'cultural' (Lewis 1969). It is based on the existence of a 'vicious circle of poverty' and a culture of poverty. Accepting the existence of a culture of poverty will influence the action of the fight against poverty. To be efficient, it must be based on representations, values and identities. Therefore, cultural interpretation is a tool used to understand the infernal universe of the poor.

However, its excessive determinism is, in some way an obstacle to finding a way out of poverty, for it tends to minimize the capacity of poor individuals to generate new practices to overcome difficulties in their surroundings and defeat poverty.

This first interpretation is rejected by the structuralist approach which precisely attacks its determinism. Poverty is perceived and understood by structuralists as a social and economic phenomenon congenial with institutional forms and a specific political and economic environment. It is experienced in a particular way by certain social categories and tends to designate a certain social condition because it first of all refers to low incomes in a social and economic context. Moreover, it can induce extra-material consequences such as lack of access to education and a reduced possibility to transmit to one's children a cultural capital to enable them to enjoy real professional and social integration. In this respect, the poor are somehow excluded, but this is part and parcel of an institutional logic, and precisely for this reason, the 'vicious circle of poverty' can be broken by appropriate policies and interventions. This aspect clearly shows the importance and necessity of social policies.

After clarifying the phenomenon, let us now go back to its manifestations in Senegal. Statistical data regarding the magnitude of poverty in Senegal are unambiguous:

- 32 per cent of households live below the poverty line, defined as the amount necessary for the acquisition of 2,400 calories per day per person in the household. 75 per cent of poor households are found in rural areas and 58 per cent of rural households are poor. Moreover, in rural areas, the average annual income per household is 3.5 times lower than that recorded in urban areas.
- In urban areas, living conditions have become very precarious: the level of access to basic services has remained low with only 33 per cent of households connected to water supply facilities, 58 per cent using electricity and 52 per cent living in houses which do not belong to them.
- Over 50 per cent of the poor in urban areas are concentrated in the city of Dakar where insecurity has risen to alarming levels.

These statistics also confirm the presence and magnitude of some of the best known manifestations of poverty.

Child malnutrition[13] and the still high maternal and infant death rates (respectively estimated at 510 for 100,000 live births and 69.4 per cent). This nutritional and health situation is all the more disturbing since the health coverage rate is still low in relation to development demands and the standards set by WHO.[14] For example, between 1980 and 1990, resources allocated to the health sector represented 1 per cent of the GDP. Diseases such as diarrhoea and malaria are particularly aggravated by malnutrition. The devaluation of the CFA franc in 1994 exacerbated the nutritional and health situation. Poor households which hitherto devoted 70 per cent of their income to food, were, because of the collapse of their purchasing power, compelled to lower their food intake both qualitatively and quantitatively. For the same reason, medicines had become inaccessible to most of the population.[15]

If the continuation of SAP has largely contributed to increasing poverty in Senegal, it must be pointed out that this was made easier by other variables like the demographic structure and situation of groups.[16] Furthermore, the average household size is 8.7 persons and dependent persons represent 62.50 per cent. The size of poor families is bigger, with a large proportion of young children not attending school.[17] This demographic configuration weakens women and children and makes them more permeable to the progress of poverty.

In that case, how do people react to continuing reforms and advancing poverty? The presentation of this phenomenon in its essential dimensions logically leads us to examine people's responses, either in the form of resistance or adaptation. Two observations can be made at this stage. First, there were no popular riots against adjustment measures such as the CFA franc devaluation. But this absence of violence and mass demonstrations is far from meaning that people's resistance is weak. This resistance can be observed in the communal and associative phenomenon whose dynamism appreciably contributed to increasing the income of the poor. One can observe a strengthening of the social link and a recentring of the roles and functions of social solidarity structures. In their search for revenue, the latter have practically substituted for the state, which obviously is no longer able to adequately fulfil its traditional function of provider of employment for the youth.

Paradoxically, the relative calm observed at the national level is permanently disturbed by manifestations of urban insecurity, generally perceived as the reaction of a youth severely hit by the negative effects of SAP, i.e. idle youth without any future prospects. The national unemployment rate is estimated at 10.3 per cent in Senegal and 27 per cent in the Dakar urban area. It affects 28 per cent of the active population, mostly the youth (63.61 per cent of the unemployed are 15 to 34 year old youths). It affects youths of both the urban and rural areas (ESP 1993).

Secondly, on several occasions, the government itself has expressed satisfaction about its collaboration with the trade unions in reform implementation.[18] On another level, the formation of several government coalitions during the adjustment period suggests that many political parties among the most representative have, at one time or another, supported most of the reforms[19]. These political choices on the part of parties and trade unions are factors that explain the weakening of the social front in the face of adjustment. Another explanatory factor is, according to some analysts, the strong Islamic brotherhood configuration of Senegalese society.

These various observations make it possible to understand the relative calm observed in the context strongly dominated and marked by the implementation of adjustment measures since 1980.[20] The government has undertaken to fight against poverty while taking into account certain constraints, the most important of which are:

- the need to pursue reforms to ensure the reorganization of the macro-economic framework;
- the will, even the obligation to rely on the outcome of all its intervention policies and that of its partnership with donors; and
- the taking into account of essential changes in the social context which in the last few years, have been marked by increased social communication, the development of a private and public press favourable to plural expression and the reinforcement of civil society's community and associative movement.

The first constraint, i.e. the continuation of political and economic reforms seems to be decisive. It should be perceived as a condition, a conditionality from the donors' point of view, for access to the necessary financing of social policies. In 1988, when confronted with the SAP's weak economic impact and in the face of its perverse social effects, the World Bank launched its 'social dimension of the adjustment' projects (SDA) and engaged in a reform consolidation logic (Serageldine and Noel 1990; Johnson-Sirleaf 1996; Garrier 1998). The purpose of the SDA programme is twofold and quite unambiguous: on the one hand, to 'prevent structural adjustment and economic reforms from causing excessive difficulties to the poor and vulnerable' and, on the other hand, to 'integrate these populations into the economic activity' (World Bank 1990: 1). The programme is reassuring for countries under adjustment: they can obtain financing for social programmes which will enable them to ease social and political tensions resulting from adjustment. In exchange, the influence of donors in the definition of social policies should be accepted. In this respect, the communal and participatory approach is a method of operating social projects, imposed by development partners, essentially the World Bank.[21] Therefore, by putting the SDA programme into perspective, we can understand the choice of social programmes, on the one hand, and the project management form, on the other.

Finally, one is entitled to wonder about the relationship between African governments under adjustment and social policies. What forms does this relationship take? What are the essential elements of its dynamics? Let us examine these various questions, on the basis of a case study: the fight against malnutrition in Senegal.

## Local Communities and the Fight against Poverty

### *Communal Participation as a Means to Make Social Programmes Profitable*

#### *The Fight Against Malnutrition, a New Approach*

In 1995, the government of Senegal, supported by its development partners, initiated the Communal Nutrition Project (CNP). This project is conceived and perceived as an efficient tool in efforts to eradicate malnutrition.[22] Its objective is threefold: to stop the deterioration of the nutritional state of the most vulnerable groups in underprivileged urban areas, to ensure drinking water supply for these groups and finally to improve food security in certain targeted zones in urban and rural areas during critical vulnerability periods.(World Bank 1995).

The CFA devaluation measures, taken in 1994, aggravated the social and nutritional situation that was already a concern. Regarding malnutrition, more specifically, the following facts have been established:

- weight deficiency (weight/age index): 21.8 per cent of 6-56 month-old children are concerned, i.e. more than 1 out of 5 children;
- underfeeding or loss of weight (weight/height index) mostly affecting (11.8 per cent) 6-35 months age group;
- delayed growth (height/age) affecting 23.3 per cent of 6-59 month- old children. The situation is particularly serious in 10 per cent of the 12-59 months age group (World Bank 1995).

Generally, the infant malnutrition rate remained relatively constant during the 1980s. According to the results of the Survey on Priorities, 29 per cent of children under 5 are chronically undernourished; with the malnutrition rate estimated at 34 per cent in rural areas and 23 per cent in urban areas. 63 per cent of undernourished children suffer from iron deficiency.

Besides poverty, which is often the cause and consequence of infant malnutrition, the latter may also be due to other important factors such as food insecurity, total ignorance of satisfactory feeding practices, endemic diseases, lack of drinking water and poor hygienic conditions.

The government could not remain indifferent to the emergency nutritional situation without risks. For the World Bank, the CNP, because of its experimental character in sub-Saharan Africa, had precise, clear and real stakes.[23] Its experience must, on the one hand, show that the communities themselves are able to realize well targeted and efficient nutritional interventions with regard to costs, and, on the other hand, it must prove that it is possible to implement a poverty alleviation programme through a private body.

The notions of profitability and private sector are central to World Bank philosophy in its interventions in general. Its SDA programme for the elimination of poverty is no exception.

The World Bank is perceived as an efficient instrument for globalization in the sense that it has the power to impose its demands (the promotion of growth, encouragement of liberalization and privatization) on developing states. The will to reduce the role of the state and give a central place to market rules is an essential characteristic of globalization. In that sense, the constraints of globalization and the pursuit of structural adjustment compel the state to resort to private enterprise in the implementation of its social policy. However, besides these notions usually localized in production projects, there appears another one, which is very present in programme management policies—that of the community (the beneficiary of the project). The involvement of local communities in the fight against malnutrition seems to be an innovative experiment in Africa. It is also interesting in many respects and for certain reasons, the most important of which are:

- the complexity of malnutrition as a social and economic phenomenon: its relation with poverty, with other factors such as food insecurity, its scanty knowledge or total ignorance of feeding practices respecting sanitary standards, the existence of endemic diseases, lack of drinking water and the poor hygienic conditions[24] make it one the most revealing phenomena of poverty;
- the failure of previous interventions in the fight against malnutrition: the evaluation of the various nutrition programs have in fact shown the inefficiency of public health structures, their inability to efficiently fight malnutrition. This assessment rather argues for decentralizing nutrition issues to the community level. Therefore, in that sense, the active implication of communities, in particular women's associations, is an element that can positively contribute to the fight against malnutrition. In this respect, the outcome of the various nutrition programmes argues in favour of local development as a relevant framework to fight against poverty and its various manifestations such as malnutrition; and
- the conclusive experience, according to the World Bank, of the Agency for the Execution of Works of Public Interest Against Under employment (AGETIP), an NGO whose essential mission is to promote employment;[25] this World Bank approval somehow legitimizes the new experiences based on self-management and the opening towards the private sector so as to ensure the success of projects.

If one refers to these various elements, the CNP's basic principle seems to rest on the following gamble: the local communities have the capacity to take charge as full actors in development and social policies.

In line with this gamble, and for the sake of coherence, those who benefit from the fight against malnutrition should no longer be considered as passive recipients but as active agents. The finality of this approach is to create the conditions for mobilizing local actors and also for the emergence of new actors.

Neighbourhoods which benefit from CNP must be collective learning places for the techniques required to improve the people's nutritional state. In that sense, the community approach adopted by the CNP is in total opposition to the hierarchical approach in classical projects. However, its implementation is somehow linked to the existence of local intermediary organizations and the capacity of these organizations to act as support structures.

These various observations lead one to think that the CNP can be considered as a materialization of the SDA programme formulated by the World Bank in 1987. The question now is whether it can serve as an impulse for local development.

Another way of asking the same question is whether the CNP, as a social programme, is an efficient instrument in the fight against poverty and malnutrition. Recalling some elements of history regarding social policies on health and malnutrition could facilitate the response to this question.

## History of Social Policies in the Area of Nutrition and Health

From independence to date, national health policies have developed significantly. The National Health Policy (NHP), adopted in 1989, constitutes a break in the state's approach to health. From 1960-1988, health policy was guided by two major principles: the right to health for all citizens, on the one hand, and the uniqueness of the health system from the local health centre to the University hospital, on the other (Ly et al. 1999). As a result of these constraints brought forth by economic reform implementation, the NHP attempts to give new directions to State intervention by involving the population in the financing and management of health services. The rationalisation of human, material and financial resources and the control of demographic variables are an integral part of the objectives of the NPH which are, to a large extent, based on the population policy declaration, adopted in 1988.

The government's determination to change the health funding structure through a better involvement of local authorities and the population, has been the main health policy factor since the early 1990s. The share of the national budget attributed to health had continued to decline: 9 per cent in the early 1970s, 6 per cent in the early 1980s and 5 per cent in the early 1990s. In these conditions, community participation and local development become meaningful as a strategy for adapting social policy to the ongoing reforms.

Social policy on nutrition certainly existed but with real limitations. The government had introduced the nutrition component in the nutritional and health protection programme (NHPP), implemented between 1973 and 1988.[26] The various programme evaluations have established that the NHPP performance was poor due to several factors. The most important were: the poor targeting of undernourished children; the inevitable nature of health centres as instruments of implementation; and an inappropriate definition of the role of the committee of mothers in relation to the health committee.

In the early 1990s, the five year (1991-1996) implementation of a national nutrition programme was announced, but it has never really been implemented. The staff of already overburdened health centres was not well equipped to implement this programme. It was on the basis of these various elements that the CNP was conceived as an efficient instrument for the fight against malnutrition. But is it really? The interpretation of survey results provides part of the answer.

## Is the Communal Nutrition Project an Efficient Social Programme?

Observations on the field show the reality of the involvement of communities benefiting from the CNP. This involvement appears in terms of commitment of these communities first at project management level, then at project operation level and finally at the level of its realisation.

At the local level, i.e. at the level of the CNP site, nutrition centres and public water fountains which constitute the backbone of the project, are managed by local NGOs from the community itself and these NGOs are trained by AGETIP, which is in charge of implementing the project. This formula,, which consists of entrusting the recipient community with project implementation, on the one hand, strengthens local capacity to provide nutrition and health services. On the other hand, it allows for the injection of monetary revenue into the community which participates in the supervision of project activities in the district through its voluntary and elected representatives. The latter also benefit from training to strengthen their management capacity and facilitate participation in implementing the project, and it should be recalled that such is the CNP's mode of operation.

As regards the operation of the project, the direct beneficiaries of the project, i.e. pregnant and breast-feeding women, are actively invited to participate in the fight against malnutrition through training, and more precisely nutritional education activities. Therefore, the fact that they attend the nutrition centres together with their children is the most significant indicator of the smooth operation of the project. The centres are places of real collective learning whose primary objective is to bring about change in the women's feeding and health behaviours. These new activities will initiate better child-feeding practices, which can contribute to durably improve their nutritional state. IEC (Information, Education, Communication) activities directed to women beneficiaries in fact reach a wider audience, with these women serving as efficient relays.[27] In this respect, the CNP can be considered as an 'influence project' in the sense that, beyond the target groups, the whole community can benefit from it.

By facilitating the improvement of health and nutritional behaviour, CNP activities are an integral part of the fight against malnutrition. As already pointed out, this struggle is dependent on both underlying factors such as cultural and social behavioural factors and food security, and on economic factors. In this regard, CNP is partly based on the active responsibilization of the communities in the management of their health through sound nutrition.

Finally, concerning CNP implementation, there is close collaboration between the executing Agency (AGETIP), local intermediary bodies and the public structures operating on the CNP site.

Obviously, the multiplicity of interests due to the various social positions gives rise to conflicts in the CNP site (de Sardan 1995: 176). However, thanks to conflict management and collaboration, the social link is maintained by promoting the development of a synergy favourable to local development.

From the various elements showing the level of involvement of beneficiary communities, it is easy to observe that the CNP can, in certain respects, be perceived as a response to malnutrition. It makes a bet on the communities' ability to generate new practices aimed at solving all the problems related to malnutrition, including cultural problems. Thus, as a social programme, its ability to face up to malnutrition is real but limited. The question arises as to the people's reaction after the completion of the project. Will taking it over be enough for them to take up on their own the fight against malnutrition? These are questions to which it is difficult to respond immediately in view of the limitations of our case study. However, they certainly introduce the problem of the relationship between community participation and poverty in a context of adjustment.

Whatever its ability to respond effectively in the face of poverty, it is important to remember that it is a solution proposed, and in certain circumstances, imposed by the donors.[29] From this perspective, it can be interpreted as a strategy of donors perceived as a strategic group which has interests to defend through political and social action (de Sardan 1995: 179). In that case, what 'cards and rules' do the donors play with? According to what 'music score'? In the last part of this paper, we will analyse the role and political function of communal participation in the implementation of social programmes in a context of adjustment. In other words, it involves determining the limitations of social programmes based on privatization.

## The Privatization of Social Programmes: Impact and Limitations

The World Bank's position in implementing CNP is significant in many respects. With 65 per cent of the project financing, it naturally can set its conditionalities[30] and it does.[31]

The idea of good governance defended and popularized by the World Bank compels the State to streamline itself. It must 'privatize' itself and 'de-statize' itself by reinforcing private initiative. It must, therefore, consolidate the basis of a market economy (Mbembe 1999). The decision to entrust the private sector and not the state's public health bodies with implementing the CNP, a social programme, is in line with this World Bank view. With the CPN experience, the Bank hopes to show that it is possible to reconcile adjustment with social policy, precisely by transferring the implementation of social programmes to the private sector. The underlying idea is that the fight against poverty can also be efficiently followed up in the framework of economic reforms. One of the conditions of this political choice is precisely to adopt community participation, to introduce dynamics that favour breaking up the traditional relationship between the state and the people. In this respect, certain analysts have noted renewed interest in local development and the participatory and community models. In relation to this renewed interest in Sahel countries, Gado (1997) writes:

> Grassroots development and the participatory approach are two fashionable concepts among development operators. In all Sahel countries, during seminars on intervention strategies in rural areas or meetings with project officers, the participatory approach leitmotiv frequently crops up. Operators consider the participatory approach as a 'new' mode of intervention that meets the real needs of the people and is capable of promoting grassroots development (219).

However, regarding the participatory approach, one cannot really talk about 'novelty' as Gado does, but more precisely about 're-actualizing', or 'updating' with a view to facilitating the continuation of structural reforms.

The World Bank is quite aware of the importance of the participatory approach when it advocates giving 'powers to the poor and women, by encouraging grassroots organizations and agricultural organizations, cooperatives and women's groupings and so on' (World Bank 1989: 6-7).

This viewpoint partly clarifies the political function of community participation. It can, in some respects, be understood as an instrument for reinforcing economic reforms, since it promotes an 'acceptable and profitable management' of poverty, which as one can see, does not tackle the very essence of the poverty issue but rather contributes to easing social tensions.

The communities, particularly women beneficiaries, have developed a sense of ownership of the project and an ability to protect it. They believe this project is theirs and have recognized its usefulness for the social development of the area. Thus, they fully participate in implementing the project and justify this participation as a condition for the CNP's success.

On the other hand, the actual impact of the project on the recipient community can be observed through several indicators. The increase in community demands for health benefits and environmental management is the most important. This impact can also be measured by the strong pressure exerted by the people on CNP, a nutrition project, in order to transform it into a classical development project. The recipient population is of the view that the CNP would be more useful for its neighbourhood if it could also take on an economic role by embarking on activities that can substantially increase household revenues.

Special attention should be given to this latter aspect of the impact of CNP activities on the community. In fact, even if the project, through its community approach, is an instrument for the collective learning of new attitudes and behaviours in the face of malnutrition and health problems, it also shows its objective limitations in the fight against poverty by creating in the community an intense need to divert the set objectives. Basically, the people's message can be read as the expression of a clear awareness of poverty in all its complexity. The community's dread of poverty is the basis of a strong belief that to be efficient, the fight against poverty must rest on a global, not sectoral, policy. The community's warning to public authorities seems to be: is it possible to fight against malnutrition without a policy which aims, among other things, at increasing household revenue?

This attitude of the communities regarding the project, though surprising in certain respects, enables one to obtain a better understanding of the complexity and ambiguity of such a project. In fact, by facilitating the emergence of new actors, CNP dynamics have, at the same time created the conditions for its demystification as an efficient tool of local development and social change. The analysis of power relations and actor strategies make it possible to understand better the function of the communal approach which is the very basis of the privatization of social programmes (Teisserene 1994).

The basic principle of CNP is to break with the hierarchical and directive approach of the classical development projects, through its action strategy. However, this objective is not easy to achieve given the history of national development efforts which, on the whole, were essentially supported by the almighty welfare state. For example, CNP operation reveals the existence of ambiguous relationships of conflictual collaboration between the various actors, the communities, the intermediary organizations and the executing agency.

One of the stakes of this conflict concerns the control of resources. Who should bear the project costs? For the beneficiary communities, association leaders in particular, communal commitment and active participation in the implementation of the project cannot be dissociated from a financial motivation logic.[32] But for the Bank, the decision to rely on local communities and the private sector follows first and foremost the logic of profitability and efficiency. The cost of a project, however social, has to be minimized, according to the Bank. Therefore, by questioning volunteer work, albeit in a concealed manner, community leaders indirectly denounce the Bank's pattern of intervention and its option to privatize social programmes, its sole objective being profitability.

Power struggles also affect the various factions of the target-community, which, one has to remember, is not homogeneous. In the daily management of the project, conflicts naturally crop up which mostly result from the difficulty of implementing the participatory approach which requires great negotiating and listening capacity. Difficulties in negotiations between local project-implementing NGOs and the community mainly stem from shortcomings in terms of training and the influence of the political and socio-economic environment. The structure of local social relationships is also an element influencing power struggles in the project. Participation encourages democratic management, a reconstitution of power relations within the community and in the case of CNP, the reconstitution is done in favour of women and youths.

This very often creates contradictory collaboration and conflict relationships between men and women, on the one hand, and between men and youths, on the other hand. The women are deeply committed to the struggle for CNP control.

In reality, the private and participatory management of social projects, in the case of the CNP, has contributed to reinforcing the role of women in the community. On the basis of nutritional education CNP has strengthened women's capacity as local development actresses and has consequently facilitated appropriation of social change activities and thus the process of perpetuation of the fight against malnutrition.

All these behaviours and attitudes of the communities towards the CNP must be considered as following a coherent logic. By asking that the CNP be transformed into a development project, by rejecting volunteer work, the communities expose donor strategies in the direction of the CNP which is, as we have mentioned, a device well adapted to a context dominated by the pursuit of economic reforms.

These community behaviours and attitudes also raise, albeit in particular terms, the whole issue of local development in Africa (Ferfera 1996). They seem to indicate that for the communities, the success of local development depends above all on the intervention of the state and its partners. With communities that have, for decades, benefited from welfare state assistance, a break in the form of reorientation can only be seen as painful. Moreover, the state is aware of the importance of resources and means to promote local development. And yet, in a context of adjustment, that is what is most lacking!

In view of all these elements, social programmes conducted according to the participatory pattern in a context of adjustment appear in the final analysis as a rather complex political choice. To a certain extent, they provide communities that are heavily hit by poverty with tools to reinforce their technological and scientific capital and therefore the means to acquire political autonomy. The break and even the weakening of the hierarchical and bureaucratic model of relations between the state and the communities has ushered in an era in which traditional power relations are reconstituted in favour of certain social categories such as the women and youth.

But the state's partial withdrawal from the formulation and implementation of social programmes weakens its system of political legitimacy (Aina 1997). The communities benefiting from social programmes occasionally show their gratitude to NGOs and the World Bank, represented in certain communities as an institution for financing projects for the poor, not as one of those responsible for their state of destitution. And this is how we have a blurred, parasitic image, which enables the World Bank and other 'development partners' to devise 'the best way' to recover the poor countries' debt!

## Conclusion

In this paper, our main objective was to reflect on the significance and determinants of social policies in a context marked by the pursuit of economic reforms and the constraints of globalization. This reflection is justified by the fact that the state, redefined in its role and essential functions, loses its capacity to manage social policies in the best interest of the people. These policies, just like all other government policies on the whole, follow the logic of reforms; the strategic objective being to facilitate the country's integration into the global market.

In spite of its methodological limitations, the case study, i.e. the programme for the fight against malnutrition in Senegal, enabled us on the one hand, to describe the social repercussions of adjustment policies and, on the other, to present what we have referred to as the social policy 'project approach' in order to understand its significance and general outline.

These are the main results we have obtained: first the adjustment programme implemented since the early 1980s practically functioned as a tool for social demolition, and the expansion of poverty within Senegalese society.

On the basis of this observation, all policies aimed at fighting against poverty and applied within the framework of this same adjustment have appeared suspicious. Second, the private and participatory model of social programmes has enabled the government to conform to one of the requirements of globalization relayed by the Bank, i.e. respecting the principle of rationalization of activities. In their definition and major orientation, social policies function as a tool to reinforce reforms. In setting the scene for the globalization of exchanges, and in the process of integrating African countries in the global market, social policy management is, to a certain extent, transferred to local communities thus called upon to play a central role in the reform support mechanisms under donor surveillance.

## Notes

* Department of Sociology, Université Gaston Berger, Saint Louis, Senegal.

1. Among these constraints are: the persistent difficulties in the agricultural sector, the tightening of constraints on industry, budget austerity policies with their negative impact on the market and economic stagnation.
2. For example, the percentage of girls in full-time education is 81 per cent in the urban areas and 22 per cent in the rural areas. As for boys, these figures are 92 per cent and 47 per cent respectively.
3. See Ministry of Health, Department of Public Health, Statistics Division: Health and Demographic Statistics 1996, July 1998
4. For example, between 1990 and 1993, the average annual GDP growth was 0.9 per cent, while it was 5.2 per cent between 1995 and 1998.

5. There is an abundant bibliography on the consequences of SAP on Senegalese populations. For this also refer to the bibliography composed by Diop, M.C., 1996.
6. We borrow this beautiful expression 'works site of social demolition', which admirably accounts for the social repercussions of globalization, from Serge Halimi (1995).
7. M. Diouf (1998) proposed a research programme whose objective is to elaborate an African contribution to the theory and practice of democratic transition. He starts with the opinion that Africa's economic crisis and the way out of it, on the one hand, and the intensification of social movements in the face of social and economic deterioration, on the other, combine to bring the debate on democratization back to the centre of the African debate. Through certain proposed research themes (the economic crisis and governance, social movements, Public Administration) one can assess the actuality of the social policy issue in Africa.
8. Regarding what we can call the sectoral social policies, we can cite: the programme of struggle against poverty, the National Action Plan for Nutrition, the Senegalese Woman National Plan and the National Plan for Struggle against Maternal Mortality. Concerning social programmes, we can cite: the Programme for the Prevention of Maternal Mortality, The Vaccination Programme, the Programme of Struggle against Women's Malnutrition, the Programme of Struggle against Trouble Due to Iodine Deficiency, the Programme of Community Nutrition, the Programme of Struggle against Diarrhoeic Diseases, the Family Planning Programme, the STD and Aids Programme, and the Malaria Programme.
9. In a text giving an overview of Senegal's regionalization policy, Diagne (1997) exhaustively presents the political evolution of decentralization since 1960. According to Diagne, the reform successively involved urban areas and rural communities. The objective of regionalization was to rectify the major weaknesses of pre-decentralization policies, i.e. bringing the Administration closer to the administered to adequately take into account the people's basic aspirations, which is the fundamental principle of the decentralization policy.
10. From a methodological point of view, we have essentially relied on the results of investigation conducted in two surveys of the Community Nutrition Programme, in which we took part. This investigation was conducted in 1997 and 1998. Cf. PNC. AGETIP. 'Etude sur la stratégie IEC de contingence 1997 and Evaluation de la participation communautaire au PNC', 1998. We have also widely used official statistics and documents.
11. The concept of the Human Development Indicator (HDI) invented by UNDP and calculated annually since 1990 for some 70 developed and developing countries is based on 3 basic parameters: life expectancy at birth, level of education, actual per capita income. According to their HDI, the countries are classified into 3 categories: high HDI, median HDI and low HDI.
12. On the definition of poverty, see Salama and Valier (1994) and Lautier and Salama (1995).
13. See the document National Action Plan for Nutrition (1997-2002) Ministry of Agriculture, Ministry of Public Health and Social Action, October 1996; also the

reference document Demographic and Health Survey in Senegal (EDSII 1992-1993, Ministry of Economy, Finance and Planning, Directorate of Forecasting and Statistics.

14. For example, concerning medical staff, the numbers decreased by 19.15 per cent between 1989 and 1994. One can also read, in a Ministry of Health report that 'One notes in terms of passive coverage, one doctor for 13,210 inhabitants, one midwife for 6,142 child bearing age women and children aged 0-4 years, one nurse for 4,570 inhabitants. This is below WHO standards, i.e. one doctor for 5,000 to 10,000 inhabitants, one midwife for 300 inhabitants and 0-4 years old children, one nurse for 300 inhabitants'. See the document Demographic and Health Statistics, 1996. Ministry of Health. Directorate of Sanitation and Public Health. Division of Statistics. July 1998.
15. The spending structure of a poor household is dominated by food products (70 per cent, with over 5 per cent for rice, sugar and cooking oil). Expenditure for health follows with over 17 per cent, and education counts for only 2 per cent.
16. Out of an estimated population of 8.5 millions in 1995, youths under 20 represent 58 per cent, 5 to 14 years 28 per cent, and under 4, 19 per cent. The demographic growth rate of about 2.7 per cent has a rapid increase in urban areas where it reaches 3.9 per cent. In spite of fast urbanization, 60 per cent of the Senegalese still live in rural areas. For more information on the demographic question in Senegal, see Gilles Pison's book (1997).
17. For example in town, poverty is more important with large households (12 persons as against 7.7 for the non-poor in Dakar) whose head is poorly educated, has a little or not mechanised job and has uncertain income (only 24 per cent of poor income in Dakar and 13 per cent in other towns, are wage-earners).
18. The good collaborator is the most representative trade union which is affiliated to the ruling party and is logically supportive of the Government.
19. The example is often given of the former Minister of Basic Education, a former trade-union leader and one of the leaders of a left-wing party represented in Parliament. He was the one who implemented the 'volunteer teacher' programme which is part of the Civil Service reform aiming at generalizing 'contract civil servants'.
20. Nevertheless, we must note that election time is a moment of strong political and social agitation. This was the case in 1988 and 1998. Some think it is precisely the adjustment context that fuels this agitation with, of course, other more political motives such as lack of transparency of the electoral process.
21. Basically, this strategy rests on a few major principles: invest in human capital; increase productive assets, therefore the poor's income; increase return on assets; promote gainful employment; and make the poor take part in economic and social life.
22. Senegal's partners in the project implementation are: the International Development Association (IDA), the World Bank, the World Food Program (WFP), the Kreditanstalt für Wiederaufban (KWF) or the German Government's Credit Agency for Reconstruction.

23. According to the Bank, 'the CNP aims at introducing an innovative approach through profitable targeted actions in nutrition, conserved in close collaboration among all partners, and implemented not by Government but by private sector institutions' (World Bank 1995: 10).
24. For example, regarding feeding practices, researchers have confirmed their decisive role in the child's feeding. This research has shown that there are still efforts to be made concerning breastfeeding and the practice of weaning in Senegal.
25. AGETIP is a special agency, with the status of a private firm. It is an NGO, an independent body whose Board of Directors is composed of the General Manager, from the private sector, representatives of employers, mayors and the building industry. Also, thanks to its efficiency, highly appreciated by the Bank, it has been duplicated in the whole West African sub-region.
26. The PPNS was funded by the USAID and the Catholic Relief Services.
27. There are 14 IEC themes: food groups, growth monitoring promotion, breast-feeding promotion, infant feeding, proto-energetic malnutrition, culinary demonstration, vaccination, the struggle against diarrhoea, water and sanitation, pregnancy monitoring, the promotion of birth control, the struggle against anaemia, Malaria prevention and the promotion of systematic deparasiting.
28. For all development projects, the main objective is to bring about sustainable and autonomous change in target populations on the basic of activities limited in both time and space. In this respect, the relevance of a development project is in its positive long term effects, in its ability to emancipate the people from aid and foreign players, i.e. in the appropriation of the changes effected. Appropriation, which is the project's ultimate objective, is defined by Mokolo and Ouedraogo (1990: 2) as being, 'A highly complex integration approach whereby the populations themselves succeed in mastering, through their own decisions, the sustainable change process on which they were embarked or embarked themselves in order to control the functioning of their lives or communities, which they did not or no longer do. It is an approach which takes into account and reorganizes all levels of social life. Its first objective is to perpetuate interventions i.e. to be viable, these activities must be assimilated and maintained after the external financing without excessive cultural, economic, social and political cost. Therefore, appropriation is an integration approach which addresses target-populations in several respects' (2).
29. We are alluding here to the recombination of the power structure it implies, the local communities' and authorities' new position in relation to the state, which explains the reluctance with which the latter sometimes approach community participation.
30. The conditionality is the set of measures a country must accept to be eligible for foreign economic support in the case of interdependent economies.
31. The total cost of the project is estimated at 28 million dollars and the financing plan goes as follows: 65 per cent for IDA, 18.57 per cent for WFP, 10.71 per cent for KWF and finally 5.71 per cent for the Senegalese government.

32. For example, the notabilities of beneficiary districts are in general implied in its activities. However, in their vast majority, they openly complain that they do not receive any financial quid pro quo for their commitment, as is the case with their political commitment in the district.

## References

Abdemalk, L. et Cowlet, C., 1996, *Les nouvelles logiques du développement, globalisation versus localisation*, Paris: l'Harmattan.

Aina, T.A., 1997, *Mondialisation et politique sociale en Afrique*, document de travail, février, Dakar: CODESRIA.

Antoine, P. et al., eds., 1995, *Les familles dakaroises face à la crise*, Dakar: IFAN/ORSTOM/CFPD.

Assidon, E. et al., 1996, La fin du Tiers Monde? Paris, La Découverte, Les dossiers de l'Etat du Monde.

Aubin B., 1991, *Aménagement des terroirs et participation populaire: éléments du débat sur les approches participatives*, série Dossiers No. 15, Québec: Centre du Sahel.

Banque Mondiale, 1989, 'L'Afrique subsaharienne. De la crise à la croissance', Etude prospective à long terme, Washington D.C.

Banque Mondiale, 1990, 'Les dimensions sociales de l'ajustement: Programme d'action', Washingtion D.C.

Banque Mondiale, 1995, 'Rapport d'évaluation, République du Sénégal', Projet de nutrition communautaire.

Bernfeld D., 1983, *Un nouvel enjeu: la participation*, Paris: UNESCO.

Benoit-Guildot, O., 1991, 'Les acteurs locaux du développement local: y a t-il un 'effet localisé?" in *Sociologie du travail*, XXXIII, Vol. 4.

Biarez, S., 1990, *Le pouvoir local*, Paris: Economica.

Bierschenk Th. et Le Meurs, P.Y. eds., 1996, 'Le développement négocié: courtiers, savoirs, technologies', *APAD*, Bulletin no. 12, Décembre.

Blanchard, A. et al., 1987, *Pauvres et pauvretés dans la France méridionale à l'époque moderne, Actes du Colloque de 1987*, Editions Université Paul Valéry.

Bloch-Laine, F. et Garrigou-Lagrange, J.M., 1988, *Associations et développement local*, Paris, LGDJ.

Bop, C., 1994, 'Les femmes chefs de famille à Dakar', in *Africa Development*, Dakar: CODESRIA, pp. 51-58.

Bourdieu, P., 1993, *La misère du monde*, Paris: Seuil.

Bourgoignie, G., 1990, 'La problématique sociale', in *Ajustement structurel et réalités sociales en Afrique*, Canada: Université d'Ottawa, Collogue de l'IDIC.

Brisset, C., 1996, *Pauvretés*, Paris: Hachette.

Castel, R., 1995, *Les métamorphoses de la question sociale. Une chronique du salariat*, Paris: Fayard.

Coquery-Vidrovitch, C. et al., eds., 1988, 'Pour une histoire du développement', Etat, société et développement, Paris: l'Harmattan.

Defarges, PH., M., 1993, *La Mondialisation: Vers la fin des frontières*, Paris: Dunod.

Diagne, M., 1997, 'Aperçu sur la politique de régionalisation au Sénégal, Communication au Forum sur la Gouvernance locale, Bakel, 16-18 juin.

Diemer, G. (eds.), 1997, *La négociation sociale des dispositifs techniques pour le développment*, APAD Bulletin no. 13, mai.

Dieng, A. A., 1997, 'Gouvernance et développement', in Institut Africain pour la Gouvernance, 1997, Bonne Gouvernance et développement en Afrique, Dakar, pp. 101-109.

Diop, M.C., 1996, *La lutte contre la pauvreté à Dakar, vers la définition d'une politique municipale*, Accra: PGU.

Diouf, M., 1998, Libéralisations politiques et transitions démocratiques: *Perspectives africaines*, Dakar, CODESRIA, Nouvelles pistes No. 1.

EDS II-Sénégal, 1994, 'Enquête démographique et de santé au Sénégal 192-93', Direction de la Prévention et de la Statistique, DHS.

EDS III-Sénégal, 1997, 'Enquête démographique et de la santé au Sénégal, Direction de la Prévention et de la Statistique, DHS.

Ela, J.M., 1994, 'Afrique, l'irruption des pauvres. Société contre ingérence', *Pouvoir et argent*, Paris: l'Harmattan.

Fall, B., 1997, *Ajustement Structurel et emploi au Sénégal*, Dakar, CODESRIA.

Ferfera, M.Y., 1996, 'Le développement local, ses institutions et son statut dans le modèle algérien de développement', in Abdelmalki, L. et Courlet, C., 1996, *Les nouvelles logiques du développement. Globalisation Versus localisation*, Paris: l'Harmattan, pp. 335-349.

Gado, A.B., 1997, 'Développement à la base, stratégie d'intervention et participation paysanne au Sahel', in P. Tersiguel, et Becker, C., *Développement durable au Sahel*, Paris: Karthala, pp. 219-232.

Gazier, B., 1981, *La pauvreté unidimentionnelle*, Paris: Economica.

Garrier, C., 1998, *Défense des populations et développement, un enjeu pour la Banque Mondiale*, Paris: l'Harmattan.

Geremek, B., 1987, *La potence ou la Pitié. L'Europe et les pauvres du Moyen âge à nos jours*, Paris: Gaillimard.

Grémion, P., 1979, 'Les assoviations et le pouvoir local', in Esprit, novembre.

Halimi, S., 1995, 'Sur les chantiers de la démolition sociale', in *Monde Diplomatique*, Manière de voir no. 28, Les nouveaux maîtres du Monde.

Henry, P.M., 1990, *Pauvreté, progrès et développement*, Paris: l'Harmattan/UNESCO.

Institut Africain pour la Démocratie, 1997, *Bonne gouvernance et développement en Afrique*, Dakar: Editions Démocraties Africaines.

Johnson-Sirleaf, E., 1996, 'La lutte contre la pauvreté comme axe central de la stratégie de développement durable', in *Journal des actes du Conseil Economique et Social du Sénégal*, pp. 7-15.

Lautier, B., 1996, 'Pauvretés au Sud, pauvretés au Nord', in Assidon, E. et al., *La fin du Tiers Monde?*, Les dossiers de l'Etat du Monde, Paris: la Découverte.

Lautier, B. et Salama, P., 1995, 'Pauvretés', *Revue Tiers Monde*, no. 142, Paris, PUF-IEDS, avril-juin.

Lewis O., 1966, 'The culture of poverty', *Scientific American*.

Makolo P.N. et Ouedraogo H.B., 1990, 'L'appropriation des actions du développement: une réflexion', Série Notes et Travaux no.15, Québec: Centre du Sahel.

Meister A., 1974, *La participation dans les associations*, Paris: Éditions Ouvrières.
Meister A, 1977, *La participation pour le développement*, Paris: Éditions Ouvrières.
Monde Diplomatique, *Manière de Voir*, no. 28, 1995, Les nouveaux maîtres du Monde.
Monde Diplomatique, *Manière de Voir*, no. 32, 1996, 'Scénarios de la mondialisation'.
Paugam, S., 1994, *La disqualification sociale, Essai sur la nouvelle pauvreté*, PUF.
Pison, G. et al. 1997, *Les changements démographiques au Sénégal*, PUF, IED, NAS.
Salama, P. et Valier, J., 1994, 'Pauvretés et inégalités dans le Tiers Monde', *La découverte*, Paris.
Sarr, F. 1998, *L'entreprenariat féminin au Sénégal*, Paris: l'Harmattan.
Séralgeldin, I., Noël, M., 1990, 'S'occuper des dimensions sociales de l'Ajustement en Afrique', *Finances et Développement*, Vol. 27, n° 3, pp.18-27.
Sine, B. 1997, 'Introduction', in *Bonne gouvernance et développement en Afrique*, Dakar: Éditions Démocraties Africaines, pp. 14-16.
Sow, F., 1993, 'Les initiatives féminines au Sénégal: une réponse à la crise?', in *Africa Development*, vol. XX, No. 3, pp. 89-115.
Teisserenc, P., 1994, *Les politiques développement local. Approche sociologique*, Paris: Economica.
Tersiguel, Ph. et Becker, CH., 1997, *Développement durable au Sahel*, Paris: Karthala.
Tinguiri, K., L., 1996, 'Economie politique d'une réforme macro-économique. Un essai de bilan social de la dévaluation du franc CFA', *Démocraties Africaines*, no. 6, avril-mai-juin, pp. 19-44.
UNRISD, 1995, *État de désaroi. Les répercussions de la mondialisation*, Genève: The United Nations Research Institut for Social Development (UNRISD).
Vallado, A.G.A., 1993, *Le 21ème siècle américain*, Paris: La découverte.
Wechters, S., 1987, *État, Décentralisation et territoires*, Paris: l'Harmattan.

# 7

# Urban Development Policies and Infrastructure in Nigeria

**Mohammed-Bello Yunusa***

## Introduction

Social services provision has direct links with the state of well-being of individuals and groups, as it supports and sustains socio-economic activities needed for development. Access to basic services and facilities is crucial to improved welfare. However, differential access (based on factors of socio-economic status, gender and age) is more the norm than exception in urban areas. Differential access has implications for and crystallises differences in livelihood and welfare among the urban populace.

The gap in access to urban infrastructures widened under the structural adjustment (SAP) regime. In this period urban services were made available to those 'who were willing and able to pay the price' (Sirken 1979: 1). This market principle as applied to urban infrastructure became imperative for cost recovery purposes.

This paper demonstrates access to urban infrastructure by socio-economic status, gender and age categories, and discusses the implications of such access for the livelihood and welfare of urban dwellers. In order to do so, a study was carried out in Kaduna, a colonial town that was the headquarters of the Northern Nigeria regional government up to 1967. It is located between 6° and 8° East and 10° and 12° North. It had a population of about 40,000 in 1952, 150,000 in 1963 and 461,000 in 1984. Kaduna has served as the seat of regional administration from the colonial period. The Kaduna urban area is managed and controlled by Kaduna North, Kaduna South, parts of Igabi and Chikun Local Government Councils.

The development and management of urban Kaduna is the responsibility of many agencies such as the Kaduna State Urban Development Agency, Local Government Councils, Kaduna State Environmental Protection Agency together with the active participation of some international agencies and private sector. As far back as early 1970s, the United Nations Development Programme ran a pilot project for a sewage and drainage system in the city.

Two wards inhabited by various socio-economic categories were identified for the survey. The wards were Tudun Wada and Badiko. In each ward clusters of residential areas were demarcated using major streets. From the clusters, a cluster was randomly sampled in each ward. In each cluster, every fiftieth household from the starting point that was randomly identified was interviewed. In the households, any adults (i.e. 18 years and above) who were available were interviewed.

In this way, 92 (73 per cent) persons were interviewed in Tudun-Wada and 35 (27 per cent) were interviewed in Badiko. Descriptive statistics were generated from the data to show the characteristics of respondents and distribution of access to infrastructure amongst the various social groups (income, age, gender etc.).

## The Context of Urban Development Policies

Policy intervention in urban development dates back to the colonial period. From the 1904 cantonment proclamations to the 1917 Road and Township ordinance, the focus of such interventions was residential segregation, land acquisition, enforcement of hygiene laws and categorisation of urban settlements. The outbreak of bubonic plague in Lagos in 1928 expanded the frontier of urban development policies to cover slum clearance, land reclamation and the development of industrial and residential estates, particularly in Lagos.

The creation of administrative frameworks by establishing Town Planning Committees for the southern and northern region in 1924 was strengthened by the enactment of the Nigerian Town and Country Planning Ordinance in 1946. This ordinance enabled planning institutions to plan and implement development schemes. It remained the nation-wide urban development law as adopted by the regions until the enactment of the 1992 urban and regional planning law.

From independence to 1981, national development plans only provided for town and country planning, and institutional capacity building was rigorously pursued. The 1981-85 national development plan specifically spelt out basic objectives of urban and regional planning for Nigerian towns and cities. These notwithstanding, the level and state of urban infrastructure development remained poor. On the infrastructure sub-sector of urban development, the federal government of Nigeria admitted that the rate at which community infrastructure and social services are provided has not been commensurate with the pace of population growth and urban expansion. As a result, infrastructure problems now plague all urban centres in Nigeria.

These include irregular water supply, poor drainage, inefficient waste disposal systems, grossly over stretched intra-city, inter-city and inter state transportation systems, etc. (Central Bank of Nigeria 1997: 46).

The situation of urban infrastructure is an indicator that the ideals of Nigeria's declaration of education, health, housing, etc. for all by the year 2000 cannot be attained. Indeed, in Nigeria the provision of social services expanded during the era of the boom in oil production, but shrank thereafter with dwindling oil revenues. As state expenditures on recurrent subheads were cut, consumables in schools, health clinics and even the quality and quantity of water available to the citizens were adversely affected. The overall situation is that Nigeria is currently faced with problems of inadequate social service infrastructure and the poor quality of services where available at a high cost.

In recent times, a major macro policy environment that shaped the urban development policy is the economic crisis management policy. By early 1980, Nigeria's external debt was estimated to be over 20 million Naira (Usman 1986). The global oil glut only aggravated Nigeria's fiscal problems (Usman 1986; Ihimodu 1991), and adjustment in the sense of restructuring public expenditure, adoption of realistic pricing and exchange rate policies, rational use of resources and commercialisation and/or privatisation of public enterprises were inevitable.

The adjustment policies, primarily put together by the industrialized nations through the World Bank and the International Monetary Fund were aimed at managing developing countries' economic problems, and attaining global co-ordination and co-operation in securing payment of debts (Ould-Mey 1994).

The SAP represented an epoch in Nigeria's twisted development process and it meant the expansion of capitalist economic space and the establishment of political domination by powerful capitalist nations over the developing countries (Zeleza 1989).

Adjustment policies presented two worries. First, the level of involvement of these agencies in any domestic economic management was a function of the magnitude of the financial problems of those economies. The adjustment loans and the devaluation of the local currencies only heightened net transfer of funds to the stronger capitalist countries (Zeleza 1989) and increased the debt burden of the benefiting countries. This strategy strengthened integration of debtor countries into the capitalist system and worse, with a weak status. Secondly, adjustment policies reduced state power in terms of control and management of exchange regimes, articulation and implementation of social policies and even budgeting (Ould-Mey 1994). Indeed, with the adjustment policies in place, the state withdrew and left behind weak institutions that were incapable of delivering public goods at minimum cost to the citizens. This situation underlines the assertion that increased globalization of the economy erodes state power (Griffen and Khan 1992) and its ability to meet basic requirements of citizens for a sustained socio-economic performance and improved conditions of living (Meagher and Yunusa 1991).

## Basic Infrastructure in Urban Areas

### *Policy Context of Infrastructure Provision in Nigeria*

Nigeria has articulated polices and programmes that are aimed at providing basic social services: for instance, the national free and compulsory primary education in the early 1970s, a national policy on primary health care and preventive services, housing and environment, etc. Though the actual development of urban infrastructure did suffer greatly between 1980 and 1985 due to economic recovery programmes, the situation has become worse in recent time. Roads, water supply, telephone, refuse collection and transportation infrastructure could not be maintained or refurbished due to dwindling resources. With the adjustment policies, economic evaluation and prioritisation in terms of cost recovery became part of urban development policy.

The development of basic socio-economic infrastructure in towns and cities is the concern of individuals, regional and national governments, corporate bodies and international agencies. Indeed, urban policies as 'interventions in social life for the purposes of ensuring the basic needs and well-being (health, education, fuel, housing, water, food, sanitation, etc.) of the majority of peoples' (Aina 1996) have national and international ramifications. Inadequate infrastructure impinges on the cities' ability to perform their functions for residents and visitors.

Development policies in Nigeria from 1986 involved the governments' (local council, regional and federal) open abdication of responsibilities to citizens. Health, electricity, telephones, water, among others were either commercialized or had subsidies on them reduced or removed. The situation naturally jeopardised living conditions and people's access, (particularly disadvantaged groups such as women, children and the aged) to basic infrastructures (Mollenkopf 1995).

### *Urban Infrastructure, Productivity and Welfare*

Basic infrastructure as conceptualised in this study includes health, education, refuse collection facilities, water supply, electricity and household fuel, roads and transport, housing (which embodies the structure and the living environment, foreground, toilets, courtyard, sewage and drainage, etc.), and market stalls. Pricing of these infrastructures enhances or inhibits access to them as well as the degree of individual and group productivity and well-being in urban centres.

The quality and quantity of infrastructure available has often fallen short of demand due to rapid rate of urbanization (population growth and expansion of socio-economic activities), shortage of funds, poor institutional arrangements and prioritization, shortage of qualified manpower, equipment and so on. To this end, Nigerians in colonial and pre-colonial towns like Kaduna were faced with problems of poor infrastructure services as indicated by electrical overload and failure, unsanitary dwelling, overcrowding, intermittent water supply and congested roads among many others.

The poor policy framework and infrastructure base, aggravated by the high rate of urbanisation and the entire adjustment policies triggered by industrial capitalist crises (Zeleza 1989 and Yueng 1995), undermined urban development, livelihoods (Yueng 1995) and welfare. An examination of access to basic infrastructure is therefore significant in understanding the dynamics of urban livelihood, productivity and welfare.

## Urban Development Policies and Programmes in Nigeria

The urban crisis in Nigeria is enormous (Onibokun 1989; Schlyter 1996). Jibrin (1994), notes that Nigeria is highly urbanised. About 36 per cent of its population are living in towns of around 20,000 people and above. Another source, (World Bank and Nigerian Collaboration 1995), puts the proportion of the urban population at 38 per cent.

Conceptually, urban development policies and projects involve improvements of the physical and social conditions of towns and cities (Diamond 1991) through the development and management of social, economic and physical infrastructure. Urban development policies and projects in Nigeria started with the colonial administration mainly for providing colonial administrators with a minimum level of comfort. The first colonial development plan for Nigeria (1946–56) recognized the need for urban planning as a means of promoting development and welfare. Within the plan period, some towns and villages were redesigned and provided with modern facilities and services such as water, electricity and health facilities.

The first national development plan of the post-independence government (1962–68) consolidated the colonial urban policies. The plan provided for urban water supply, healthcare, and town and country planning. The town and country planning component included housing, transport, sewage, market stalls and site and services programmes. These programmes and projects remained the crux of urban policies and projects in the second (1970–74) and third (1975–80) national development plans with emphasis on drainage and sewage.

Nigeria never had a national urban policy until in 1997 when it was realized that 'a bleak future for Nigerian urban settlements (is unavoidable) unless constructive remedial measures are taken' (Federal Republic of Nigeria 1997: 6). To this end, the national urban development policy of 1997 sets out 'to develop a dynamic system of urban settlements which will foster sustainable economic growth [and] ensure improved standard of living and well-being for all Nigerians' (Federal Republic of Nigeria,1997: 17).

In Kaduna, it is common to find several government agencies and parastatals providing a range of urban services. Nation-wide, various agencies of federal, state and local Governments are involved in the construction and maintenance of urban services. The multiplicity of agencies involved in the provision and running of urban services makes provision of urban facilities prone to duplication, institutional conflict and inefficiency.

The sole agency charged with the development of urban services in Kaduna is the Kaduna Urban Development Board, which later became the Kaduna State Urban Planning and Development Authority (to cover all urban centres in Kaduna State). The edict establishing the authority was issued in 1972. Other agencies like Kaduna Property Development Authority, Kaduna State Water Board, Kaduna State Ministry of Works and Housing, Kaduna State Health Management Board, the National Electric Power Authority and Nigeria Telecommunication, in addition to numerous private establishments and individuals, are active participants in the development of Kaduna town.

## Development of Urban Facilities in Kaduna

Kaduna, from inception, has always exhibited residential segregation with the delineation of separate areas for Europeans, and non-European reservation areas for the native population, as well as non-residential areas. The segregation was to avoid contamination and social conflict among the various social categories in the town. In 1917 Kaduna was declared a second class town and the area of the town was expanded. As a result, transport facilities were extended into ethnic settlements. Thus, Tudun Wada, became part of Kaduna Township as a non-European residential area. The later development and expansion of Kaduna incorporated such villages like Karma Marshi, Badiko, and several neighbouring settlements.

With the introduction of urban services in Kaduna from about 1917, the first hospital was established in the European reservation areas. For the Africans, the first clinic was established in 1924. In 1929, pipe borne water and electricity supplies were introduced into Kaduna.

Residential segregation now exists in the form of high-and low-income residential areas. The high-income areas have better facilities, services and utilities and therefore provide greater opportunities for efficient socioeconomic activities and improved well-being than the low-income residential areas.

Taxation policy is a major tool for effective income re-distribution and poverty reduction. Nigerian taxation policies generally encourage progressive taxation to reduce the tax burden on the poor, stimulate economic growth, combat inflation and encourage diversification of the macro economic system. It can be observed that the rich generally pay more tax than the poor but also that the poor have less ability to pay for urban services under inflationary conditions. In any case, the poor neighbourhoods of Tudun Wada, Ungwar

Sarki and others are inadequately provided with urban services compared with the wealthy neighbourhoods, as in the case of the government reservation areas (GRAs) of Ungwar-Rimi, Malali, Barnawa, etc. The supply of utilities like water, electricity and telephone services is hardly disrupted in the GRAs, mainly due to the socio-economic and political status of the their inhabitants.

## The State of Urban Infrastructure in Kaduna Town—A Review

The Kaduna Capital Development Authority is charged with implementing the Kaduna Urban Development Plan of 1965, as well as to 'co-ordinate the developmental activities of various organisations in Kaduna' (Yashim 1984: 2). The efforts of the authority in discharging its responsibilities notwithstanding, serious problems regarding water supply, sanitary conditions, the overcrowding of households into single rooms, and poor drainage are common (Seymour 1980).

### *Transport*

The Kaduna State Transport Authority, a state agency charged with the responsibility for public transport provision and management within Kaduna metropolis, functioning as public transport carrier in Kaduna town, has been phased out as its buses have been declared unserviceable. This leaves intra-city transport service to private sector operators of taxis and mini-buses. The urban transport problem was graphically described by Ogwude (1989) as follows:

> transport infrastructure in the cities has become severely overloaded, due to population growth...the price of new vehicles have increased three fold beyond what most could afford, and there were shortages of spare parts to repair existing stock of vehicles (Ogwude 1989: 5).

As a result of these shortcomings, a taxi trip that cost 0.50 Naira in 1985 now costs 10.0 Naira. Also, the rise in transport fares is linked to the price of vehicles and the cost of maintenance. These changes are overwhelming for urban households and the local economy.

A core policy that affect transportation is the petroleum product pricing. The state charged the Petroleum Products Marketing Company (PPMC) with the responsibility of fixing prices for petroleum products. Between 1985 and 1995 the pump price of petrol, a major input in the transport industry, went from N 0.20 to N 11.00 per litre representing a 5,500 per cent increase in ten years. The pump price that was N 20.00 in 1999 is currently N 22.00 per litre. The increase induced inflation, as prices of most goods and services are tied to transport. The increase deepened urban poverty in the sense of greater destitution, powerlessness and vulnerability to vagaries of living.

The impact of the general pricing policies in the transport sector was summed up in the Central Bank of Nigeria 1997 annual report as follows:

> Available data showed that vehicles registered in 1997 stood at 81,443 compared with 63,418 in the previous year (1996) indicating an increase of 28.4 per cent. The rise is attributed mainly to increased patronage of low second hand vehicles. - However the stock of vehicles in operation continued to experience high cost of spare parts replacement and maintenance. The cost of engine oil, brake fluid, fuel and air filters, spark plugs edged up substantially above the previous years' levels—These prices have consequently raised the costs of transportation (CBN 1997:124).

## *Housing*

Housing, as an embodiment of welfare facilities, was only provided to public servants and produced for sale by the Kaduna Housing Authority (KHA). The KHA was involved in urban renewal, direct provision of housing units and provision of housing loans to civil servants of the state. In 1989, it completed only 10 housing units with loans from a commercial bank and grants from the state government. These houses were sold to the general public in 1991 at 300,000 Naira each. The staff housing loan was then pegged at a maximum of 40,000 Naira and later raised to 80,000 Naira. From this it is apparent that the price of government housing units puts housing beyond the reach of urban poor and even the highest paid public officer. The value of housing loans to civil servants would not enable completion of a house either. Therein lies the predicament of public servants and the poor in urban Nigeria.

## *Water Supply*

Kaduna was served with pipe borne water and electricity in 1928, (Bryant undated). In the 1975-80 development plan period, the Kaduna urban water supply was expanded by about 45 million litres per day in addition to the existing 72 million litres. To ensure a constant water supply, it was further expanded by 150 million litres per day with 102 million Naira during the 1981-85 development plan period. Of this sum, 67 million Naira was a loan from the World Bank.

Data on quality and quantity of water supplied and consumed in Kaduna were not readily available at the time of study. However it was observed that water supply lines are extended to the government, private and corporate premises on a simple request without due regard for the capacity of the supply system to meet the demand. In a 1984 assessment, it was observed that the actual water supply in Kaduna metropolis was less than 50 per cent of the total demand (Yashim 1984). All three water works in Kaduna North and South Local Government Areas performed below capacity of 126.42, 19.46

and 14.46 million litres per day respectively in 1991. The result of this short fall is dry taps across the metropolis and the frequent search for water by women and children.

The 150 million litre per day Kaduna North water project (which was started in 1981 and was commissioned in 1991 when 89 per cent of the project was completed), was a joint project of the World Bank (US $92 million), Kaduna state government (24.79 million Naira), and Kaduna State Water Board (18.45 million Naira). Between 1985, and 1987, the World Bank invested 272.68 million Naira in urban water projects in the entire Kaduna State.

## Health Facilities

From the state statistical records, Kaduna metropolis has 10 per cent of all the health facilities in the state as of 1985. A substantial proportion of this was provided by private individuals (33), Local Government Council (14), industries and corporate bodies (12) and state government (8). In addition to involvement of the three tiers of government in the provision, running and management of health facilities, external agencies are involved in aiding Kaduna State in the health sector. For instance, the USAID donated hospital equipment worth 10 million Naira to the state, the Johns Hopkins University trained family planning personnel for about 0.63 million Naira and the United Nations Population Fund co-funded a 2.05 million Naira project with Kaduna State. A major constraint in gaining access to health facilities is the cost of drugs, which has gone up in recent times.

### *Telephone Facilities*

As a major economic and social facilitator, the telephone has increasingly become too expensive for most people. The cost of procuring and using telephones has gone up astronomically particularly during the past six years. In 1980, for private and business use, a telephone line was installed for 110 Naira. In 1996, the minimum required for installing telephone in a private house was 2,490 Naira, and business lines cost 3,090 Naira. The 1998 price was 29,505 Naira and 34,020 Naira for private and business lines respectively. These are only the official costs of installations. There are other charges by the staff which are off the record.

In the same vein, making local calls in 1982 had a fixed rate of 0.10 Naira, while trunk calls could be made at between 0.30 to 2.00 Naira per three minutes depending on distance. In 1996, it went up to between 0.60 and 1.80 Naira per minute.

Other than the cost of using this facility, the location of call points poses another problem of accessibility to users. Despite the rising costs, up to 1997, call points were easily accessible in physical terms to the people. By 1997, the private call points, business centres, were closed down to enhance the monopoly of the state corporation. With a military decree, the Nigerian Telecommunications took over the responsibility of providing call points and phone cards. The call points became too few and far from residential areas. To illustrate this, the whole of Kaduna, at the time of the survey, had only two call points and Zaria has only one. All these steps made it difficult to access telephone facilities in Kaduna.

### *Energy Supply*

An effective energy supply is a requirement for economic activities and comfortable living. For the purpose of this study, it suffices to note the dramatic changes in the costs of installation and consumption of electricity. The cost of consuming a unit of electricity went up from a flat rate of 0.6 Naira to between 1.30 and 1.51 Naira charged in residential areas and between 1.80 to 1.90 Naira for commercial and industrial areas in 1995. In the same year, the connection or installation fee went up from a minimum of 1,600 Naira to about 14,600 or 38,300 Naira, depending on the number of phases. Note that both telephone and electricity services were commercialised from 1986. Again, these charges are the official rates. The unofficial rates charged by officials off-record are much higher. The ability of citizens to afford these costs in the face of devaluation, high inflation levels and low income is doubtful.

From the above, it is clear that there is a general inadequacy of the facilities, services and utilities and inability of citizens to pay and access them. This has been acknowledged in documents of the state. For instance, the Central Bank notes that:

> telecommunication services deteriorated in 1997...The decline in telephone and telegraphic messages reflects largely the inability of potential users of the services to pay prevailing tariffs given low purchasing power (Central Bank of Nigeria 1997: 125).

Scanty as these statistics are, two things can be observed. First, the provision of urban infrastructure, for instance housing, is designed to benefit a few. Second, funding for urban infrastructure development has for a long while come from the governments, private sector and international capital market as facilitated by the World Bank and other international agencies. Despite the sourcing for funds nationally and internationally, there is no coherent policy on the provision of urban facilities, services and utilities to benefit the mass of the people.

## Socio-Economic Characteristics of Respondents

This section focuses on household data obtained through the survey. The respondents were interviewed in 84 households. In the sample, 41.7 per cent (55) were females and 58.3 per cent (77) were males. A substantial majority of the respondents were below 30 years of age (49.2 per cent), others were between

30-50 years (39.4 per cent), and 11.4 per cent above 50 years. This is a normal urban age distribution given the tendency for youth to migrate to towns and the older generation to move back home.

The areas covered by the survey were inhabited by the Hausa (28.8 per cent), Yoruba 18.2 per cent), Ebira (13.7 per cent), Gwari (4.3 per cent), Fulani (3.8 per cent) and such others like Igala (5.3 per cent), Igbo (6.1 per cent), Idoma, Jaba, Kagoro, Kataf, Nupe and Tiv. The sample was composed of mainly Muslims (69.7 per cent) and Christians (30.3 per cent).

The respondents were in various occupations, both primary and secondary, as in Table 2.1. In the sample, a majority were self-employed in the informal sector (tailoring, barbing salon, carpentry, auto-mechanic, electronics and other repair services). This occupational structure indicates the decline of urban formal employment and the growth of self-employment. In fact, the existing policy of rational application of resources mainly reduced the number of public sector employees and induced the growth of the informal sector employment (Mustapha 1991; Meagher and Yunusa 1991). All the small businesses and artisanal economic activities require urban infrastructure to enhance their productivity.

The educational qualifications of respondents were as follows: 14.4 per cent had received quranic education, 3 per cent had no education at all and 0.8 per cent of the sample had no Western education. 15.2 per cent of the sample had obtained university education. Yet about 18.9 per cent of the sample possessed no practical economic skills. All others enjoyed some level of skill in traditional crafts, modern crafts, repair of machines, equipment and household appliances, trading in specialised articles (auto and machine spare parts, medicines, etc.) and other activities such as hairdressing and dry cleaning.

The analysis o774f age, sex, education and income of respondents provides some basis for a further analysis of urban dwellers' needs for and use of basic infrastructure as a requirement for productive economic activities and social well-being.

## Livelihood Strategies of Respondents

Livelihood strategies entail all activities that are carried out for the purpose of making a living. Respondents were involved in a wide range of economic activities. The primary livelihood activities of respondents included civil service employment (in the sense of working in the government bureaucracy and corporate establishments), petty trading, big businesses, and farming. Only 2.3 per cent of the sample were dependants due either to schooling or unemployment. A majority (53 per cent) were self-employed. Those in petty trade were involved in street food, front door retail sales and local restaurants (bukateria). Manual workers included people engaged in the repair of household appliances (radio, refrigerator, television sets) or vehicles. Some operated hairdressing salons and similar small enterprises. More than half of the respondents (56.8 per cent) started their primary economic activities from about 1985 to 1997, but a third (37.1 per cent) entered the various economic activities after 1990 when the economic environment became harsher.

In addition to these economic activities, respondents were participants, simultaneously, in other economic activities in order to gain additional income. These others are the secondary livelihood opportunities of respondents. A little more than a third of the sample (37.1 per cent) are self-employed in the urban informal economic activities, and this is almost half (46.7 per cent) of the proportion of respondents engaged in secondary economic activities. A fifth of the sample have no secondary economic activities. Over all, 68.1 per cent of respondents engaged in secondary activities started between 1990 and 1998.

Under the prevailing economic climate, intensifying income earning activities is desirable to meet personal and household demands. The expected intensification was measured by hours spent at income-earning activities. Indeed, respondents have increased hours they spend at work. In the sample, 39 per cent of the respondents increased, 13.8 per cent decreased while 43.9 per cent responded no change in the number of hours they spend at work. Intensification of hours at work, though does not necessarily mean greater labour application and higher earnings. It may be directed at increasing possibilities of more potential clients calling on them and therefore generating more future income.

Despite the drive for increased income which could be expected given the high rate of inflation, income generation abilities of individuals significantly vary. A wide gap was noticed in the monthly income of respondents in both primary and secondary occupations. Earnings from primary occupations ranged between 50 to 75000 Naira a month, though 6.8 per cent of the sample could not state their incomes. The mean monthly income from primary activities was about 5,000 Naira.

As for the monthly earning from secondary occupations, it ranged between 50 to 30,000 Naira with a mean of 3500 Naira. In the sample, 31 per cent did not have or did not state earnings from secondary sources. When earnings from the two sources were added, the gap between the lowest and highest earner decreased marginally. Total earnings of the respondents ranged between 250 and 57,000 Naira a month with a mean of 8700 Naira. The skewness of the earning among households surveyed can be observed in the fact that 71.3 per cent of the respondents earn less than 10,000 Naira month. Indeed, 44.3 per cent of the households have less than 500 Naira per capita monthly income.

Income earnings of females and males in the sample were virtually the same. But the younger generation earn far less (1931.25 Naira) than the oldest generation (5437 Naira). Of interest is the fact that education may have nothing to do with income generation. Respondents with quranic education earn less than those with no education at all. Also respondents with quranic education earn more than those with secondary or post-secondary education. Respondents with no education or no Western education at all earn about the same income as those with primary education. However, those with university education earned the highest income, 11,275 Naira per month.

## Access to Urban Facilities

The study assessed respondents' need for and access to some fundamental facilities that support or promote economic activities and improve the welfare of urban inhabitants. Infrastructure so considered includes roads, open spaces, house courtyards and frontal space, health, transport, telephone, water supply, electricity, kiosks and market stalls. From Table 7.3, it can be observed that other than roads, open spaces, water supply and market stalls, all respondents seem to have access to virtually all the facilities indicated. In fact, not all respondents who have access to these facilities require them for economic activities. In the same vein, relatively, respondents that needed frontal space, health facilities, cheap transport, telephone, electricity and kiosk do not find them readily available for their various activities. It was observed that inaccessibility to some of these facilities created other problems in the use of other urban infrastructure. For example inadequate space in front of houses leads households to encroach on public spaces, particularly streets and pavements and thus obstruct traffic flows. It was also noticed that the inability to obtain electricity prompts illegal connections, particularly in houses and workshops (especially welding workshops). This has caused fire disasters and transformers to short circuit due to over loading. This further induces interruption of the already epileptic electricity supply.

Access to and need for this basic infrastructure are not the same across education, age, income and gender groups. Respondents with a medium level of education have the greatest need for such infrastructure as roads (43.8 per cent) open space (40 per cent), transport (45 per cent), telephone (40 per cent), water supply (41.2 per cent), electricity (46.5 per cent), kiosks (40 per cent) and market stall (53.3) as compared to the low educational group (about 16 per cent to 23 per cent) and high educational group (about 5 per cent to 24 per cent). In the same vein, the low income group (those earning under 10,000 Naira a month), have the greater need for this urban infrastructure for economic activities than both the medium and high income earners (Table 7.4).

Respondents that started their economic activities before the adjustment years have more needs for space in front of the house and health facilities than those who started their activities between 1986 and 1991. It was found that those that require health facilities are essentially respondents that trained as health workers and needed to work in health institutions and others who needed the facility on the grounds of ill health.

In the sample, those that set up between 1985 and 1987 have the greatest need for kiosks and household spaces (foreground or courtyards). According to a respondent, 'economic hardship has made it imperative to augment our household income. The easiest way we found was setting up retail business in front of this house, since we can not pay shop rents'. When a look is taken at those that set up between 1989 and 1993, it is apparent that their needs for virtually all the basic infrastructure, except electricity, is high.

The data further revealed that females, more than males, need space in front of the house (50 per cent) and market stall (67.7 per cent) possibly because the females are much more involved in petty and small scale retail business than men. The latter are generally involved in contract business, modern crafts and services and artisanship. Also, the females' need for space in front is linked to their household responsibilities which require that they stay around the house. With respect to age group, respondents under 30 years have greater need for courtyards (66.7 per cent), health facilities (50 per cent) and telephones (50 per cent), transport (50.7 per cent), water supply (66.7 per cent) and kiosks (61.2 per cent). Those aged between 30–50 years of age only have a higher need for road and market stall for the pursuit of livelihood activities in urban areas. The need of those above fifty years for the infrastructure is generally lower.

Considering the year economic activities were started by the respondents, those that started in or before 1985 only have easy access to one basic infrastructure (health). And those that set up between 1991 and 1996 have greater access to a lot more facilities (roads, health, foreground, transport, water supply, electricity, etc.) and shared equal levels of accessibility to market stalls with those that started their economic activities between 1985 and 1988. Those that set up the economic activities between 1991-1995 did so in the middle of the economic crises and amidst high competition among small business operators. Thus, to cope, they had to locate or source all basic infrastructure needed for the effective operation of their activities. This was observed in setting up hair-dressing salons as niche businesses with an attractive environment to attract a greater number of customers.

On gender basis, females have greater access to what they desire most for economic activities, front house space and market stalls. Males have greater access to all other facilities listed. Even when it appeared that both sexes have about the same mean income, the females in petty retail and small scale business activities have less ability to pay the cost of gaining access to this other infrastructure than the males.

## Respondents' Assessment of Urban Infrastructure

It was observed that there are overlaps between the infrastructure needed and the infrastructure easily available to the respondents. For instance, for such facilities as open space, courtyards, telephones, water and kiosks, respondents under the age of 30 years had easier access to them than they needed for economic activities. Indeed, for females, there are more respondents accessing health facilities than they needed to function in their places of economic activities. Males generally have greater access to road, open space, courtyard, foreground, transport, water and kiosk than they would need to support their economic venture. Based on facilities at their disposal, the males have a higher possibility to easily diversify their economic activities using the infrastructure than females.

According to the respondents, some facilities have collapsed over the years. This is a major constraint for livelihood purposes. Most respondents indicated that some urban infrastructure has worsened in the past six years. This included housing, school and health facilities (Table 7.5). Second order deterioration is indicated for telephones, transport and refuse collection, and health and school facilities became more expensive for the average urban dweller. A particular school that was really short of teachers requested an additional 15 teaching staff. Days later, the head teacher received notices of dismissal for 22 teaching staff on the grounds of inability to sustain their monthly remuneration due to poor government finances.

The deterioration observed is not so much in the physical condition of the facilities as in escalation of tariffs and prices which virtually put these facilities beyond the reach of urban dwellers. This seems to be the case wherever adjustment policies have been adopted, as it has been graphically illustrated by Mensah (1984) with respect to price changes in the provision of facilities, particularly health, in Ghana.

While refuse was allowed to accumulate, the water and electricity supply became more erratic. The worsening infrastructure is blamed on the government policies (76.2 per cent) of spending, structural adjustment programme, maintenance and management attitude of agencies responsible. Some respondents (10.8 per cent) explained the deterioration of infrastructure to have resulted from general public misuse, the Nigerian attitude to the use and maintenance of facilities and non-payment of tariffs on public facilities, particularly water, electricity and telephones. Interviews with respondents revealed that people consume these utilities and collude with their managing officials through meter reading and tampering with records to avoid payments.

The deterioration of urban infrastructures notwithstanding, some of the infrastructure, particularly roads (72.48 per cent) is said to have improved due to the activities of such federal agencies as the PTF that was set up in 1994 to maintain and re-build urban and rural infrastructure. The PTF activities are more noticeable in the rehabilitation of urban infrastructure possibly to cushion urban political agitation and demands on the government. A majority (67.3 per cent) of the sample said that the government is responsible for the minimal improvements in urban infrastructures and were emphatic on the point that the PTF has done a good job in enhancing the condition of urban infrastructure, particularly roads and health institutions. Note that road re-surfacing has not translated into better or more equipment on the roads and reduced fares in Kaduna town.

According to the respondents, the state of urban infrastructure has differing impacts on economic activities. The improvement or worsening of some of the infrastructure may either enhance or hurt economic activities. When asked which facility enhances their livelihood pursuits, more than half of the women indicated that the state of the infrastructure is devastating to their economic activities (by increasing the costs of operation) while it generally enhances males' economic activities of about the same proportion. Discussions with some respondents revealed that even when the infrastructure is getting worse, the males are more able to cope (in terms of payment for the services and relating to officials of agencies, making illegal connections to service lines to sustain their supply) than the females.

## Housing Condition of Respondents

Housing is essential to economic productivity, well-being and general conditions of living. Housing is an embodiment of facilities which serve both economic and welfare purposes. The respondents are housed in buildings with an average of 3.7 sleeping rooms. In the sample, 43.2 per cent are living in their own houses, while 56.8 per cent are tenants. The mean rent paid by the sample is 1,849.82 Naira a month. Given the income of respondents, these rents represent significant proportions of urban dwellers' income. By implication, after rent payments, the disposable income of respondents will be far from meeting the basic needs of a majority of the sample.

The houses have varying types of facilities (Table 7.6) some of which also have various types of problems. Over half of the sample have all the facilities in the houses except for telephones, which only 28.8 per cent possess. In any case, facilities in the houses are hardly problem free.

According to the respondents, toilets are not maintained by landlords (39.8 per cent), and there are too many people to a toilet (50.9 per cent). Piped water is either too costly to connect, or taps are often dry (50.9 per cent)—little wonder that 64.4 per cent of the sample have wells in their houses. Waste collection is irregular (38.6 per cent) and yet charges by collectors are high (27.2 per cent). Electricity supply is both erratic (47.9 per cent) and expensive (52.1 per cent). And finally, a majority can not afford telephone lines (66.1 per cent) and others that have been able to install this facility complain of lack of dial tones and frequent breakdowns (26.8 per cent). It suffices to note here that urban households do not generally have basic housing facilities, utilities and services. Where they are available, a range of problems renders their usefulness to the people very minimal.

## Asset Holding of Respondents

The state of the welfare of the people was measured by levels of production and household assets holding and sales by respondents. To measure this, respondents were asked to indicate durable assets they have acquired since 1985. The data showed that acquisition of assets included household electronic consumer appliances (transistor radio, radio-cassette players and television sets), landed properties (farmland, house plots and houses), income generating equipment, (photocopying machines, welding machine, carpentry and painting equipment, auto-repair tools, etc.) and machines (grading, motorcycles, which can be used privately or as public transport, etc.). Ownership of assets such as cars, taxis, lorries, tractors, etc., all of which are capable of generating income, appears to be low among respondents in the sample. Despite this low ownership of production assets, some of the equipment is not in a working state.

Generally, less than 20 per cent of equipment and machines owned by respondents are faulty, due to the inability to procure spare parts needed for maintenance. Under inflation, the prices of spare parts have sky-rocketed. A majority of respondents tend to use assets for their own economic and social returns—even the motorcycle is used for public transport.

Across board, some respondents have sold some of their assets in the past 10 years. In fact, among those that own these assets, 11.8 per cent sold farmland, house plots (9.4 per cent), houses (8.8 per cent), equipment (12.3 per cent), grinding machines (14.1 per cent) motorcycles (11.1 per cent), motor cars (8.2 per cent), lorries (3.2) tractors (3.3 per cent), sewing machines (7.2 per cent), transistor radios (19.3 per cent), cassette players (15.2 per cent) and television sets (6.4 per cent). The disposal of these assets indicates an inability to maintain them. This trend can reduce respondents' production and income generating capacity and adversely affect their welfare. This is the more so as assets were being disposed due to lack of spare parts, high cost of maintenance or household demands for cash.

## Consumption Pattern of Respondents

With limited access to infrastructure within and outside houses, and the inability of respondents to keep production and household assets, what is happening to respondents' consumption of basic food items and social services? This question is pertinent to further understanding the state of urban inhabitants' welfare.

Respondents were asked to indicate whether their consumption of certain critical items has altered in the past ten years. From Table 7.7, it is apparent that consumption of various items has altered in some ways. Relatively few respondents have completely stopped consumption of the items indicated to them except for bread, eggs and tea, as well as utilisation of schooling facilities. Use of such social services as schools and health facilities is dependent on the stage of one's social development and dependents' levels of schooling and frequency of illness within households. Despite the noted variations in the consumption patterns of respondents, most drastic is the decrease in consumption of meat and fish and even cooking oil, which 7.9 per cent have stopped completely. These two items are the main sources of protein, and to stop their consumption can affect urban dwellers' health.

## Social Activities

Social activities are livelihood support systems through which individuals are able to organize and meet certain social obligations. About a third of the sample indicated no change in their participation in basic religious, rotating credit activities and assistance to relations. Nearly half of the sample indicated attendance of ceremonies (naming, marriage, burial, etc.) and professional guilds and unions. Further to this, it was observed that 40 per cent have reduced visits to home places and relatives, as transportation has increasingly become expensive and home people's demands tend to increase with frequency of visits (Table 7.8). Most striking is the increased intensity of participation in religious activities, which of course is expected among the generality of the people in periods of hardships. Religion provides spiritual and psychological comfort that is desirable in coping with stress.

## Summary and Conclusion

Urban development in Kaduna dates back to the colonial period. Since then, government and its agencies have been the main producers of urban infrastructure, except for housing that is predominantly supplied by individuals and the private sector. As at now, there is a multiplicity of agencies involved in the provision and management of infrastructure.

Beyond the myriad of agencies, participants in urban development include the government, private individuals as investors and international donor or funding agencies like the United Nations organs, and the World Bank. Datashow that urban development agencies are involved in garnering resources from private and public sectors nationally and internationally to implement urban programmes.

Furthermore, the analysis of the current state of infrastructure in Kaduna town revealed that available facilities, services and utilities are inadequate as indicated by the problems of each type of infrastructure. The study has noted the high prices of facilities, services, and utilities, and the under-capacity, weak performance and poor location which makes accessibility to them problematic. These, as the respondents claimed, inhibit economic activities. This is apart from problems generated by inaccessibility—illegal connections of service lines, obstruction of traffic flow and fraud—that further complicate access to and use of infrastructure.

As the poor are seeking illegitimate access through illegal connection of service lines of various services, utilities and facilities, the influential, powerful and rich evade payment of tariffs on services, utilities and facilities. This clearly illustrates a situation in which the people who need government and government services do not have political power. The ones who have political power do not need government services and do not want to pay for it (*Time* 1995: 31)

Access to and use of the basic services and infrastructure are not the same for all income, age, educational and gender groups. Some have greater needs for and access to the infrastructure than others and this has variously impacted on their living conditions. The study has demonstrated the deteriorating state of urban infrastructure which respondents link to government development policies. As infrastructure in the wider urban environment is collapsing, basic facilities within households are inadequate or delapidated.

On consumption and social activities, individuals, faced with economic crisis, household pressure and devalued income, are cutting consumption, selling off durable and production assets and shying away from extended family responsibilities. Though revenue collection is desirable, a situation where urban residents have to pay dearly for services, facilities and utilities is counter-productive and devastating to the welfare of citizens.

On the whole, the cost recovery principles of adjustment policies impaired urban dwellers' access to basic infrastructure even for economic activities. If this is allowed to continue in the years ahead, urban infrastructure will deteriorate further, and access will be hampered, spelling the collapse of the urban economy and heralding sub-standard living conditions for residents.

In the face of population and activity agglomeration in urban areas in developing nations, the cities are faced with problems of physical degeneration and insufficient quantity and quality of basic infrastructure. Policies on the development, management and provision of basic services, utilities and facilities are uncoordinated and therefore inimical to the needs and welfare of the generality of urban populace. The extent to which social services and physical structures can support sustained economic activity and improve welfare is undermined by pricing and general macro-economic policies. Yet, access to the limited available infrastructure is subject to diverse socio-economic and gender factors.

The problem of accessing available infrastructures is further compounded by the shrinking economic opportunities for urban inhabitants, through the moratorium on state employment, retrenchments and so on. In addition, hardship is accentuated by the decline in real income due to devaluation of the Naira and the high inflation rate. The opportunities for multiple modes of existence are slim due to the lack of production and investment resources. Indeed, the multiple modes of existence (Mustapha 1991) require the existence of multiple opportunities and strong currency to make incomes so generated worthwhile. These are the contradictions in the life of urban citizens. These contradictions tend to become graver as infrastructure degenerates and becomes inaccessible.

From all these, it is apparent that national policies on education, health and international declarations on environment and housing in the 1980s and 1990s notwithstanding, Nigeria is far from meeting the infrastructure needs of urban dwellers at present time. It is imperative to articulate a body of policy on the development, provision and management of urban infrastructure as public goods.

Since the government alone can not shoulder the responsibility of providing and managing urban infrastructure, partnerships between the government and urban community based organisations, non-governmental organisations and the private sector are desirable. To forge these relationships, the government is required to create an enabling environment and enhance the capabilities of these organisations as co-participants in urban development. Indeed, it is important to strengthen these structures as a basis for enhanced provision and management of the infrastructure and the promotion of access to it. To enhance such partnerships and private investor opportunities in urban development, it is necessary to break the monopoly of state corporations charged with the responsibility of developing and managing infrastructure, and to allow for private investor participation. Though this is in line with the principles of deregulation, it will remain necessary for the state to regulate management and pricing policies of infrastructure providers to guarantee access to the poor. This will maximise poverty reduction capabilities in urban development.

**Table 7.1: Schedule of Infrastructure Responsibility of Three Tiers of Government in Nigeria**

| |
|---|
| **Federal Government**<br>General transmission, distribution of electricity telecommunication, public housing commercial facilities, roads, education and health. |
| **State Government**<br>Distribution and transmission of electricity, water supply, sewage, drainage, solid waste collections, public housing, commercial facilities, land servicing, education and health. |
| **Local Government**<br>Distribution of electricity, sewage, drainage, solid waste collection, roads, land servicing, education and health. |

**Table 7.2: Occupation of Respondents**

| Occupation | Primary (N=129) | Secondary (N=105) |
|---|---|---|
| Industrial Workers/Civil Servants | 30.2 | 19.0 |
| Small business/petty trade | 13.2 | 25.7 |
| Farming | 2.3 | 8.6 |
| Handwork | 54.3 | 20.5 |

**Sources**: Author's field work, 1998.

**Table 7.3: Basic Infrastructure Easily Accessed and Needed for Economic Activities (N=132)**

| Infrastructure | % that need facilities for economic activities | % that have easy access to the infrastructure for economic activities |
|---|---|---|
| Road | 68.8 | 73.8 |
| Open spaces | 55.0 | 58.5 |
| Court Yard | 16.5 | 17.2 |
| Fore Ground | 49.5 | 47.8 |
| Health | 39.6 | 33.0 |
| Cheap Transport | 70.9 | 65.6 |
| Telephone | 30.9 | 28.0 |
| Water supply | 50.5 | 63.0 |
| Electricity | 69.2 | 67.0 |
| Kiosk | 26.5 | 21.1 |
| Market Stall | 32.3 | 38.9 |

**Sources**: Author's field work, 1998.

**Table 7.4: Infrastructure that has Improved or Worsened 1992–98**

| Facilities | % of respondent (improved) | % of respondents (worse) |
|---|---|---|
| Water | 48.8 | 40.5 |
| Electricity | 61.5 | 41.9 |
| Telephone | 28.2 | 67.6 |
| Refuse collection | 38.5 | 52.8 |
| Road | 72.4 | 44.3 |
| Transport | 33.2 | 59.5 |
| Health | 31.4 | 73.4 |
| School | 23.6 | 77.2 |
| House | 28.9 | 69.4 |
| Drainage | 46.7 | 39.5 |

**Source**: Author's Fieldwork, 1998.

**Table 7.5: Facilities in the House of Respondents (N=132)**

| Facilities | Available (%) | Not available (%) |
|---|---|---|
| Pit toilet | 59.8 | 40.2 |
| Well | 64.4 | 35.6 |
| Water closet | 51.3 | 48.5 |
| Piped water | 72.7 | 37.3 |
| Sewage/Drainage | 52.3 | 47.7 |
| Electricity | 87.9 | 12.1 |
| Telephone | 28.8 | 71.2 |
| Enough space | 72.0 | 28.0 |
| Waste collection | 70.5 | 29.5 |

**Source**: Author's Fieldwork, 1998

**Table 7.6: Levels of Consumption of Various Food, and Social Services by Respondents (1988–1998)**

| | Levels (%) | | | |
|---|---|---|---|---|
| Items | increased | decreased | stopped | no change |
| **Food** | | | | |
| Rice (128) | 43.8 | 34.4 | 4.7 | 7.2 |
| Bread and Tea (125) | 23.2 | 35.2 | 20.8 | 20.8 |
| Beans (129) | 42.6 | 25.6 | 6.2 | 25.6 |
| Yams (121) | 22.3 | 32.2 | 9.9 | 35.5 |
| Cooking oil (126) | 30.2 | 23.0 | 7.9 | 38.9 |
| Meat/Fish (120) | 22.5 | 50.0 | 2.5 | 25.0 |
| Household fuel (118) | 28.0 | 26.3 | 1.0 | 24.7 |
| Maize (126) | 46.0 | 25.4 | 4.0 | 24.6 |
| **Clothing** | | | | |
| Cloth (127) | 40.2 | 37.8 | 3.1 | 18.9 |
| **Social services** | | | | |
| Electricity (129) | 48.8 | 17.8 | 3.1 | 30.2 |
| Health (124) | 36.3 | 27.4 | 8.1 | 28.2 |
| School (115) | 34.8 | 18.3 | 20.0 | 27.0 |
| Transport (128) | 37.5 | 33.6 | 3.9 | 25.0 |

**Source**: Author's Fieldwork, 1998.

**Table 7.7: State of Social Activities of Respondents (1988–1998)**

| Social Activities | State | | | |
|---|---|---|---|---|
| | increased | decreased | stopped | no change |
| Visit to home place (125) | 36.0 | 39.2 | 10.4 | 14.4 |
| Visit to relations (127) | 31.5 | 40.2 | 4.7 | 23.6 |
| Attendance at ceremonies (129) | 29.5 | 16.3 | 8.5 | 45.7 |
| Attendance at the professional Unit (125) | 20.0 | 12.0 | 26.4 | 41.6 |
| Attendance at Ethnic Unit (125) | 24.0 | 12.0 | 28.0 | 36.0 |
| Attendance at the religious functions (128) | 58.6 | 4.7 | 3.1 | 33.6 |
| Participation in credit Unions (121) | 19.8 | 12.4 | 33.9 | 33.9 |
| Assistance to relations (124) | 37.1 | 26.6 | 0.8 | 35.5 |

**Source:** Author's Fieldwork, 1998.

## Note

* Department of Urban and Regional Planning, Ahmadu Bello University, Samaru-Zaria.

## References

Adedeji, A. & Rowland, L., eds., 1973, Management Problems of Rapid Urbanisation in Nigeria, Ile-Ife: University of Ife Press.

Agabi J.A. Abang, S.O. and Animashaun, 1989, Module Two: Nigerian Environment, Macmillan Nigerian Publishers House.

Aina T., 1996, 'Globalization and Social Policy in Africa', CODESRIA Bulletin, Number xx.

Ayeni, M.A.O., 1978, 'Pattern, Processes of Urban Development', in J.S. Oguntoyinbo, O.O. Adeola and M. Filani, eds., Geography of Nigerian Development, Heinemann Educational Books Ltd.

Baulch, B. 1996, 'The New Poverty Agenda: A Disputed Consensus', IDS Bulletin, Vol. 27, No. 1.

Becker, C.M. deBodisco, C. N and Morriso A.R., 1995, 'Urban Africa in Macroeconomic and Microeconomic Perspective: Issues and Options', World Bank Discussion Paper, Report No UDD - 97.

Bryant K.J., Kaduna, Nigeria, Gaskiya Corporation undated.

Central Bank of Nigeria, 1986, Annual Reports And Statement of Accounts.

Central Bank of Nigeria, 1987, Annual Reports And Statement of Accounts.

Deacon, B., Halse M. and Stubbs P., 1997, Global Social Policy: International Organisations and the Future of The Welfare States, Sage Publishers.

Diamond D.R., 1991, 'Managing Urban Change', in Bemelt, R. and Estall. R., ed., Global Challenge: Geography for the 1990s, London: Routledge.

Dreier, P., 1995, 'Putting Cities on National Agenda', *Urban Affairs*, Vol. 30. No. 5.

El-Shakhs, S. and Obudho R., ed., 1974, Urbanisation, National Development and Regional Planning in Africa, New York: Praeger Publishers.

Federal Republic of Nigeria, 1997, National Urban Development Policy, Federal Ministry of Works and housing, Abuja, October.

Gandonu, A., 1983, 'Planning Implication of the Metropolis in Nigeria', National Conference on Development and Environment, Ibadan: Nigerian Institute for Social and Economic Research.

Gans, H.J., 1968, Peoples and Plans: Essays in Urban Problems and Solutions, Basic Books Inc.

Goldsmith, Michael, 1980, Politics, Planning and the City, London: Hutchinson.

Griffin, K and Khan, A.R., 1992, 'Globalization and The Developing World', United Nation Research Institute for Social Development Report 92.3.

Hamer, Andrew Marshall, 1986, 'Urban Sub-Saharan Africa in Macroeconomics Perspective: Selected Issues and Options', World Bank, discussion paper, Report No. UDD - 96.

Harvey, D., 1973, Social Justice and the City, Edward Arnold.

Heilbrun, James, 1974, Urban Economics and Public Policy, New York: St. Martins Press.

Ihimodu, I.I., 1991, 'A Review of the Nigerian Macro Economic Environment and the Planning Experience', National Centre for Economic Management and Administration, Ibadan Seminar on Sectoral Management.

Imbroscio, D.L., 1995, 'An Alternative Approach to Urban Economic Development', *Urban Affairs*, Vol. 30, No. 6.

Jibrin, I., 1994, Population Dynamics in Contemporary Nigeria: Economy, Society and Politics, OCDE/OECD, September.

Kabeer, N., 1996, 'Agency, Well-being and Inequality: Reflections on The Gender Dimensions of Poverty', *IDS Bulletin*, Vol. 27, No.1.

Kaduna State Government, 1985–91, Achievement of Military Administration in Kaduna State.

Kaduna State of Nigeria, undated, Activities of Kaduna State Housing Authority.

Kaduna State of Nigeria, 1972–73, Kaduna Capital Development Board Annual Report.

Kaduna State of Nigeria, 1982, Kaduna State in Perspective.

Kaduna State of Nigeria, 1982, Kaduna State Water Board in the New Social Order, September.

Kaduna State of Nigeria, *The Tasks Accomplished in Kaduna and the Tasks Ahead.*

Kaltho, J.B., 1982, 'Planning for the Urban Poor', Association of Town Planning Students of Nigeria, Zaria: Ahmadu Bello University.

Kulshrestha, S.K., 1984, 'Trends in Development of Kaduna Metropolis: A Case for Review of the Existing Master Plan', Workshop on Problems of Physical Planning and Plan Implementation in Kaduna State, Kaduna State chapter of Nigerian Institute Town Planners.

Mabogunje, A.L., 1968, *Urbanisation in Nigeria*, African Publishing Corporation.

McNamara, S. Robert, 1985, The Challenges for Sub-Saharan Africa, Sir John Crawford Memorial Lecture, Washington D.C., November 1.

Meagher, K and Yunusa, M.B., 1991, 'Limits to Labour Absorption: Conceptual and Historical Background to Adjustment in Nigeria's Urban Informal Sector', United Nation Research Institute for Social Development, DP. 28.

Mensah, S.N.A., 1989, 'The Impact and Prospects of SAP in Ghana', conference on SAP and the Future of Nigeria, Zaria: Centre for Social and Economic Research, Ahmadu Bello University.

Mollenkopf, J., 1995, 'What Future for Urban Federal Policy?' *Urban Affairs*, Vol. 20, No. 5.

Mosha, A.C., 1989, 'Planning and Development of Human Settlement in Tanzania', Review of Rural and Urban Planning in Southern and Eastern Africa.

Mustapha, A.R., 1991, *Structural Adjustment and Multiple Modes of Social Livelihood in Nigeria*, United Nation Research Institute for Social Development, DP26.

Nwaka, G.I., 1989, 'Doubts and Direction in Nigerian Urban Policy', *Public Administration and Development*, Vol. 9.

Ogwude, I.C., 1989, 'Transport Sector Under Structural Adjustment Programme', National Workshop on SAP and the future of Nigeria, Zaria: Centre for Social and Economic Research, Ahmadu Bello University.

Ojowu, Ode, 1991, Planning in the Nigerian Macroeconomic Environment, National Centre for Economic Management and Administration, Ibadan.

Okpalaeke, D. and Ijediogor, 1998, 'Fuel Crisis: Appropriate Pricing, Disproportionate Agony', *The Guardian on Saturday*, Dec. 26.

Onibokun, A.G., 1989, 'Urban Growth and Management in Nigeria', in Stren, R.E and White R.R., eds., *African Cities in Crisis: Managing Rapid Urban Growth*, Boulder: Westview Press.

Ould-Mey, M., 1994, 'Global Adjustment Implications for Peripheral States', Third *World Quarterly*, Vol. 15, No. 2.

Palen, John, J., 1981, *The Urban World*, McGraw-Hill Book Company.

Schlyter, A., 1996, 'The City Summit, Habitat', *NEWS From Nordiska Afrikainstitutet*, No. 3, October..

Seymour, Tony, 1980, 'Housing Policy and Income Distribution in Kaduna', Centre for Social and Economic Research, Ahmadu Bello University, Zaria, reprint paper No. 4.

Sirken, A. Irving, 1979, *The Pricing of Public Urban Services*, Washington: World Bank.

Smelser, N.J., 1994, *Sociology*, Blackwell Publishers.

*Time International Magazine* July 3, 1995.

Usman, Y.B., 1986, *Nigeria Against the IMF: The Home Market Strategy*, Vanguard printers and publishers, Kaduna.

Witzling, L.P., 'Urban Planning', *The Encyclopaedia Americana*, Vol. 27, pp. 807–811.

World Bank with Nigerian Collaboration, 1995, *Restoring Urban Nigeria.*

World Bank, 1996, *Nigeria: Poverty in the Midst of Plenty. The Challenge of Growth with Inclusion*, A World Bank Poverty Assessment, Reprint No. 14733. May 31.

World Bank, 1987, The Urban Edge, January.

World Bank, 1991, *The Urban Edge*, Vol. 15, No. 2 March.

Yashim, D.Y., 1984, 'Organisational Framework for Effective Urban Development', in Kaduna State Paper to a Workshop on Problems of Physical Planning and Plan Implementation in Kaduna State.

Yeung, Y., 1995, 'Globalization and World Cities in Developing Countries', in R. Stren, and J.K Bell, eds., *Urban Research in Developing World Vol. 4: Perspectives on the City*, University of Toronto Press.

Zeleza, T., 1989, 'The Global Dimensions of Africa's Crisis, Debts, Structural Adjustment and the Workers', *TransAfrican Journal of History*, Vol. 18.

# Part III

# Globalization, Women's Work and Citizenship

# 8

# Globalization, Women's Work Intensity and Household Well-Being in Nigeria

**Chukwuemeka U. Okoye & Uzoma O. Okoye***

## Introduction

In recent years 'globalization' has become a catchword among economists, sociologists and political scientists trying to explain the dramatic retreat of autonomous space all over the world. Defined as a coalescence of varied transnational processes and domestic structures, allowing the economy, politics, culture and ideology of one country to penetrate another (Mittleman 1994), globalization portends as yet largely uncharted trajectories for nation states and civil society. Globalization received a massive boost in the 1980s. During those years, the transformations that have accompanied globalization, arguably to some extent intentional, have exhibited six consistent trends that continue to have a tremendous impact on global, national, and local social and institutional structures. These are the spread of liberal democracy, the dominance of market forces, the integration of the global economy, the transformation of production systems and labour markets, the high speed of technological change, and the media revolution.

While the globalization debate centres more on the implications of the contraction of the state for macroeconomics, for the development of a new world system as well as for control of the unfettered civil society, the whole vital question of the impact of globalization on grassroots labour processes, and the well-being of poor households, remains largely unbroached. A strand of the debate on globalization holds that it promotes inequality between and within countries (Griffin and Khan 1992; Williamson 1997), and that this rising inequality is often expressed in declining wages, employment instability, etc., for certain parts of the world.

Analyses of the consequences of adjustment-led economic globalization have strongly linked it with real income and job losses. In terms of gender dimensions, it has been observed that women are over-represented in the low end of the subsistence informal economic activities that have mushroomed under liberalisation. During the import substitution industrialisation era (up to the late 1970s), local production and labour regimes and structures were incorporated into world-wide (and globalized) supply, demand and price fluctuations. The rapid growth of the Nigerian informal sector during this period, from 50 per cent to 65 per cent of the urban workforce between the late 1970s and the late 1980s (ILO 1988) may not have been a coincidence. The vulnerability of the sector to international market conditions has persisted under economic adjustment despite its continued expansion, diversification and the energetic character of the economic agents that operate it. Gender concerns have grown concurrently with the ascendancy of economic globalization. But the gender dimensions of the impacts of globalization have not received adequate analytical treatment. High work intensity or the simultaneous performance of two or more tasks induced by economic, social, and cultural globalization are important dimensions of women's working lives (Elson 1993; Moser 1991; Beneria and Feldman 1992) but it is not so obvious how this is promoted by the forces of economic globalization. Yet given the pivotal role of women in the household, the implications of work intensification for household well-being, particularly among the poor, and the health of the whole economy are likely to be significant.

This paper discusses the key issue of how globalization-induced work intensification has impacted on the labour force participation and the well-being of Nigerian women and their households. The broad focus is on how the desire to satisfy household resource needs under conditions of rapid globalization determines women's time allocation strategies, and ultimately affects the welfare of their households. The specific questions that we attempt answering here include: what are the causes, incidence and extent of work intensity among the women? Why are women engaged in overlapping activities? What is the role of state institutions in mediating between globalizing forces and the women at local levels? How can we use the knowledge gained from answers to the above questions in broader social policy making? There is a need to accumulate knowledge about the influence of globalization on local populations so as to help develop efficient social policies to target social expenditure to the poorest and most vulnerable. The empirical basis of the following discussions comes from a survey carried out in Opkoko, a low-income squatter area of Onitsha, Anambra State in the South East of Nigeria. The sample of 200 women/households was selected by means of random route sampling technique.

The paper is divided into four parts. Part one is the introduction. Part two presents a review of the concept and phenomenon of globalization, and its linkages to labour force issues. It also focuses on the specific causes, incidence, extent, and socio-economic patterns of globalization-induced work intensification among women in Nigeria. Part three is an attempt to analyse the effects of the lengthening of work day and work intensification on the well-being of poor women and their households. Finally, in part four we conclude with suggestions regarding policy measures for the more productive use of women's time for enhanced household well-being under globalization.

## Socio-economic Context

### *Socio-economic and Labour Force Participation Profile*

The respondents in this study were selected by means of random route sampling through the streets of Okpoko, a low-income squatter area of Onitsha in Anambra State, Eastern Nigeria. The choice of this area of the city effectively restricted the survey to the low-income population segment of the area. The socio-economic and labour force characteristics of the respondents are displayed in Tables 8.1 and 8.2. A key point of interest in this profile is the relative youth of the sample, with a mean age of 41 years. The mean household size of 5.9 is higher than the national average for urban households in 1992 (5.7). On the average, the women completed a total of 6.9 years of formal schooling, indicating a relatively low literacy level.

**Table 8.1: Socio-economic Profile of Respondents**

| Attribute | Range Mean | 1992 | Value |
|---|---|---|---|
| Age | 24-62 yrs | 41-0 | - |
| Number of household heads (29 %) | | | 13 % (**) |
| Number of non-household heads (71 %) | | | 87 % (**) |
| Household size | 1-13yrs | 6-1 | 5-7 (***) |
| Years of residence | 1-33yrs | 10-8 | - |
| Years of formal schooling | 0-20yrs | 7-4 | - |
| Annual income (N) (*) | 12,000-90,000 | 5,865-0 | - |
| Monthly household expenditure | 833-6,000 | 2,677-0 | - |
| Per capita monthly household expenditure (N) | 94-1,950 | 506-8 | 802 |

**Source**: Field Survey, 1999.

(*) Nigerian Naira 98=US $1
(**) Nigeria-wide data (FOS, 1992)
(***) Awotona 1993.

### *Major Occupations*

Most of the women (82 per cent) are own account workers, while the rest (18 per cent) worked either in government or the private sector. Among the wage earners, the following categories were observed: casual labourers who worked for different employers on a daily contract basis, wage labourers in small (mainly distributive) trading enterprises, self-employed producers of goods and services, peri-urban farmers, etc. The petty trader category constitutes by far the largest occupational group covered in this study (62 per cent) and includes market women, stall holders and shop keepers who tend to have a spot where they sell consumer items mainly of everyday use, such as sweets, razor blades, toilet paper, cigarettes, matches, bread, stimulants like kola nuts, local gin, analgesic drugs, antibiotics, herbal preparations, etc. Most often the only assets of the women were a small table, a stool, a small wooden bench and sunshade material (waterproof, cloth or other discarded material from factories).

The occupational distribution of the respondents is shown in Table 8.2. Analysis of occupational distribution here is very important because it is the women's functioning in the context of these occupations that reflects the extent of their work intensification. The size of the petty trader category reflects the relative ease of entry by women into the sub-sector. The food vendor roves the street carrying various food items which she has either prepared at home or has purchased from small fast food operators. Both the street vendors and fast food operators depend on wholesalers with whom they maintain tight credit relationships. There were also sales clerks in a number of private, often informal business enterprises. Operators of roadside food kiosks, including confectioners of local delicacies such as fried bean paste ('akara' in Igbo), roasted plantain, and roasted corn constitute the catering category.

The civil servant category in the sample was made up of primary school teachers, messengers and cleaners in government ministries and departments. The civil service has become an unenviable place to work these days because of the very low salaries. Things have improved since September 1998, when an enhanced minimum wage was approved for the country. Women who remain employed in the civil service often supplement their earning by engaging in other activities. In the artisanal category are hairdressers, knitters (tailors) and seamstresses. The casual labour category involving work at construction sites is often seen as a temporary resort by women who are trying to survive shocks such as losing their husbands, having had their husbands retrenched or having lost their jobs themselves. Other casual workers are found in the markets doing odd porterage work.

**Table 8.2: Occupational Distribution of Respondents**

| Occupation | Main Occupation (% of sample) | Own account workers (% of sample) | Employees (% of sample) |
|---|---|---|---|
| Petty trading | 59-0 | 54-0 | 5-0 |
| Street vending | 3-0 | 3-0 | 2-0 |
| Civil servant | 2-0 | | 2-0 |
| Clerical | 6-0 | | 6-0 |
| Catering | 13-0 | 10-0 | 3-0 |
| Artisanal services | 11-0 | 9-0 | 2-0 |
| Urban farming | 3-0 | | 3-0 |
| Casual labour | 3-0 | | 3-0 |
| Total | 100-0 | 82-0 | 18-0 |

**Source**: Field Survey 1998.

## Linking Globalization with the Local Labour Force Process

Most of the women in the sample were involved in more than one income-earning occupational activity. The major and minor occupations of the women are often unrelated.

What then are the causes, the mechanisms, and the possibilities of globalization for transformation of the work habits of ordinary people? Where can one focus the analysis in order to capture this change? To Mittleman (1994) an appropriate avenue of inquiry in the study of globalization is the nature of the labour process and its products on a global scale. This, he emphasises, is because conflicts between capital and labour (the classical antagonists in capitalism) and commerce and consumer tastes, all reflect what is produced and how it is produced. Micro-scale analysis that seeks to find out how whole societies and their constituent groups try to influence and/or adjust to changes in the organisation of production equally fills very important knowledge gaps in the study of globalization. By relativising human conditions, globalization creates conditions of economic, social and cultural dependence and hence inequality between nation states, and, particularly important in this study, within nations. The local labour process probably generates most easily the empirical facts that support the inequality thesis because the ability to cope with vulnerability may depend, among other things, on social/work status. Here, it also is appropriate to comment on the intentionality or otherwise of globalizing forces. Many of these forces are impersonal and beyond the control of any individual, but many others, as well are intentional and reflexive (e.g. global marketing planning by multinationals or the actions of the environmental and feminist movements). Withdrawal of uncompetitive products by multinationals usually opens up some niche for low-cost, local resource-using indigenous informal operators. On the other hand, where macro-economic difficulties hold down industrial capacity, liberalized importation of cheaper alternatives alters the labour force profile in favour of commodity merchandizing operations, retailing and the services.

There are several avenues through which globalizing forces have reportedly permeated local labour conditions in Nigeria and influenced the outcomes. The relevant global forces include exchange rate reviews (specifically currency devaluation) which increased the cost of imports, trade liberalization which encouraged flooding of the markets with finished foreign goods and job rationalizations in the public and private sectors which released job-seeking entrepreneurial individuals into the market. These factors have in turn sped up the process of informalization by deepening the informal sector—in making it more competitive through the infusion of relatively well educated and technically competent persons from the formal sector, particularly for low-level self-employed operators whose labour is always supplied jointly with entrepreneurship. It has also made the sector relatively more profitable given the increased relevance and acceptability of low-level technical and service-oriented activities.

Another remarkable response of the informal sector to globalization is in terms of the level and profile of technologies employed and other inputs that are brought into the production process by small operators. These technologies, by being relatively cheap, divisible and largely locally developed, have promoted independence among women entrepreneurs and enhanced their ability and ease to enter the market, especially in the area of food processing. This conforms with the conceptual distinction of the informal sector on the basis of free entry and mode of production. Furthermore, the informal sector exhibits wage flexibility, and because of the globalization-induced formal sector employment freeze and the ensuing surplus labour availability, the supply price of labour in the informal sector has almost always been below the prevailing wage, thus encouraging small operators to employ others with whom they can negotiate the pay. In addition, the response of the informal sector to economic downswings following adjustment seems to have been expansionary both in terms of the diversity of activities and the prevailing hours of work. In either case, the net effect has been the increased labour force participation of women which has grown pari pasu with informalization. Other effects include the convergence of work roles between men and women and the blurring of the divide between domestic and market production despite the dramatic increase in the latter.

Informalization has also been instrumental in smoothing the transition from import substitution industrialization to an adjustment dictated liberal regime. According to Oman (1994), what emerged over time with import substitution industrialization was a modern sector capable of absorbing only a small fraction of the domestic labour force combined with excess industrial capacity, and high inflation. Today all these characteristics are still evident and even further heightened by Nigeria's structural adjustment programme (SAP), except that the increase in informal sector employment has acted as a safety valve to some extent. At the same time, according to the theory (Mazumdar 1989: 70), incomes ought to have fallen by a greater proportion in the informal than in the formal sector (in response to economic globalization), but this has not been so because of the rigidity of wages in the formal sector. Furthermore, economic recession, exchange rate and trade liberalization policies rendered import-substitution industrialization inefficient and unprofitable thereby creating a products and services supply gap which low-skilled informal sector enterprises are filling with cheaper alternatives.

The policy bias against peasant agriculture contributed to the growth of the informal sector, especially in the urban areas. With privatization and restructuring came several important changes in the nature of work for women in particular. These included the loss of well-protected jobs in both the civil service and private sectors and the expansion of female employment in low-paid, insecure and unskilled jobs, increasing entry of women into the labour market often as the main wage-earner of the family. Meagher and Yunusa (1996) assessed labour force participation characteristics under SAP and found that there was an overwhelming concentration of female participation at the low end of the informal sector in Zaria, Nigeria and that 96 per cent of female entrepreneurs were involved in low-income activities.

## Time Use and Work Intensification

### *Time Use Categories*

An understanding of the criteria for delineating women's time use may be helpful in appreciating the dynamics of work intensification. As such, before exploring forms of work intensification, we shall first of all, for analytical purposes, define the time use categories within which, theoretically, we are able to capture all the activities that women engage in at Onitsha. By looking at all tasks, whether performed at home (the so-called reproductive tasks) or in the market place, as 'productive', we brush aside connotations or judgmental considerations regarding which of the two categories is more important. The four time use categories are: time in household (home) production activity, time in market production activity and time in household as market production activity, and time in leisure activity.

Time in household production activity includes periods spent in the core reproductive tasks of women such as child bearing and care, home management and food preparation. Time in market production covers periods which women spend on income-yielding endeavours whether based at home or outside of it, but excludes cases where market-related work is taken home and executed there. Time in leisure activity includes time spent in activities like conversations/ chatting, attendance at social functions, social networking and community organizing including attendance at religious fellowships, which is very common among Christian women in Nigeria. To the women, there is nothing like a special time meant for leisure per se, such as going on holidays or taking days off. Leisure time is often intertwined with, and interposed between, either home or market production activity or both. This is the case, for instance with the time market women spent taking naps within the confines of their stalls or trading spaces.

### *Forms of Work Intensification*

The manner in which an individual allocates time reflects the level of work intensification experienced by that person. The intensification of time use occurs in three key ways. These are the increase in time spent working per day (i.e., the lengthening of workday), the intensification of activity combinations (i.e., overlapping of activities such that two or more of them are executed simultaneously) over time and intensification of enterprise combinations over time and space. The activities that were considered in the analysis of activity combinations were taken from five activity clusters, namely, child and personal care, food preparation, market production, leisure and social networking. We can assume here that if work day lengthens, and the number of activities and enterprises combined per unit of time increases, there ought to be labour intensification as an inevitable accompaniment, and this would have direct biophysical as well as indirect socio-economic implications for the woman and her household.

### Lengthening of Work Day

The workday of a respondent is deemed to have lengthened if the time spent by the subject working per day increases. The average workday of the women at Onitsha was estimated to have risen by up to 23 per cent since 1988 (Table 8.3).

### Overlapping of Activities

The number of hourly overlapping activities as used in this study is defined as the number of times the respondents reported having to carry out one or more activities from the five activity cluster groups defined earlier, simultaneously in one day to the extent that they had to switch attention between those activities as they were being executed. However the activities we considered for classification as overlapping are those in which the period of overlapping lasted for at least as long as ten minutes, and there was noticeable switching time between them (which could have occurred several times within the period considered). In the domestic sphere, the most frequent overlapping took place between child/personal care, food preparation, food processing and social networking. In the market sphere we saw overlapping occurring mostly between food processing/preparation for both domestic use and for sale, childcare, market work and leisure. Overall, it was estimated that in 1988 the number of hourly activity combinations was 1.6, and that in 1998 it was 2.7, a rise of more than 167 per cent.

For the overlapping activities, a key concern is the switching time between them, which can have negative impacts on the woman's overall effectiveness. Switching time for our respondents ranged between a few seconds to as much as 15 minutes. Women whose enterprises were in different locations or located far away from their houses obviously reported higher switching times.

Among women in catering and artisanal production activities where resources, as intermediate products, have to be mobilised across the boundary between the home and market domains, there was a high level of overlapping. Shopkeepers among the women who have their shops attached to their homes spent almost all the workday, and in fact all their time there, in home and market production-related activities combined.

## Multiple Modes (Enterprise Combinations)

The multiple mode strategy operates within the home domain and in the market domain differently. In the home domain, overlapping of household functions, or home production activities such as sweeping, cooking, scouring the dishes and processing food, prevails and was found to be dependent on, among other factors, the family size and level of use of househelps and household appliances. Here we concentrate only on multiple modes in the market domain, that is, on income-earning enterprise combinations. But it is necessary to add that market enterprises have a way of increasing the range of home production activities because of the interlinkages between the two domains as a result of resource exchanges between them. For instance, this has become particularly noticeable as a result of adjustment-inspired exploration of new, cheaper food sources by women both as a coping strategy and as an income-earning enterprise. This includes, for example, the processing of soya beans, which, until relatively recently, was hardly a Southern Nigerian staple, but which has gained importance as a cheap protein supplement in the face of the high cost of meat and milk products. In the market production environment, market functions such as selling, scouring wares, etc., also overlap apart from the increase in the number of enterprises which women engage in. Not to be neglected is the fact that, as hinted about soya milk making, market production activities are often taken home and executed together with home production activities, just as home production activities also come into the market domain and overlap with market production activities.

## Summary of Key Indicators of Work Intensification

Table 8.3 shows averages of key parameters of work intensification for 200 women for 1988 and 1998. Figures for 1988 were approximated from recall data. The year 1988 represents a low-intensity globalization period when, even though SAP had been implemented, its effects were not yet too significant. The three indicators have increased significantly.

**Table 8.3: Key Indices of Work Intensification**

| | 1988 | 1998 |
|---|---|---|
| Average length of work day (hrs) | 10 | 14-9 |
| Average number of hourly activity combinations (overlapping) | 1-6 | 2-7 |
| Average number of enterprise combinations | 0-9 | 3-0 |

**Source:** Field Survey 1998.

## From Globalization to Work Intensification: The Empirical Paths and the Evidence

Theoretically, economic globalization influences women by impacting on three fundamental and substantive arenas of social life (Waters 1995). The first is the economy, defined as social arrangements for the production, exchange, distribution and consumption of goods and tangible services. For instance, in Nigeria, since 1986, restructuring and liberalization, working through employment rationalization and exchange rate changes result in the net decrease in real incomes and other resources available to the family. Also, government tariff policies discourage production but encourage the services sector as well as merchandising/distributive trade.

The second is the polity, i.e., social arrangements for the concentration of power, especially in so far as they involve the organized exchange of coercion and surveillance (military, police, vigilantes, local government authorities), as well as such institutionalized transformations of these practices as authority and diplomacy. The ways in which Nigerian local government officials have used security, coercion, authority, force, surveillance, legitimizing and appeals for loyalty and obedience have been particularly felt by women. For instance, the galvanizing power of the First Lady at federal, state and local government levels in the framework of the Family Support Programme (FSP) and its key poverty alleviation project, the Family Economic Advancement Programme (FEAP) is enormous and has been deployed in attempts both to empower women and to manipulate them for political gains.

The third arena is culture, i.e., social arrangements for the production, exchange and expression of symbols that represent facts, effects, meanings, beliefs, preferences, tastes and values which liberate relationships from spatial referents. Ample evidence of this can be found in the symbolism of the Nigerian feminist movement and local women empowerment initiatives which, for instance, have encouraged women to challenge some socially-constructed norms long considered inimical to the well-being of women and their children particularly in the areas of sexuality/family planning, widowhood and women's ownership of landed property.

In the following section, we provide evidence on the causes of work intensification among women in Onitsha. We consider that this evidence can best be sorted into four broad categories, namely; factors related to greed and entrepreneurial drive (the two basic characters of capitalism), market-related alterations of incentive structures, public and private sector job losses and vulnerability.

The line between the first two sometimes seems vague. Vulnerability, as we shall discuss shortly, is however the most fundamental explanation underlying the other two less praiseworthy aspects. Each of the factors discussed below integrates elements of the economy, the polity and culture dimensions of social life referred to above. These three dimensions (i.e., the economy, the polity and culture) have structural linkages which give them mutual strengthening.

### Socio-political/Cultural Movements

While social networks were breaking up in Nigeria, the government was able to galvanise the redundant energies of women in programmes of economic empowerment such as the Better Life for Rural Women Programme (BLP) and the Family Support Programme (FSP), amongst others. Both the BLP and FSP also gained impetus from a desire by the Nigerian Federal government to shore up the economic status of Nigerian households which had suffered serious real income declines due to adjustment policies introduced in 1986. Although these programmes were primarily conceived and implemented as SAP relief initiatives, in practice they became tools of social and political control in the hands of the wives of military heads of state, state administrators and local government chairmen. But a crucial point to make here is that the global desire to give adjustment programmes a human face was supported by another contemporary tendency, in this case, the feminist movement and its associated gender ideologies. Various women empowerment programmes and campaigns have had their take-off from the prescriptions and advocacy of the global women's (feminist) movement. Of particular interest in this regard is the 1995 Beijing international conference to which a number of our respondents made very clear references in support of their newfound will to become more challenging of some of the household/community norms that are thought to discourage female entrepreneurship. Through oral communications, publications, performances, oratory, teaching, displays, public demonstrations, entertainments, propaganda, advertisement, data distribution, exhibition and spectacle, the BLP and FSP have been able to influence certain attitudes to enterprise development and business ownership that have increasingly restructured gender relations in Nigeria.

Financial support for BLP and FSP projects by bilateral and multilateral agencies such as ILO, UNDP, WHO, UNICEF, MacArthur Foundation, and UNFPA among others added some impetus to the adoption of some globalized ideological and administrative and implementational approaches to skills and entrepreneurship development among women in Nigeria. Skill development programmes that equip women for new roles, micro credit/cooperatives that give them business capital are all parts of why women's work has intensified. Micro-credit programmes that have eased the credit needs of women who want to start new ventures in Onitsha include those by the Catholic Women Organisation, United Bank for Africa Credit Scheme for Women, Peoples Bank of Nigeria, the community banks, etc. Local responses to economic globalization have included the variety of informal financial intermediation techniques (daily savings syndicates) developed among petty traders, which encouraged small savings for business development. Local government administrations in Nigeria have in no small measure aided this process by setting up bazaars called Better Life Markets (Fairs) where products of women's groups and skill development centres were exhibited and sold to the public. Interviews with our respondents revealed that those of them who did not belong to BLP groups were replicating some of the exhibits, which ranged from crafts to confectioneries on their own, and setting up small businesses. Eighty-seven per cent of the respondents have in one way or another either taken part, or are planning, to take part in the BLP or FSP activities.

### Greed and Entrepreneurial Drive

Entrepreneurship could be viewed as greed moderated by rule of law and conscience. Much of the observed multiple modes dynamic among poor women in response to the adversities of SAP is propelled by a desire on their part to be like their more successful neighbours, without the necessary training and innovating instincts. The mushrooming of fashionable women-focused enterprise and skill development programmes based on locally sourced materials, following the global resolve to give SAP a 'human face' has succeeded in unleashing a surge of entrepreneurship among women. Some of these women who graduated from one skill acquisition course or another, making soaps, candles, soya milk beverages and confectioneries have been quite successful. But at the same time, a lot more women who have sought to imitate these successful ones without first acquiring the necessary functional skills have suffered serious setbacks, failing in one enterprise and rising to try their hands in yet another in which, most often, as a result of the aforementioned lack of training and skills, they are again unsuccessful. And the cycle continues to exacerbate the intensification of their work life.

### Market Saturation and Product Crowding

The quantum growth of the informal sector in recent times, as noted earlier, is partly a spin-off of economic globalization. The free entry[1] character of the informal sector, while a blessing for the many women who could not get a job in the formal sector, may also be seen as the inadvertent promoter of multiple job holdings and work intensification among the women. This is because increased awareness due to greater information flows has bred a tendency for most women to adopt similar coping strategies. The regrettable thing however, is that many of those jobs are, on the balance, either barely productive, outrightly unproductive, or even possibly destructive, in the classic Baumaol (1996) sense. For instance, in the area of small scale food processing, those women producing locally made beverages such as soya milk are now so many that the market is almost saturated and there are almost more sellers than buyers in many neighbourhoods. Amid the resultant oversupply, limited absorption capacity of the local economy and loss of glamour in these fads it often suddenly dawns on these women that the trade into which every body is jumping is not so rosy after all. Soon, the more enterprising ones among the women have had to quickly either move away completely from particular trades or expand into other business interests in order to hedge against possible shocks, thereby exacerbating the multiple modes dynamic and heightening work intensification. Over 50 per cent of the women interviewed for this study have had this type of experience. There were some women who sincerely would have preferred to do less and let their husbands do the struggling, but had to start new businesses or expand existing ones 'in order to be like their friends and neighbours' and avoid being seen as liabilities.

The same thing can be said of those selling used clothing, imported jewellery or loin cloths in offices. Similarly, there is an amazing proliferation of small shops in neighbourhoods where there is hardly an adequate population concentration to support any reasonable level of sales and profitability. The result is that the women are constantly seeking additional avenues for generating extra income while most often still clinging to the less remunerative one(s) they have already ventured into.

### Divisibility and Availability of Consumer Products

The fizzling out of protection for erstwhile import substitution industries under trade liberalization has disrupted many entrenched consumer products oligopolies resulting in non-competitiveness, loss of market share, excess capacity, rampant scarcities, and thence to widespread importation and distribution of a large variety of divisible, relatively cheap but often sub-standard consumer goods mainly from South Asia. Traders with small means are able to engage in the retailing of these products on account of the product's divisibility, cheapness and availability. Multinational companies like Lever

Brothers PLC, Patterson Zochonis, etc., are facing very serious challenges from these imported products, not least because of the large army of willing (mainly women) retailers who are ever ready to open very small retail outlets. It is no surprise that petty traders made up 59 per cent of the sample for this study. But at the same time, the interest in local sourcing of raw materials, traditional medicines and maintenance culture which grew in the late 1980s and early 1990s stimulated the growth of numerous micro-enterprises dealing in unique, special niche agricultural processing, medicinal plant formulations and general services which have strong work-intensifying implications.

### Deregulation and Primary Commodity Price Instability

The deregulation of primary commodity marketing (represented mainly by the abolition of commodity boards), and trade liberalization in general has led to wide seasonal fluctuations in prices, thereby encouraging the growth and deepening of speculative activity in primary commodity trading. For instance, women were heavily involved in the speculative storage and sale of a wide variety of primary agricultural products including kola nuts, maize, beans, palm oil, irvingia spp. seeds, etc. The point of interest here is that while these products demand relatively little care during storage, they drain a lot of shared time when being retailed. One hundred per cent of the women who were found to engage in speculative trading do so on a part time basis. The intensification of activities in primary commodity trading is linked with the efforts of some multinationals and indigenous companies to use cheaper alternative raw materials as they became less competitive due to liberalization and deregulation. Thus the interest of women in the storage of castor oil seeds and maize for example arose reportedly from the strengthened internal demand for them by the food seasoning and poultry feed industries respectively.

### Low Bank Interest Rates and Disappointing Results of Financial Deregulation

Financial deregulation and the failure of the Washington Consensus have encouraged reversals aimed at addressing the problem of fragmentation of the financial market in Nigeria. As such, the growth of both formal and informal micro-financial intermediaries has increased women's access to credit for enterprise development. But two related factors which scuttled the hopes of realising financial integration led to greater work intensity among women. First, when the banking sector was deregulated in 1986, many dubious finance houses otherwise called wonder banks because of the incredibly high savings interest rates they paid (up to 60 per cent per month) collapsed. Second, by the time the Abacha government sanitized the Nigerian banking system, interest rates dipped to very low levels. Most of these aforementioned wonder banks eventually crashed in the mid-1990s, with many people losing their savings. This led to an unprecedented level of illiquidity preference, particularly among small savers, many of who were women, and forced them to invest in speculative activities such as storage, trading, etc., as mentioned earlier, rather than keeping their money in banks and finance houses. Women reported a boom in the buying and stocking of such products as kola nuts, palm oil, maize, irvingia spp, melon, garcinia kola'aku inu' in Igbo, etc. Consequently, those women engaging in these practices as secondary occupations have additional responsibilities.

### Changing Norms/Attitudes to Participation

It is generally believed that women in Nigeria are overworked, even in traditional societies, doing unrecognized household duties in combination with market production. The situation has probably even grown worse in Nigeria under globalization, in line with Roldan (1985) and Beneria's (1992) assertion that where resources are scarce, the resulting draconian allocation rules forced on households exert greater pressure on women to perform overlapping activities.

To many women, until recently, it was fashionable to either be a complete housewife, or at most, have only one income-earning enterprise. Complete 'housewifery', however, was never a normal traditional practice in the culture of most nationalities in Nigeria. It probably only crept in with the advent of Islamic conquests among Northern Nigerian Moslems, and reinforced with the practice of 'purdah'. Among the Southern nationalities such as the Igbo, Yoruba, Efik, etc, complete 'housewifery' was embraced by men in white collar colonial employment who wanted to demonstrate their elevated status, and convince their in-laws that their daughters knew no suffering. In the South, while education subsequently bred career women, the less educated were stuck with this practice until economic problems set in during the 1980s. Thus before this change, women working used to be seen as a reflection of poverty. Holding more than one occupation was perceived as even a stronger confirmation of poverty, although probably not in all cases. And husbands were keen to avoid the associated opprobrium. But today, these perceptions seem to have changed, thanks to some attitude changes induced by hardships accompanying economic globalization. Specifically, entrepreneurial and skill development programmes of the earlier-mentioned international feminist movements, by developing a combination of propaganda, demonstrations, spectacle, etc., seem to have succeeded in justifying and normalising the involvement of women in income generation activities. This is true to the extent that husbands now seem to object less to their wives working. Women have taken up some of the tasks that were traditionally outside their domain either as a result of the men providers being no longer capable of contributing adequately to household income because they have lost their jobs, or as a result of the fact that returns on their effort are too low (Lado 1992). In effect, the local norms pertaining to participation of household members in the labour market seem now to approximate a global pattern, as obtains in economies in which structural adjustment has been implemented. However, whereas the emerging trend portends greater economic freedom for women, it also leads to further intensification of women's labour.

### Privatization and Deregulation of Labour Markets

Bakker (1994) and Elson (1991) have demonstrated that deregulation widens the 'gender gap' and increases the exploitation of women's paid and unpaid labour. There is evidence that this has increased pressures on women to supplement family incomes with additional earnings, resulting in work intensification. Some of the women recognize the insecurities associated with deregulation, privatization and increased labour flexibility. For women employed in sole proprietorships, etc., there is often no question of their employer adopting any labour standards/rights or codes of conduct regarding working conditions. This may be a major cause of involuntary labour intensification because avenues for successful resistance are non-existent, prompting those who can to start an enterprise in which they would be under nobody's control. Labour laws are grossly inadequate, ignored or unenforced, and the women cannot form unions.

### Proliferation of Coping Strategies

In addition to economic restructuring and its consequent job losses, one of the most devastating blows to household well-being since SAP in Nigeria has been the removal of subsidies on basic social services (e.g., water, electricity, fuel, fertilizers, etc). Coupled with an inefficient and crumbling infrastructure, the impact has been devastating, calling on the most basic survival instincts of the people. Social change in response to prevailing economic conditions exhibits a specific evolutionary direction and possesses a logic or dynamic that drives it. The social change in question relates to alterations in life styles and labour force participation strategies engendered by economic restructuring. That logic is adaptation or striving to be compatible with the forces of global change (restructuring, liberalization, downsizing of labour, devaluation of currencies and loss of real income). The ways the poor use household resources and the ways they respond to adverse circumstances and opportunities constitute their coping strategies, and these strategies are known to be determined by the external economy of the household, intra-household relations and bargaining norms and lifestyle characteristics, as well as the household's embeddedness in a wider set of social relations. For the purposes of our work here, we would like to further define coping strategies as actions less in scope and depth than mainline occupations of people. They are repetitive actions carried out on daily basis. These strategies can be classified in three ways: strategies for creation of new resources, those for conserving and improving the use of existing resources and extended family and migration strategies. Another analytical perspective on the categorization of coping strategies is to divide them into two, namely, those embarked upon to reduce vulnerability by increasing one's access to access to protective social capital and entitlements, and those embarked upon to increase income and economic assets. But because of the general failure of most social infrastructure in Nigeria and the persistence of official corruption, women have almost no access to protective social capital. Ninety-three per cent of the respondents bought water for daily use. Of the 70 per cent that had access to electric power from the national grid, about one half complained of being blacked out most of the time. Access to state-supported healthcare is very low. If they attend government clinics, the women do not obtain any prescribed drugs there because the drugs are not available. In view of all these shortcomings, the livelihood strategies of the women are based on a constant search for means of accumulating cash with which to reduce their vulnerability. It would seem, from the responses to questions as to how to reduce their feelings of vulnerability (table 8.4), that in practical terms, the poor believe that increased accumulation of monetary income alone is capable of reducing the vulnerability.

**Vulnerability**

Feelings of vulnerability among women are one of the main reasons they engage in multiple occupations in order to lessen such feelings by hedging against risks and uncertainty. Economic, social, political and environmental risks and uncertainties (shocks, cycles) whether community-wide or idiosyncratic, are known factors that expose people to risks and uncertainties.

There are price and market risks for products from competitors. There is exchange rate devaluation and the trickle-down effects to those using imported capital equipment. Next to food shortages, perhaps the greatest daily fear among the women is inability to pay house rent. The landlords are merciless, being equally subject to high inflation as well and ever ready to posit that justification for the frequent upward revision of house rents. Fear of such contingencies can elicit varied reactions from different people.

Our interviews revealed some contradictions in the coping strategies of the respondents. Either in combination or singly, some coping strategies would always produce a net negative return to effort. Consider, for instance, the strategy of purchasing consumables in small quantities which does not confer any benefit from economies of scale. Closer examination of the strategies in table 8.4 reveals that most of them would have the unintended effect of directly or indirectly further marginalizing the women through either paying more per unit of item or through loss of efficiency or both. This is a kind of 'strategy peonage'. A few women were able to analyse the dilemma that buying cheaper food items sometimes means buying those that demand a longer cooking time and increased consumption of kerosene, their major cooking fuel. The emerging picture is that barring good luck or well-organized support efforts, most of these women and their families may survive increasing urban crisis but may not escape poverty, and the strategy peonage effect would translate into ever-increasing intensification of effort.

## Globalization, Work Intensity and Household Well-Being

### *Conception of Well-Being*

One of the issues that is potentially contentious is the definition of 'well-being', or conversely, situations, conditions and states of ill-being. This is a practical as well as empirical question, one that requires contextualized answers, not least because as it were, one man's meat could be another man's poison. The World Bank (1990) argued that well-being is a product of adequate consumption of goods and services, and of health, status, achievement, and security. Since most of these are theoretically attainable in the market, we can measure well-being using available income as a proxy, since income is supposed to give access to these commodities.

Standard economic notions of well-being usually focus on material goods and services with little or no attention given to the way people make use of their time. The more time one has, the more utility one can create for one's household if one possesses appropriate knowledge and energy, and is healthy enough to carry out many tasks at the same time and/or for long periods of time. The length and intensity of work time are important, but often ignored, dimensions of well-being (Floro 1995b). Engaging in overlapping activities generally results in a person working harder for a given unit of time through an intensification of labour, with no increase in productivity, only an increase in energy (mental and physical) expended by the worker. Baruch et al. (1987) have shown that an intensification of work time creates stress and leads to an eventual deterioration of health. Time use is therefore a determinant of the quality of life not just for the woman but for her household as well. Time and the ways in which it is used have opportunity costs. The choice of enterprise which structures the way time is used also has opportunity costs.

**Table 8.4: Coping Strategies/Mechanisms for Reducing Vulnerability (Sample Size= 200)**

| Coping Strategy | Percentage of Respondents |
|---|---|
| Purchasing shorter-cooking, fuel, conserving food items | 42 |
| Buying smaller quantities of consumable items from the neighbourhood | 83 |
| Making more frequent trips to the market to purchase consumables | 76 |
| Having fewer meals per day | 28 |
| Working for longer hours | 87 |
| Engaging in more than one occupation at a time | 59 |
| Combining paid employment with private business | 4 |
| Combining market and housework | 90 |
| Combining wage, market and housework | 6 |
| Reduced house work in order to earn more from market work | 54 |
| Taking credit to expand business | 63 |
| Organizing 'esusu' with friends | 13 |
| Withdrawal from group/association (i.e., reduced networking) | 33 |
| Rise in spirituality and membership of Christian fellowships | 88 |
| Renting shared accommodation for business premises | 23 |
| Cultivation of small gardens (market gardening) | 18 |
| Increased emphasis on assets maintenance | 95 |
| Sale of household assets | 33 |
| Shedding extended family responsibilities | 14 |
| Allowing husband to do 'women work' in the home | 45 |
| Doing men's work (i.e., increased bread-winning functions) | 61 |
| Trading within office premises | 3 |

**Source**: Field Survey 1998.

## Conceiving Work Intensification and its Key Well-being Implications

The woman were questioned with structured interview schedules about their perceptions around well-being in the context of a lengthening of the work day, changing activity combinations, and changing enterprise combinations. The women's perceptions of the opportunity costs of using time in a particular way or of choosing a particular enterprise have definite implications for their state of well-being. For instance, non-economic but essential tasks impose an overhead of appropriated time on women the reduction of which may have well-being/health opportunity cost (Palmer and Weeks-Vagliani 1987) for the woman, her children or for the general family welfare. Thus, the women's perception of the opportunity costs of lengthened workdays include deterioration of personal health, exposure of family to extraneous agents and risk of household instability, among others. More than 80 percent of them reported deterioration in personal health and a breakdown of norms (Table 8.5).

On the other hand, having to carry out a number of activities simultaneously involves the expense of switching time and its associated costs (in terms of energy, stress, etc.), and has caused a deterioration in health for 68 per cent of the women. Women whose enterprises (mainly food processing) have to be carried out in the home environment report noticeable pollution of their living space by both equipment and wastes, demanding more attention, which means more stress, to keep in order. This is particularly serious in view of the already very inadequate (mostly one to two room apartments) that these women occupy, and the absence of piped water or even any water at all, and any waste disposal arrangements. In many of these places, stagnant pools of sludge and waste, largely from the women's activities, surround the homes.

The third scenario is that in which a woman manages more than one enterprise. In that case apart from lengthened workdays, the woman does not spend vital hours in home management. There is the tendency for undesirable social influences when children accompany them in these spells. Some 35 per cent of the respondents expressed the fear that their children were being exposed to behaviours like smoking, pickpocketing, etc. Reducing time spent on household coping strategies may have an infant health opportunity cost or a general family welfare opportunity cost. So there is no easy or straightforward way to restructure time use in order to achieve a higher scale of well-being. An important point to note at this juncture is the contradiction between the objective of coping strategies and the eventual net outcomes of some of those strategies. In fact, in some cases, the nature of coping strategies deployed by the women had a net welfare-depleting effect over the medium term.

Recent evidence that women's welfare has deteriorated as a result of the economic recession in Nigeria includes a study by Guyer and Idowu (1991), which supports earlier assertions to that effect by Onimode (1989). Meagher and Yunusa (1996) found that in Nigeria, the burden of household pressures under adjustment is falling disproportionately on women at the same time as support networks institutionalised in the extended family are weakening.

We have seen how globalization has lengthened women's workday, increased the number of activities they execute simultaneously, and the number of income-yielding enterprises that they engage in. The effects of work intensification and the lengthening of work day were reported in five key domains, namely the woman's personal health, her children's health, her housekeeping, quality of her output, and her social life.

**Table 8.5: Work Intensifications and Key Well-being Implications (Sample Size: 200)**

| Aspects of Work Intensification/Frequency of Reported Well-Being Impacts | | | |
|---|---|---|---|
| Reported Well-Being Impacts | Lengthening of work day | Activity combinations | Enterprise combinations |
| Deterioration in personal health | 83 | 68 | 43 |
| Exposure of family to extraneous control | 51 | - | - |
| Risk of household instability | 78 | - | - |
| Exposure of children to street delinquency | 40 | - | - |
| Exposure of family to negative public menerisms | - | - | 35 |
| Break down of household norms | 87 | - | 41 |
| Loss of control in routine household management | - | 40 | - |
| Attention loss and poor quality output | - | 40 | - |
| Pollution of living space | - | 37 | - |

**Source**: Field Survey 1998.

## Break Down of Social/Support Networks

Kinship, neighbourhood and religious associations feature very prominently in the provision of informal safety nets for the poor in Nigeria. The component of total work time spent on social activities may lead to the enhancement of well-being through social capital formation. But except for Christian religious fellowships, evidence exists that women's interest in social networking has waned generally. The erosion of networking or community-level association as a result of women launching into multiple occupations or into working longer hours in order to survive the recession has the effect of reducing social capital and increasing the household's vulnerability. In the last 2 years, 65 per cent of the women interviewed for this study have abandoned at least one social network, while 89 per cent and 13 per cent enlisted in a Christian religious fellowship and other associations respectively. Inquiries show a rapid decline since the late 1980s, which they attribute to 'lack of time' and/or lack of resources to meet their membership obligations in such associations or the irrelevance of such associations in terms of assistance for livelihood sustenance, etc.

In turn, a reduced amount of time spent socialising means the maintenance of fewer friends and acquaintances, which circumscribes women's ability to build new social capital that is often crucial for overcoming vulnerability.

### *Changes in Households Norms*

Both neo-classical and Marxist economic conceptions of the household regard it as an undifferentiated unit allowing economic interests to operate on, but not within it (Folbre 1986). Accumulating evidence on the nature of households now shows the need to account for risk and transactions within households—the relative bargaining power of its members, etc. (Bruce 1989). This is a vital issue because we know that for a majority of married women, access to income, whether earned by themselves or their husbands, often reflects intra-household decisions which have been known to create gender asymmetries in bargaining power between household members. The question here is to what extent has globalization influenced, affected, restructured or transformed intra-household relations, and what are the implications for household well-being?

It was found out that the well-being implications of globalization in this context depended to a great extent on the extent to which the women's ability to reallocate their labour time between different tasks and task domains was affected, restructured or curtailed. Our findings confirm the position of earlier writers on the constraints that women face in their ability to reallocate their labour time in order to improve their earnings and well-being. To begin with, they are generally constrained, relative to men, in their attempts to respond to changing price signals (Gladwin 1991; Lele 1991; Common Wealth Secretariat 1989). This relative immobility stems from the peculiar nature of their obligations, rights and bargaining positions within the household (Collier 1988; Haddad, Hoddinot and Alderman 1994). For instance, our respondents had limited access to strategic information emanating from the media (radio, TV, and newspapers) simply because they had either been socialised not to read, listen to, or watch, or they were too busy to do so. Women's time use is further constrained by the fact that there is often an intertwining of social activities with work (Szebo and Cebatorv 1990), thereby leaving very little room for the lengthening of their work day purely for income generation, and as a survival strategy.

It is not only patriarchal structures that ensure that control and distribution of resources within the household are unequal among its members. We found out that there are also other less obvious norms of bargaining within the household. In particular, we note the influence of women's empathy towards their children; a kind of matriarchal submissiveness to the children's wishes which also diminishes the woman's personal resources and time. Good mothering in Igbo tradition often equates to the tendency to deny or overstretch oneself in order to satisfy the family. This is a kind of invisible norm which promotes complicity in self-subordination to the extent that, in the context of per capita distribution of resources in the household, the woman reallocates her share of personal resources among her children. Thus, as family real income declines, mothers may be internalising the costs of poverty and adjustment. And the effects of dwindling household incomes on the children's well-being may be underestimated, particularly if these and children's consumption levels do not decline significantly. This is an aspect of a wider system of socially constructed, gendered, self-negating thought patterns within which women generally unknowingly accept self-subjugating (restraining) realities, without feeling or complaining. In addition, in many cases, the level of household consumption and well-being appears to have been sustained, more or less, as a result of the women working longer hours and earning extra income. Of course, the long-term implications of these outcomes for the well-being of the children and the family can only be negative, as the hen that lays the egg gradually shrivels due to over-work and under-nutrition.

Another important aspect of household relations that may influence household well-being is the widely-held opinion among women that men are conceding some of the ground they had always held when it came to household decision making, and taking up some of the erstwhile 'women's work' in the home. This was so in the opinion of 72 per cent of the respondents. But a few others pointed out that their husbands only concede these rights because they recognize the strategic nature of the women's enterprise for household livelihood security. Thus they may take up some of the traditional functions of the woman in the home such as deciding what to eat, what groceries to buy, sweeping, scouring utensils, laundry work, cooking and looking after the children. Husbands who are temporarily out of work, or are much less busy than their wives are said now to accept, without feeling embarrassed, taking on more of the responsibility for directing home affairs, children, etc., particularly where access to househelps is limited. The usual assumption is that involving men jointly in home management would have a positive impact on family well-being through the balancing of burdens between husbands and wife. But some 'traditional' opinions regard it as irresponsible on women's part to 'abdicate' their responsibilities, and that it has a net negative effect on the man's well-being through loss of status and social esteem. The key question is whether this outcome is a transformatory 'gain' or a transitory one for women? It begs the question, how resilient can socially constructed household structures and bargaining norms be in the face of economic pressures? If the net result of these changes is positive, they probably would be adjudged one of the alleged, if dubious, well-being gains for women, of the current economic crisis, at least in the urban areas of Nigeria. But concerns ought still to be raised as to whether the 'unfettering of women', as it were, does not pose more medium-to long-term dangers for household well-being and stability.

### Inefficiency, Ineffectiveness, Poor Quality Output

The need to combine new tasks may result in the quality of output in each of the four activities becoming sub-optimal. A meal may be burnt or lower sales may result, or the child may be exposed to unsafe and unstimulating environments. So many micro-enterprises have floundered because the attention of their women owners was too divided between different activities. In many cases either the product is of poor quality or the owner's helpers cheat her or are not devoted or hardworking enough lacking proper supervision.

### Child Neglect

This is a very serious consequence of work intensification, one that could inflict irreversible damages on children. Various kinds of child neglect were reported. Sixty-three per cent of the respondents said that they had to stop breast feeding their babies earlier than they used to. Thirty-five per cent of them lamented their inability to detect disease or ill-health in their children, while another 43 per cent agonised over their inability to assist their children with homework.

Poorly supervised children have dropped out of school (20 per cent), or joined anti-social gangs (15 per cent). Poor supervision was also linked to a decline in nutritional status because the women's absence created problems with balancing the meals, with children going on quick fix poor nutritive snacks such as garri, in addition to the meal times being irregular.

### Passive Child Labour

The problem of children working with their mothers when they should be in school, at play, studying or asleep was a phenomenon that has always existed but has expanded tremendously along with informalization and increasing women's work force partic ipation. A slightly different issue is that of children just sitting around in their mother's business premises unattended and, not necessarily working, but battling with sleep while sticking out the long hours with their mother whose working day has become trebly extended. Then there are very young ones who cannot work. Such children often catch colds, are bitten by disease-bearing insects such as mosquitoes, or inhale a lot of smoke from either the wood fire or crude lanterns which the women use. Many of the confectioners interviewed who bake akara or fry dodo, fish and other fast foods by the road side, at night, reported this problem. The problems are compounded in the night bazaars that characterize slum areas in Nigerian cities which have become breeding grounds for sundry delinquent acts. Sending these children on errands to and from the house and the business premises exposes them to real dangers such as kidnapping, abduction and rape. Having very young kids around as the woman transacts her business reflects in many cases the lack of a secure home environment or reliable domestic help or grown-up children who could look after the younger ones. If globalization persists in creating conditions that increasingly intensify women's work for a long time, then the danger of intergenerational transfer of welfare loss liabilities becomes real.

## Sense of Place and Well-being

Central to many urban dwellers' feeling of well-being is the perceptual relativity of 'rural' and 'urban' in terms of social amenities and employment prospects. For a lot of people, a key reason for migrating to the urban areas has always been to be able to help their kith and kin left behind in the village. If you must leave the rural area and go to the city, you must defend that choice. Thus, in their view, if one's living conditions in the urban area are not superior to those of relatives who remain behind, one loses the respect that rural people usually accord urbanites. Urban dwellers who are sensitive to this kind of reasoning consider themselves victims of a special kind of vulnerability. This is particularly the case where failed hopes of prosperity make it difficult for the urbanite to send remittances of money and essential commodities to their rural relatives, and when children of the rural relatives cannot visit their city-dwelling relatives on holiday. Many women lament this kind of powerlessness, irrelevance, and vulnerability and see it as having increased with the coming of structural adjustment in Nigeria. The concern of the women is that their work regimes do not leave them enough time to visit the village as often as they used to. But more tellingly, in spite of their intensified efforts at income generation, they still find it difficult to save reasonable amounts for remittance to the village. This situation is one reality of urban poverty that haunts many people more than they are willing to reveal, and it tremendously influences the determination of individuals as they struggle to make ends meet.

## Policy Implications and Conclusion

Globalization is an important feature of contemporary social, economic, political, cultural and technological reality with yet uncharted consequences for the Third World. While the macroeconomic effects of globalization are easily appreciated, the micro-level impacts remain obscured. The complex redistribution of resources and power which the phenomenon kindles is noticeable within households, social networks and the informal sector. The challenge to African social policy makers is how to harness the dynamics of globalization to strengthen long-term productivity growth, create new employment and reduce wage disparities between the sexes on a sound, lasting basis. But the challenge is also how to protect the vulnerable from unproductive entrepreneurship expressed in increasing work intensification with adverse household effects.

Increasing work intensity could be viewed as a measure of livelihood insecurity and as an indicator of the extent of the deterioration in household well-being. It is certainly not a definitive expression of women's capacity to achieve sustainable access to resources because the progress of the types of enterprises they engage are often rocky. They receive little or no support either from the state or women's crumbling social networks. These enterprises depend on personal capacities, a fact which supports the claim that crises of urbanization in the 1980s have been beneficial in unleashing women's entrepreneurial talents. Still, talent which generates capital that enjoys little or no support in a rather hostile environment, as in Nigeria, often dies an early death. We should not be deceived by the observed vibrancy of informal activities which creates the impression that there are few business failures. The fear of vulnerability and the struggle for survival keeps pushing women into new ventures all the time, many of which face serious uncertainties, are marginal and cannot withstand incidental, not to mention community-wide, crises and shocks.

Evidence points to the fact that women usually intensify their labour force participation within the informal sector. Informalization has been seen by some researchers as evidence of deteriorating labour market conditions (see Boyd 1988). On the other hand, with evidence from this study, we are persuaded to regard informalization, to the extent that it increases women's labour force participation, as a means of restitution of labour market asymmetries that have existed even before liberalization pressures gained researchers' attention. We must resist the temptation to reach the rather contestable conclusion that liberalization has benefited women through increased labour market participation. It is contestable in the sense that the quality of that participation is in doubt given the marginal nature of most women's business enterprises.

One important policy consideration which arises from our analysis in this paper is whether women's ability to diversify activity types and coordinate them indicates effective agency. Perhaps it is just a band wagon effect, a trend which will fade away sooner than later, as the wind of globalization slows down. Could encouraging enterprise diversification lead to sustainable empowerment for women? There is no doubt that the intensification of work and nurturing of multiple enterprises have had both positive and negative effects on household well-being. But the balance of effects (higher household income but compromised child care, for instance) cannot be determined at this stage. In addition, we cannot be sure whether globalization has had any transformatory effects on women's conditions within the household, and on their empowerment in general.

That globalization promotes inequality is evidenced here, where despite women's increased work intensification and income earning, household norms may still come between them and the use of the resources they create. If globalization and work intensification are not accompanied by favourable changes in household norms, women will become increasingly overworked outside the home without any significant reduction in household burdens. This will lead to a double jeopardy, and the household will be the worse for it.

## Notes

* Centre for Rural Development and Cooperatives, University of Nigeria, Nsukka, Nigeria.

1. This is in the sense of the relative absence of a state regulatory presence which could dissuade people from starting a new business. However, once in the business, the women have to contend with sundry taxes imposed by the local government as well as entrenched barriers from market associations, and ethnic or kinship interests protecting niches they perceive as their own domain.

## References


Awotona, Adenrele, 1993, 'The Urban Poor's Perception of Housing Conditions', in W. Robert ed., *Urban Development in Nigeria*, Avebury: Aldershot.

Bakker, I., 1994, *The Strategic Silence: Gender and Economic Policy*, London: Zed.

Baruch, G. and Barnett R. , 1987, 'Role Quality and Psychological Well-being', in Faye Crosby, ed., *Spouse, Parent, Worker: on Gender and Multiple Roles*, New Haven: Yale University Press.

Baumol, W. J., 1996, 'Entrepreneurship: Productive, Unproductive, and Destructive', *Journal of Business Venturing*, Vol. 11, No. 1.

Beneria L. and Feldman F., 1992, eds., *Unequal Burden: Economic Crises, Persistent Poverty and Women's Work*, Boulder: West View Press.

Bruce, J., 1989, 'Homes Divided', *World Development*, Vol. 17, No. 7, pp. 979-991.

Collier, P., 1988, 'Women in Development: Defining the Issues', Policy, Planning and Research Working Paper WPS 129, Washington DC: World Bank.

Elson, D., 1991, *Male Bias in the Development Process*, Manchester: MUP.

Elson, D., 1993, 'From Survival Strategies to Transformation Strategies: Women's Needs and Structural Adjustment', in Beneria L. and F. *Unequal Burden: Economic Crises, Persistent Poverty and Women's Work.*

Floro, Maria, 1995, 'Women's Well-Being, Poverty and Work Intensity', *Feminist Economics*, Vol. 1, No. 3.

Folbre, N., 1986, 'Cleaning House: New Perspectives on Households and Economic Development', *Journal of Development Economics*, Vol. 22, pp. 5-40.

Gladwin, C., ed., 1991, *Structural Adjustment and African Women Farmers*, Gainsville, FI: University of Florida Press.

Haddad L. Hoddinot J. and Alderman H., 1994, 'Intra-household Resource Allocation: An overview', Working Paper 1255, Washington D.C.: The World Bank.

ILO/JASPA, 1988, African Employement Report, Addis Ababa.

Lele, U., 1991, 'Women, Structural Adjustment, and Transformation: Some Lessons and Questions From the African Experience', in C. Gladwin, ed., *Structural Adjustment and African Women Farmers*, Gainsville, Fl: University of Florida Press.

Mazumdar, D., 1989, *Microeconomic Issues of Labour Markets in Developing Countries*, The World Bank, 70.

Meaghter K. and Yunusa M., 1996, 'Passing The Buck: Structural Adjustment and The Nigerian Informal Sector', UNRISD, discussion paper 75, Geneva.

Mittleman, J. H., 1994, 'The Globalization Challenge: Surviving at the Margins, *Third World Quarterly*, Vol. 15, No. 3, pp. 427-443.

Moser, C., 1991, 'Adjustment From Below: Low Income Women and Time and The Triple Role in Guayaquil, Ecuador', in H. Afsha and C. Dennis, eds., *Women, Recession and Adjustment in Third World Cities*, London: Macmillan.

Oman, C., 1994, *Globalization and Regionalisation: The Challenge for Developing Countries*, Development Centre Studies, OECD.

Onimode, B. ed., 1989, *The IMF, The World Bank, and African Debt: The Social and Political Impact*, London and New Jersey: Zed Books Ltd for The Institute of African Alternatives.

Palmer I. and Weekes-Vagliani W. , 1987, 'Gender Issues in Food Policy Research: The case of Java', Development Centre Papers, Paris: OECD.

Roldan, M., 1985, 'Industrial Outworking, Struggles for the Reproduction of Working Class Families and Gender Subordination', in N. Redclift and E. Mingione eds., *Beyond Employment: Household, Gender and Subsistence*, Oxford and Cambridge: MIT Press.

Szebo L. and Ceboatorev E., 1990, 'Women's Work Patterns: A Time Allocation Study of Rural Families in St. Lucia', *Canadian Journal of Development Studies*, Vol. 11, No. 2, pp. 259-278.

Williamson, J. G., 1997, 'Globalization and Inequality, Past and Present', World Bank Research Observer, Vol. 12, No. 2, pp. 117-35.

World Bank, 1990, *Making Adjustment Work for the Poor - A Framework for Policy Reform in Africa*, Washington, D.C.

World Bank, 1990, 'World Development Report', The World Bank.

# 9

# The Structural Adjustment Programme and Urban Poverty among Wage Earners in South Eastern Nigeria

**Edlyne Anugwom** *

## Introduction

The Structural Adjustment Programme (SAP) can be conceived as one great dimension of the massive wave of globalization in developing nations. Globalization despite its various conceptualisations (Mittelman 1995, 1994; Sakamoto 1994; Griffin and Khan 1992) can be seen as the complex process of change and interchange of ideas, resources, goods, technologies etc among the various nations of the world. However, globalization also implies the global triumph of capitalism or capitalist hegemony over all other modes of socio-political organization of societies. One issue regarding globalization is the spread of poverty. Poverty which afflicts both urban and rural dwellers can be seen as likely more intense among urban dwellers because of the lack of group solidarity and gross atomization that marks urban life. In this sense, the urban poor may lack the coping mechanisms provided by a social unit like the kinship group in the rural areas. This may have informed the contention by Herrick and Hudson (1981), that urban agglomerations provide the medium for other processes that generate or sustain poverty. Thus the urban area is seen as a centre likely to exacerbate poverty as these authors found in the case of Costa Rica. In Nigeria, the incidence of urban poverty may have been worsened by the Structural Adjustment Programme (SAP) and the inability of government to deal squarely with the problem.

The Structural Adjustment Programme was introduced in Nigeria in 1986 as a macro-economic policy aimed at halting the worsening economic fortune of the country. Following the global recession of the 1980s, the SAP was recommended by the International Monetary Fund (IMF) as the appropriate cure for the economic situation in many African countries. However, the premises and logic underlying the IMF therapy of structural adjustment have been found wanting (Adesina 1994). Being an externally imposed programme, economic structural adjustment may be argued to reinforce existing social distinctions while at the same time deepening inequality in Nigeria.

It is however necessary to point out that the gradual erosion in the socio-economic status of the average Nigerian started before the introduction of the Structural Adjustment Programme. The point, as has been made in the case of Malawi, may be that SAP worsened the general socio-economic situation and in this instance may not have created poverty but have deepened it (Kutengule 1993).

This study apart from its interest in the general poverty of workers during SAP, focuses on the influence of SAP on social policies targeted at workers. Hence it addresses the following questions: What is the impact of SAP on urban wage earners in Nigeria? What is the relationship between SAP and workers' social policies in Nigeria? Is there any difference in the gender impact of SAP?

The socio-economic reality facing the Nigerian workers has been well articulated by Usman (1985), who has stated that the past military governments have been incapable of addressing the situation. It is no wonder that Bafyau (*Newswatch* 1992) concluded that the expectations around SAP have been dashed and that poverty is more widespread. Agreeing with this line of thought, Hugon (1989) argues that austerity measures in developing countries have, in fact, penalised the poorest members of the society. Anugwom (1994), in an investigation of labour-management conflicts during economic recession has found that wage earners bear the brunt of economic hardship consequent upon SAP. According to the UNRISD (1995), the stabilization and adjustment inherent in SAP have led to hardship. Even though the conceptualization of poverty has presented contentious issues among scholars, poverty is a social fact that can be seen or perceived.

The principal aims of this study are to ascertain (i) how SAP has generally affected urban wage earners (ii) and more importantly, how SAP has impacted on social policies meant to benefit wage earners, in Nigeria. For the purposes of our study, the impact of SAP on four of these policies was examined. The four policies are:

- National Housing Policy
- National Provident Fund
- National Policy on Employment and Promotion
- National Policy on Wages and Salaries

In pursuit of the first aim, data was collected from a randomly selected one hundred and fifty worker sample in the Federal Secretariat Enugu, Enugu State, through the use of a questionnaire. Only workers (both sexes) employed before 1986 when SAP was adopted were included in the sample. Also the Focus Group Discussion (FGD) was employed to obtain in-depth information from 40 respondents purposively selected from our original 150 respondents. For the second aim, which is the core objective of this work, documentary sources of data were exploited.

## The Urban Wage Earner, Income and Welfare Under Structural Adjustment

In a study focusing on poverty, income is a very crucial variable. After all, the access of an individual to economic resources which is used in defining poverty (see Atkinson 1991) is dependent on the income available to that individual. Eitzen and Zinn (1989) see the poor as those who spend over two-thirds of their income on food.

For our study, this becomes a relevant indicator of poverty. This is born out of the realization that SAP-induced deprivation has led many Nigerian workers to be unable feed themselves daily. It is this fact that led Adesina (1994) to argue that SAP has induced urban food poverty among Nigerian workers. Given this scenario, we asked our respondents to indicate what percentage of their income they spend on food and luxury items (or non-food expenditures) in both pre-SAP and SAP periods. The responses are presented in Table 9.1 (taking the averaged expenditure pattern):

**Table 9.1: Respondents' Expenditure Pattern**

| Period | Expenditure | | | Total |
|---|---|---|---|---|
| | Food | Non-food | Savings | |
| SAP | 80 % | 18 % | 2 % | 100 % |
| Pre-SAP | 60 % | 32 % | 8 % | 100 % |
| Total | 70 % | 25 % | 5 % | 100 % |

**Source**: Author's Field work

This Table shows that on the average, the Nigerian workers in our sample spent over two-thirds of their income on food, less than a fifth on non-food items, and had little left to save in the SAP period. This contrasts with the pre-SAP period when the workers spent only slightly more than half of their income on food and had something left for savings and non-food expenditure. However, when the expenditure is reconfigured around what can be termed essential needs, the Nigerian worker's salary is inadequate. As the workers reported, non-food expenditure is money spent on paying school fees, hospital bills, house rent, transportation, etc.

From the foregoing, it is obvious that the welfare of the urban wage earners has worsened under the SAP. Apart from an inability to cope with essential needs, luxury and leisure have been sacrificed. On being asked to comment on their welfare in the SAP period, respondents reacted with aggression towards the Focus Group Discussion moderator. It was as if the workers were saying: 'Why ask us, are you not living in this country?' However, a middle-aged woman was forthright in explaining that her family's welfare has grossly deteriorated under SAP due to the inadequacy of earnings. Asked to expatiate, she argued that her children now go to inferior schools, wear second hand or used clothes, do not have Christmas dresses, the family car is dysfunctional and they have been living in a deteriorating flat for over ten years. For another male worker, 'there is no question of welfare for the Nigerian workers. SAP is killing us all gradually'.

All the same, in order to extract the relationship between SAP and welfare, especially in terms of access to social services like pipe-borne water, electricity, public health institutions and education, the workers were asked to estimate the efficiency of these social services in the last ten years (i.e. SAP period). Their responses are provided in Table 9.2.

**Table 9.2: Distribution of Respondents by Rating of Social Services' Performance**

| Opinion | Social Service | | | | Total |
|---|---|---|---|---|---|
| | Water | Electricity | Health | Education | |
| Very efficient | - | - | - | - | - |
| Efficient | 12 (48%) | 4 (10.8%) | 6 (17.1%) | 8 (32%) | 30 (24.6%) |
| Undecided | 6 (24%) | 12 (32.4%) | 14 (40%) | 8 (32%) | 40 (32.7%) |
| Inefficient | 4 (16%) | 10 (27%) | 8 (22.9%) | 6 (24%) | 28 (23%) |
| Very inefficient | 3 (12%) | 11 (29.8%) | 7 (20%) | 3 (12%) | 24 (19.7%) |
| Total | 25 (100%) | 37 (100%) | 35 (100%) | 25(100%) | 22 (100%) |

**Source**: Author's Fieldwork

The crux of the matter here is that of assessing the effectiveness of these services to which, as tax payers, workers are entitled. The picture that emerges from the above is that urban wage earners are faced with inadequate earnings and uncertain social services. Given this fact, it is easy to conclude that the welfare of the average wage earner in Nigeria has deteriorated severely in the prevailing SAP climate. This period has seen the devaluation of the currency, the commercialization of social services, while at the same time there have been partial embargoes on promotion. Hence, workers are the immediate victims of the negative implications of SAP (Anugwom 1994; Adesina 1994).

## The Structural Adjustment Programme and Workers' Social Policies in Nigeria

In this part of this paper, we focus on the relationship of SAP, which is a manifestation of globalization, with social policies aimed at workers. The importance of social policies as any student of social welfare will agree is the balancing power they exert in curbing misery and privation while reinforcing citizens' belief in the collective will of the state.

In the case of Nigeria, while the pre-SAP social policies may have been informed by non-profit and social legitimation considerations, the SAP era policies or the modifications of pre-SAP policies were driven by other factors. In this regard, it is important to point out the two main elements distinguishing the SAP era workers' social policies. These were the lessening of emphasis on social services provision and the re-orientation of social policies.

The SAP era in Nigeria began with a gradual but determined withdrawal of government from the provision of social services and infrastructure. It was as if the government defined the privatization component of the SAP process to mean total withdrawal of government from its social responsibilities. Therefore, provision of social services was de-emphasized and instead 'self reliance' and 'independence from government' became the catch-words. Government denied full responsibility for employment creation but assumed a facilitating role in a self-employment exercise championed by the National Directorate of Employment (NDE). As a result, there was a total embargo on fresh employment in government and its parastatals, along with an initial freeze on promotion. A Wages and Salaries Commission was set up and mandated with the task of harmonizing rewards in the civil service. However, this commission turned out to be a more or less diversionary tool.

In addition, the orientation of social policies in the country changed drastically. Social policies became market oriented, i.e. economic viability and the profit motive became the key determinants of the ingredients of workers' social policies. Thus, these policies were re-evaluated on market principles and user charges were demanded for a less than satisfactory service. However, all these steps were taken without a grasp of the cushioning effects of these policies when properly implemented. Social policies are ideally driven by the need to cushion hardship and express government's interest in the welfare of its citizens. From a labour perspective, social policies are meant to enable workers to cope with the challenges of living and come to terms with the privations of a capitalist society.

Social policies are generally part and parcel of the welfare measures of the state. Indeed, social policies targeted at the workers are usually welfarist in nature. And, of course, the inextricable link between welfare (or its lack) and poverty cannot be over-emphasized (Midgley 1984). But the 'charitable' nature of these policies and access to them is determined principally by the orthodox definition of welfare by the state. Although social welfare services can be seen as a normal 'first line' function of modern society, social marginalists advocate a very limited state role in social welfare. They hold strongly to such doctrines as individualism, private property and free market, a minimum government role and the conceptualisation of welfare as charity to the unfortunate (Pusic 1972). This orthodoxy seems to have informed the nature of social policies in Nigeria in the SAP era. The following examination of particular social policies in the SAP era will highlight the dominance of this 'neo-liberal' orthodoxy and its failure to effectively contribute to poverty reduction for the Nigerian wage earner.

## The National Housing Policy

Shelter can be seen as one of the most basic human needs which impacts on the life style as well as self-fulfilment of people. Housing, in this regard, encompasses the physical structure itself and the necessary or ancillary services like water, electricity, roads, habitable environments and proximity to a human community. The National Housing Policy could be viewed as having been made up of time-tested housing policy thrusts of government, all of which were crystallized in the National Housing Policy of 1980, but modified in the period between 1989 to 1992.

This policy emanated from the recognition of the severe housing problems in most of Nigeria's urban areas. Accordingly, the policy took cognisance of both the qualitative and quantitative nature of this problem, viz. the huge shortage of houses and existence of sub-standard housing marked by over-crowding, lack of utilities and poor environmental conditions (The National Housing Policy 1980). This policy itself was informed by the acknowledged need for comprehensive and explicit guidelines on housing in order to resolve the housing problem in a way compatible with the demands of other sectors. The policy was essentially long term in perspective.

Some of the specific objectives of the policy directed at workers included:

- To ensure that the provision of housing units were based on realistic standards which the prospective house owners could afford.
- To give priority to housing programmes designed to benefit the low-income group.
- To encourage every household to own its own house by providing more credit. In addition, the policy was meant to tackle the menace of spiralling urban rents.

While this policy underwent various amendments periodically from different governments in Nigeria, especially between 1989 and 1992, the basic philosophy, with the later full incorporation of a role for the private sector in 1992, has been the same. However, the type of attention given to this policy by successive governments has been greatly influenced by the economic notion that housing constitutes non-productive, durable consumption which requires a high capital outlay. But, it is instructive to appreciate the fact that the social cost of not investing in housing may greatly outweigh this economic rationalization. In fact, housing also generates its own economic gains in terms of employment creation and labour sector effectiveness.

In a major move between 1989 and 1992, the government re-launched the National Housing Policy and established the National Housing Fund (NHF) and the mortgage institutions decree, aimed at providing housing for all by the year 2000 (*Newswatch* 1992b). The Housing Policy was intended to work by pooling resources from both the public and private sectors while at the same time limiting government's direct participation. Under a mandatory scheme, workers were to compulsorily contribute 2.5 per cent of their monthly salaries at an interest rate of 4 per cent into a National Housing Fund [NHF] to be withdrawn in old age as retirement benefits plus accrued interests at commercial rate. Also, banks, insurance and other corporate firms in the private sector were encouraged to invest their loans, advances and other reserve funds in the Federal Mortgage Bank of Nigeria (FMBN) and also encouraged to become involved in the NHF. The National Provident Fund also participated in the NHF directly by investing a substantial portion of its total investment portfolio in it.

Thus, two very visible ingredients of the SAP era housing policy were the massive involvement of the private sector and the advent of the NHF component. The National Housing Fund was a compulsory contributory scheme for housing finance (Oghifo 1997). In this scheme, the private sector in the form of Primary Mortgage Institutions (PMIs) empowered by the mortgage decree bridged the gap between the FMBN and the contributor (employers and workers). The PMIs are the primary lenders with a responsibility to evaluate each loan application from the individual contributors to the scheme. The ceiling for loans to individual contributors was pegged at half a million naira and was usually jointly financed by the PMIs and the FMBN.

Thus, there arose a novel two-tier mortgage finance structure in which the FMBN was to serve as a pool for mortgage finance and the PMIs as the retail outlets. The PMIs were seen by Decree 53 of 1989 as specialised financial intermediaries empowered to accept money from the public, pay interest on it, and in the case of certain types of investment, allow them to be withdrawn on demand or on short notice. These PMIs could go by different names such as building societies, state housing corporations, housing co-operatives and home savings and loans associations (Federal Government of Nigeria Mortgage Institutions Decree 53 of 1989; National Housing Fund Decree 3 of 1992).

The picture that emerges from the above is that SAP era housing de-emphasized both the role and involvement of the central government in particular. Ironically, the policy at its inception was supposed to increase the involvement of government in housing rather than leaving it to the private sector. Apart from this, the loan ceiling to individual contributors has been seen as inconsistent with cost realities of the SAP era (Okupe 1997). Also, the participation of the private sector has been severely curtailed by problems of accessibility to urban land (the Land Use Decree of 1978 vests all land in government), finance facilities (housing is costly), hindrances arising from government policies, regulation and even by laws. Given this scenario, it is not surprising that such problems as the organic growth of slums, spiralling urban house rents, high occupancy rates, limited mortgage financing and unaffordable housing which the Housing Policy set out to curb have really multiplied.

**Table 9.3: *FMBN Lending Operations, 1985-1989**

| Year | Volume of Loan Applications | Total Loan Approved* | % of Approvals of Applications |
|---|---|---|---|
| 1985 | 25.437m | - | - |
| 1986 | 79.429m | 8.552m | 10.76 |
| 1987 | 71.136m | 61.611m | 86.61 |
| 1988 | 130.196m | 42.214m | 32.42 |
| 1989 | 126.585m | 19.286m | 15.23 |

**Source**: FMBN, Lagos, Nigeria.
(*) This was before the commencement of NHF in 1992.

Therefore, the housing situation of the urban wage earner has worsened, and the palliatives of government in this regard have been blunted by placing economic rationality in the forefront. Paradoxically, housing units developed by private sector participants and government recently have been out of the reach of the average honest worker. Thus, the policy on housing has been pursued with insensitivity to the plight of the workers in the SAP era. A judgement on the efforts of the government in housing provision for the workers seemed to have been passed when a former Works and Housing Minister, Mamman Kontangora commented that Nigeria's housing programmes had been marked by 'partial successes and monumental failures (West Africa 1991: 345)'.

Workers' unions like the National Union of Banks, Insurance and Financial Institutions Employees (NUBIFIE) and even the central National Labour Congress (NLC) passed a vote of no confidence in the scheme (*Newswatch* 1992b). More recently, the NHF is under threat arising mainly from its inability to keep faith with the desires of the workers and private sector employers. Eight industrial groups under the Nigerian Employers Consultative Association (NECA) enjoined the association to stop deductions from employees' salaries for the fund (*Business Times* 1998). According to the Business Times (1998) since 1992, only 6.72 million naira (about $672,000 US$) have been disbursed by the FMBN under the fund while over 2.7 billion naira were contributed. A leading figure of the NECA, Victor Eburajolo, argued that the workers have come to believe that 'there is no way they could benefit from the above scheme especially, the low income workers who form up to 80 per cent of the working population of the country (*Business Times* 1998: 4)'. This assertion by a representative of the private sector employers glaringly exposes the inherent weakness of the policy in mediating the harsh realities of SAP.

## The National Provident Fund (National Social Insurance Trust Fund)

The National Provident Fund (NPF) was established by the National Provident Fund Act, Cap 273 in 1961. It was established by the government as a sort of pooling mechanism where workers and employers of labour make monthly or regular contributions to the fund headed by a government appointed Director under the Ministry of Finance. Workers were supposed to benefit from the fund in terms of their contributions and interest accruing thereon when they attained the retirement age of fifty-five, or subsidiary benefits in time of severe sickness or withdrawal from the fund because of emigration or on the presentation of evidence of no more employment (Laws of the Federation of Nigeria 1990, Vol. XVII, Cap 273).

According to the Act, contributions are at two levels, viz from the employer of the worker at his own expense and in relation to the number of staff employed, and deductions from the workers' salaries. However, the Act exempts workers employed in such public departments or parastatals where they are 'entitled to the benefit of any scheme of pensions on terms substantially similar to those prescribed by the Pensions Act (Laws of the Federation of Nigeria 1990, Vol. XVII, Cap 273: 10973)'. Deductions start from the moment the worker's employment is confirmed. The worker and his employer are expected to contribute equal amounts monthly to the fund. By the Act, the deduction is fixed at 6 per cent of the employee's salary. Any private sector organization with at least ten permanent staff members is a compulsory participant in the scheme.

Thus at the onset, the NPF scheme was born out of a genuine desire by the government to safeguard the interests of workers engaged mainly in non-pensionable and mostly private sector jobs. The Act establishing it made it a compulsory saving scheme for private sector workers. The general idea was for the savings to provide a bulwark against privations for the worker at retirement.

The problems militating against the effectiveness of the NPF predate the SAP, even though the SAP has worsened these problems. Some of these problems include evasion of contributions by employers; misrepresentation of the NPF by workers; bogus bureaucracy in the NPF; evasion of registration by firms; and evasion of payment and rigorous pre-payment demands by NPF. The Fund also suffered from the debilitating internal problems of poor staffing, low wages and low morale which affected workers' performance and predisposed them to corruption. In the SAP era this tardiness identified by Agwudagwu (1987) multiplied. In part this was because of the inability of the employers, groaning under bleak economic conditions, to keep to their commitments to the scheme, as well as the inability of the government to fundamentally restructure the NPF or its operating principles to take cognisance of the SAP.

The NPF has been able to honour only a small number of its obligations over the years. The number of beneficiaries seems to have been getting less and less in spite of the increasing contributions at the disposal of the Fund. In fact, workers generally complain of their inability to obtain the stipulated benefits from the fund. It was this reluctance to settle worker contributions to the fund that led the mass media to dub the scheme 'operation robbing Peter to pay Paul' at the onset of the SAP (*Newswatch* 1987).

A critical examination of the philosophy of the NPF will show that a period of gross structural changes demands a re-evaluation of the tenets of the policy. In this sense, the government should have reacted to the SAP influence by creating a consolidated fund especially for private sector drawing in meeting NPF commitments. This fund would have acted as a SAP period credit to the firms in that sector. Alternatively, the workers' contributions could have been waived for a period of, say, four years in order to lessen the social impact of SAP on these workers. The government's inability to do any of these may be seen as conforming to the prevailing orthodoxy distancing government from welfare and social policies in the SAP era. And this created a situation where many workers who suffered SAP-induced retrenchment and those whose firms closed shops because of SAP were left without any help from a largely comatose NPF.

In fact, an employee of the scheme described it as gradually becoming irrelevant and a breeding ground for official corruption as a result of the huge financial resources available to the Fund. The promise of the one-time Labour and Productivity Minister, Ike Nwachukwu, to harmonise the operations of the NPF with the new social security scheme being put together by government has not really materialised. But it was this thinking that led mainly to the changing of the nomenclature of the NPF to the Nigerian Social Insurance Trust Fund (NSITF) in July 1994. The new name has changed neither the orientation of the fund nor its discharge of its obligations as billions of naira lie with the scheme while some of the contributors are dead and others are languishing in misery without receiving their benefits. Thus, the famed social security scheme has remained a pipe dream for the workers.

**Table 9.4: NSITF Basic Claims and Payments**

| S/No | Types of Benefit | Qualification Conditions | Benefit Payable |
|---|---|---|---|
| a | Retirement Grant | Employee who had attained the age of 60 and above and retired from employment having 12 monthly paid contributions. | A lump sum payment equivalent of the final monthly contribution multiplied by the number of months of paid contributions. |
| b | Retirement Pension | Employee who had attained the age of 60 and above and retired from employment. Having at least 120 monthly paid contributions. | Minimum of 30 per cent and a maximum of 65 per cent of final average insurable earning depending on number of contributions paid. Amount equal to the final monthly contributions multiplied by the number of months of paid contribution. |
| c | Invalidity Grant | Employee permanently incapable of working. At least 12 monthly contributions paid. | An amount equal to the final monthly contributions multiplied by the number of months of paid contribution |
| d | Invalidity Pension | Employee permanently incapable of working. At least 36 monthly contributions paid out of which he is expected to have worked continuously for 12 months. | A minimum of 30 per cent and a maximum of 65 per cent of final average insurable earnings. In either case amount payable not to be less than 80 per cent of National Minimum Wage. |
| e | Survivors Pension | Death of an employee receiving retirement or invalidity pension with dependent as survivors. | 100 per cent of deceased employee's pension. |
| f | Survivor Grant | Where a dependent is not entitled to survivor's pension but deceased employee had at least 12 monthly paid contributions. | Equivalent of the deceased employee's invalidity or retirement grant. |
| g | Funeral Grant | Death of employee receiving invalidity or retirement pension | 2,000.00 for meeting funeral expenses. |

**Source**: Coverage and Compliance with the NSITF Scheme.

As the Table9.4 shows, both the NPF and the later NSITF were conceived from solid ideas to ameliorate private sector workers' hardship in periods of severance from employment. But the implementation of the scheme has characteristically suffered from official misappropriation, bureaucratic red-tapism and ambivalence on the part of government.

**National Policy on Employment and Promotions**

It is difficult to pinpoint the actual SAP era employment policy direction of various governments in Nigeria. Suffice it to say that the SAP era started with wide ranging curtailments of labour sector privileges. One of these was the directive embargoing employment in the public service at the federal level and the retrenchment exercises of the SAP period which was aimed at achieving a SAP recommended 'downsizing and rightsizing' of the bureaucracy.

However, it is pertinent to point out that employment issues are to be considered against the background of other labour market realities, especially the unemployment trend. Prior to the advent of the SAP, the unemployment level in Nigeria was at an abnormally high rate. This necessitated a call on government to live up to its responsibility of providing jobs for the teeming numbers of unemployed. The government of General Ibrahim Babangida responded to this call by establishing the National Directorate of Employment (NDE) in 1986. The NDE, according to its decree, was mandated to train unemployed youths between the ages of 15 and 21 in various self-employment skills. The NDE was inaugurated on Nov.ember 20, 1986 (Times International 1987). Realities have subsequently drawn the NDE into attempting to facilitate self-employment for university graduates, but it has no role to play in solving the unemployment problem of other adults or in providing succour for workers displaced or retrenched in the wake of economic restructuring of the SAP era.

Against this background, one can look at the employment policies of the government in terms of efforts or lack of efforts at maintaining the existing labour force as well as attempts at curbing general unemployment, which was the main task of the NDE. The rationale behind the NDE seems to underline the philosophy informing government's employment policies. The NDE was created to direct employment away from the government. Individuals, under a SAP-inspired propaganda of self reliance, were now responsible for their employment. Thus, the NDE was supposed to act as a facilitator of self-employment for Nigerians and not as an agency for creating government employment for the qualified and unemployed. But interestingly, the advent of the NDE coincided with the emergence of SAP. In popular parlance, the SAP era called for a tightening of belts among Nigerians, i.e. a period of hardship and decreased government spending power. Given this reality, one wonders how self employment through the acquisition of practical skills and government backed NDE credits could have off-set unemployment in a depressed economy with low purchasing power.

Put differently, self-employment works well in a buoyant and expanding economy but not in an economy in transition or one in which factories are being closed down and workers are constantly retrenched. Once an existing economy does not expand, there is little room for self-employment. All the same, the Nigerian government has an established employment exchange unit as well as the Professional and Executive Registry of the Ministry of Labour and Productivity, whose function is mainly to register and place job applicants in government employment (Annual Labour Report 1989). However, the job of this unit is merely academic, as there are no independent records documenting the performance of actual placements during the period of SAP.

The SAP had as one of its principal aims the curtailment of unproductive investments in the public sector and the revitalization of the private sector. In Nigeria, this translated into the relentless retrenchment of public sector workers. The practice was fruitless, since the retrenchment of one set of workers was matched by the employment of others on the basis of patronage (*Newswatch* 1998).

This retrenchment exercise provided a ready tool for the intimidation and cowing of workers by government and was carried out with a ruthless vigour that showed the not the least concern for the welfare of the worker. According to Onah (2000), civil service reform in Nigeria included a downsizing component which meant the rationalization and retrenchment of staff and affected not only the civil service but staff of government parastatals and other extra-ministerial agencies.

In spite of this, one can however agree that the period between 1989 and 1991 witnessed a gradual reduction in the rate of retrenchment in the immediate SAP era. It was however the case that retrenchment was subsequently pursued and re-invigorated under the administration of late General Sani Abacha, leading to the establishment of the Ayida Commission on Civil Service Reforms in 1997. The Ayida Report put forward a drastic reduction of the strength of the civil service, which it saw as negating productivity. It actually recommended that about 150,000 workers out of an estimated half a million federal civil servants should be retrenched (Chigbo 1998). This portrays the ironic tendencies of a government engaged in a cosmetic management of unemployment through the NDE but vigorously pursuing a mass retrenchment agenda in the civil service. The implication of such an agenda for urban poverty cannot be over-emphasized. Nigerian labour history is replete with rampant cases of government's inability to honour its contractual obligations to both retirees and retrenched workers.

Thus, workers are disengaged from formal employment and left at the mercies of the vagaries of a depressed economy. The Nigerian government's legacy in mishandling the settlement of disengaged workers can be aptly illustrated by the now notorious Nigerian Railway Corporation case where some people disengaged even twenty years ago are yet to get their entitlements.

The government's attitude towards employment can be further illustrated by an examination of the SAP era employment trend in a typical government parastatal (Table 9.5). The practice which is the same in almost all government parastatals is that of a steeply decreasing work force. Thus, as the number of people looking for employment increased, the number of jobs created or available decreased. This explains why the unemployment figure in Nigeria is constantly on an upward trend.

**Table 9.5: Number Employed by the Nigerian Railway Corporation (1990-94)**

| Period | Department | | | | Total |
|---|---|---|---|---|---|
| | Civil Engineering | Mech. Engineering | Operation or Commercial | Admi-nistration | |
| 1990 | 9,859 | 6,094 | 5,163 | 4,384 | 25,500 |
| 1991 | 9,076 | 5,683 | 4,790 | 4,210 | 23,759 |
| 1992 | 7,841 | 4,716 | 3,968 | 3,628 | 20,153 |
| 1993 | 4,002 | 2,644 | 2,146 | 2,554 | 11,346 |
| 1994 | 3,973 | 2,599 | 2,114 | 2,664 | 11,355 |

**Source**: Federal Office of Statistics, Lagos, Nigeria.

The economic rationality behind most SAP directives regarding government employment also affected the issue of promotions for workers. The 1986 SAP measures kicked-off with a total freeze on promotions. This was later changed to a partial embargo which has more or less operated until the present. Even in establishments and ministries where this policy directive remains undisclosed, workers can generally testify to the stagnant upward mobility which has characterized the SAP era. This stagnation, however, was often offset through political or military patronage, which provided an easy route to appointments into higher offices.

This attitude to promotion can be seen as largely complementing the embargo on employment foisted on most government ministries and parastatals. It was only in 1998 that the former Head of State, Adbul Salami Abubakar, lifted the embargo on employment in the Police through a presidential decree. The previous SAP era practice has been the use of mainly contract or casual workers by government establishments.

## National Policy on Wages and Salaries

Wages and salaries in Nigeria have been subjected mostly to the determination of wage commissions, particularly in the pre-SAP era. However, the use of wages commissions negates the process of collective bargaining, which is the effective democratic tool in modern industrial relations. Thus, while the government and employees have agreed on the overwhelming need for collective bargaining procedures, the reality reveals the opposite. Salaries and wages policy in Nigeria has been mainly the exclusive preserve of the government.

The era of military rule has not in any way aided the evolution of an enduring collective bargaining legacy. As a result, the government has, as usual, exhibited an overbearing deterministic tendency in wages affairs. The period of SAP did not help matters. Government in the SAP period undertook a wages and salaries policy regime which emphasised a partial or total freeze on wage increases and a tendency on the part of government to use obnoxious military decrees in checking the agitation of the workers.

It is only against this background that one can appreciate the unrealistic payment of 250.00 naira monthly as a minimum wage to workers in Nigeria. This was at a time that the value of the naira had depreciated by over 800 per cent. No wonder the past President of the NLC, Paschal Bafyau, commented that most of the expectations about SAP have not been met, and poverty has become even more widespread in the land (*Newswatch* 1992a). The pervasive nature of poverty among urban wage earners in Nigeria during SAP and the spill-over effect of this on urban economies led to the popular SAP riots in major urban areas in Nigeria championed by University students, unemployed youths and urban workers in 1989. The Babangida government responded to this popular agitation by characteristically doling out short-term palliatives rather than tackle the source of the problem. In addition to this, an upward review of minimum wages from 125.00 naira set by the civilian government of Shehu Shagari pegged them at 250 naira in 1991.

While retaining the starvation wages and salaries paid workers, the government of General Sani Abacha in 1997 came up with the ideas of re-emphasizing the National Wages and Salaries Commission and the restructuring of the existing uniform wages regime. In the new dispensation, government announced a deregulation of wages policy in which the state governments were mandated to work out their respective wage structure on the basis of their individual capacity to pay (*The Guardian on Sunday* 1997). This deregulation spirit could still be seen in the wages review of the Abubakar administration. The principle of wage deregulation, which is very common in the private sector, emanates from an economic rationale which sees a sector employer as paying as much as he thinks he can afford or on the basis of what is deemed the marginal productivity of the worker in spite of wage-related developments in other sectors.

Deregulation may work in a developed economy where the welfare of the employees and employers reconciled within a collective bargaining framework. But in a developing country where dictatorial government, corruption, misappropriation and diversion of public fund are the order of the day, deregulation leads to the oppression of workers. In Nigeria, deregulation has been used by government not only to divide workers along sectoral and state lines but also to justify the penchant for ad-hoc salary reviews unilaterally.

The Abacha-sponsored National Salaries and Wages Commission wound up its sittings in 1997 acting subtly as a rubber stamp for the view of the military on the wages issue. Ironically, the submissions of this commission, apart from speculations in newspapers (see, for instance, *The Guardian on Sunday*,

July 6, 1997), have not been made public. The 1998 upward review of wages carried out by the administration of Abubakar was not informed in any way by this commission. But the wage review was aided by the work of the nascent National Income, Wages and Salaries Committee.

It may be important to highlight the fact that while government has shown a disposition to use committees and commissions to tackle the issue of wages and salaries, none of the recommendations of these committees has been followed to the letter. Thus, from the Bridges Commission of 1941 to the Udoji Commission of 1975 and even the 1990s commissions, the government has always gone ahead with its own agenda. And this is the main problem with this arrangement, not only is it anti-collective bargaining, but it provides government with a rubber stamp and government takes only what it likes from their recommendations, which are usually not open to debate.

Be that as it may, the inadequacy of income has been the lot of urban workers in the SAP era in Nigeria and to a large extent explains the excruciating poverty confronting these workers. A good measure of how far down the poverty ladder Nigerian workers have gone is glaringly shown by the realization that despite the fact that the 1998 Abubakar review led to an over 500 per cent increase in minimum wage for federal workers, the urban worker is still groaning under poverty. This is because the government and employers of labour in Nigeria have over the years ignored the International Labour Organization's guidelines which stipulate that workers' salaries should be reviewed whenever the consumer price index rises. The SAP era has encouraged ad-hoc anti-collective bargaining wages arrangements by government which are largely insensitive to the plight of the urban wage earner in Nigeria.

## Pre-SAP Versus SAP Era Social Policies in Nigeria: A Summary

It is difficult to attempt a straight- forward comparison between pre-SAP and SAP era policies. This is because of the different socio-economic situations confronting each period in Nigeria. For instance, while the pre-SAP period (before 1986) witnessed some semblance of democratic governance and an economy with substantial petroleum oil revenues, the SAP period (1986 onwards) was the era of military rule and witnessed a decline in state income from oil. These two factors—the nature of governance and the position of oil as the hub of Nigeria's mono-economy—structured the nature and dynamics of relevant social policies in both eras. However, it is pertinent to state that the brute force which pervaded the SAP era military government and the excessive pandering to the dictates of the Bretton Woods Institutions went a long way in shaping the SAP era policies (Fashoyin 1990; Adesina 1994).

Hence the SAP era policies were driven by the ethos of privatization and/ or commercialization, as one of the bedrocks of the SAP. But the pre-SAP policies were born out of a genuine, even though poorly executed, desire to ameliorate social privation through social provisioning. This fact can be further strengthened when it is realized that even though the four policies we have considered more or less predated SAP, their strategies and mechanisms were drastically modified to suit the market logic of SAP. In other words, these social policies were largely affected or eroded by the dictates of globalization.

The reality is that these existing policies were modified and given more prominence out of the ostensible desire of the government to 'mitigate' the adverse affects of adjustment. But the sum of these policies was the further erosion of the urban workers' socio-economic position and the intensification of poverty.

## Concluding Remarks

One would have favoured a wages philosophy driven by collective bargaining and economic realities. Thus, the SAP policies on wages and salaries should have been motivated by the need to enable workers meet their economic demands. Instead of this, the SAP era wages were a result of the need to curtail government public sector spending. In fact, this much was apparent in the SAP declaration itself (*Newswatch* 1992). The same attitude also drove the policy on housing, especially the modifications between 1989 and 1992 which led to the establishment of the National Housing Fund. It is instructive that the Obasanjo government in 2000 declared the NHF a failure.

Despite the metamorphosis of the NPF into the NSITF, the benefit of the fund is yet to be felt. In this sense, rather than weighed down by bureaucracy, the Fund should have been driven by workers' needs. The employment scenario of the SAP era appears to be the most destructive. The SAP occasioned the closure of many existing firms, as well as the pruning down of the work force in both private and public sectors, which was in line with the short term objectives of the programme. However, the unfortunate thing is that after a decade of SAP, the envisaged economic regeneration or revival did not materialize and successive governments in Nigeria have faced the daunting challenge of providing jobs for a teeming unemployed population.

Social policies in the SAP era were not tailored towards elevating the social status of workers, rather they were guided by the rationale to be self-sustaining or profitable to the provider-government. Apart from this, the government tactically abandoned its responsibility of social provisioning which usually is a first line obligation of governments, particularly in periods of economic recessions or structural changes. Rather, it saw social policies as feasible only when they could be made profitable, commercial and involve the financial participation or involvement of the beneficiaries. This belief partly explains why poverty has remained endemic in urban Nigeria. A recent World Bank Report on poverty eradication (*Newswatch* 1998a) stated that poverty was widespread and severe in Nigeria, while purchasing power continued to decline with high inflation. Globalization can be conceived as the renewed march of capitalist hegemony in the post-cold war period.

## Note

* Department of Sociology, University of Nigeria, Nsukka.

## References

Adesina, J., 1994, *Labour in the Explanation of an African Crisis*, Dakar: CODESRIA Books.

Agwundagwu, S., 1987, 'Robbing Paul to Pay Paul', *Newswatch*, December, Vol. 21, pp. 36-37.

Akintoye, S., 1997, 'Challenges of New Wages Structure', *The Guardian*, January, Vol. 19, pp. A15.

Annual Labour Report, 1989, Labour Office, Federal Ministry of Labour and Productivity, Lagos.

Annual Labour Report, 1988, Labour Office, Federal Ministry of Labour and Productivity, Lagos.

Anugwom, E.E., 1994, 'Economic Conditions and Industrial Conflict in Nigeria: A Study of Pre and Structural Adjustment Periods (1981-1992)', unpublished M.Sc thesis, Nsukka: University of Nigeria.

Anugwom, E.E., 1997, 'The Public Sector and Industrial Conflict in Nigeria: Facts and Issues', *Nigeria Journal of Public Administration & Local Government*, Vol. 8, No. 1.

Anugwom, E.E., 1998, 'Organisation and Environment in Nigeria: The Corruption Potency', *Nigerian Journal of Management and Social Sciences*, Vol.2 No. 1.

Anugwom, E.E., 2000, 'Militant Labour Unionism: A Viable Option to the Nigerian Crisis', forthcoming.

Atkinson, A., 1991, 'Comparing Poverty Rates Internationally: Lessons from Recent Studies in Developed Countries', *The World Bank Economic Review*, Vol. 5, No. 1.

Badjan-Young, Janet, 1996, 'Collective War Against Poverty', *A.M. News*, Thursday, April, 11.

Bafyau, Paschal, 1992a, quoted in *Newswatch.*

Batchelder, A., 1971, *The Economics of Poverty*, New York: John Wiley.

Bates, R., 1981, *Markets and States in Tropical Africa: The Political Basis of Agricultural Politics*, Berkeley: University of California Press.

Bourguinon, F; de Melo J. , Morrisson C., 1991, 'Poverty and Income Distribution during Adjustment: Issues and Evidence from the OECD Project', mimeograph, The World Bank, Country Economics Dept.

*Business Times*, 1998, 'Private Sector Moves to Dump NHF', October, Vol. 26, pp. 1&4.

Chigbo, M., 1998, 'From Udoji to Abubakar', *Newswatch*, October, Vol. 26, pp. 10-11.

Coverage and Compliance with NSITF Scheme (n.d.), Abuja: NSITF.

Deininger, K. and L. Squire, 1996, 'Measuring Income Inequality: A New Data Base', mimeograph, The World Bank, Policy Research Dept.

Demery, L. and Squire L., 1996, 'Macroeconomic Adjustment and Poverty in Africa: An Emerging Picture', *The World Bank Research Observer*, Vol. II, No. 1, February.

Dorosh, P. and Sahn E.xc, 1993, A General Equilibrium Analysis of the Effect of Macroeconomic Adjustment on Poverty in Africa, Ithaca, New York: Cornell University Food and Nutrition Policy Programme.

Eitzen, D.S. and Zinn, M.B., 1989, *Social Problems*, Boston: Allyn and Bacon.

Eteng, I.A., 1995, 'Populism and Rural Development in Nigeria', in C.O. Nwanunobi; C.C. Ukaegbu; and E.U.M. Igbo, eds., *Innovative Approaches to Rural Development in Nigeria*, Enugu: Auto-Century Pub.

Fashoyin, T., 1990, 'Nigerian Labour and the Military: Toward Exclusion', *Labour, Capital and Society*, vol. 3, No. 1, April.

Griffin, K. and A. Khan, 1992, *Globalization and the Developing World: An Essay on the International Dimensions of Development in the Post-cold War Era*, Geneva: UNRISD.

Grootaert, C., 1983, 'The Conceptual Basis of Measures of Household Welfare and their Implied Survey Data Requirements', *The Review of Income and Wealth*, Series 29, No. 1.

Grootaert, C., 1993, 'The Evolution of Welfare and Poverty under Structural Change and Economic Recession in Côte d'Ivoire, 1985-88', mimeograph, The World Bank, African Technical Dept.

Hayami, Y, Subbaro K., and Otsuka R., 1982, 'Efficiency and Equity in Producer Levy of India', *American Journal of Agricultural Economics*, Vol. 64.

Herrick, B. and Hudson B., 1981, *Urban Poverty and Economic Development: A Case Study of Costa Rica*, New York: St. Martins Press.

Hugon, P., 1989, 'Social Effects of Structural Adjustment Policies', *Third World*, Vol. XXX, No. 17.

ILO, 1977, *Meeting Basic Needs: Strategies for Eradicating Mass Poverty and Unemployment*, Geneva: ILO.

Kutengule, M., 1993, 'The Structural Adjustment Economic Reform Programme and Urban Poverty in Malawi', in N. Hall, ed., *Social Development and Urban Poverty*,. Zimbabwe: School of Social Work.

Lanjouw, J. and Lanjouw P., 1997, 'Poverty Comparisons with Noncompatible Data', mimeograph, The World Bank, Policy Research Dept.

Laws of the Federation of Nigeria, 1990, The National Provident Act, Vol. XVII, Cap. 273.

Lele, U. and Adu-Nyako R., 1991, 'Integrated Strategy Approach for Poverty Alleviation: A Paramount Priority for Africa', *African Development Review*, Vol. 3, No. 1, June, 1-29.

Lipton, M., 1977, *Why Poor People Stay Poor: Urban Bias in World Development*, London: Temple Smith.

Lipton, M., 1983, *Labour and Poverty*, Washington D.C.: The World Bank.

Midgley, J., 1984, *Social Security, Inequality and the Third World*, New York: John Wiley.

Mittelman, J., 1994, 'The Globalization Challenge: Surviving at the Margins', *Third World Quarterly*, Vol. 15, No. 3, September.

Mittelman, J., 1995, 'Rethinking the International Division of Labour in the Context of Globalization', *Third World Quarterly*, Vol. 16, No. 2.

Modo, I.V.O., 1997, 'Cultural Devaluation of Women in Sokoto Metropolis: A Cog in the Wheel of Sustainable Development', in Y. Oruwari, ed., *Women, Development & the Nigerian Environment*, Ibadan, Vantage.

Morris, D.M., 1979, *Measuring the Conditions of the World's Poor*, New York: Pergamon.

*Newswatch*, 1992a, 'What Future for SAP', Vol. 15 No. 8, February,pp. 24.

*Newswatch*, 1992b,. 'Striking Towards 2000AD', October, Vol. 19, pp. 26-31.

*Newswatch*, 1998, 'Minimum Wage, Maximum Crisis', October, Vol. 26, pp. 8-17.

Ogbugwo, Y., 1996, 'Tightening the Noose', *The Guardian*, March, pp. 24.

Oghifo, B., 1997, 'Delay of NHF Statement of Accounts Deliberate', *This Day*, October, 15, pp. 26.

Ojha, P.D., 1970, 'A Configuration of Indian Poverty', *Reserve Bank of India Bulletin*, January.

Okeibunor, J.C., 1995, 'Traditional Institutions and Social Mobilization in Rural Areas', in E. Eboh; C. Okoye and D. Ayichi, eds., *Rural Development in Nigeria: Concept, Processes and Prospects*, Enugu, Auto-Century Pub.

Okoli, C., 1992, 'Nigeria: Social Implications of SAPs in Africa', in N. Hall, ed., *Workshop Report: The Social Implications of Structural Adjustment Programmes in Africa*, Proceedings of a Workshop held at University of Zimbabwe, Harare: School of Social Work and International Association of Schools of Social Work.

Okoye, U.O. and Echezona I., 2000, 'Increased Economic Responsibilities of Child-Bearing Rural Women: the SAP experience in Nigeria', in E. E Anugwom; V. Okeke; R. Asogwa and I. Obasi, eds., *Social Sciences: Issues and Perspectives*, Nsukka: Fulladu.

Okupe, L., 1997, 'The Construction Process: Methods & Cost Implications', paper presented at the Workshop on Implementing the NHF, Lagos, October 11.

Olomolaiye, F., 1986, Research Methods and Statistics, Jos: Fab Anieh.

Onah, F., 2000, 'Contemporary Issues in Nigerian Public Administration: Foundations of Civil Service Reforms', in E.E Anugwom et al., eds.

Palmer, I., 1992, 'Gender Equity and Economic Efficiency in Adjustment Programmes', in H. Afshar and C. Dennis, eds., *Women and Adjustment Policies in the Third World*, London: Macmillan.

Pusic, E., 1972, *Social Welfare and Social Development*, The Hague: Mouton.

Rakesh, M., Wagner W.; and Garcia J., 1981, 'Measuring Urban Malnutrition and Poverty: A Case Study of Bogota and Cali Colombia', *World Bank Staff Working Paper*, No. 447.

Ravallion, M., 1994, *Poverty Comparisons*, Chur: Harwood Academic Pub.

Ravallion, M. and Chaudhuri S., 1996, 'Risk and Insurance in Village India: Comment', *Econometrica*, Vol. 66.

Reutlinger, S. and Selowsky M., 1976, *Malnutrition and Poverty*, Baltimore: John Hopkins University Press.

Sahlins, M., 1972, 'Stone Age Economics', quoted in *The Courier*, 1994, No. 143, January-February.

Sakamoto, Y., ed., 1994, *Global Transformations: Challenges to the State System*, Tokyo: United Nations University Press.

Sen, A., 1987, *The Standard of Living*, Cambridge: Cambridge University Press.

Srivastara, D., 1975, 'Poverty: Its Concepts and Definition', in Poverty in Nigeria, Proceedings of the Annual Conference of Nigeria Economics Society, Ibadan: NES.

*The Courier*, 1994, 'Fighting Poverty', No. 143, January-February.

The Federal Military Government of Nigeria, 1992, The National Housing Fund Decree No. 3.
The Federal Military Government of Nigeria, 1989, The Mortgage Institutions Decree No. 53.
*The Guardian*, 1996a, 'Twenty Per cent of Mortgage Banks May Draw From NHF', April 21, pp. A13.
*The Guardian*, (Lagos), 1996b, 'Realistic Public Sector Wages', September 22.
*The Guardian*, 1997, 'Govt. May Pay 1000 Minimum Wage', July 6, pp. 1-2.
*The National Housing Policy*, 1980, Lagos, Government Printers.
The World Book Encyclopedia, 1991, Vol.15, Chicago: World Book Inc.
Times International, 1987, 'Babangida's Labour Policy', August 31pp. 14-15.
UNRISD, 1995, *States of Disarray: The Social Effects of Globalization*, UNRISD Report for the World Summit for Social Development.
Usman, B., 1985, 'Understanding and Resolving Current Economic Crisis in Nigeria', *Africa Development*, Vol. X, No. 112.
Vickers, J., 1991, *Women and the World Economic Crisis*, London: Zed Book Ltd.
Watkins, K., 1995, *The Oxfam Poverty Report*, Oxford: U.K,Oxfam.
Wescott, C., 1996, 'Civil Service Reform: Lessons from Africa', *Poverty* & *Development: Analysis* & *Policy*, The Hague: Netherlands.
*West Africa*, 1991, 'Housing Squeeze', March 11-17, pp. 344.
World Bank, 1981, 'Accelerated Development in Sub-Saharan Africa: An Agenda for Action', Washington D.C.: World Bank.
World Bank, 1990, *World Development Report*, New York: Oxford University Press.

# 10

# Globalization and Refugee Policy in Africa: Reflections on Contemporary Humanitarianism

**Okechukwu Ibeanu***

## Introduction

Research literature on the African refugee crisis has for long recognized a link between global political and economic processes and the problem of refugees in the continent (Gordenker 1983; Ferris 1985, 1992; Dowty 1987; Lawless and Monahan 1987; Gordenker 1987; Gasarasi 1988; Loescher and Monahan 1990; Ibeanu 1990). For instance, until recently, superpower rivalry in the Horn of Africa was a very important factor supporting the chronic problem of refugees in that region (Makinda 1985; Hasci 1991; Waldron and Hasci 1994). In southern Africa, the bygone apartheid regime in the Republic of South Africa, its strategy of destabilizing neighbouring, black-ruled states and the liberation wars in which the super powers and their proxies intervened, were for many years the immediate causes of the refugee crisis in the region (Ibeanu 1990). Expectedly also, the momentous changes and restructuring that the world system has been undergoing in recent times, particularly since the end of the cold war, have impacted profoundly on African refugees. The gamut of these changes may be called globalization (Aina 1996).

In spite of these changes, the crisis of displacement in Africa remains enormous. Of 22,729,000 people who fell under the mandate of the United Nations High Commissioner for Refugees (UNHCR) by the first of January, 1997, 8,091,000 or 35.6 per cent were Africans. Although the figure declined by about 2.6 per cent in 1998, the population of Africans that fell under the mandate of the UNHCR remained outrageously high at 7.38 million (Table 10.1). These figures exclude the 30 million internally displaced people, about 60 per cent of which were in Africa.

**Table 10.1: People of Interest to the UNHCR by Region, 1997 and 1998**

| Region | Total of Concern 1 January 1997 | Total of Concern 1 January 1998 |
|---|---|---|
| Africa | 8,091,000 | 7,385,100 |
| Asia | 7,925,000 | 7,458,500 |
| Europe | 5,749,000 | 6,056,500 |
| Latin America & Caribbean | 169,000 | 103,300 |
| North America | 720,000 | 1,294,900 |
| Oceania | 75,000 | 78,000 |
| Total | 22,729,000 | 22,376,300 |

**Source**: UNHCR, 1998a: 2

The persistence of Africa's crisis of population displacement in the face of far reaching contemporary global changes raises the issue of how globalization has affected refugees and refugee policy on the continent. To address this, we need first to review the way the problem of refugees has been studied in the last half century. Second, we should evaluate the conditions of African refugees as dictated by the prevalent global humanitarian regime, which has been shaped largely by globalization. This paper is, therefore, an attempt to analyse contemporary social policy on refugees and displaced people as shaped in the cauldron of globalization. It analyses the impact of globalization on refugees and refugee policy, and explores how this has shaped contemporary humanitarianism in Africa.

## Why Population Displacement Occurs

In the past half century, the dominant perspective on why displacement occurs locates it as a problem of 'forced/involuntary migration'. This perspective is based on a force-subject-migration reasoning. Implicit in it is the idea that force (war, ethnic conflict or religious persecution) acts as an externality on a person (subject) as a push factor, leading to a rational, albeit kinetic/coerced decision to relocate. This type of migration is usually distinguished from 'voluntary migration' in which the force-subject-migration matrix is mediated by a 'positive motivation' to move based on a rational assessment by the subject that life will be better in a new place. Here, force acts on the subject as a pull factor from the destination (Kunz 1973, 1981; Hansen 1981: 190; Suhrke 1983: 164-5).

The force-subject-migration perspective on population displacement has many inherent weaknesses. In the first place, it treats force as being of the same magnitude in all cases. We do not know if different forces in all circumstances or the same force in different circumstances yields the same result, that is migration. Second, it does not consider the different capacities of subjects to absorb or contain force. Third, it treats all displacement as involving relocation and assumes this to involve a movement from vulnerability to safety.

Furthermore, the epistemological principles of subjectivism and the 'rational actor' which inform this perspective are flawed. As a subjectivist outlook, it treats displacement as an individual matter, rather than a group one. This distorts the fact that individuals act principally as agents of social ensembles, and that the relationship between a social group and its individual members is a complexly structured one. Related to this is the problematic of the rational actor as the basis of social action. In this regard, 'voluntary migrants' are distinguished from displaced persons on the basis that they have time to assess the situation rationally, unlike displaced persons whose movement is coerced and kinetic, like atoms in motion. The problematic of the rational individual as the basis of social action leads sociological research to a search for eschatological (finalist) explanations founded on the motivations of the conduct of individual actions, rather than the conflicting interests of social ensembles (Poulantzas 1978).

For one thing, the subjective will and motivation of individuals need not take precedence over their objective distribution into social ensembles with delineable interests and practices. Individuals are located in these ensembles as their agents, and in the final analysis, the collective interests and practices of a social ensemble are not equal to the sum total of the interests and practices of individuals situated in it. For another thing, it is not particularly correct to assume that decisions are ever made under conditions of full information in which all possible alternatives are considered in a 'rational-comprehensive' manner. As such, neither displaced people nor the so-called voluntary migrants have full knowledge of 'conditions' and 'alternatives' in the destination before relocating. Also, to suggest that displaced people lack a 'positive motivation' to relocate does not help very much. The fact is that there is always a threshold for any threatened group (and individuals as their agents) beyond which continued stay in the current abode is an unacceptable option. Whether it is ten minutes before an invading army arrives or five years within which a wage level is incapable of sustaining a decent life is not very material. Above all, the distinction between 'push forces' and 'pull forces' as motivations for migration is also inadequate. It overlooks the dialectical relationship between push and pull factors. A push is at the same time a pull. Negative and threatening changes in the place of origin are assessed in terms of expectations and belief that life will be better and more secure in the destination. Therefore, we cannot distinguish displaced populations based on the push-pull matrix.

A proper understanding of population displacement in Africa should locate it within a broad socio-historical perspective at the heart of which is the process of state making. This perspective privileges the practices of social ensembles in struggle over force acting externally. Existing knowledge is inadequate for understanding population displacement because it pays inadequate attention to a number of social, economic and political factors that are fundamental. A central issue in population displacement is threat or perceived threat to group security—security of livelihoods, food security, security of identity, security from social exclusion, environmental security and, above all, physical security. These threats arise mainly from contradictory claims on finite resources. Deriving from this is group conflict. The contradiction of group interests inherent in population displacement means that social antagonisms from time to time boil over into physical conflicts and violence. When this happens, relocation becomes an inevitable option. The dynamics of group security and conflict are structured in the process of state making. This is because the state frames, focuses and mediates social antagonisms. Its role is always to keep such antagonism within the bounds of order, which is preventing them from boiling over into open conflicts and physical violence. To achieve this, the state must always rise above the interests of social groups, forging consensus and acting as a guarantor of the security of every group. By so doing, the state appears as autonomous, the representative of the collective and corporate interests of all groups—the people-nation. Population displacement is, therefore, most likely to occur in situations in which the state is unable to perform these functions. Notably, this occurs in situations where state making encounters serious problems.

State making involves both vertical and horizontal relations (Ake 1997). The first set of relations has to do with the imposition of domination over independent social formations by bringing them together into one polity dominated by the centralizing power. These relations include:

- the imposition of a chain of command;
- extraction of political allegiance and social surplus;
- making and enforcement of laws;
- transformation of the subordinated social formations into a coherent economy and polity; and
- elimination of the resistance of the subject formations to the hegemonic-centralizing power.

On the other hand, horizontal relations have to do with struggles for domination and subordination among constituent social forces in the emergent state. These find expression in:

- the renewal of primordial identities and solidarities;
- communal competition among subject communities for access to central power, especially competition among communities that were antagonistic prior to their common subjugation to the centralizing power;
- strategies for evading the state's demands and coercion;
- alliances and projects for local empowerment;

- cultivation by groups of new exclusivist identities and solidarities; and
- manoeuvres for forms of exclusivity by which the elite of particular groups and communities attempt to disable potential competitors.

These horizontal and vertical relations are to be historically situated in the establishment of the state in Africa, which has genealogical affinities with the history of global capital accumulation. Like all organic systems, capitalism has historically grown or expanded both intensively and extensively, the former usually preceding the latter. The period of intensive growth of capital was characterized, among other things, by the emergence of an integrated national market under a single central state. The intensive growth of capitalism, which occurred principally in Europe between the sixteenth and seventeenth centuries, is clearly distinguishable from the economic fragmentation and the parcelling out of state power as prebends characteristic of feudalism.

The stage of extensive growth of capital, on the other hand, is the stage of 'internationalization' and colonialism. Propelled principally by economic crises 'back home', it was based on a logic of accumulation with measured social transformation and minimal social responsibility. At this stage, there was really no need for the complete dissolution of pre-capitalist social forces, institutions and solidarities as in the stage of intensive growth of capital, when these were systematically wiped out (Zolberg 1985; Ibeanu 1993). Consequently, in the colonies there was a great deal of preservation effect on the pristine order in a new symbiosis with capital, especially where the pre-capitalist order supported accumulation without responsibility. As a result, the emergence and hegemony of the market-oriented, formally free and autonomous individual as the subject of economic and political organization was only partially realized. Thus, the vast majority of colonized peoples at this stage of expansion of capital, whether in the urban or rural areas, continued to exist as agents of primary social forces and solidarities. In Africa, the strongest manifestations of these social forces linked to population displacement are ethnic groups. Communalism also takes the forms of race, religion or a combination of cultural factors.

One problem with these primary solidarities is that they have a tendency to be exclusive and totalitarian. They invariably define people as 'in-group' and 'out-group', and lay claim to the total control of the lives of members of the 'in-group'. They became even more exclusivist and totalitarian as a new capitalist culture and solidarity, which tended to threaten their exclusiveness and contest the control of their members, assailed them. This was worsened by the divide and rule strategy of colonialism, which sought to keep the various communal ensembles apart in order to dominate them. Above all, the massive power of both colonial capital and the colonial state, which in many cases was used only to breach the liberty and well-being of the colonized, served to heighten anxiety and drive people deeper into the embrace of communalism. Paradoxically, this anxiety of the colonized had a dialectical character. On the one hand it was marked by a proclivity to avoid the Leviathan colonial state, while on the other hand it was marked by a predilection to make a fetish of its power and nurse a deep desire to inherit it on behalf of sectional, primary interests.

As part of its specific historical constitution as a moment of the global domination of capital, the colonial state generally did not exist as an objective force standing above society and holding its antagonisms in a balance. This is quite unlike the state that emerged from the stage of intensive growth of capitalism in Europe (Ibeanu 1993). Historically, the constitution of capitalism was always an authoritarian project. From the 'enclosures' in Europe through the 'conquistadors' in Latin America to the colonial pacification of Asia and Africa, force, brutality and repression, rather than dialogue, discussion and bargaining were the initial driving forces behind the spread of capital. However, once constituted by an initial act of force, economic domination becomes increasingly routinized and autonomized through the market. At the political level, the emergent 'community of commodity bearers will necessarily evolve executive power as an independent public force administered in strict conformity to the rule of law' (Ake 1985: 2). In this way, a 'civil society' emerges and political domination is institutionalized and legitimized.

Contrariwise, in the colonies, indigenous people were seen neither as the equals of Europeans, in the sense of being commodity bearers, nor were they integrated into a national market. Instead, they were perceived as occasional petty commodity producers and consumers of European finished products. At the political level, only the white-settler population, initially, and much later a few indigenous urban dwellers, were part of civil society and therefore subject to the rule of law. Consequently, the vast majority of the indigenous peoples of the colony remained outside of civil society and subject to the rule of force. This gave the colonial state a dual character. One part, a smaller part, was for the citizen, and was autonomized and functioned according to the rule of law. The larger part, organized under the rubric of Native Authority, existed for the colonial subjects, who were organized into communal groups, and functioned principally to conquer and keep these native-subjects down (Mamdani 1996). In this part of the colonial state, state violence reigned supreme. Unfortunately, at independence it was the Native Authority part of the colonial state, rather than the civil authority part that survived. Because it was never really accepted by most groups as the guarantor of their collective security, its constitution and functioning remain widely contested. This contest is expressed both vertically in the relation between the state and constituent groups, principally communal groups, and horizontally in the relation among communal groups.

Because of its history, there was no question of evolving, routinizing and institutionalizing principles for the non-arbitrary use of the Native Authority part of the colonial state. In the post-colonial era, this state passed into the hands of a pseudo-capitalist class that was seeking to become economically dominant. It then became for its controllers a powerful instrument for acquiring private wealth, and a monstrous instrument in the hands of individuals and communal ensembles for pursuing private welfare to the exclusion of others. The major task of state making in Africa in the post-colonial era is to transcend this anti-democratic Native Authority state that is partisan, violent and sustains communal conflicts that lead to population displacement. The violence and aggression of this state is at heart of population displacement in Africa. State violence expresses the violence of the state against targeted groups. This aggression occurs in the routine business of projecting power, carrying out policies without consultation or negotiation or spreading terror (Ake et al., n.d.: 9). Often, state violence is used in support of the claims of one social group against those of others, rather than as part of the legitimate, institutional use of public coercion. This arises because a major problem of state making in most parts of Africa is the inability of the elite, usually purporting to represent ethnic groups, to evolve and sustain ground rules for the non-partisan use of the state they inherited from colonialism.

## State Making and Africa's Crisis of Displacement

Problems associated with the process of state making are at the heart of Africa's crisis of refugees and population displacement. The 1969 OAU Convention Governing Specific Aspects of Refugee Problem in Africa (OAU, 1969) recognized this early on, when it built into the definition of refugees factors like persecution based on race, religion, nationality, membership of specific social groups and political opinion. It also included such conditions as external aggression, foreign domination, events 'seriously disturbing public order' and the inability of persons to avail themselves of the protection of their state of nationality. When that Convention was adopted on September 10, 1969, most African countries had hardly experienced ten years of independence from colonial rule. Since then, the contradictions of state making in Africa have deepened. In fact, in the last days of colonial rule the emergent post-colonial state had shown itself to be as arbitrary, authoritarian and exclusivist as the colonial state. At independence, the post-colonial state was grossly unable to manage incipient ethnic and other communal conflicts that colonial rule and a bungled nationalist movement left behind. The phalanxes used by the elite to wage these conflicts were ethnic-based political parties and associations.

In Nigeria, the fission of the nationalist movement into three ethnic political parties—the National Council of Nigerian Citizens of the Igbo, the Action

Group of the Yoruba and the Northern Peoples Congress of the Hausa-Fulani—was at the heart of the crisis that culminated in the civil war. In the three-year civil war (1967-70), about three million people perished, while another 10 million were displaced. Since then, intermittent conflicts among the over 250 ethnic and religious groups in Nigeria have caused further population displacement. The lasting tension in the North between the predominantly Muslim Hausa-Fulani and predominantly Christian autochtonous ethnic minorities such as the Atyap and Sayawa is a looming source of violent conflict and population displacement. Added to this is the fault line between the Hausa-Fulani and a large population of Christian migrants groups, especially the Igbo, which was a prime issue in the 1967-70 civil war. The massacre of thousands of Igbos in the North in 1966 was one of the triggers of the civil war. Since the civil war ended, ethno-religious violence has occurred in northern cities like Bauchi, Kano, Kaduna and Maiduguri.

The most recent of these violent clashes took place in February and March 2000 in Kaduna Sate. It followed the introduction or intended introduction of the Muslim legal code, the Sharia by some Northern State governments. Zamfara State had set the ball rolling by enacting the law earlier in the year. Among other things, the law abolished prostitution, consumption of alcohol and barred men and women from sharing taxis, buses and other public facilities. Although the Governor of Zamfara State, Sani Yerima, insisted that non-Moslems would not be subject to the law, except where government-provided facilities were involved, there were growing tensions in the State between Christians and Moslems. In fact, many Southerners were forced to flee parts of the North as a result. Condemnations of the introduction of Sharia in Zamfara State were widespread among Christians across the country. The tension upped tremendously when other States of the North like Sokoto, Kebbi, Kano and Kaduna began to unfold plans to join Zamfara. The introduction of the Sharia in Kaduna State, a very cosmopolitan area both in religion and ethnicity, sparked the violence and killings across the country in February/March 2000.

In Angola, divisions among the anti-colonial political movements along ethnic and class lines were particularly responsible for the prolonged civil strife that has produced one of the world's worst refugee emergencies. The division between the indigenae and assimilados instituted by the Portuguese colonialists formed the undercurrent of the post-independence internecine wars. The United Party of Northern Angola (UPNA) formed to restore the freedom and independence of the Bakongo Kingdom, which later became the bulk of the National Front for the Liberation of Angola (FNLA), had its social base in the Northern Bakongo peasantry. The Popular Movement for the Liberation of Angola (MPLA) on its part, was the party of assimilado intellectuals, mulatos, liberal whites and the urban proletariat. Finally, the

National Union for the Total Independence of Angola (UNITA) founded by Jonas Malheiro Savimbi, who was a prominent member of FNLA and served in its Revolutionary Government in Exile (GRAE) drew its support from the Ovimbundu of the Central region (Kambwa et al., 1999). These social cleavages were deepened by struggles by the elite for the control of resources such as crude oil and diamonds. The inability of the elite to evolve and respect state structures and institutions capable of acting as frameworks for building consensus among these fissiparous tendencies left Angola in the throes of a twenty-five year old civil war in which millions of Angolans were displaced. In 1998, in spite of recent refugee repatriations, Angola was among the top six producers of refugees in Africa. By the end of 1997, there were 262,900 Angolan refugees. This increased to 314,700 representing an increase of almost 17 per cent (Table 10.2). In fact, Angola was one of a handful of African countries where there was an increase in refugee population between 1997 and 1998, and with the exception of Sierra Leone, which recorded an increase of 20 per cent, Angola recorded the highest percentage increase.

**Table 10.2: Angolan Refugees by Country of Asylum, 1997-1998**

| | End-1997 | | End-1998 | |
|---|---|---|---|---|
| Country of Asylum | Total | UNHCR Assisted | Total | UNHCR Assisted |
| Brazil | 1,300 | 130 | 1,300 | 870 |
| Congo | 20,600 | 5,900 | 20,000 | 5,900 |
| D.R.C. | 87,700 | 47,000 | 137,000 | 74,200 |
| France | 1,600 | - | 1,600 | - |
| Namibia | 2,200 | 1,900 | 2,500 | 2,500 |
| South Africa | 2,300 | - | 2,500 | - |
| Zambia | 147,200 | 26,800 | 149,800 | 29,300 |
| Total | 262,900 | 81,730 | 314,700 | 112,770 |

**Source**: UNHCR – http://www.unhcr.ch/world

In both Burundi and Sierra Leone, conflicts carried over from the colonial period have dogged the process of state making in the post-colonial period and have been central in the crisis of population displacement in both countries. In Burundi, ethnic divisions instigated by Belgian colonial authorities set the stage for successive violence arising from political intrigues, coups d'état, assassinations and genocide as Tutsi and Hutu politicians sought dominance over one another. The assassination of moderate Prime Minister Pierre Ngendandumwe in 1965, presumably by Tutsi extremists, created a deep cleavage between Hutu and Tutsi members of the ruling UPRONA party. Subsequently, many Hutu politicians in UPRONA joined forces with the Hutu-controlled People's Party to form the Jeunesses Populaires Ngendandumwe. Coming in the wake of the May 1965 election, these events marked a threshold of ethnic violence from which Burundi has never recovered. Other large-scale ethnic conflicts in which thousands of Burundians either died or were forced to flee their homes followed in 1972, 1988, 1991 and 1993. In June 1993, the resounding victory of the Hutu hardline FRODEBU party in both legislative and presidential elections deepened anxieties among the Tutsi. When the newly elected President, Melchior Ndadaye was assassinated in October 1993 after only 102 days in office, the country was plunged into a deep crisis which persists till today and which has led to the displacement of hundreds of thousands of Burundians (Gahama et al. 2000).

In Sierra Leone, ethnic and other communal divisions created and/or nurtured in the process of establishing colonial domination have shaped current cleavages and violent conflicts. The establishment of a Protectorate in 1896 brought together many ethnic groups of the hinterland and the Krio, a communal identity developed among the freed slaves in Freetown over whom the British had established a colony in 1787. The tendency of the colonizer to cast the Krio as superior to the peoples of the hinterland such as the Mende, Temne, Mandingo and Fula contributed to ethnic conflicts. In addition, the colonizer's arbitrary creation of Chiefdoms, whimsical imposition and deposition of Chiefs and exaction of crushing taxes, for instance the Hut Tax of 1898, increased disaffection and conflicts during the colonial period.

**Table 10.3: Burundian Refugees by Country of Asylum, 1997–98**

| | end-1997 | | end-1998 | |
|---|---|---|---|---|
| Country of Asylum | Total | UNHCR Assisted | Total | UNHCR Assisted |
| Dem. Rep. of the Congo | 47,000 | 6,000 | 20,000 | 1,100 |
| Rwanda | 6,900 | 2,300 | 1,400 | 1,400 |
| United Rep. of Tanzania | 459,400 | 259,400 | 473,800 | 273,800 |
| Zambia | 1,700 | 1,400 | 1,500 | 1,100 |
| Total | 515,000 | 269,100 | 496,700 | 277,400 |

**Source**: UNHCR, http://www.unhcr.ch/world

In the post-colonial period, these conflicts have been worsened by struggles for control of resources, particularly diamonds by successive political leaders who conduct political mobilization along ethnic lines. In the decades after independence in 1961, these struggles were waged between the Sierra Leone People's Party (SLPP) of Sir Milton Margai, which drew much of its support from ethnic groups in the South and East and Siaka Stephens' All People's

Congress (APC), which drew support from the North. In time, the military joined the struggle, itself divided along ethnic lines. In the 1967 election, the Head of the Army, Brigadier Lansana, an Easterner supported the SLPP of Sir Albert Margai, while his Deputy, John Bangura, a Northerner, supported APC. This was followed by successive political actions by the military culminating in some junior officers staging a coup and installing Siaka Stephens in 1968, who subsequently turned Sierra Leone into a de facto one-party state. All these problems of state-making climaxed in the guerrilla war began in March 1991 by the Revolutionary United Front (RUF) led by Forday Sankoh, a renegade ex-army Corporal who was jailed for a coup attempt by the APC government in the 1970s (Laggah et al., 2000: 81-84). The consequence of Sierra Leone's turbulent process of state making, particularly Foday Sankoh's war, has been unprecedented bloodletting, massive violation of human rights and population displacement.

**Table 10.4: Sierra Leone: Refugees by Country of Asylum, 1997-98**

| | end-1997 | | end-1998 | |
|---|---|---|---|---|
| Country of Asylum | Total Refugees | UNHCR Assisted | Total Refugees | UNHCR Assisted |
| Gambia | 5,400 | 660 | 5,400 | 1,500 |
| Guinea | 192,200 | 180,200 | 297,200 | 297,200 |
| Liberia | 126,800 | 25000 | 103,000 | 38,900 |
| Total | 319,000 | 205,200 | 400,200 | 336,100 |

**Source**: UNHCR, http://www.unhcr.ch/world

These high figures of refugees exclude the so-called internally displaced persons (IDPs). These are people who have been forced to relocate from their habitual homes, but who have not crossed an internationally recognised boundary. These people are not generally treated as refugees and so the UNHCR rarely have responsibility for them. I have elsewhere made a critique of the tendency to link displacement with whether victims cross an international boundary or not (Ibeanu 1990). As we shall argue later, the shortcomings of this tendency are all too glaring, especially in Africa where the state and its boundaries remain seriously contested issues. The numbers of IDPs in Africa have been growing steadily as numerous conflicts surrounding state-making have worsened. Table 10.5 shows that those countries in which state-making has been particularly problematic in recent times also account for most of the continents IDPs. These countries include Sudan with 2.6 million IDPs, Angola with 1.2 million and the Democratic Republic of Congo (DRC) with 1 million. As we shall also argue, one failing of contemporary humanitarianism is the continued insistence in separating IDPs from refugees, thereby placing them outside the protection of the international community and squarely under the same state which is responsible for their plight.

**Table 10.5: Major Conflict-induced Internal Population Displacements in Sub-Saharan Africa**

| Region | Country | Internally Displaced Persons |
|---|---|---|
| West Africa | Ghana | 20,000 |
| | Liberia | 725,000 |
| | Mali | 110,000 |
| | Nigeria | 470,000 |
| | Senegal | 5,000 |
| | Sierra Leone | 200,000 |
| Central and East Africa | Kenya | 100,000 |
| | Uganda | 328,000 |
| | Rwanda | 180,500 |
| | Burundi | 470,000 |
| | DRC | 1,000,000 |
| | Congo | 240,000 |
| Horn of Africa | Sudan | 2,600,000 |
| | Ethiopia | 15,000 |
| | Eritrea | Unknown |
| | Somalia | 350,000 |
| Southern Africa | Angola | 1,200,000 |
| | Mozambique | 50,000 |
| | South Africa | 20,000 |
| | Total | 1,620,000 |

**Source**: Adapted from J. Hampton, ed., 1998, *Internally Displaced People: A Global Survey*, London: Earthscan., pp. xiv.

It is not only the case that problems of state-making generate refugee flows. Refugee flows also worsen the problems of state making. As a result, state making and refugee flows have a negative mutually reinforcing interaction. In the first place, refugees bear the brunt of conflict and so retain bitter memories of deprivation, loss and death that can last many generations. In this way, social distance and political cleavages are transmitted. This situation is at the background of many revenge attacks and killings that we have seen in many African countries. In Burundi and Rwanda, memories of past atrocities harboured by both ethnic Hutu and Tutsi have been responsible for the persistent genocide mentality that characterizes politics there. Those memories are strongly expressed in the way the two groups interpret political events in

Burundi. For instance, the widespread violence of 1972 in which about half a million Hutu refugees fled the country has been interpreted by the Hutu as having been sponsored by the government as a continuation of a Tutsi genocide agenda, which began in 1965. They point to the massacre of Hutus across the country although the disturbances happened in a few regions of the South. On their part, the Tutsi interpret the violence as the result of attacks on Tutsi population by Hutu rebels, and argue that only Hutu extremists were affected by the reprisals. In the same vein, the assassination of President Ndadaye in 1993 is interpreted by the Hutu as a clear example of the refusal of the Tutsi to accept democracy. For them, Ndadaye was the first democratically elected President of Burundi. To the contrary, Tutsis saw Ndadaye as an ethnic leader who was assassinated by his fellow Hutus within FRODEBU who wished to carry out genocide against Tutsis (Gahama et al., 2000:96-97).

Secondly, in many refugee-generating internal conflicts, refugees settle just across the border, usually among people of the same ethnic origin (Clapham 1996: 218-219). Often, refugees link up with insurgent and irredentist elements and refugee camps become recruitment and training bases for protagonists of civil wars. For instance, the SPLA is known to be very active in refugee camps in both Ethiopia and Uganda, prompting Khartoum to describe the refugee camps as SPLA training bases and legitimate targets of military reprisal. In Central Africa, the ethnic affinities which both Tutsis and Hutus have in neighbouring countries like Uganda, Zaire, Rwanda and Burundi have supported persisting conflicts in the areas. For instance, the continuing activities of the Intarahamwe would not have been possible without the support it draws from exile Hutu elements in countries of the region.

Thirdly, refugees compete for resources among their hosts. This constitutes a double jeopardy for many of the host communities, which in most cases are among the poorest countries in Africa. It is paradoxical that the major hosts of refugees in Africa are not only the poorest, but also the major producers of refugees as well. In 1998, the top nine refugee-producing countries in Africa hosted more than one in every four refugees they produced. The figures are even more serious when we move beyond the major producers. Table 10.6 shows that in 1997, poor African countries hosted over 89 per cent of all the refugees from the top nine refugee-producing countries. The figures increased by over 2 per cent in 1998. The burden of hosting refugees for many of these countries worsens already dire economic conditions, which directly and indirectly feed into the problem of state-making in these countries.

**Table 10.6: Refugees Hosted by Poor African Countries**

| | 1997 | | 1998 | |
|---|---|---|---|---|
| | Hosted by Poor Countries | Total Refugees | Hosted by Poor Countries | Total Refugees |
| Angola | 257,700 | 262,900 | 309,300 | 314,700 |
| Burundi | 515,000 | 515,000 | 496,700 | 496,700 |
| Dem. Rep. of Congo | 158,900 | 166,500 | 141,730 | 149,130 |
| Ethiopia | 54,900 | 60,710 | 45,600 | 51,900 |
| Liberia | 256,000 | 485,000 | 124,200 | 257,100 |
| Eritrea | 315,000 | 315,000 | 342,300 | 344,800 |
| Sierra Leone | 324,400 | 326,270 | 405,600 | 408,900 |
| Somalia | 451,900 | 519,100 | 390,000 | 475,150 |
| Sudan | 348,590 | 350,190 | 370,500 | 372,400 |
| Total | 2,682,390 | 3,000,670 | 2,625,930 | 2,870,780 |
| % of Total hosted by poor countries | 89.4 % | | 91.5 % | |

Partly as a result of the deepening political and social crises resulting from state-making,, and partly as a result of global economic dynamics, the economic outlook in many African countries quickly moved from bleak to dire. Intensified struggles for fewer economic resources and opportunities increased social distance and deepened cleavages. Again, the net result became more violent conflicts and more population displacement. As such, political problems associated with state-making, poor economic conditions and refugee flows are mutually reinforcing in Africa. It is not surprising that the worst refugee-producing African countries are also the most politically unstable, the poorest economically and the most depressed socially. Table 10.7 illustrates the relationship between refugee production and a number of economic and social indicators for nine of the worst refugee-generating countries in Africa. Clearly, the table suggests that there is a very strong correlation between high refugee production and low ranking in the UNDP Human Development Index. The table also shows that low per capita GDP correlates strongly with high refugee flows, while refugee flows coheres with low life expectancy at birth. In 1999, three of the major refugee-producing countries in Africa namely, Ethiopia, Burundi and Sierra Leone ranked among the last four countries in the world based on UNDP's Human Development Index. The seven worst refugee-producing countries for which data were available had an average GNP per capital of about 283 Dollars in 1997, whereas the averages for Sub-Saharan Africa and the world were 500 Dollars and 5,130 Dollars respectively. At the same time, life expectancy at birth in the nine countries averaged about 48 years, standing as low as 36 years in Sierra Leone. Paradoxically, military expenditure as a percentage of GDP in Sierra Leone stood at a whopping 6.1 per cent in 1995. It was 3.0 per cent in Angola and 4.4 per cent in Burundi. Incidentally, the world average that year was only 2.8 per cent.

**Table 10.7: Refugee Production and Major Socio-economic Indicators**

| | | | GNP Per Capita | | | |
|---|---|---|---|---|---|---|
| Country | Refugees End of 1998 | UNDP HDI Ranking of 174 Countries 1999 | Dollars 1997 | Avg growth rate (%) 1996-97 | Life Expectancy at Birth (Years) 1996 | Military Expenditure as % of GDP 1995 |
| Ethiopia | 51,900 | 172 | 110 | 2.0 | 49 | 2.2 |
| Burundi | 53,898 | 170 | 180 | 1.1 | 47 | 4.4 |
| Somalia | 107,796 | N/A | N/A | N/A | 49 | N/A |
| Sierra Leone | 215,592 | 174 | 200 | 0.0 | 36 | 6.1 |
| Sudan | 431,184 | 142 | 280 | 4.2 | 54 | N/A |
| Eritrea | 862,368 | 167 | 210 | 0.0 | 55 | N/A |
| Angola | 1,724,736 | 160 | 340 | 12.1 | 47 | 3.0 |
| Liberia | 3,449,472 | N/A | N/A | N/A | 49 | N/A |
| DRC | 6,898,944 | 141 | 660 | -2.2 | 52 | 0.3 |
| Sub-Saharan Africa | - | - | 500 | 1.2 | 52 | N/A |
| World | - | - | 5,130 | 1.8 | 67 | 2.8 |

## From Exile to Containment: Refugee Policy in a Globalizing World

Globalization has scarcely alleviated the problem of state-making in Africa for it has changed very little of the political and material underpinnings of the state. If anything, globalization has made the problems of state-making in Africa more acute owing to its decompositional effect on the state (Ake 1997). Materially, Africa's position in the international division of labour has changed very little, as numerous statistics and global 'league tables' readily show. The implications of these for population displacement are twofold. For one thing, it means that Africa's crisis of population displacement will only marginally abate, if at all. For another thing, it means that humanitarian policy in Africa will continue to be dictated by extra-continental forces that control the global aid and refugee regime. This policy will increasingly disfavour African refugees and displaced people for it will be geared essentially to suit the interests of those globally dominant interests. In other words, the changes which globalization has induced in the international refugee regime will put Africa at a disadvantage. The strongest expression of this is the way these dominant forces, usually of the West, are framing migration as a problem to be controlled. Expectedly, globalization is better equipping people to migrate. In 1990, legal international migrants were estimated at 100 million, refugees 19 million and illegal migrants 10 million. However, both academics and policy makers in the West are casting migration as negative and a real threat to Western civilization because most of these immigrants come from non-Western societies, thus creating a context for a 'clash of civilizations'. In Germany, Turkish immigrants numbered 1,675,000 in 1990. By the mid-1990s up to 13 million Muslims lived in Western Europe, 4 million of them in France (Huntington 1996: 198-200). Consequently, in this era of globalization immigration has become a central political issue in most Western countries. Right wing anti-immigration governments have become a common phenomenon on the European landscape. The successes of Thatcherite Conservative Party in Britain, Kohl in Germany and the growing share of popular votes won by extreme nationalist parties in France, Belgium, Germany and Austria all reflect this negative framing of migration and refugee flows. Consequently, containment instead of exile is now the philosophy behind the international refugee regime.

The end of the Cold War created a widespread optimism that Africa's refugee crisis would begin to receive the attention it deserves. During the Cold War, superpower rivalries, which took the forms of proxy wars and ideological struggles, contributed immensely to refugee flows. Authoritarian political regimes propped up by the superpowers were also widely implicated in the 'crisis of exile' in Africa. There seemed to be firm grounds for this optimism. First, the 'peace dividend' meant that more resources would move from the arms race to human needs, including humanitarian needs. Second, it was hoped that the end of bloc politics would make it possible for the international community to conduct greater scrutiny of states. This would be particularly so for authoritarian regimes that hid behind the high walls of bloc politics to commit untold atrocities against their own people. The demands by Western countries for political liberalization as a precondition for continued financial support for their erstwhile authoritarian protégés in the Third World was widely seen as heralding this new turn of events. Related to this increased capacity of the international community was the expectation that the United Nations system would become more decisive in intervening in refugee emergencies within and between States. Third, there was also pervasive optimism that moral compulsion of humanitarianism would increase tremendously with the end of the Cold War. The wide adoption of the notion of humanitarian intervention seemed to many observers to signal this new moral capacity of the UN and the international community to intervene in refugee emergencies. The phenomenal growth in the numbers and influence of transnational Non-governmental Organisations (NGOs) working with displaced people also served to bolster this enthusiasm.

Events of the 1990s strongly suggest that the early optimism was perhaps premature, especially in Africa. Since the end of the Cold war, a profoundly different displacement dynamic has emerged. The decomposition effect which the post-Cold War phenomenon of globalization has had on the nation-state has also led to increasing internal ferment over the nationality question, access to resources, human rights and political participation. In the process, many contradictions embedded in the project of state-making in Africa have been unearthed, culminating in violent intra-State conflicts. With the increasing internalization of conflicts has grown the number of internally displaced people. While the number of displaced people crossing international boundaries (refugees) has declined considerably, the number of people displaced within their own countries has risen phenomenally. Superficially, this appears to be the result of sympathy fatigue or feeling of high cost of compassion in the publics of donor countries, leading to a reduction in the rate of acceptance of refugees. More seriously, the figures suggest that the mid-1980s, which was the period of intensification of globalization, was the period IDPs surpassed refugees. Indeed, what we are witnessing with globalization is a fundamental move in the international humanitarian regime from a policy of exile to a policy of 'humanitarian containment'. Formerly during the Cold War, the superpowers used refugee flows from hostile countries as a propaganda weapon, thereby overtly and covertly encouraging exile. In the post-Cold War era, however, a policy of 'humanitarian containment' which confines displacement within state borders and discourages refugee flows, has become dominant. As Bennett aptly observes, with containment humanitarian intervention becomes a form of disengagement for the international donor community by supporting populations in war zones, discouraging refugee flows and internalising the causes and consequences of population displacement (Bennett 1998: 17).

A second impetus to humanitarian containment is the phenomenal rise in xenophobia and racism in the North. The end of the Cold War and defeat of communism had raised hopes in the capitalist world for a new and more prosperous life for citizens of the North. However, the peace dividend did not materialise and for many people living conditions actually deteriorated. In the widespread political disillusionment that followed, foreigners, particularly refugees and ethnic minorities, became the prime targets of nationalist anger. The surge to victory of right wing and nationalist political parties in the West epitomised this period. Immigration became one of the biggest political issues of our time, the political safe haven for right wing parties and the graveyard of social democrats. Consequently for refugees, half-open borders and calculated kindness became their lot in the West. For the international refugee regime, repatriation suddenly became the best solution.

## Critique of Contemporary Humanitarian Policy in Africa

The principles behind current policy of the international refugee regime on Africa are dissuasion of exile and reduction of costs. As a result, there is a stark difference between the treatment of African refugees and refugees from other parts of the world. For instance, there are marked differences between the conditions in African refugee camps and those in other parts of the world. African refugee camps are known to hold as many as 500,000 people many of whom die daily of cholera and other public health problems. By contrast, the largest Kosovar Albanian camp in Macedonia during the Kosovo conflict had a population of 30,000 and none of the inmates is known to have died from public health problems. To illustrate further, by May 1999, the World Food Programme (WFP) had reached 70 per cent of its fund raising target for Kosovo refugees for the year. The corresponding figure for refugees in the Great Lakes Region of Central Africa was only 22 per cent and less than 1 per cent for Liberian refugees. Again, $1.60 was spent everyday on each of the refugees from Kosovo, while each of Africa's refugees received 11 cents per day.

There are three planks on which cost reduction in provisioning for refugees in Africa is built. The first is the portrayal of humanitarian assistance as gift giving and therefore the prerogative of the patron, the giftgiver. The second is the advancement of repatriation as the 'durable solution' for African refugees. The third is the internalization of displacement within national boundaries. We shall examine each of these planks.

### Eleemosynary and disaster-oriented humanitarianism

Contemporary humanitarianism, as it is applied to Africa, is flawed because it is basically eleemosynary and disaster-oriented. It tends to depoliticise humanitarian assistance, portrays it as an alms-giving process and denotes the refugee crisis simply as a humanitarian problem. This agrees with the orthodoxy of ruling groups in Africa about sovereignty, territorial integrity and non-interference in the affairs of states. For instance, based on this viewpoint the OAU Convention of 1969 urged that member states should consider asylum a humanitarian act. It also admonishes host countries to ensure that refugees do not act in any way that threatens stability in countries of origin (Article III) (OAU 1969; Ibeanu, Karadawi and Mathews 1990: 238). These have served the two purposes of shielding authoritarian and repressive regimes that produce refugees from censure, and to ensure that refugees are constantly harassed as security risks in the countries of asylum. One dangerous consequence of the eleemosynary conception of humanitarian assistance is that refugees are increasingly abandoning alms for arms. Everywhere, the Kalshnikov has become the credit card of the refugee, and the call to arms of the warlord has become more meaningful than the exhortations of the aid worker. In addition, depoliticised humanitarianism in many cases becomes a public relations stunt. Aid organizations and local recipients pose for photographs which are widely publicized. Beyond that, however, few people care.

Also, the prevalent disaster-based concept of humanitarian assistance coheres with a concept of the refugee that starts counting only when people 'vote with their feet'. Understandably, this conception gives rise to a humanitarian policy which considers intervention necessary only when people have moved, that is emergency charity to refugees (Harrell-Bond 1986). But a more productive use of humanitarian assistance should be development-oriented and should locate the refugee problem within a broader process of population displacement, a process which may or may not result in the physical relocation of people (Ibeanu 1990). The dominant tendency—which is to look out only for people who relocate, rather than for people who are displaced— misses a lot about the structural conditions underscoring the refugee problem. Humanitarian intervention based on this tendency becomes a mere palliative to cushion the effect of relocation and not a solution to the refugee problem. Extending our humanitarian attention span to all populations facing displacement, rather than just a sub-set of them (those who have relocated), is necessary if we are to develop an 'early-warning system' for containing refugee flows and providing timely humanitarian assistance. There is a need therefore to move from the use of humanitarian assistance basically as emergency relief to using it for long-term socio-economic development. For instance, it does not make sense that the United States is willing to give grain to famine victims in Ethiopia, which will take months to arrive, instead of providing money for the grain to be bought more quickly from neighbouring African countries, which will help develop their agricultural sector.

## Repatriation as the Best Solution for Africa

To be sure, repatriation as the best solution for African refugees pre-dates the current era of containment. It is one of the three so-called durable solutions in refugee studies (integration and resettlement in a third country are the others). Since Africa became a major producer of refugees, repatriation has become the 'durable solution' favoured by international refugee agencies (Zarjevski 1988: 21). It is even more so today. When the focus of the world's refugee crisis was Europe, the 'durable solution' was resettlement in a third country. Zarjevski notes that in cases in which the repatriation of African refugees was unfeasible:

> . . . plans had to be made to transfer the newcomers away from the frontier and settle them on land where they could become self-supporting through agriculture. Resettlement in a third country was considered only in exceptional cases, where refugees could not be integrated in the country of first asylum (1988: 21).

Although there had been past refugee repatriations in Africa, for instance 65,000 Sudanese (1972), 130,000 Zairians (1978–82), 150,000 Angolans (1978–82) and 80,000 Mozambicans (1974), recent repatriations seem to be more imposed, less voluntary and part of the policy of containment. Even the poorest and worst refugee-producing countries in Africa have been browbeaten into accepting repatriation as the best solution. In Bujumbura in February 1995, some of the major refugee-generating and hosting countries in Africa like Burundi, Rwanda, Tanzania, Kenya, Uganda, Zambia and Zaire, together with international aid agencies, met in a regional conference on assistance to refugees, returnees and displaced persons in the Great Lakes Region. The conference declared repatriation the best solution to the refugee problem of the area. A few months after that declaration, the UNHCR reduced its 1995 budget for the Great Lakes Region by $28.5 million. It is not therefore surprising that among the ten largest repatriations in the world in 1997 and 1998, seven were to African countries, mainly in the Great Lakes Region (Table 10.8)

**Table 10.8: African Countries Among the World's Top Ten Repatriations 1997 and 1998**

| 1997 | | 1998 | |
|---|---|---|---|
| Rwanda | 220,300 | Liberia | 235,700 |
| Burundi | 89,300 | Sierra Leone | 193,800 |
| Sudan | 63,300 | D.R. Congo | 62,400 |
| Angola | 54,000 | Somalia | 48,100 |
| Somalia | 51,800 | Mali | 23,600 |
| D.R. Congo | 45,100 | Burundi | 23,600 |
| Mali | 33,500 | Angola | 21,800 |

**Source**: UNHCR, 1998a.

Mozambique has been hailed as the success story of African repatriation. In the early 1990s, 1.7 million Mozambicans repatriated from exile within a thirty-month period, in a programme that cost the UNHCR over $100 million. The High Commissioner launched about 1,500 'Quick Impact Projects' involving the distribution of food, seeds, tool and shelter materials, and rebuilding roads, schools, health centres and wells (UNHCR 1998b). However, even this 'success story' is predicated on withdrawal by the UNHCR. In fact, the UNHCR itself ascribes the success of the programme partly to a detailed exit strategy (UNHCR 1998b: 3). No wonder that many locals complain that the aid was withdrawn too soon, a move that affected the projects negatively. By 1992/94, about half of the projects were no longer viable (UNHCR 1998b: 4).

Still, the experiences of other repatriations suggest that Mozambique was the exception rather than the rule. In many cases, refugees were repatriated back to situations that were profoundly unstable and unliveable—Angola,

Burundi, Rwanda, Sierra Leone, Liberia and Democratic Republic of Congo. In Angola, over 160,000 refugees were repatriated between 1995 and 1998, following the government-UNITA peace accord. But the situation has since deteriorated and new heavy flows of refugees are being recorded. The same is true of previous repatriations in other countries. In Liberia, the programme to repatriate 700,000 refugees had hardly started when a fresh, more bloodthirsty war began in 1996. Usually, the resumption of refugee flows after repatriation provides a justification to leave African refugees to their own devices as long as they are contained within the borders of their own countries.

## Humanitarianism and Post-conflict Peace Building

Since repatriation is now the best medicine for Africa's refugee problem, contemporary humanitarianism increasingly focuses on post-conflict peace-building. The concept of peace building that is prevalent is however flawed because it is essentially war-centric and limits itself to the aftermath of wars. But by concentrating on 'post-war' activities, it neglects processes of peace building prior to the outbreak of conflict and in peacetime. Since it is conceived in conventional war and direct conflict, this peace-building focuses on the epiphenomena of war. These include disarmament and destruction of arms, clearing land mines, repatriation of refugees displaced by war and monitoring human rights violations by the parties in conflict. This is not to suggest that these aspects are not important, but they are inadequate. By focusing exclusively on them, we gloss over structural conditions that, in most cases, generate open conflicts. Structural violence has to do with conditions such as exploitation, inequality, poverty, discrimination, repression and militarization of social life, which, as we have seen, are rife in the state-making project in Africa. The dominant conception of peace-building contributes to the militarization of life in post-conflict situations. By giving a principal role to the military in peacekeeping operations and delivery of relief materials, it elevates the military in the psyche and values of the people. In addition, there have been cases in which relief materials were used to sustain the military rather than needy refugees, thereby prolonging conflicts.

We think that the deepest threats to peace and post-conflict reconstruction are less direct violence and the epiphenomena of war as much as they are conditions of structural violence. This type of violence is indirect and is exerted through channels that are not immediately visible as violence. They are usually visited by ruling groups on underprivileged groups. Invariably, they generate confrontation between the perpetrators and the victims in the form of revolts, uprising and civil wars, which then involve direct violence on both sides (Nnoli 1987: 27). Structural violence has also been argued to be more important in understanding refugee flows in Africa than direct violence (Ibeanu, Karadawi and Mathews 1990). We think that peace-building measures should not be limited to conventional war and its effects. They should also address conditions of structural violence. Consequently, humanitarian assistance to refugees for peace building must target the elimination of these conditions in peacetime, as well as before and after a war. Unfortunately, the same global forces that control contemporary humanitarianism and post-conflict reconstruction are major perpetrators of structural violence in Africa. For instance, international financial institutions such as the World Bank and the IMF, which the UNDP in its 1999 Human Development Report alluded to as unaccountable, are today playing a central role in post-conflict humanitarianism (UNDP 1999: 9; Chimni 2000: 6-7). This is in spite of the direct and indirect role they have played in the humanitarian emergencies that African countries have experienced since independence. These institutions only function to strengthen the very conditions that generate refugees in Africa, namely, the debilitating state and economy bequeathed by colonialism. As Chimni perceptively argues:

> In view of the dominant role that transnational capital has come to play in the globalization process, the world is today coming to be divided into those societies which provide the conditions in which it can flourish and others in which these conditions are absent. The neo-liberal agenda recommended by international financial institutions has today acquired the status of a truth ... Today, in the wake of decolonisation and the collapse of the socialist world, the Third World is to be reconverted into productivity even if it takes humanitarian interventions and wars. Thus, among the first acts of reconstruction recommended by the donor states in Kosovo has been to put in place 'a healthy and predictable environment for private investment and, more broadly, an accelerated process of transition to transform Kosovo into a market economy'. They have called for the privatisation of state owned industry and invited its business communities to look for investment opportunities (2000:6).

## Internalization of Population Displacement

The inclination of contemporary humanitarian policy to contain displaced persons within State boundaries has exploded the population of the so-called internally displaced. The main concern of the international community presently is to develop a 'normative framework' for dealing with internally displaced persons. This has been the focus of the work of the Representative of the UN Secretary-General on Internally Displaced Persons appointed in 1992 (Deng 1998: 2). In 1998, the Representative, Dr. Francis Deng and his team produced a set of Guiding Principles. The Guiding Principles (GPs) remain the most comprehensive effort at global management of 'internal population displacement'. To be sure, the guiding principles are still very far from metamorphosing into an international legal Instrument. Still, they are increasingly acquiring moral force and are already shaping how the international community thinks of 'internally displaced people'. They therefore merit a critique.

The United National Guiding Principles generally follow the epistemology that has dominated the understanding of population displacement in the last half century. They define the problem of 'internal population displacement' in terms of victims and circumstances, rather than the process itself. According to the document:

> . . . internally displaced persons are persons or groups of persons who have been forced or obliged to flee or to leave their homes or places of habitual residence, in particular as a result of or in order to avoid the effects of armed conflict, situations of generalized violence, violations of human rights or natural or human-made disasters, and who have not crossed an internationally recognized State border (UN 1998).

This definition improves slightly on the definition of refugees contained in the UN's 1951 Refugee Convention in two ways. First, it recognizes the conditions of people displaced by the so-called non-political factors like 'natural disasters'. A good deal of the conceptual debate that has gone on in the past four decades over the 1951 Instrument has been about the expansion of the factors generating refugees. While many people have called for recognition of the 'non-political' factors and therefore expansion of the mandate of the UNHCR, others have tried to create new categories and labels such as 'economic refugees' and 'environmental refugees'. Second, the Guiding Principles go beyond the individualization of refugee experience that underpinned the 1951 Convention by recognizing the group character of displacement, albeit in a contradictory fashion. According to the principles, 'internally displaced persons are persons or groups of persons'. By adopting the notion of internally displaced persons, the Guiding Principles clearly set out to define individuals. At the same time, the principles speak of 'groups of persons', ostensibly recognizing that displacement also has a group dynamic. However, it seems to us that there is a contradiction in defining internally displaced persons (individuals) as groups of persons. We think that this contradiction arises from a hangover of the subjectivist and legalistic traditions of the past four decades, which creates a dilemma over the correct weight to accord to the individual and the group in displacement.

In defining legal persons (persons to be recognized as displaced), the Guiding Principles, like the 1951 Convention, are clearly addressed principally to politicians, bureaucrats and lawyers. In particular, the definition is conditioned by the concern of politicians to separate refugees from other displaced groups. Consequently, we have a definitional problem in which one social category (internally displaced) is defined based on the characteristics of another social category (refugees). In short, IDPs are refugees who have not crossed an internationally recognized border.

The Guiding Principles definition of displacement could be quite problematic in the African context, for State borders inherited from colonialism continue to be seriously contested. To define IDPs in terms of Africa's volatile boundaries could contribute to the growth of irredentism and 'affinity intervention', that is cross-border action by one state on behalf of its ethnic 'kith and kin' in other states. This would make the already unstable border relations in Africa even more precarious. Related to this, the definition could encourage the 'internally displaced' to seek to cross an 'internationally recognized border' as a means of getting support and assistance. This could heighten hostilities among African states, especially where borders divide ethnic groups and there is already a history of border problems.

Perhaps most importantly, the Guiding Principles assign the main task of assisting and protecting IDPs to states. On that, the Guiding Principles are questionable on two grounds. First, they assume that states can and/or are willing to provide such assistance and protection. This contrasts markedly from refugees for whom the international community has a principal responsibility. This could lead displaced people to opt for 'refugeehood' instead of internal displacement. The consequences of displaced people consciously heading for an internationally recognized border would be enormous indeed. Secondly, it is paradoxical that the state, which is highly implicated in the internal displacement of people, is given the responsibility of protecting its own victims. This paradox is deeply rooted in the notion of non-interference and sovereign equality of states, which fails to recognize that the process of state-making is still very much in progress in many parts of Africa. In fact, it seems that the mass of African people are far ahead of the international community in conceptualizing and addressing the problem of population displacement. While the people address the problem as one that is integrally linked to the transformation of the state (state-making), the international community tends to address it statically within existing political structures (non-interference).

Without doubt, the UN Guiding Principles on internally displaced people represent an epistemological advancement over the UN Convention on Refugees. However, we think that to problematize internal population displacement as if to constitute a separate theory outside a general theory of population displacement improves neither our academic understanding nor the legal framework for dealing with displaced people. In the last analysis, such a preoccupation only serves the desire of politicians to keep displaced people within their own countries (containment), separate from refugees (Ibeanu 1999).

Still, it is a well-known fact that Africa's internally displaced population is growing geometrically. As we saw in Table 10.6, the estimated number of conflict-induced internal displacements alone stood at over 8 million in 1997/98, excluding countries for which figures were unavailable. Sudan alone had an estimated 2.6 million people displaced internally by conflicts. These conflicts, which are embedded in the process of state-making in African countries, are being exacerbated by globalization, as groups seek the redefinition of the basis of the nation-state across the continent. In Ghana, land rights disputes between the Nanumba, Dagomba and Konkomba ethnic groups in the Northern Region between 1994 and 1995 displaced an estimated 192,000 people (Beattie 1998). In Mali, the uprising by ethnic Tuareg over marginalization by the central government led to the displacement of thousands of people in the Tombouctou, Kidai and Gao regions (Vohra 1998). And in Nigeria, conflicts over resources, especially land and crude oil, among ethnic groups and the state, as well as conflicts linked to democratization have recently led to the displacement of nearly half a million people (Ibeanu 1998, 1999a, 1999b). The same is true of most other countries of Africa.

## Conclusion

This study set out to analyze contemporary humanitarian policy in Africa as shaped by globalization. Considering the growing incidence of displacement in Africa, humanitarian policy is a very important part of social policy in Africa. The paper tries to show how globalization is shaping humanitarianism away from exile to containment. Ostensibly, resource efficiency drives this movement. However, Africa's intractable problems of state-making, which are linked to its continued subordination in the global system, means that the problems of the continent will increasingly take the back burner. Still, the situation offers African countries a rare opportunity to develop singly and collectively local capacities for social provisioning for displaced persons.

## Note

*Department of Political Science, University of Nigeria, Nsukka.

## References

Aina, T., 1996, 'Globalization and social policy in Africa', *CODESRIA Bulletin*, No. 4.

Ake, C., 1985, 'The Future of the State in Africa', *International Political Science Review*, Vol. 6, No. 1.

Ake, C., 1997, Why Humanitarian Emergencies Occur, The United Nations University WIDER, Research for Action, No. 31.

Ake, C. et al., nd., 'The causes of conflicts in Africa', Centre for Advanced Social Science, Port Harcourt, mimeo.

Beattie, I., 1998, 'Ghana', in J. Hampton, ed., *Internally Displaced People: A Global Survey*, London: Earthscan.

Bennett, J., 1998, 'Internal Displacement in Context: The Emergence of a New Politics', in W. Devies, ed., *Rights Have No Borders*, London: Norwegian Refugee Council.

Chimni, B., 2000, 'Globalization, Humanitarianism and the Erosion of Refugee Protection', RSC Working Paper, No. 3, Refugee Studies Centre, Oxford University.

Clapham, C., 1996, *Africa and the International System: The Politics of State Survival*, Cambridge: Cambridge University Press.

Deng, F., 1998, 'Flocks Without Shepherds: The International Dilemma of Internal Displacement', in W. Devies, ed., *Rights Have No Borders*, London: Norwegian Refugee Council.

Dowty, A., 1987, *Closed Borders: The Contemporary Assault on Freedom of Movement*, New Haven: Yale Univ. Press.

Ferris, E., 1992, 'Refugees', in M. Hawkesworth and M. Kogan, eds., *Encyclopedia of Government and Politics*, Vol. 2, London: Routledge.

Ferris, E., 1985, 'Overview: Refugees and World Politics', in E. Ferris, ed., *Refugees and World Politics*, NY: Praeger.

Gahama, J., Makoroka, S., Nditije, C. Ntahombaye, P. and Sindayizeruka, O., 2000, 'Burundi', in A. Adedeji, ed., *Comprehending and Mastering African Conflicts: The Search for Sustainable Peace and Good Governance*, London: ZED Books and ACDESS.

Gasarasi, C., 1988, 'The effect of Africa's Exiles/Refugees Upon Inter-African State Relations: Conflict and Co-operation: 1958–1988', PhD dissertation, Tulane University, Department of Political Science, .

Gordenker, L., 1983, 'Refugees in Developing Countries and Transnational Organization', *The Annals of the American Academy of Political and Social Science*, 467.

Gordenker, L., 1987, The Refugee in International Politics, London, Croom Helm.

Hampton, J., ed., 1998, *Internally Displaced People: A Global Survey*, London: Earthscan.

Hansen, A., 1981, 'Once the Running Stops: Assimilation of Angolan Refugees in Zambia Border Villages', *Disasters*, Vol. 3, No. 4.

Harrell-Bond, B., 1986, *Imposing Aid: Emergency Assistance to Refugees*, Oxford: Oxford University Press.

Hasci, N., 1991, 'Somali Refugee Policy and Development—An Analysis of Durable Solutions (1979–1989)', PhD thesis, John Hopkins University.

Huntington, S., 1996, *The Clash of Civilizations and the Remaking of World Order*, New York: Simon and Schuster.

Ibeanu, O., 1990, 'Apartheid, Destabilization and Displacement: The Dynamics of the Refugee Crisis in Southern Africa', *Journal of Refugee Studies*, Oxford University, Vol. 3, No. 1.

Ibeanu, O., 1993, 'The State and the Market: Reflections on Ake's Analysis of the State in the Periphery', *Africa Development*, Vol. 18, No. 3.

Ibeanu, O., 1998, 'Nigeria', in Hampton, J. (ed.) *Internally Displaced People: A Global Survey*, London: Earthscan.

Ibeanu, O., 1999a, 'Exiles in Their Own Home: Conflicts and Internal Population Displacement in Nigeria', *Journal of Refugee Studies*, Oxford University, Vol. 12, No. 2.

Ibeanu, O., 1999b, 'Ogoni–Oil, Resource Flow and Conflict', in T. Granfelt, ed., *Managing the Globalized Environment*, London: Intermediate Technology Publications.

Ibeanu, O., Karadawi, A. and Mathews, K., 1990, 'The Problem of Refugees and Displaced Persons in Africa', *Nigerian Forum*, Vol. 10, Nos. 9 & 10.

Kambwa, A., Casimiro, D., Pedro, N. and Ngonda, L., 2000, 'Angola', in A. Adedeji, ed., *Comprehending and Mastering African Conflicts: The Search for Sustainable Peace and Good Governance*, London: Zed Books and ACDESS.

Kunz, E., 1973, 'The Refugee in Flight: Kinetic Models and Forms of Displacement', *International Migration Review*, Vol. 7, No. 2.

Laggah, J., Allie, J. and Wright, R., 2000, 'Sierra Leone', in A. Adedeji, ed., *Comprehending and Mastering African Conflicts: The Search for Sustainable Peace and Good Governance*, London: Zed Books and ACDESS.

Lawless, R. and Monahan, L., eds., 1987, *War and Refugees: The Western Sahara Conflict*, London: Pinter Publishers.

Loescher, G. and Monahan, L., eds., 1990, *Refugees and International Relations*, Oxford: Clarendon Press.

Makinda, S., 1985, 'Shifting alliances in the Horn of Africa', *Survival*, Vol. 27.

Mamdani, M., 1996, *Citizen and Subject: Contemporary Africa and the Legacy of Late Colonialism*, Princeton: Princeton University Press.

Nnoli, O., 1987, 'Revolutionary Violence, Development, Equality and Justice in South Africa', *Africa Today*, Vol. 34, Nos. 1 & 2.

O.A.U., 1969, *The OAU Convention Governing Specific Aspects of the Refugee Problem in Africa*, Addis Ababa: Ethiopia.

Poulatzas, N., 1978, *Political Power and Social Classes*, London: Verso Press.

Suhrke, A., 1983, 'Global Refugee Movement and Strategies of Responses', in M. Kritz, ed., *U.S. Immigration and Refugee Policy: Global and Domestic Issues*, Lexington, Mass.: Lexington Books.

UNDP, 1999, Human Development Report 1999, (http//www.undp.org/hdro/).

UNHCR, 1998a, United Nations High Commissioner for Refugees By Numbers, Geneva: UNHCR Public Information Section.

UNHCR, 1998b, 'Going Home: Mozambique Revisited', *Refugees Magazine*, No. 112.

United Nations (UN), 1998, 'UN Guilding Principles on Internal Population Displacement', in J. Hampton, ed., *Internally Displaced People: A Global Survey*, London: Earthscan.

Vohra, S., 1998, 'Mali', in J. Hampton, ed., *Internally Displaced People: A Global Survey*, London: Earthscan.

Waldron, S. and Hasci, N., 1994, Somali Refugees in the Horn of Africa: State of the Art literature Review, *Studies on Emergencies and Disaster Relief*, Report No. 3, Refugee Studies Programme, Oxford University.

Zarjevski, Y., 1988, *A Future Preserved: International Assistance to Refugees*, Oxford: Pergamon Press.

Zolberg, A., 1985, 'The Formation of New States as a Refugee-Generating Process', in E. Ferris, ed., *Refugees and World Politics*, New York: Praeger.

# Part IV

# Higher Education and Globalization

# 11

# Higher Education Transformation and Academic Exterminism:
## The Case of South Africa

**Chachage Seithy L. Chachage***

### But You are Free to Teach the Determined Content!

This chapter is centered on higher education policies, which are increasingly being implemented by many African governments, including South Africa. The focus will be on humanities and social sciences, and more specifically on Sociology. The reasons for doing so are related to matters of principle, as well as the personal experience I have undergone since my arrival in January 1999 in South Africa at the University of Cape Town, given the attempts to transform it. Now, raising issues on the educational policies which have been introduced from above by the government or the university administration, is not necessarily an imitation of the ancient malcontents who, being suspicious all the time, used to say: *Timeo Danaos et dona ferentes!* - I fear Greeks bearing gifts! I say so because when I initially questioned the assumptions behind the 'transformations' in education soon after joining UCT, a 'colleague' cautioned that it was unwise to look negatively at the government's good intentions.

It all started sometime in January 1999, when a meeting of some members of staff (three from Sociology and one from political science) was held by the Head of Sociology. The aim of the meeting was to determine the content of an Honours course, which I was assigned to teach - Social Theory and Issues in South African Society. I was informed that the course would no longer deal with social science theories as had been previously the case: instead, I was to teach development theories, which in turn would enable students to specialize in either the Development Studies and Transformation (DST) or

Industrial, Organization and Labour Studies (IOLS) programmes. In other words, students at Honours Degree level were no longer supposed to be equipped with the fundamentals of Social Science, since the new programmes which had been introduced (as part of transformations) were geared towards responding to the 'job market'.

The whole exercise was definitely against one of the fundamental rights of academic freedom (the right to determine content and teach without any interference, subject to the generally accepted principles, standards and methods of teaching). I was to learn that the programmes had become a requirement of the university as part of the implementation of national policies. Arguing against this treatment proved futile, since the programmes had already been approved. This exercise to determine the content of the course I was to teach, as I was to interpret later (given the encounters), was an unconscious expression of what it means to join what they call in South Africa a 'historically white university', which still remains thus.

The reasons for becoming an 'expatriate' may vary among those who become so. But for some, it is the excitement of the possibility to take a challenge of participating in the 'African Renaissance', which South Africa has taken the lead in championing. The reality is different: it simply knocks one down like the stone which hit the biblical giant Goliath. Once in South Africa, an African 'expatriate' lives in a contradiction between the myth of a university as a centre of critical intellectual inquiry and the realities of conformism of those who have created programmes to safeguard their personal interests, rather than those of academia and human welfare in general. The threat of retrenchments, which hangs over some heads like the sword of Damocles, it seems, has given some 'academics' (who may be quite influential) an occasion to reassert their personal usefulness, regardless of the implications of their actions to the students and the world of knowledge in general.

Some may disagree with the following observations, as they lack the finesse of 'political correctness' which has become fashionable contemporarily. Simply, an African 'expatriate' in the historical circumstances such as those pertaining to UCT suffers the indignities of always being regarded (by some of his or her colleagues) as having been recruited because of the policy of 'affirmative action' or 'employment equity', rather than being a genuine academic. He or she has little or nothing of substance to contribute. He or she is regarded as someone who has taken advantage of such policies to move to 'greener pastures', since she supposedly comes from a world 'rife with poverty and calamities'.[1]

When confronted with a situation which dictates the content of what to teach *a priori*, you wonder whether you have become a showcase for posterity to demonstrate that there are Africans who have been recruited in an attempt to implement the policies of 'positive affirmation'! It is these experiences which have compelled me to interrogate the nature of higher education institutional transformation taking place.

## The Genealogy of Institutional Transformations

Now, there is no doubt that transformations in any scientific enterprise are historically imperative. The question, however, is, What is the basis of those transformations? What are they aimed at transforming? What do they aim to achieve as far as the issue of systematically ordered knowledge of social life is concerned? The 1996 National Commission on Higher Education (NCHE) and the UCT Strategic Planning Framework of August 1997 provide the answers to these questions. I suggest that to make sense of those answers, it is best to start with an outline of the 'world agenda' in the past twenty years or so as far as education in Africa is concerned.

Public policy debates, which still continue today, started escalating in many African countries in the 1980s. These were sparked by the 'revolution' in policy preferences which had emerged by then with the emphasis on the elimination of government regulation; reduction of taxes; provision of tax incentives for business; and cutting of welfare and privatization of the delivery of government services. These policies emerged in response to the world economic crisis that began in the early 1970s, and which had resulted in many African countries facing a balance of payments, deficit, high inflation rates, shortage of consumer goods, decline in export of primary goods and agricultural goods, under-utilization of industrial capacities, etc.

This situation was part of the global economic recession which was characterized by high interest rates, declining commodity prices and internal and external imbalances in the developed countries, which in turn created adverse conditions for the developing economies. For the developing countries, the result was endemic economic disruptions, which crippled production, distribution and financial systems. The 1980s, it was concluded, were a lost decade for African countries.

This crisis created a space for another model of development for these countries. A new turn in economic thinking and policy making began to take place in the late 1970s. When the crisis began to unfold, a number of analysts and decision makers, spearheaded by the IMF and the World Bank[2] attributed the recession to the predominance of welfare-oriented (basic needs) programmes pursued by various governments and the neglect of pure economic concerns. The perception that governments are the driving force of economic growth was increasingly being replaced by the perception of an increased role for market forces in the allocation of resources and a much enlarged role for the private sector in production and the management of the economy.

The model, which was being replaced, is what is popularly known as Keynesianism. The English economist, John Maynard Keynes from the late 1920s, developed it and British officials attempted to implement it during the second World War and post-War reconstruction. The fundamental idea in Keynesian thought is that capitalist economies systematically fail to generate stable growth or fully utilize human and physical resources because of reliance on market mechanisms of self regulation and adjustment. Accordingly, markets cannot eliminate economic crises, unemployment or even inflation. His thought validated the state taking a leading role in promoting material welfare and growth, and in regulating the civil society. Broadly, this thought inspired the macroeconomic policies, which were to be pursued by most independent governments in Africa, which advocated for state centrality in development processes. It was the same ideas, which were central in modernization thinking. It will be recalled that development plans in many of the colonies were introduced after the second World War.

There was another historical event, which justified further the replacement of the statist model of development. The collapse of the bureaucratic socialist states and their evident incapacity to reform themselves also provided stronger evidence of the unworkability and unrealism of the state-led development model to these analysts. Inspired by the long periods of conservative governments of Reagan and Thatcher, Keynesian ideas were increasingly being replaced by neo-liberalism (the free market capitalism ideas) of what have become popularly known as the New Right. The new emphasis was on supply-side economics (as exampled by what is popularly known as Reaganomics and Thatcherism).

Consequently, the new model of development which emerged became popularly known as Structural Adjustment Programmes (SAPs), which stressed the efficiency of free market allocation of resources and emphasized deregulation and export orientation so as to achieve international competitiveness based on comparative advantage. Thus, this model supported the notion of 'globalism' or 'one world', in which a single market for goods, capital, services, skills and technology prevailed. The new focus was on SAPs as the pre-condition for growth and implicitly for poverty reduction—since the benefits of growth would trickle down to the poor.

The World Bank published a number of studies since the mid-1980s, which have become the 'philosophical' basis for the so-called transformations of universities, which are being imposed by many African governments.[3] Fundamentally, these studies called for a restructuring of education, so that there can be a public cost recovery and reallocation of government spending towards levels with highest social returns. This, according to these studies, would promote higher efficiency and egalitarian distribution of education resources. They were of the view that higher education system should be made to operate at the lowest possible public cost. Accordingly, these institutions should exist by virtue of their being 'viable' and 'efficient'. By viability, it meant that they must be made to produce for the 'market' and pay for themselves. Thus, the introduction of cost-sharing. By efficiency, it simply meant that these institutions must be made to revise their syllabi to suit the 'products' for the market.

This was essentially an attack on higher forms of knowledge and research - specifically, theoretical knowledge. It was a call for the 'market' to dictate trends in universities. Thus, there would be a preference for professional as opposed to liberal faculties, and within faculties a bias towards imparting technical 'skills' rather than critical analytical ones. In other words, universities were to be reduced to the task of supply of the 'labour force'. The World Bank envisioned a stage whereby 'programmes or centres of excellence' would replace the present university systems. Rhetoric aside, this was an expression in a subtle way of the fact that universities should be turned to vocational schools in all but name!

## Transformations as Celebration of 'Globalization'

The immediate question that comes to mind when one looks for the answers to the questions I posed above is, What are the historical circumstances of the transformations that have been proposed in South Africa? NCHE answers this in terms of the transition of South Africa to democracy, 'which has interlocking socio-economic, political and educational components' (NCHE 1996: 27). What is to be transformed is the apartheid legacy of education, which had discriminatory, unequal and inefficient allocation of resources and undemocratic governance structures. This education system restricted access to Africans and Coloured. It was 'unplanned and uncoordinated with no national goals, common qualifications structure' and unresponsive to the 'economic and social needs of the majority' (27).

In this regard, the premises are that the development of higher education is bound up with the development of the overall economy. The crucial and determining factor is the question of employment and unemployment, since educational levels have an effect on employability. Thus, it would appear, the restructuring of the economy to promote economic growth would allow even redistributive programmes (such as job creation, housing, training schemes, etc.) for marginalized communities to take place. This growth is supposed to be taking place within 'the dominant feature of the late twentieth century modernization, what has been termed 'globalization'', and its 'multiple changes in economy, culture and communication in advanced economies' (27). The effect of this, according to NCHE is:

> [G]reater flexibility in production design to meet increasingly diverse global consumer needs obtained by using new computer-led technologies and employing more educated labour force in more participatory forms of work organization. These include teamwork, multi-skilling, flattening management structures and quality circles. Micro-economic strategies today are concerned primarily with adding value in production through innovation, by so-called 'smart' workers, new technologies, participatory work and continuous deployment of new knowledge (29).

The above has implications as far as the question of the social organization of knowledge is concerned. As 'a form of symbolic capital', productivity has increasingly become 'dependent on knowledge and information applied to productivity—and knowledge is increasingly science based'. The 'Knowledge society' is the characteristic of 'modern life'. It is in this regard that higher education institutions are supposed to play a central role, since they are the habitat of 'specialized knowledge' (NCHE 1996). Thus:

> If South Africa is to compete economically on the world stage, it will need increasing numbers of skilled professionals and knowledge workers with world-class skills to strengthen the enterprises. If South Africa is to build the necessary skills base many thousands of new or retrained professionals in the next generation must come from the black community (31).

Beyond this, higher learning institutions in this era are supposed to 'play a special role in creating national cohesion around citizenship. This role goes beyond the role of producing skilled workers and new knowledge' (33). Humanities and social sciences will have to make 'a major contribution to social problem-solving and socialization of new citizens with high-level social problem solving skills' (NCHE 1996).

The 'learning society' has implications as far as higher education and its role is concerned. Taking its lead from an European Union 1994 White Paper, the Commission points out that there is an increased shift from the kind of society where formal learning occurs once-off. With 'globalization, someone's education does not stop after one has obtained a qualification. Moreover, public and private organizations are increasingly taking on continuing education of their members as a major responsibility.

> This means that higher education institutions will no longer have a monopoly on the transmission of knowledge, which will become increasingly diversified, with higher education institution being only one of many organizations competing for the education/training market' (NCHE 1996).

If the higher education institutions are not to be marginalized, then the only alternative for them is to 'develop a wide range of partnerships with organizations in private and public sectors'. This depends on the extent to which these institutions become learning organizations (39).

The framework for transformation being proposed entails a movement away from academic insularity with governance structures and day-to-day operations. The government will have to become a very powerful partner 'which involves, through regulation arrangements, other institutions, bodies and agencies in governing'. Thus what is involved in these transformations are:

1) New state-higher education linkages, whereby 'the former should adopt a steering or co-ordinating role, the latter is more answerable to the demands of the treasury and civil society for accountable management and more efficient, client-sensitive educational delivery' (48).

2) New higher education-civil society relations, whereby these institutions 'adapt to the array of new demands for more recurrent, continuing and adult education, and more flexible modes of delivery (contact as well as distance and open learning)' (48).

Other issues are:

3) New higher education-economy linkages. This is related to the global economic changes and the new forms of knowledge production which require formal partnership between higher education institutions, state parastatals and private enterprises.
4) New inter- and intra-institutional partnerships. This is related to the question of 'more rational use of resources, while for teaching and research it could mean the establishment of schools—which could be transdisciplinary, interfaculty or transinstitutional. It could also entail reorganizing disciplines and faculties within institutions into programmes and schools, rather than departments and faculties' (49).

> Beyond the above, some of the other significant features in the transformation of higher education is the question of 'increased responsiveness in mass higher education systems' the shift from closed to open intellectual systems in the academic arena. Increased responsiveness entails an epistemological transition away from closed knowledge systems managed only by canonical norms and collegial authority to open systems which are dynamically interactive with outside social interests and knowledge systems' (49). In real terms, this has meant increased enrolment from a wider array of social classes and a shift in the learning function of the higher learning institutions. 'There has been a move away from the elite cultures of privileged middle classes (the traditional constituency of elite institutions) to incorporate the values of non-elite communities. Higher education institutions are now offering a greater mix of programmes, some based strictly on disciplinary knowledge and canonical norms, others emphasizing the development of professional competence in the workplace' (49).

Related to the above question of responsiveness is the need to change the traditional role of higher learning institutions—that of the generation and dissemination of knowledge, so that the 'provision of learning programmes that lead to the award of qualifications' becomes the major function' (NCHE 1996). Accordingly:

> The Commission proposes a programme based definition of higher education as a key method of delimiting the boundary between higher and other forms of post-compulsory education. Higher education programmes consist of focused sets of learning units/courses that lead to the award of a formal qualification at certificate, diploma or degree level. Programmes are by implication transdisciplinary and can be transfaculty and transinstitutional. (All programmes have a broad area of specialization and it is possible to use wider or narrower definitions of programmes for specific purposes, for example, first degrees and diplomas in engineering, bachelors degrees in engineering, B.Sc (eng) in electrical engineering, or the light or heavy current streams within the latter) (58).

Thus, redefining the role of the higher learning institutions.

As far as the research component of the same institutions is concerned, the Commission is of the view that given the 'globalizing' trends, these can no longer claim to be the 'leading sites of knowledge production'. Their pre-eminent role has been 'eroded by the development of multiple role of research and knowledge production outside the higher education system' (NCHE 1996). Their role has been eroded by multinational and private sector research laboratories, scientific and cultural councils, research councils and agencies and a plethora of individual and commercial organizations. In sum there are many other organizations, other than higher learning institutions, which are 'active in the research and knowledge business' (NCHE 1996).

> Thus, separation between what the Commission terms 'theoretical (basic) and applied knowledge, according to its view, is being contested by both the new forms of knowledge production and by new management models of research. The major change is that knowledge is not only generated in its traditional basic and discipline-driven manner in the academy, but in new forms in the market and community, and crucially in the interface between higher education and society'(77).

Related to all the above, is what are mentioned as changing education realities. It is here that the assumptions underlying this education framework and the orthodoxy of the World Bank are clearly articulated. The NCHE states that, the new vision, according to the government White Paper on education stressed 'lifelong education and training, opening access and improving equity, democratic processes, accountability, efficiency and productivity' (34). While it agrees with this vision, it is of the opinion that the implementation phase of the policies may generate 'tensions and priorities'. These are basically related to the question of public expenditure on education. According to the Commission, expenditure on education was expected to be 9 per cent of GDP in 1995/96. This it considers being already substantial by international standards. 'In 1992, for example, the total public expenditure in North America was 7.2 per cent and in the European Community the average was 6 per cent' (34). The amount of 1.1 of GDP, which was planned to be spent on higher education in 1995/96 was already substantial by international standards. Conclusion:

> ... South African higher education, with less than 70 per cent of its higher education budget coming from government funding, it is considered by the World Bank to be among those countries with a low level dependence on government funding.
>
> World Bank-led human capital theory posited that raising literacy provides a better return on investments, and indirectly productivity, than investing in higher education. Recent assessment of this policy and the new demands of the 'information' economy dictate that both are important.
>
> It does not help to raise literacy levels if this is not linked to economic growth, which in a modern economy requires high-level person-power skills. (34)

In South Africa, increasing numbers of students from financially disadvantaged backgrounds will add pressure on a scale hitherto unknown. Tension between rising social and economic demands and finite pool of public resources is experienced in every higher education system. A South African problem is that personal contributions to the costs of higher education have reached the ceiling for most. Response to these multiple demands will require various forms of public and private enterprise in higher education and possibly higher fees for those who can afford them. It will also require a reduction in unit costs through greater efficiency and more cost-effective methods of delivery. Increased participation and diversity inexorably raise questions about, and set up tensions between quality, efficiency and resources (38).

What I have attempted to do here is to merely point out what I consider to be the salient features of the National Framework. Some debates have taken place around these issues.[5] It seems that there are some that even sounded the warning that a slip 'into a generalist curriculum and research paradigm' is not necessarily the route to coherence (Bawa 1997: 49). However, the question is to what extent were such suggestions or issues taken into consideration in the implementation of such policies. My experiences at the University of Cape Town show that major efforts have been towards implementation. The University of Cape Town's Strategic Planning Framework, as demonstrated by its conceptual framework, clearly accepts with very minor modifications the National Framework. Its starting point is the 'global' changes. In the spirit of the National Framework, the UCT Framework reasserts the position that,

> Universities can no longer be seen as privileged points of access to knowledge, nor can a University be seen as just a repository of knowledge, nor has a university graduate any longer an automatic expectation of a single job lasting a lifetime. More and more, graduates' careers will involve many changes, including changes of direction. 'Knowledge workers' will prosper according to the extent to which they continue to learn and put their knowledge to work; they will be rewarded not for owning a static corpus of knowledge, but for problem-solving skills, creative thinking, and adaptability (Stratégic Planning Committee1997: 1).

The University of Cape Town is even able to predict the future by the use of impressionistic indicators, which lack a solid foundation of a sociology of knowledge.

The basic points of departure for UCT was encapsulated in the Mission Statement of the broad institutional goals: 'to be an outstanding teaching and research university, educating for life and addressing the challenges facing our society' (1). Thus the vision is to be 'a world-class African University'. The university is to be a multidisciplinary and interdisciplinary institution, an institution of excellence and relevance, which is responsive to regional and national issues; etc. The document stated that this process of change, besides making information available, would be consultative and a subject of 'rigorous debates'. One of the major goals was to make UCT a multi-disciplinary institution without necessarily 'on *a priori* grounds alone eliminating any field of scholarship from consideration as a possible degree programme or project'(1).

In meeting the national and institutional goals, besides merging some faculties, programmes were also introduced in 1999. The Faculties of Humanities and Social Sciences became the Faculty of Humanities and 21 programmes were introduced to meet the requirements of a programme-based education.

## What is the Big Deal in these Transformations?

There is nothing heretic in summing up the results of the above by stating boldly that the higher education policies fit squarely into those of the World Bank, even though they were tailored for Sub-Saharan Africa. Many governments in Sub-Saharan Africa seem to have accepted this position, and have been busy attempting to implement them with varying degrees. The World Bank/IMF policies, for many of these governments have provided a justification to deal with the so-called 'armchair' or 'ivory tower' academics (often branded as elite-type). That is, essentially a war against those academics that question the crust of post-independence privileges—those who try to raise questions that seek to transcend the existing arbitrary relationships. It is an attack on those who attempt to give their societies their images, by both reflecting upon and crystallizing the woes and concerns of their people—those who are marginalized, exploited and oppressed.

These 'institutional transformations' have introduced notions of 'viability', 'relevance', 'equity' (couched in the language of trade-off between investment in literacy and that in research and development!) and 'efficiency'. The tying of education to the apron strings of the 'market' is essentially an imposition of restrictions on those forms of knowledge that aim at raising larger social and political issues. These 'transformations' demand that higher learning institutions must work with the governments to produce 'person power' for the economy - an essentially technicist conception of education. The fundamental objectives of the university—scientific inquiry, pursuit of knowledge and the search for the whole truth in the interest of social transformation and human emancipation—are increasingly being relegated to the position of what cynics of institutions of higher learning consider to be mere 'ivory tower' ('elite', 'luxury' and 'esoteric') activities.

The African intellectuals and academics reacted to this situation by producing 'The Kampala Declaration on Intellectual Freedom and Social Responsibility' in November 1990.[6] This Declaration started by affirming the rights of the people; basically taking into consideration the fact that African states are parties to international and regional human rights instruments. The first and foremost to be proclaimed was the right of people to wholesome education.[7] Some of the other rights were those of freedom of movement for intellectuals; the right to pursue intellectual activity 'subject only to universally recognized principles of scientific inquiry and ethical professional standards of education'; the right to security of tenure of the intellectual community; etc.

Beyond this, the Declaration reaffirmed the independence and autonomy of the higher learning institutions from the state or any other public authority 'in conducting their affairs, including administration, and setting up their academic, teaching, research and other related programmes'. It also set out the obligation of the State, one of them being 'to continuously ensure adequate funding for research institutions and higher education'. The intellectuals also set out in clear terms the social responsibilities of intellectuals. To quote some:

> **Article 19**: Members of the intellectual community are obliged to discharge their roles and functions with competence, integrity and to the best of their abilities. They should perform their duties in accordance with ethical and highest scientific standards.
>
> **Article 22**: The intellectual community has the responsibility to struggle for and participate in the struggle of popular forces for their rights and emancipation.
>
> **Article 23**: No member of the intellectual community shall participate in or be party to any endeavor which may work to the detriment of the people or the intellectual community or compromise scientific, ethical and professional principles and standards.

The concern of the African intellectuals is, as the world enters the twenty first Century, of how to transform African social formations and transcend the historically - (national and international) formed arbitrary social relations. This is a very different starting point from those of governments, development organizations such as the World Bank, IMF, and the United Nations Institutions which were more concerned with the fetishism of 'globalizing' developments—global communication industry, multinational enterprises and global financial markets. The African intellectuals were expressing those more significant 'globalizing trends' which were being silenced or marginalized by those tendencies so dear to the hearts of governments and 'development' organizations. These were in the form of increased awareness of planetary social problems such as, individual and human rights (expanded from legal to the political to the economic—the latter incorporating the question of minimum material standards of living); environmental destruction and global warming; issues of inequality (gender, class, race, ethnic, cultural, national, economic, social, political, etc); and, peace and security.

What was this, if it is not a response to human needs and sensitivity to human predicament? But, of course, whether in Africa or the world over, not all intellectuals shared such concerns. There are some, in the Atlantic world, for example, who have been enjoying affluent styles of living from grants of so-called 'applied' branches of science and research, which is claimed to be an application and development of 'pure' knowledge of the academy.[8] There are those who are even employed by branches of the state and industry, thus making research a big business. This tendency for 'academic entrepreneurs' to emerge has over the years been accompanied by the prominence of centres, bureaus, institutes, programme-based teaching, etc.

In those countries, a successful academic, naturally, is not one whose research is 'acceptable' to his or her profession or relevant to human needs, but one whose research is capable of attracting the greatest funds or controls a research institution capable of distancing itself from the purely teaching structure of the faculties and departments. Financial sponsors are the ones who determine the form of knowledge, and accepted knowledge in turn is increasingly that of 'research technicians' or 'professional researchers' rather than scientists. For these 'academic entrepreneurs', the definition of knowledge has increasingly been restricted to the so-called called 'pragmatic' teaching disciplines/programmes, research and 'specific practical concerns'.

It is in this way that they have been able to proclaim loudly and proudly that 'in a such a worldwide informational economy, investment in what is called 'human capital' becomes strategic [and] universities become fundamental tools for development' (Castells 1993: 66). They have further proclaimed that, as we approach the millennium, knowledge is increasingly no longer a cognitive appropriation of socially-determined material transformations for life processes. Instead, it has become simply a post-industrial force of production, since the real substance of knowledge is informed by the so–called developments in science (global cyberspace, theories of everything and progress in genetics and its aims); and the triumph of liberal democracy and a free market economy. The world is entering an era whereby cosmologies of the human subject are not the real thing, since technology and economics have fused/merged, appearing under labels such as computer economy, electronic, services, information, etc. In sum, it is an era of the celebration of the end of history (as Francis Fukuyama would put it), even though all other histories are excluded.

Popular, academic and political thinking in Africa has increasingly ceased to debate on emancipatory politics—those politics which would lead to the transformation of societies so that we reach a stage where one's humanity is not contested. Permanent critique of reality from the point of view of liberation from domination and exploitation in all their forms has become less fashionable. The most fashionable debates are those around issues on how our African countries are being 'globalized'. It is more the dominance of a universalistic cult of a programme of desired goals (simply right wing utopianism) than an empirically supported understanding of more general trends with regard to the various activities regionally and internationally.

Simply, our knowledge can only be as good as the questions we ask. 'Globalization', as a central concept in contemporary thinking, has a pedigree traceable to the 'civilization analysts'—'modernization' and 'post-modernist' analyses of the transition of human societies. It is those theories, which almost always implied the universalization process they explain. It is supposed to be a process which is directly a consequence of the expansion of the Atlantic culture, within particular patterns of capitalist accumulation/expansion. Globalization is simply an answer to welfarism, nationalism, socialism, and so on.

It is this euphoria of post-this–and-that and globalization, which is ahistorical, reifies facts and fetishizes systems of empiricism; a euphoria celebrating the dehumanization and desocialization of relationships which some academics have also internalized in Africa. This 'fine' tradition was already becoming dominant by the 1980s. Increasingly, meritocracy was becoming dominant in the 1980s rather than a search for knowledge and truth - among both students and academics. This was a time when even the concept of a university as faculty was being transformed to that of the administration being the university and faculties becoming mere subsidiaries, à la business organizations! Traditionally, the faculty has always been the university, while the administration has played a supportive role.

With meritocracy, it became a matter of the pursuit and provision of degrees and certificates. Career advancement became the norm to the extent that it was even possible to marginalize good scholarship and research. This opportunity thus provided for some academics an excuse for pursuing private interests to the neglect of public and social responsibilities. Increasingly there arose a category of academics who began to live off the academy rather than for it. The university had become a way of getting ahead in the world economically or otherwise, since there is a market of donors, NGOs, international donor organizations, local and international consulting firms, etc., to which one can vend his or her skills. Exploiting the human predicament has become the norm among these. In the name of responding to international imperatives, these academicians have accepted the transformation of education from outside the academia (given the 'findings' of some consultants—including themselves or some 'international' organizations).

The National Framework itself does not conceptualize the problems facing the education sector in terms of the problems facing South Africa, including their history of emergence and becoming; but with what it considers to be a transition which is in turn posing new challenges as far as participation in the global economy is concerned (termed new technologies and expanding opportunities). It is a question of how to prescribe educational policies that will make it possible to have a curriculum, which will enable the country to participate in such an economy. Nothing is said in terms of the forms of knowledge, for example, which had been predominant during apartheid, and the actual role that the education and higher learning institutions played. What type of education existed then? What type of history, sociology, economics, psychology, biology, etc. was being taught? To what extent did these reinforce the social, economic and political relations? There is a resounding silence with regard to these questions. There is also hardly anything said about how higher education is supposed to contribute to dealing with problems related to health and sanitation, disease, misery, unemployment, displacement, landlessness, shelterlessness, social exclusion, alienation, violence, coercion, domination, injustice, delinquency, corruption in public authorities and among the rich, racism and prejudices, imbalances and inequalities (related to gender, class, age, ethnicity, power and distribution, etc.), misinformation (so-called news management as a result of the information revolution), environmental degradation, conflicts, and so forth.

The fact is, constant changes/transformations are not only necessary but also imperative, especially in the education sector. The issue is, if the conceptualization of changes in the education sector was to start from the point of view of the problems facing people and their history, the questions posed would have related to how to make it effective in improving the human condition. That is, how to bring about forms of knowledge that enhance the chances of mutual survival by dealing with the problems just mentioned. To pose questions from that point of view is in essence to take account of the fact that the revolution in communication (so beloved by the 'market fundamentalists' in justifying their arguments on alternative forms of knowledge) is the one that has ignited the awareness of the planetary problems. Therefore, the fundamental issue would have been to what extent is the education system playing its role in dealing with societal problems?

From this point of view, the search would be for an education system that equips people with the necessary tools to master/mistress knowledge and concepts necessary for the survival of the human race in this rapidly changing world. In other words, those that enhance an emancipatory and transformational mode of social activity. Such forms of knowledge and concepts definitely go above and beyond the 'job market', or 'person power requirements'. 'Job markets' as a conventional assumption underlying the role of education, are a constriction on creativity, scientific inquiry, and fidelity to the pursuit of truth and intellectual freedom in general.

Important to note here is the fact that the so-called response to the 'market forces' and 'global forces' for some of the academia is nothing more than an ideologically determined position, which would like to turn the university into a supermarket without any long-term considerations of the national and societal needs in general. The historical conditions in Africa and South Africa in particular require an unhampered greater ferment of ideas and a sense of commitment to the interest of social transformation and human emancipation today more than ever before.

Taking such a position as far as education transformations are concerned means viewing education from the point of view of fundamental human rights. An equitable provision of education cannot be guaranteed if the link of the education institutions and the society is simply a matter of finance. There is nothing like 'free' education or social services in the world, as those who advocate the commercialization or privatization of social services want the world to believe. All governments in the world derive their revenue from taxation. It is for this reason that they are supposed to be responsible for the provision of social services and infrastructure. In other words, it is society and not governments, which finance social services. Therefore, to talk of free services is to mask the truth. To talk about government assistance (or so-called cost-sharing) to those who cannot afford, is a mystification since those who cannot pay are the majority, to the extent that it makes no difference if the minority who can pay does not pay. Simply, an education system which treats knowledge production as an industry tends to reinforce inequalities and hierarchization.

## Transformations and Sociology at UCT

There were 26 programmes proposals by May 1998 for the Faculty of Humanities, of which 21 were established by early 1999. All the programmes which were established had seemingly fulfilled the conditions set by the University Framework - educational objectives, outcomes, quality assurance, streams, marketability, etc. These were supposed to be linked to high-level and budget planning based on student demand, planned enrolment, etc. What does the actual reality show? The first thing to note is that there has generally been a shift in student profile in that the number of black students has dropped (of course, there has been a drop in enrolment of students in the country in general). What is characteristic about the enrolment in the Faculty of Humanities at UCT, is the fact that there are fewer students from what are termed 'disadvantaged' groups, but their 'preparedness' is higher than the white students. There is to some extent a number of students from outside South Africa (especially Zimbabwe). It is further reported that about 90 per cent of the students are concentrated in five 'programmes'. Table 11.1 shows the distribution among those programmes.

There are other programmes that did not fare badly, such as B.A Fine Art (68 students) Music and Social Work (separate figures for first years were not available by then), according to one of the participants in the enrolment exercise. There is a dramatic drop of figures of students in the rest of the programmes, to the extent that some have almost no students at all.

**Table 11.1: Faculty of Humanities 1999–Stream+Programme Enrolment (22/03/99)**

| Programme | Stream |
|---|---|
| Cultural & Literary Studies | 178 |
| English Studies | 33 |
| African, Colonial & Postcolonial Literature and Culture | 2 |
| European and Mediterranean Studies | 6 |
| Film, Media and Visual Studies | 137 |
| Law and Humanities | 149 |
| Law, Politics and History | 72 |
| Law and Psychology | 26 |
| Law, Psychology and Economics | 16 |
| Law, Philosophy and Language | 35 |
| Industrial, Organization & Labour Studies | 119 |
| Labour, Industry and Management | 7 |
| Labour, Industry and Management Extended | 29 |
| Industrial Restructuring and Industrial Policy | 1 |
| Industrial Organization, Psychology and Industrial Relations | 43 |
| Human Resource Management | 39 |
| Economics (BsocSc) | 96 |
| General Economics | 21 |
| General Economics Extended | 52 |
| Philosophy, Politics and economics | 22 |
| Labour and Development | 1 |
| Psychological Studies | 96 |

**Source**: Minutes of Faculty of Humanities Board, March 25, 1999.

The same academic, who participated in the enrolment exercise, reported in a meeting of the Sociology Department that most students had two concerns as far as choice of their programmes was concerned. One was whether the degree was transferable to Europe, which is why most of the students desire to have a degree, which would enable them to work outside South Africa. Put crudely, what it means is whether the degree was responding to the needs of Europe and not South Africa! The other was whether it would lead to public or private sector employment. According to him, many students did not want to have anything to do with the public sector. He also noted that in some ways, students were concerned with keeping some of the traditional 'specializations'. One could interpret this to mean that students chose courses that had more relevance for Europe and were anti-public service (those that did not have anything to do with working for the public)!

There has been a significant drop of enrolment from 'disadvantaged' groups. This is very significant (a phenomenon observable in virtually all universities). It simply demonstrates the fact that marketization of university education and issues of equity are incompatible. Higher education is very expensive anywhere in the world. It is only the minorities who are rich and can pay who can afford it. The majorities who are below the 'poverty line' cannot afford it! Moreover, the preference for a degree that leads one to go to Europe implies that 'programmes' which are marketable are those which are preferred by the 'advantaged'.

What is more significant in virtually all the programmes is the fact that they do not necessarily meet the requirements of transdisplinarity or transfaculty. What the designers of the programmes have done is to selectively put together two or more disciplines and close all possibilities of students crossing those boundaries. Thus, a student who is doing Law and Psychology, for example, cannot have an option to take a course in sociology or gender studies. Rather than open up more options, these programmes narrowed the choices! Then, of course, the programmes are designed in the same manner as discipline-based departments, with all the streams. One wonders why are departments (with Heads) and programmes (with Co-ordinators) operating simultaneously? Isn't this a contradiction in terms?

As a result of the establishment of these programmes, the discipline of Sociology is supposed to be among the main losers as far as enrolment of students is concerned. Sociology courses appear under two programmes: Industrial Organization and Labour Studies (IOLS, with 119) and Development and Social Transformation (DST, which got a total of 29 students). In the former, it is offering only courses that have traditionally been taught as part of industrial sociology. In the latter, it is courses dealing with development theories.

Thus, with the establishment of these programmes, all courses dealing with social issues in general and social problems in particular have been abolished. Not only that, but even those courses which used to deal with social science theories have virtually been scrapped. In reality, *the establishment of programmes has meant the abolition of sociology as a discipline.* This is not accidental at all. One of the things I have come to learn is the fact that those who participated in the establishment of those programmes which are supposed to have a 'sociological component' from the Sociology Department, do not have a sociological background as such. They have a background in economics and development studies, respectively![9] More interesting is the fact that a sociology-based programme by one who has such a background was rejected for not having strong justifications!

Sociology departments in other higher institutions of learning of South Africa have remained with a substantial number of enrolments (within the general trends of drops in enrolment). Now, I am not trying to suggest that sociology would have been more 'marketable' for UCT than these programmes. Nor am I necessarily advocating for narrow disciplinary specialization or defence of the status quo. My concern is with the implications of abolishing a discipline without regard to its societal relevance and the social epistemological issues of science in general. For the novices and those who are unacquainted with issues of social sciences, let them be reminded that it is simply unimaginable to talk about the so-called 'knowledge society' without a sociology of knowledge and historical sociology! It is sociology which has historically been influential in social thought, because of its preoccupation with the nature and first principles of social sciences (philosophies, theories and methodological issues in general), and thus being the focal point of debates. It has also been central in conveying into more specialized disciplines a sense of social context. In many ways, it has been traditionally working with other disciplines, and thus the existence of spheres (not in UCT, of course!) such as 'economic sociology', 'political sociology', 'development sociology', 'social policy and welfare', 'rural sociology', 'urban sociology', 'sociology of crime and deviance', 'industrial sociology', 'environmental sociology', 'social psychology' the list goes on.

Therefore, any transformation process of a discipline would need to do so from the point of view of its development as historically occurring practices within societal and scientific contexts. For sociology, the pertinent question would be: what does it actually mean to transform a discipline, which ranges over a vast field—from philosophy of science to the microscopic investigation of bizarre forms of human activity—in order to shed light on the general human conditions and forms of social life? To what extent is the structure of the discipline limiting as far as the new pathways of production of knowledge are concerned? If the structure is limiting, could an 'interdisciplinary' or 'multidisciplinary' mode assist in smashing those limits? In this case, what does an 'interdisciplinary' or 'multidisciplinary' programme mean for sociology? Does it mean that one can not have a discipline? Does that mean a possibility of one being a Jack/Jane or Juma/Mwajuma of all trades and master/mistress of none?

History has never been kind to idlers! In case there are those who are unaware, these issues of 'interdisciplinarity' and 'multi-disciplinarity' have been raised before in an attempt to develop alternative modes of perceiving reality through science. In the West, multidisciplinarity ended up by bundling together 'haphazardly several present disciplines that have congealed as particular responses to the West's historical development', as was noted by Susantha Gooatilake way back in the 1980s (1987: 21-22). The result of this was the constituent disciplines (with their existing channels of perception) ended up leaving many areas of the physical reality unexplored. Thus, multidisciplinarity and interdisciplinarity do not necessary lead to a breakthrough or new structured knowledge:

> We know that unlike the assumptions of a conventional mechanistic view of science, cross flows of metaphors had occurred often in creative situations. Thus, especially at paradigm breaks, the intellectual elements that nourish a discipline constitute a surprising collection. These elements include a-priori orientations of scientists which encompass also mystical and 'extra-scientific' beliefs, modes, metaphors and orientations from other often unrelated disciplines and perspectives, as well as beliefs drawn from social ideas of every day.
>
> Displacement of ideas across disciplines has been recorded by many. Thus, the impact of Malthus on Darwin and Darwin on Social Darwinism, social ideas on organic chemistry (?) are few. However, it should be noted that although science in its growth takes its external elements outside a discipline, it is structured socially and a social perspective governs implicitly the process of discovery.
>
> Drift of metaphors from one discipline to another, a very fruitful source of new ideas should not be confused with conventional multidisciplinary and inter-disciplinary studies. Drifts of metaphors where it is valid could be a source of creativity (21-22).

What then, it may be asked, are multidisciplinary and interdisciplinary programmes/studies? In my understanding, each of the disciplines involved in a multi-disciplinary programme uses its own concepts and methods. It is only the general subject or question involved which remains the same. The philosophical or theoretical backgrounds of those involved and their conceptions about society may be quite different. Therefore, the outcomes of such a programme involve an interpretation on levels of each separate discipline. This is very complex in terms of comparison, since it is practically impossible to have a synthetic point of view, and even if one is achieved, it will be only superficial.

An interdisciplinary study/programme involves an attempt to deal with a given issue simultaneously from different angles to take into account diverse aspects of the subject matter at the same time. This is more united and more concentrated than multidisciplinary work. Here, it is possible to even formulate or share a theoretical edifice. This kind of programme enables a holistic, synthesized understanding of the issue being dealt with. What is needed in this type of a programme is some kind of a 'meta-language', a language based on a shared perspective on people, society (and its basic essence) and the question at hand, which will express the holistic view. In other words, a close relationship is required between the philosophical background of the disciplines and their ways of formulating scientific questions and hypotheses.

Being part of multidisciplinary or interdisciplinary study/programme/research presupposes that one already belongs to a discipline, thus contributing to dealing with an issue (in many cases practical) from different angles. In which case, such studies/programmes/research may be possible only at a higher level when one is already grounded in a discipline. In the case of universities, this implies the post-graduate level. In this case, they usually aim at the application of knowledge, rather than production of new knowledge. The history of programmes where research has become an industry demonstrates this fact. Programmes in many European countries have always been at the postgraduate level. I believe that if programmes must be established, then it should be on the basis of long-term national and societal needs, the intrinsic scientific value of the branches of knowledge in question and the programmes' expected contribution to the intellectual stature of the university before anything.

Were the above aspects taken into consideration in the formulation and introduction of programmes at UCT? As it will be demonstrated by the manner in which the exercise was implemented in the Sociology Department, the answer is no. Those who formulated the programmes in Sociology simply took what is popularly known as a 'human capital investment approach' à la the World Bank, uncritically. They were following the lead of the University executive and the Academic Planning Committee who initiated the move to programmes. This approach assumes that students enrol in courses that are in demand and are rewarded by the market. Therefore, students' choices should be the strategy for establishing programmes. But again, even in this regard, no research was conducted to determine what students wanted, or what the market needed or wanted. Unfortunately, experience in many universities all over the world demonstrates that students and parents seek degrees less for any additional skills than mainly to entitle them entry to higher status jobs, rather than to the actual content and standards. There is ample evidence from many universities which demonstrate that at times students simply choose the easiest route to degrees; thus more often than not, they pressurize academic members of staff to become lax in their grading. In which case, students' choice-based planning in many cases encourages 'fadism'. This, in the long run, is very costly, inefficient and detrimental to the whole enterprise of knowledge production.[10]

It is certainly very important to produce graduates who are employable. This is one of the fundamental roles of any university in the world. Universities should seek to impart skills which are usable in the labour market. However, unlike in the vocational training schools or polytechnic tradition which produce operatives, universities are primarily charged with the task of cultivating analytic skills and developing critical faculties/thinking in the students. In other words, training in professional skills goes hand in hand with the development of students' ability to generate ideas and engage in critical analysis. Once this is successfully done, then the rest falls in place.

It is with the necessary analytic tools that students are able to refine their skills and acquire new ones with a measure of resourcefulness, originality and creativity. In this regard, there are disciplines such as philosophy which may appear unusable to the superficial, but which are very critical to the students in all fields of specialization for the development of critical and analytical skills. It is inconceivable to imagine an environment with a vibrant intellectual life, for example, in a situation where poetry, philosophy, literature, aesthetics, etc. are simply viewed from the point of view of their connection to a 'national framework' or their 'marketability'.

A look at the way programmes were formulated leads to one conclusion: some individuals, without necessarily involving other members in the debates have established them. These individuals have done so, not in response to changes, but to the preservation of their own narrow specializations, in the course forcing other people to be subject to their narrow dictates. The programmes have been set up without regard to what does it actually mean to be multi-disciplinary or inter-disciplinary and the implications, as far as knowledge dissemination and production are concerned. The names of the programmes are quite attractive, and they are seemingly 'practically oriented'. In reality, they are a death knell to the basics of the scientific enterprise.

This is clearly demonstrated by the way the programmes were established—throwing away all the fundamental issues relating to problems of knowledge, philosophies and theories of social sciences, etc. What the Department of Sociology has done is to relegate the fundamental objectives of knowledge production to the background in favour of certain restrictions without involving all academic members in the debates. No democratic debates and principles were employed in establishing these programmes. I think, academicians have no right to preach democracy to others if they cannot practice it themselves. In the academia, undemocratic practices tend to breed petty antipathies, bad conscience and brutal mediocrity.

As I stated above, transformations in any scientific enterprise are necessary. To repeat what I pointed out earlier, the questions, however, are: What is the basis of those transformations? What are they aimed at transforming? What do they aim to achieve as far as the issue of systematically ordered knowledge of social life is concerned? What does such a process entail for a discipline which ranges over a vast field from the philosophy of science to detailed minute investigation of human activities? These are not bizarre questions, since, at stake in any discipline is an account of the transformations in methods, problematics and subject matter practices—including the socio-scientific transformation of concepts. Science is historically occurring practices before anything. In which case, one-sidedness cannot be entertained, since specific methods are required for dealing with specific contradictions. It is in this regard that it is necessary to sustain a pluralist conception of science which takes into account the question of unity in diversity in both method and subject matter.

Being part of a historically white university, the Sociology Department at UCT has since 1974 confined itself to teaching what is called general and industrial sociology, in response to the dictates of narrow technocratic social, economic and political circumstances prevailing then. In this case, transformations should have, in the first instance re-examined and summed up this past history (including the type of knowledge which was being imparted) and subjected it to a critique. The next move would have been to consider the historical trajectory/context in which it is operating.

Within the above context, another question that should have been dealt with is that of what distinguishes one discipline from another. That is: What is the subject matter of a discipline that makes it distinguishable from another, and how does it relate to those others? For sociology, for example, it is social problems and social movements, which have historically been of prime significance in stimulating sociological imagination. It is social issues, which are of central concern. And these cannot be addressed from the simplistic point of empiricism and the logic of the market.

By following orders from above, the formulators of the programmes in Sociology Department violated this fundamental point of departure. They have taken that the point of departure is the question of industrial and economic development in general. They have done so in response to development organizations such as the World Bank, International Monetary Fund, United Nations Development Programme, etc. These organizations, Governments and Development Studies per se have mainly concerned themselves with economic development. Thus, globalizing developments—global communication industry, multinational enterprises and global financial markets—have been the defining sources of the programmes. This has been done to the detriment of social issues. They have ignored or forgotten the fact that even those organizations, have over the years come to acknowledge the importance of taking into account issues such as social impact of economic, industrial and development policies in general.

More serious is the fact that they have ignored the real tendencies and issues regarding 'globalization'. That is the tendency towards an increased awareness of planetary social problems, which I pointed out in the preceding section. A programme, which claims to be incorporating sociological aspects and does not take into account these historical circumstances, signals academic exterminism. Transformation of programmes in this regard, must start from conceptualization of problems facing Africa and South Africa in particular; without on any account losing sight of their global context. To formulate a programme in response to the so-called global dictates is to ignore completely issues of societal relevance. Aimé Cesaire rightly stated in the 1950s that 'there are two ways of losing oneself: through fragmentation in the particular or dilution in the 'universal' (quoted in Hountondji 1983). The starting point should be the numerous social problems facing South Africa and African countries in general. To mention some: civil strife, ethnicity, racism, corruption, terrorist governments (both civilian and military), unemployment and labour exploitation, landlessness and environmental destruction, rural/urban migration, homelessness and displacement, crime and violence, sexual harassment, sexual abuse and rape, abuse and violation of children, alcoholism and drug abuse, etc.

All the above processes entail possession of adequate knowledge about social relationships and other factors given the societal goals or partial ones. This means, those involved in dealing with social problems must be well-trained researchers and analysts. They must be equipped with a systematically ordered knowledge of social life, which can provide an empirical and rational basis for social policy-making. The conceptualization of modes of politics and social life which would lead to more humane organization of societies is more wanting now than ever, given the generalized crisis (socially, culturally, politically, economically, etc). Such conditions necessitate the formulation of a programme which is strong theoretically (within a local and international context) and rich in fundamentals (from textbooks) and concrete research in response to societal problems.

Such a programme would have to provide skills and critical faculties among students so that they are sensitive to the human predicament and able to work in communities and organizations, while remaining committed to the pursuit of truth and redressing historical and contemporary social imbalances (inequalities and distribution of power). It would have to produce students who, besides being able to gather facts and establish the basis for policy formulation, will be in a position to put together patterns of action that have occurred with some regularity and construct explanation to help in the understanding of social relations and social behaviour. At the individual level, it would have to give them a wider consciousness of human society.

Within this context, a programme which can provide an objective analysis of the dimensions of social problems, assess their potential consequences for individuals, communities and societies in general, which can suggest strategies for dealing with them, and show the possible side effects of reducing the damage, requires an approach from four angles. The first is a sociology of knowledge-based one. What it implies here is one has to know the processes by which reality is socially constructed. That is, one has to grasp how and why one rather than the other harmful condition is thought to be a social problem. Related to this is a social anthropological angle. Important here is the one which has practical applications, mainly focusing on the links between cultural processes and economic, political and sociological ones. It mainly emphasizes cultural aspects of cognition.

Another angle is a social psychological one. This takes into consideration the ways in which people interact with one another, how they influence their groups and how others influence them. This angle, for example, should be able to help one specify how individuals' parents and friends, etc. influence them to be poor, drug abusers, gangsters, or in any action identified as a social problem. Finally, the social structural angle. The focus in this angle is on the way organizations influence behaviour. Examples here include: the impact of industrial and agrarian or land policies, urban policies, the electoral process, welfare policies and other factors which may explain why the individual is becoming poor. Often, such factors seem to have very little to do with the particular individual. The structural angle makes one grasp the manner in which social structures influence the rates of those things which are defined as social problems. It helps one to uncover the hidden/essential dimensions of society, related to distribution of conflicting interests and benefits.

Thus, such a programme would have to provide a comprehensive knowledge of how to study emerging social problems in contemporary society. The focus would have to be on basic concepts, methods, and theories for studying social problems and approaches to social problems from global, regional, national and local perspectives. Moreover, it would have to provide a comprehensive social theory/analysis knowledge which provides an introduction and overview of the full spectrum of social theory and which concentrates on teaching students how to apply theory to make sense of social problems and to offer practical suggestions for the improvement of social life. Other issues involved would be a comprehensive provision of historical, economic and political background for analyzing emerging social problems in South Africa and other African contexts; and a comprehensive social policy education which covers the full range of practical and substantive issues linked to policy formulation, implementation, evaluation and analysis.

## In lieu of a conclusion

What I have done in this chapter is to try and show the problems of transformation of higher education, as far as the question of production of knowledge is concerned. I have not taken to task the government's position on the role and mode of financing higher education. I do not intend to do so, since I fear that the so-called practical people will claim that I am being impractical. Therefore, I chose to hide behind the words of a former teacher (by profession) and President of Tanzania up to 1985, Mwalimu Julius K. Nyerere, which he pronounced in the commemoration of the 25th Anniversary of the University of Dar-es-Salaam in 1995. I feel tempted to quote in extenso in lieu of a conclusion:

- Yet, whatever the national difficulties, and whatever ideologies or policies have been adopted by current governments on behalf of the people who elected them, some things remain constant, A nation finances a university for its own national purposes. In doing so it expects that university to fulfil three functions, to transmit advanced (and advancing) knowledge from one generation of mankind to the citizens of another generation; to provide the educated and trained high-level manpower needed by that society; and to be the centre for the national endeavor to advance knowledge.

- This means that a University—any University—has to be relevant to the society within which it exists; further, it must be seen to be relevant. It must relate its thinking and its teaching to the needs, the aspirations, and the problems of that society. This is a difficult thing to do at any time, for the international environment is constantly changing the needs and problems of every developing country. Nor is 'planning' ever perfect! But at times of 'transition' towards a more 'laissez faire' economy, the difficulties of forecasting future needs multiply. This does account for the fact that even now some graduates from this university are finding it difficult to get employment. If it stopped trying to be relevant to the society the position would be worse!?
- In choosing to have one or more Universities, a nation and its governments have accepted commitments. At the minimum, it has undertaken to provide sufficient resources for the universities to function effectively. So what happens if, as things change, a government finds it absolutely impossible to do that?
- ... [N]o government is completely free in its choices. Within the education sector, a government cannot decide to close down primary and secondary schools so as to make money available for the University, because the latter needs qualified entrants as well as money! Nor can it decide to privatize Universities (that is, to leave the provision of tertiary education to 'the market') without abandoning even the shadow of a commitment both to equal opportunity for all its citizens, and even to genuine university education. An understanding of 'the market'—and indeed usefulness in 'the market'—may well be aspects of relevance in the determination of University courses or teaching; but I fail to see how the prime purpose of making a profit is consistent with the academic freedom and excellence which is an intrinsic part of being a university.
- In a real financial crisis, where public revenue is insufficient to meet the minimum requirements of the existing Universities, what could—or should—the government do? Should it decide to close one or all of them? Or should it cut University budget allocations below the minimum...?
- Yet it can be argued that there is another possible response to such a crisis. It is that the government should look again at its priorities and the possibility of extending the range of its possible choices. In other

words, a government in this position should re-examine the priorities which have determined budgetary allocations, and should also re-examine the balance between the nation's private and public expenditure. The latter point is really a euphemistic way of asking whether the government is raising—and collecting—as much revenue in taxation as it needs to do or could do!

- For in considering the problem of financing universities, a related argument is that the bulk of a university's unavoidably heavy recurrent costs is really an investment in the future. It is an investment in people and knowledge, and thus in the creation of a resource essential for overcoming the national economic and financial crisis (Nyerere 1995: 4-7).

He is from a poor country. Those who think wisdom can not be drawn from those who are poorer than they are should remember that it took a child to remind the king that he was naked! Grownups kept pretending that the king was dressed.

## Notes

* Department of Sociology, University of Dar es Salaam.

1. Paul T. Zeleza has noted similar experiences in some of the Atlantic world universities. See his, *Manufacturing African Studies and Crises*.
2. The discussion on IMF and World Bank policies is mainly based on the following: World Bank, Towards Sustainable Development in Sub-Saharan Africa: A Joint Programme of Action, World Bank, Washington D.C., 1986; Peter Gibbon & Adebayo Olukoshi, *Structural Adjustment and Social Change in Sub-Saharan Africa: Some Conceptual, Methodological and Research Issues,* Nordiska Afrikainstitutet, Research Report No. 102. Uppsala, 1996; P. Gibbon, K. Havnevik & K. Hermele, *A Blighted Harvest? The World Bank and African Agriculture in the 1980s*, James Currey, London, 1993.
3. Among these are: Financing Education in Developing Countries, 1986; Education and Adjustment: A Review of the Literature, 1991; Education in Sub-Saharan Africa: Policies for Adjustment, Revitalization, and Expansion, 1988, 1988; Issues Related to Higher Education in Sub-Saharan Africa, 1985; Why Educational Policies can Fail: An Overview of Selected African Experiences, 1990.
4. NCHE, A Framework for Transformation of Higher Education System, Governance and Funding, Pretoria, April 1996, P.27. References for this document will be indicated in the text in order to avoid many footnotes on the same source. Use of so many quotations is unavoidable, since the aim is to present the arguments and the phraseology faithfully.
5. See, for example, N. Cloite, J. Muller, M.W. Makgoba & D. Ekong (eds.), *Knowledge, Identity and Curriculum Transformation in Africa.*
6. Reproduced in Mamadou Diouf and Mahmood Mamdani (eds.), *Academic Freedom in Africa.*

7. Earlier (April 1990) the higher learning institutions in Tanzania had produced the Dar-es-Salam Declaration on Academic Freedom and Social Responsibility of Academics. (also reproduced in *Academic Freedom in Africa*). This Declaration is more explicit as far as rights to education and the basic principles are concerned. Some of the basic principles of this Declaration stated:

   * Every human being has a right to wholesome education. Education shall be directed to the full development of human personality.
   * Access to education shall be equal and equitable.
   * Education shall prepare a person to strive for and participate fully in the emancipation of the human being and society from oppression, domination and subjugation.
   * Education shall prepare a person to strive to overcome prejudices related to gender, race, nation, ethnicity, religion, class, culture and such like. Education shall inculcate in every person respect for all human culture developed by humankind.
   * Education shall develop critical faculties, inculcate the spirit of scientific enquiry and encourage the pursuit of knowledge and the search for the whole truth in the interest of social transformation and human liberation.
   * Education shall be secular. Religious instruction shall be separate from secular education and imparted to those wanting to partake of it voluntarily.
   * Education shall make every person conscious of ecology and the need to protect the environment.

8. Allan Bloom's The Closing of the American Mind, 1987, is one of those books which document how higher education has failed democracy and impoverished the souls of students in America. It points out some of the things I mention here. As far as Britain is concerned, see E.P. Thompson ed.
9. Some of many want to retort that Max Weber was trained as a lawyer and contributed to economics, history and sociology - especially in the establishment of the latter. Or that Durkheim's background was in psychology and not in Sociology. That is precisely the point. These did not remain grounded in their backgrounds. They transcended them and became preoccupied with the study of social life as an objective reality, in all aspects, amenable to a sociological mode of enquiry. What I see as the determining factor in the two programmes from 'sociology' here is the stamp of those individual's background. Development Theories are only a small part of social science or social theories; even industrial restructuring and management is not necessarily the same as those sociological studies which deal with industrial relations, labour relations, workers' participation, labour movements, etc.
10. Susantha Goonatilake, 'Transfer Systems in Science and Technology and Indigenous Intellectual Initiatives', in Philosophy and Social Action (Special Issue on Social Problems of Scientific Knowledge), Vol. XIII, No. 1-4, Jan.-Dec. 1987, P. 21-22.
11. In an article forwarded to me by a colleague, Jon Temin, a 3rd year student at Swarthmore College, Philadelphia, USA, who spent a semester at UCT in 1998, published an article in the Boston Globe (01 17 199) titled: 'This is Africa' (College student finds Cape Town eye-opening). Here are some of his observations: 'What

seems strange in retrospect, though, is that almost everything I learned was derived by simply living in South Africa, and not from my experience at UCT. The university itself was perhaps the only disappointing part of my time there. UCT is not shy about its ambition to become 'a world-class African university', but it seems far from realizing its goal. I enrolled in three classes there, in Archaeology, History and Political Studies departments. The classes ranged in size from roughly sixty to one hundred and twenty people, although those are hard estimate to make because attendance never approached full capacity. Simply put, many UCT students never go to class – 'Of course this happens at any university, and I am not one to preach the virtues of perfect attendance, but I was stuck by the frequency with which some students skipped entire weeks of classes, not to mention individual days. What's worse, though, is that some professors seem to have come to accept this behaviour. I had a fifteen-person tutorial with my history professor once a week. The first week we had almost a full attendance, but each week thereafter fewer and fewer students 'pitched up', ... In the final week I was the first person in the classroom, the professor entered a minute later, and that was the extent of the attendance'.

## References

Bawa A., 'Knowledge Production and Curriculum Research Strategies in South Africa', in N. Cloite et al. eds. *Knowledge Identity and Curriculum Transformation in Africa*, Cape Town: Longman, p. 49.

Gibbon P. and Olukoshi A., 1996, *Structural Adjustment and Social Change in Sub-Saharan Africa: Some Conceptual, Methodological and Research Issues,* Research Report No. 102. Uppsala: Nordiska Afrikainstitutet.

Gibbon P. , Havnevik K. and Hermele K., 1993, *A Blighted Harvest? The World Bank and African Agriculture in the 1980s*, London:: James Curry.

Hountondji P., 1983, *African Philosophy: Myth and Reality,* Bloomington: Indiana University Press.

Manuel Castells, 'The Informational Economy and the New Division of Labour', in Martin Carnoy et al. (eds.), *The New Global Economy in the Informatioon Age: Reflections on our Changing World,* Penn State University Press, Pennsylvania, 1993, p. 66.

Strategic Planning Committee,1997, 'Strategic Planning Framework', University of Cape Town, 22 August , p. 1.

'Speech by Guest of Honour', in *The Dar Graduate: Journal of the Convention of the University of Dar-es-Salaam,* Vol. 2, Special Issue 1995-96, Dar-es-Salaam, 1996, pp. 4-7.

World Bank, 1986, *Towards Sustainable Development in Sub-Saharan Africa: A Joint Programme of Action,* Washington D.C.

Zeleza Paul T. , 1997, *Manufacturing African Studies and Crises,* Dakar, CODESRIA Book Series.

# 12

# Globalization and University Education in Nigeria

**Ogoh Alubo***

> We cannot accept the unique authority of the few nations (seven or eight richest) that claim it is their right to make decisions for the whole world, or of the[ir] monetary institutions that claim all human activity should be subservient to their interest—Giovanni Berlinguer (1999: 592).

## Introduction

University education commenced in Nigeria with the opening of the University of Ibadan in 1948, prior to which all higher education was obtained abroad. Since then, the number of universities has grown rapidly to the present forty-four. The growth in the number of universities is meteoric, averaging more than one per year since independence in 1960 (Fafunwa 1997: 20).

Universities in Nigeria are reckoned by their age of inception as first (1948–62), second (63–75), third (76–81), fourth (1982–1993), and now fifth generation (1994–1999) universities (Chizea 1983; Bako 1994: 154). The first generation universities have more elegant infrastructures, are generally better staffed and equipped, and are also better known nationally and internationally. The second-generation universities do not match the first in terms of staff strength, facilities and reputation. The former are however ahead of the third, fourth and emerging fifth generations. In this sense, generation goes beyond chronological age, they correspond with changing levels of reputation. Until the first quarter of 1999, licenses were granted to four non-state proprietors (Musa 1999). Two of these are run by missionaries, the Seventh Day Adventist and the Catholic Church, and the other two by private individuals, including General Babangida, Nigeria's military ruler, 1985–1993.

In their contemporary forms, universities as classified are conventional and specialized universities. The first group runs courses in all fields including 'specialized' areas, while the latter concentrates on broad disciplines like agriculture and technology. The federal government exclusively owns the specialized universities, but shares ownership of conventional ones with the state governments, and now missionaries and private individuals. However, in addition to being longer in the business, the federal government owns about two-thirds of the universities.

Irrespective of generation, the federal government controls all universities through the National Universities Commission, NUC, and the Joint Admissions and Matriculation Board, JAMB. The first is the superintending organ over administration, finance, and broad policy issues, while the second coordinates all admissions (Alubo 1999a; Adelakun 1999). The Ministries of Agriculture and Technology coordinate the universities of the same name, while the state ministries of education (NUC 1994) oversee the state universities. There was no information on the structure of private universities at the time of writing.

As might be said of other aspects of development, the growth of universities received a boost from the oil boom whose unprecedented earnings funded most of the increase. In addition to numerical increases, those already in existence experienced a wholesome expansion in newer academic programmes, absorptive capacity in student's intake, facilities and in staff strength. The majority of the teaching staff during the period were expatriates.

Until recently, the general policy thrust of Nigerian universities was expansion to cope with demand for university education. Part of this clamour was to train the skilled labour force needed for the public and private sectors of the Nigerian economy, and to place people in better positions to improve their lives. In addition to this practical need, the university in particular, and tertiary education in general, are regarded as a final rite of passage for the elevation to 'senior service' or high status in society (Ayandele 1974). University degrees were, in consonance with this conception, called national meal tickets. Consequently, university admissions are keenly sought after both by Nigerian nationals and West African neighbours who take advantage of relatively more available places.

Universities in Nigeria have, as might also be said of other sectors of the public service, started to receive the universal therapy of rationalization and adjustment. As part of this policy, Universities have discontinued some services such as subsidized feeding for students, and commercialized others such as intra-campus transportation. It has similarly imposed levies on sport, health services, examinations and sundry services. While there are officially no tuition fees, these sundry levies add up to substantial amounts of money. To be sure, their financial outlay weighed heavily and sufficiently on students to precipitate popular student protests in January 1997 (Obiagwu 1997). More fundamentally, the hitherto operating philosophy seems to have yielded to the new one of 'efficiency' and cost recovery as the driving force. What is more, mergers, perhaps outright closures in the pursuit of this emerging philosophy, threaten the university system. A presidential panel on Tertiary Educational Rationalization headed by the Estu Nupe which had been at work since October 1996 and had submitted its report in the last quarter of 1997 had the express mandate to close, merge and recommend tuition fees in line with what is called economic reality. At a 1998 graduation ceremony, apparently as a kite flying act, the then Minister of Education, Dauda Birma, said that federal universities would be pruned by more than 70 per cent to no more than six. These merger proposals have obvious implications for access to university education.

Whatever aspect is examined, there are telling tales of changes away from the previous era of stability, growth, and autonomy. However, the nature of these changes and what they portend for national development have not been systematically examined. This essay is an attempt to address the impact of these changes on university education in Nigeria. More specifically, it focuses on budgetary allocations to the universities, the staffing situation and students' admissions in the past decade, 1988–1999. What is the level of financial support for the universities now and how has this changed over time? What is the impact on students' admission and staff strength, and how have these changed?

The three areas of funding, student intake and staff strength are important to the survival of any university. This is because whether and how well the main primary functions of teaching/research, publication and community service are performed largely depend on these factors. Funding, its availability and quantum, for instance, has wide ramifications for the number and calibre of staff, nature of facilities, as well as research and community service. Funds also influence the nature of facilities, and as such, the capacity for students' admissions. Staff strength and the quality of staff recruited and retained, are among the factors for which a university gains reputation. In an increasingly competitive and globalized market, funds also circumscribe income and other benefits, which influence the ability of universities to retain or attract valued staff. Finally, both the availability of funds and staffing strength circumscribe students' admissions as well as the quality of teaching and learning. In this way, the three areas of focus have profound implications for the nature of universities, what is thought and learnt, and indeed the nature and dissemination of knowledge.

The essay is in four sections; the first outlines data sources, while the second sketches a conceptual framework for understanding globalization and the changing context of university education in Nigeria. In the third, attention turns to the impact of globalization on the funding, admission and staff strength, while the fourth discusses the implications of these changes for Nigeria, and other countries experiencing similar political and economic changes.

## Methodology and Data Sources

The essay is based on both primary and secondary data. The first derive from questionnaires administered to key functionaries in four universities, namely Ahmadu Bello University Zaria, University of Jos, Abubakar Tafawa Balewa University of Technology, and Benue State University. The four universities represent first and second generations, a state university, as well as a university of Technology, in that order. Questionnaires, which were the main instrument for primary data covered areas of funding, students' admission, staffing position, how each of these have changed, the impact of such changes, as well as adjustments being made. In each university, data were sought from the bursar, registrar staff matters (personnel), the director of academic planning, and deans and heads of Department. The purpose was to investigate how broad policies from the centre were impacting on academic programmes at the level of individual universities.

The secondary data came from the National Universities Commission and the Joint Admissions and Matriculation Board, the two agencies which superintend universities. In keeping with bureaucratic practice, the written permission of the Registrar of JAMB and the Executive Secretary of NUC was sought and obtained. However, due to an apparent backlog in compilation, more recent data are not available from either agency. JAMB made available admission figures for only 1990 to 1994, while NUC Annual Reports which covered a wide range of issues are available for 1988 to 1996. It is noted that these Annual Reports are often late, supposedly because of compilation problems and late statistical returns from individual universities. The 1995 report, for instance, was issued only in 1997.

There were, however, some limitations in the data. First, the response to the questionnaires was poor. In spite of regular follow-ups by field assistants, only fifty questionnaires were obtained from the four universities, and none from key functionaries of Bursar, Registrar staff matters and Director of Academic Planning. Second, important sections were left blank in many of those returned. Third, the permission of the Executive Secretary of the National Universities Commission, and the Registrar of the JAMB was required to obtain necessary data from these regulatory bodies. In spite of the permission, problems with the relevant units in charge of statistics frustrated all attempts to obtain more recent data. We therefore relied mostly on the annual reports, which were not always comprehensive or consistent. In the end, available data do indicate trends in all three focal areas.

## Globalization and the Changing Context of University Education: A Conceptual Framework

Through formal colonization and the activities of European merchants, which preceded the political conquest, Nigeria was incorporated into international capitalism. At the initial stage—post slave trade—it was primarily a source of raw materials as well as a sales outlet for manufactured goods (Williams 1980; Onimode 1983; Parfit and Reiley 1989). The emerging market was externally propelled through cash crops whose demand and price were controlled from outside.

This externally controlled economy was inherited at independence in 1960. For the first decade as a sovereign nation, Nigeria was a basically agrarian economy and relied on groundnuts, cocoa, and palm produce for its foreign exchange (Onimode 1983). All economic policies reflected this agrarian base until the early 1970s when oil replaced agricultural produce as the foreign exchange earner averaging $25 billion annually between 1973-1980 (Parfit and Reiley 1989: 3). Oil enormously boosted Nigeria's revenue base, which led General Yakubu Gowon, the then military ruler, 1966-1975, to boast that Nigeria's problem was not the availability of money but how to spend it (Alubo 1985). The oil wealth propelled enormous growth in all sectors of the economy, including the founding of new universities and the expansion of existing ones (Fafunwa 1997; Jega 1997).

The oil boom, both real and imaginary, did not change the structure of the economy; rather like agricultural produce, it also reflected dependency. And hence, when oil prices dipped in the international market in 1978/79, the Nigerian economy felt the impact. This was the period that austerity, now a household word, was first introduced into the Nigerian political economic lexicon, and when Nigeria obtained its first major foreign loan of $2 billion. This initial crisis normalized until 1982/83 when prices collapsed again. As oil prices plummeted, so did revenue and the attendant fiscal crisis; foreign debts began to mount.

The unabating crisis has constituted a major economic problem for all regimes in Nigeria since 1979. Recent governments in Nigeria (such as Babangida 1985–1993, Abacha Abubakar 1993–1999, Obasanjo May 1999 to date) have responded to the crisis by imposing austerity programmes prescribed by clubs of finance capital, especially the London and Paris clubs, the IMF and the World Bank. Enunciated in recent policy documents as Structural Adjustment Programmes (SAPs), the thrust has included currency devaluation, trade liberalization, removal of subsidy and commercialization of hitherto free welfare services, privatization of public enterprises and wage restraint measures (Federal Government of Nigeria 1986, 1989; Ohiorhenuan 1989; Agbese 1992).

These events have combined to pile enormous pressure on political stability and national unity (Ake 1996). The past decade also witnessed the most rapid decline in aspects of social, economic life such as roads, water supply, health sector, and the value of the national currency, the naira (Alubo 1990). The Naira collapsed from N1 to US $0.50 at the inception of SAP in 1986, to US $1.00 to N85 in the first quarter of 1998, and to US $1.00 to N105 by the second quarter of 1999. This collapse precipitated high inflation and the general decay in social services. The decline in national revenue was equally rapid from $ 1000 in 1988 to $ 260 in 1998 within a decade. This led to a reclassification of Nigeria from a middle to a low-income country. It is within the context of this decline and the adjustments attendant on it that globalization in general and its impact on university education in particular are to be understood.

Not coincidentally, the period in question is when the globalized therapy, the Structural Adjustment Programme (SAP) was formally initiated in Nigeria (Federal Government 1986; Agbese 1992; Olaniyan and Nwoke 1990). This period was also when the erstwhile socialist block collapsed, marking the end of the Cold War. This development transformed the world in accordance with the supremacy of market forces and its ideologues. As the late Claude Ake has argued, this imposition of Structural Adjustment and the overall hegemony it is a part, were facilitated by the end of the Cold War and emergent new world order of unipolar international power:

After the Cold War, there is only one power block whose leaders act as though might is right. There is only one ideology, liberal democracy, only one religion, market forces (Ake 1996: 5).

The emergent New World order is what Walden Bello (1994) has appropriately described as constituting a Dark Victory. In his words, SAP is a 'Sweeping strategy of global economic roll back unleashed by Northern political and corporate elite to consolidate corporate hegemony in the home economy and shore up the north's domination in the international economy' (Bello 1994: 2-3).

This market ideology is reinforced by the leading Western countries and presented to the rest of the world as 'freedom' and the only viable path to development. This process has been considerably enhanced by developments in communication particularly via the Internet. This innovation makes its possible to trade in stocks, goods and services from far-flung territories at the mere click of a mouse. But like other aspects of development, access to the Internet is not evenly distributed. Africa and other regions of the third world have less access than other parts of the world (African Research Bulletin 1999). But irrespective of attempts to present globalization as a natural and inexorable course of human history which is turning the world into a 'global village', its class character and links with those who control the world market cannot be obfuscated (Sawyerr 1998; Navarro 1998). Responses to the pertinent questions, of whose globalization, and what ultimate objectives, therefore become clear because:

> What now passes as globalization is a specific type of internationalization of capital, labour, and knowledge, characterized by an unrestrained and regulated search for profits and greatly enhanced by the public policies initiated by the governments of President Reagan and Prime Minister Thatcher (Navarro 1998: 743).

As part of this process, the policies of the 'free world' have spun threads to ensure that poor countries will remain in bondage, of which the situation in Tanzania is illustrative:

> But in view of the short-term restructuring targets, benchmarks and the tight budget that are the standard prescription for economic reform and growth, even existing school do not have teachers, books, and other teaching aids. It is not unusual to find 50 pupils sharing text books you could count on the fingers of one hand; or to find a school with hundreds of students but less than 5 teachers! Yet, I have hundreds of unemployed graduate teachers. I have science students with no science laboratories. Are they getting the kind and quality of education that will prepare them for the challenges of the new century? (Mkapa 1999: 15)

This is the sense that Giovanni Berlinguer's (1999: 580) statement that SAP is a de facto human experiment with the peoples of the third world but without informed consent becomes most apt.

The university system could not obviously be shielded from these changes. But just how have these changes impacted on the university? How have the universities made their own 'adjustments' and with what implications? To these and related issues, we now turn.

The focus here, as earlier indicated, is on how these changes might have impacted on funding, the staffing position and student intake. It is important to examine each of these areas in some detail.

## Globalization and 'Adjustments' in the Nigerian University Systems: The Changing Nature of University Funding

A careful reading of available data as depicted in the table above, shows that funding has declined since the inception of SAP, as reflected in the lower figures between 1989 and 1990. Allocations to the universities also show fluctuations, especially in capital grants in which the 1994 amount was less than half of the previous year. In a similar manner, the average allocation to each university in 1991 was less than half of that of 1989. This trend and the general decline are more glaring when the total amount of funds in 1991 is compared to the two previous years, even when the number of institutions increased by three. The seeming increases in recurrent expenditure from 1991 are accounted for by supplementary votes following reviews of conditions in the universities. In 1991, the federal government adjusted the minimum wage and allocated N84, 295,664.43 million to the universities to accommodate its implementation. There was a similar supplementary allocation of N1, 394,884,030 billion in 1992 following the report of the Longe Commission on tertiary education. The substantial increases in the recurrent vote since 1993 were due largely to an agreement between the Academic Staff Union of Universities and the Federal Government which, in addition to improved salaries and staff benefits, also provided for improvement in teaching facilities and libraries (ASUU-FGN 1992, Jega 1994). Finally, per institution, analysis shows that universities experienced little improvement, particularly in the context of the rapid decline in the value of the naira. Indeed, a conversion of the annual allocations shows a continuous decline. In effect, the universities were progressively rendered incapable of meeting their requirements for journal holdings, textbooks and equipment, all of which are mostly imported. Funding of universities had therefore remained a problem, and as discussed later, central to the struggles by the ASUU to make the system more functional.

At the level of individual universities, funding has impacted on academic activities in the following ways. First, because of the low level of salaries, the more experienced staff migrate to greener pastures, many of them to countries in Southern Africa, Western Europe and North America. Second, funding is central to the shortages of basic essentials such as chemical reagents, down to the stationary to produce course syllabi. Third, the low level of funds has translated to shortages in the availability of books, journals and other reading materials, which are mostly from the West and therefore require foreign exchange. Finally, many activities integral to the curriculum such as field trips, practicals and teaching practice are either not carried out at all, or cut short because of funds.

In all four universities, the revenue situation is being addressed by mounting saleable courses either on a part-time basis, or through the growing phenomenon of satellite campuses. The University of Technology is for example offering business courses at the diploma, baccalaureate and masters' levels in Jos and Lagos study centres even though these are not available as part of its normal academic programmes. Whereas such adjustments may beef up revenue, there are other implications for the quality of education, as staff in many of these study centres do not go through the regular process of recruitment. Furthermore, the criteria for admission into academic programmes, as discussed in more detail below, are also watered down. In this way, the adjustments currently being made would seem to further contribute to the declining quality of education in Nigeria.

## The Staffing Situation in Nigerian Universities

Nigerian universities have experienced problems of decline in academic staff as shown by Table 12.1. There are declines both in absolute numbers but especially in reference to non-teaching staff. The latter has continued to grow steadily in comparison to teaching staff.

**Table 12.1: Staffing Situation in Nigerian Universities, 1989 to 1996**

| Year | Academic Staff | Non-Academic Senior Staff | Non-Academic Junior Staff | Total Non-Academic Staff | Academic as % of Non-Academic |
|---|---|---|---|---|---|
| 1989/90 | 12,289 | 11,533 | 35,071 | 46604 | 26.36 |
| 1990/91 | 13,645 | 11,498 | 36,785 | 48,283 | 28.26 |
| 1991/92 | 12,927 | 12,321 | 84,981 | 97,303 | 13.28 |
| 1992/93 | 11,089 | 10,570 | 84,165 | 95,551 | 11.60 |
| 1993/94 | 11,947 | 10,584 | 86,543 | 97,1271 | 12.30 |
| 1994/95 | 12,326 | 12,009 | 34,064 | 46,073 | 26.75 |
| 1995/96 | 12,432 | 13,980 | 31,263 | 45,243 | 27.47 |

**Source**: Compiled from NUC Annual Reports, 1990-1996.

One consequence of this is the heavy work burden on the few available teaching staff. In general, the prescribed teacher/student ratio is not met (NUC 1993, 1994). In the 1992/1993 session for example, 'The staff/student ratio computed across the twenty-one Federal government Universities shows that only one of the twelve major disciplines, Veterinary Medicine, has met the NUC approved ratio of 1:6.' Ten disciplines have ratios less than the approved guidelines indicative of inadequate number of teaching staff and consequently higher workload for the available teachers' (NUC 1993: 42-44).

An important feature of the staffing situation is its unstable nature. In the 1994/95 academic year, neither Veterinary Medicine nor any discipline met the stipulated ratio. Indeed, the ratios are remarkably different between disciplines, with some within over 100 per cent in deficit (National Universities Commission Annual Report 1994). In 1995/96, the last year for which data are available, only the discipline of education attained the required ratio as shown in the table below.

The primary data from the four universities reveal the same situation; none of the 50 heads of departments had adequate staff. In addition, there are problems with attracting and retaining senior categories as well as in some of the specialities as reflected by the frustration of the head of department:

The staff strength is poor (i.e., only 8 academic staff) and the quality is average. Qualified staff are either attracted to other more lucrative jobs, or go abroad for better pay. Up till now, vacancies in Climatology, Geomorphology and Economic Geography have not been filled and staff teaching load is very high. The quality of teaching has dropped particularly in areas where specialists have not been found. There is so much teaching to be done by the few staff that hardly any research work is going on at the moment. The university does not provide research grants.

The situation in this state university is replicated in others. In a Social Science Department in Ahmadu Bello University, the head of the department observed that staff strength has dropped from 30 in the middle 1980s to less than 20 in 1999. He lamented that 'most of the senior people have been drained away'. In a similar vein, there were only three PhDs out of a staff strength of sixteen in a department in another university. Of the four universities, the staffing situations in the University of Technology and the State University were more critical.

'Adjustments' to the situation have taken the form of intellectual incest whereby graduates of the department are absorbed and trained internally using the same inadequate facilities. This situation is particularly rife in the University of Technology where loud complaints of inadequate staff and poorly equipped laboratories have not deterred a growing postgraduate training programme.

**Table 12.2: Mean Staff/Student Ratios by Discipline for the Federally Funded Universities 1995/96**

| Disciplines | Ratio in the Universities | NUC Guidelines |
|---|---|---|
| Administration | 1:42 | 1:20 |
| Agriculture | 1:14 | 1:9 |
| Arts | 1:16 | 1:20 |
| Education | 1:24 | 1:24 |
| Engineering | 1:20 | 1:9 |
| Env. Design | 1:19 | 1:10 |
| Law | 1:34 | 1:20 |
| Medicine | 1:11 | 1:6 |
| Pharmacy | 1:19 | 1:10 |
| Sciences | 1:13 | 1:10 |
| Social Sciences | 1:22 | 1:20 |
| Vet. Medicine | 1:8 | 1:6 |

**Source**: NUC Annual Reports 1996: 47

In a situation of raging inflation, the declining salaries do not help matters, and hence all heads of department in the four universities indicated that they were short staffed. For many, teaching positions in the university are used as a stopgap between postgraduate training and better paying employment, and hence the shortage. This pattern is consistent with Yusuf Bangura's finding that 'data from 9 universities prepared by the National Universities Commission reveal that 1,128 academic staff left the university between 1988 and 1990' (1994).

In a reaction to the poor conditions of service, the government has made special supplementation for expatriate staff. Through the National Expatriate Supplementation Scheme foreign lecturers and Professors receive supplementation in foreign exchange (NUC 1996: 26). It has also marginally increased the salaries of workers, including university staff. Such increases, which are usually wrested by the unions, especially ASUU, bring earnings closer to a living wage. However, the unions seem to face a non-win situation as increases are frequently followed by macro economic policies which lead to higher inflation. In May 2000 for example, a 35 per cent increase in wages was followed two weeks later by a 50 per cent increase in the prices of petrol (Guardian June 1, 2000). The rationale of easing the burden is thus negated.

## Students' Admissions and Changing Access to University Education

Data on student admission into Nigeria universities are available for the 1990/91 to the 1993/94 period. There is a gradual decline in student admission. Overall, less than 17 per cent of applications are placed, resulting in an over 80 per cent unsuccessful rate in applications. Even though there are no data on the numbers that meet admission requirements, it seems clear that increases in the number of federal universities have made little difference in the availability of places.

Admission into universities in Nigeria are further restricted by the stipulated 60:40 Science/Arts ratio. The logic is supposedly to beef up the sciences to enable the technological take off of the country. In practice, there might be empty places in Science while those for Arts might be overflowing. Universities are punished or rewarded (through bonus, or withholding of part of funds) according to the extent they meet the NUC enforced Arts/Science ratio. As has been noted elsewhere (Alubo 1999a), this quota is part of the centralized control of universities along similar lines of military establishments.

The data on admission shows a declining access to university education in Nigeria, a development which has been interpreted as part and parcel of a World Bank master plan for education in indebted countries (Bako 1994; Jega 1994). According to this view, the World Bank favours more technical education, possibly to service the envisioned industries, and fewer university places whose training includes more critical thinking. The Nigerian government seems to be implementing these blueprints and hence, in spite of rapid increases in number of universities, admission has remained low to the frustration of applicants and parents.

**Table 12.3: Students Admission into Federal Universities**

| Year | Number of Applications | Number Admitted | Percentage |
|---|---|---|---|
| 1990/91 | 289,572 | 47,504 | 16.40 |
| 1991/92 | 398,215 | 60,479 | 15.18 |
| 1992/93 | 357,950 | 57,685 | 16.11 |
| 1993/94 | 429,657 | 64,684 | 15.37 |

**Source**: *JAMB News* May/Aug 1994:8

Data from the NUC Annual Reports provide further information on the trend in student enrolments. This set of data, which is based on actual head count (it differs from JAMB data, which are based on numbers offered admission some of which may not be registered) shows the following for the 1988 to 1996 period:

**Table 12.4: New Entrants to Nigerian Universities, 1988-1996**

| Year | Number of New Entrants to 1st Degree Program | Number of Institutions | Average Intake Per Institution |
|---|---|---|---|
| 1988/89 | 45,231 | 31 | 1459 |
| 1989/90 | 42,024 | 31 | 1355 |
| 1990/91 | 50,125 | 33 | 1518 |
| 1991/92 | 60,882 | 32 | 1902 |
| 1992/93 | 51,059 | 32 | 1585 |
| 1993/94 | 40,593 | 21 | 1933 |
| 1994/95 | 42,209 | 26 | 1623 |
| 1995/96 | 47,300 | 21 | 2,252 |

**Source**: NUC Annual Reports 1989-1998.

The low numbers admitted into federal universities are central to the clamour and subsequent emergence of state universities, particularly in southern Nigeria, from where about three out of every five applicants come. It is therefore no accident that all Southern states with the exception of Kwara and the three created in 1995 have state universities. In addition to the relief provided by state universities, all of which are fee paying, federal universities have responded to the admission problem through commercialised study centres. Across Nigeria, the satellite campus phenomenon has flourished where a wide range of courses in highly subscribed disciplines such as law, computer and business sciences are offered. As discussed in more detail below, these 'business courses' seem to place profit before academic content. It is simultaneously an avenue for revenue generation as well as of meeting the needs of 'customers'.

The issue of satellite campuses seems destined to remain a source of friction between the universities and the NUC. The former argues that it provides more access to tertiary education and therefore fulfils an existing need. It is also a source of additional revenue. The latter allege that satellite education is effectively watered down and effectively legitimizes low standards. By October 1999, the NUC had banned satellite campuses (Akhaine 1999). The various universities involved in running satellite campus seem to have simply ignored the ban. In addition to satellite campuses of Nigeria universities, other 'satellites' or virtual universities are available through the Internet, over which the NUC has no control.

## Other Impacts of SAP on the Universities

In addition to the previously mentioned areas, globalization has impacted on the universities in other ways. One of the first causalities of SAP in Nigerian universities was catering services for students, which have been discontinued since 1985/86. In their place, private sector initiatives have sprung up where students are, as if to be reminded of the overall philosophy of globalization, forced to turn to the food vending market. Across university campuses, students either cook in their hostels, or purchase food from the emerging campus food markets including mobile vendors (Alubo 1999b). On many campuses, the universities have built shopping complexes, which are rented to private sector initiatives for catering and other business purposes.

Transportation services, within and between campuses, which were hitherto free have also been commercialized. As part of the growing market in the universities, transportation services are also run by private sector operators, some of who use motorcycles.

The primacy of the market has also affected course offerings such that programme in philosophy, classics and psychology have either been 'rationalized' or merged with other departments. In Benue State University, for example, the Department of Psychology has been merged with Sociology with all degrees under the latter auspices. But just as some courses are being discontinued, others—such as marketing, business administration and computer science—are being expanded in celebratory reminder of 'economic determinism'.

As part of this economic determinism, courses which attract high patronage are now widely available through a novel phenomenon of satellite campus. These de facto business centres are located in large urban areas and cater to those who want to study in the evenings or on weekends. However, the admission criteria in most of these campuses are watered down; there is also no guarantee of the calibre of staff. Furthermore, many of the universities run courses for the market that are not available in the their regular programmes; herein lies the proof for the market driven nature of the satellite phenomenon. For the most part, the nature of facilities, calibre of staff and teacher-student ratio are overlooked, so long as revenue is generated. Like the traditional market, the consumer—in this case the student—is king.

Perhaps, because of the obvious implications of satellite campuses for the quality of education, they have drawn the wrath of the regulatory agency. Indeed, the NUC has fought a spirited, but so far unsuccessful, battle with universities over satellite campuses (NUC Newsletter 1999). A recent meeting of the National Board of Education, Nigeria's highest policy body on educational matters, described the satellite campus as 'wanton proliferation of illegal university campuses across the country'. The NUC was directed to shut them down within three months (*The Guardian* 1999: 1).

Running the universities as markets has included regular awards of honorary degrees. This long-standing practice to recognise achievements has been commercialized and incorporated into the internal revenue generation's scheme of universities. This programme of honours for sale, has, as Obaro Ikimi puts it,

> Became part of internal revenue generation. University A wants to build a classroom block, it will cost ten million naira. So it looks around for a couple of millionaires and offer honorary degrees to them at a price. The price settled, it is no problem getting beautiful citations prepared?It does not matter how those to be honoured made their money, just provided the university can also get [its share of] the loot (1998: 9).

This process of revenue generation or adjusting to budget cuts takes other forms whose impact on the integrity of the university, as centres of learning, are equally severe. In the last years of military rule, the strategy involved pandering to the powerful by awarding them honorary degrees and naming auditoria and other campus landmarks after them. According to Wole Soyinka, 'Vice Chancellors are compelled to know how to kow-tow to the first military ladies for funds to run their institutions, bribe them with honorary degrees or rename libraries and students' hostels after these arrogant spouses' (1998: 28).

The combined impact of these changes has led to the rapid decline and decay in the university system. There have been sustained reports (Adekeye 1999b, (The Guardian 1994) about decay in all facets of the university system: physical structures, academic programme and autonomy. With particular reference to physical structures, Alubo has noted that 'Existing facilities are in a state of disrepair. Open sewers, gaping cracks in buildings, blown off roofs and naked electrical fittings are common. Nearly all buildings in the university system need urgent repairs' (1997: 7).

This situation is reflected in the four universities from where primary data were obtained. At the Ahmadu Bello University, the once elegant buildings have deteriorated with age and poor maintenance. Facilities like water fountains and swimming pools are now relics. In the University of Jos there are shortages of classroom spaces and poorly maintained municipal services. The situation in the university of technology and the State University were similar. In all four universities, the infrastructural decay was in addition to unreliable power, water, and electricity supply. The issue of water poses a formidable public health problem as the large numbers on each campus depend on what is notionally a water closet system.

The decay of municipal services across Nigerian Universities is an urgent problem with wide ranging implications for public health as well as the sustenance of academic programmes. Research activities in laboratories are, for instance, hampered by water and electricity supply problems. For Nigerian universities, the situation of municipal services further compounds the crisis. Many have parallel water supply systems, while others rely on the public system; either way, huge financial outlays are involved. Some universities now charge 'municipal fees' to their students. For most of the May to August 1999, for example, the University of Ibadan (Olonade 1999) was shut down following riots triggered by the high municipal fees being charged by the university. The situation is a recipe for turmoil because on the one hand, the low funding from the centre precipitated a decline in municipal services, which the university has sought to remedy through charges. On the other hand, the levies are clearly above the means of most students who, in addition to non-available scholarship loans or grants may be unable to raise money from parents most of who are either retrenched, receive meagre salaries or are subsistence farmers. The University of Ibadan was asking for N 11,00 per annum, an amount which the going minimum wage earners would require three and half month savings of the total wage to meet. The students, understandably, opposed these increases with resultant clashes with security forces and closure (Fabowale 1999). The issues of revenue have led to imposition of tuition fees in Nigerian universities. At the beginning of the second quarter of 2000, the federal government, apparently under pressures from the World Bank, asked the universities to charge fees as part of 'autonomy' (Daniel 2000).

The impact of this decay on scholarship, especially teaching and learning, is pervasive and profound. Across Nigerian universities, there are such gross shortages of classroom space that it has become 'normal' for half of the students to stand or hang out from the windows during lectures. Worse, many of the laboratory-based sciences are, due to a combination or shortage of space, reagents and staff, unable to complete up to half of the required practical sessions. In many instances, frustrated staff have contented themselves with what is called 'the theory of practical'. This applies to medical schools where some students in anatomy classes climb on stools to watch dissection sections they ought to have been carrying out (Alubo 1997; Jega 1994; Bako 1994).

We conclude this section by noting that the changing policies have been stoutly opposed by various segments of civil society, primary among which ASUU is prominent. ASUU has continuously opposed the commercialization of education and other forms of the impact of SAP on the universities (ASUU

1986; ASUU-FGN 1992). These struggles have taken various forms such as public enlightenment through the media, dialogue with the key government functionaries, and strikes. ASUU's struggles (Jega 1994; ASUU-FGN 1992) are part of broad agenda for a democratic and more equitable society.

Both as a reaction and as a challenge to some of these changes, the universities have been restive. Strikes by the constituent members of the university system, academic and non-academic staff and demonstrations by students have become frequent. As testimony to the impact of these forms of resistance, no single session has ended without major disruptions in individual universities or in the overall system in the past decade. One consequence of these disruptions is the multiplicity of sessions running concurrently within the system. More telling still, the 1995/96 academic year was nationally declared lost—apparently to the strikes and disruptions.

The ASUU has consistently opposed the new policies, although not always successfully. It has engaged in four nation-wide strikes in the past eleven years: 1988, 1992, 1996 and 1999. It has struggled for improved working, and university autonomy. It wrested an agreement with the military government in 1992, which was conceived as a comprehensive package for the revitalization of the decaying system (ASUU 1992). The government began to implement this agreement which brought more funding as well improved income for university workers. However, many aspects of the agreement were ignored; what is more, when it was time for a review, the government balked and interpreted all efforts to bring it to the negotiating table as challenges to its authority (Jega 1994; Alubo 1999a, 1999b). Union leaders were subsequently arrested and detained, other academic staff were forcibly ejected from their houses, salaries were also stopped. All but the most recent strike received a similar reaction from the military rulers. With the return to a democratic polity in May 1999, the ongoing strike was devoid of any harassment, arrests or detentions.

## Conclusion: Globalization and the Future of Nigerian Universities

University education has expanded rapidly in Nigeria within the last three decades. Globalization and its policy of SAP are now circumscribing this expansion which was motivated by the need for a skilled labour force. Universities in Nigeria are passing through a period of ferment in which new concepts and values such as cost recovery, 'efficiency' and sellable courses, have been introduced as part of the process of globalization. Academic programmes must now primarily transform into sources of revenue; the intellectual content of such programmes is now relegated to the back burner. Similarly, engaging in business which before was thought to be incompatible with academic pursuits has become the fulcrum around which the system revolves. In a word, the university system has become an extension of the market. Thus, programmes, which do not measure up to the new criteria, are rationalised and discontinued. This development raises important concerns for knowledge (what is taught, and by implication the direction of research) which now becomes what attracts the market rather than a process of enlightenment to further increase the frontiers of light.

As this essay has shown, this policy has led to reduced funding, declining staff strength and, consequently, lower student intake in a situation where number of universities has made little difference in student numbers. In this way, access to university education has become more difficult in the last years of the century than a decade previously.

Those admitted are confronted with commercialized welfare in the university system, particularly the question of food services. Many students are unable to eat regularly; a balanced diet is out of the question. It had been found that these circumstances are part of the factors compelling female students to engage in piecemeal commercial sex work for survival, all at a time that the threat of HIV/AIDS looms large (Alubo 1998; Osakwe et al. 1995).

The changes have also impacted on the quality of teaching, learning and academic work in general. With fewer staff, including shortages in various specialities, many important areas are not taught. The required number of laboratory and practical sessions are also not carried out due to a combination of staff shortages as well as non-availability of needed reagents or equipment. In this way, recent graduates of the Nigerian University system are victims of trained incapacity. The implications for development are profound, as graduating doctors, lawyers, engineers and teachers and others on whom future generation will depend might be severely incapacitated by the circumstances of their education. These university-trained workers would have no alternative than to reproduce the incapacity in their employment careers and future generations. The situation also limits the ability of Africans to compete for jobs with those who had the benefit of a more adequately endowed educational system. This is already happening through a growing culture of inbreeding in many of the departments within the university system, and several other public and private organizations.

The most insidious change of all is the transformation of the university from centre of learning and a civil society institution to a market. This transformation is dictated by globalization, prescribed by the IMF and World Bank and enforced by 'independent' African governments. As part of this process, new concepts and values of commerce, hitherto foreign and considered inimical to the academic calling, are now the dominant ones in the university (Currie and Newson 1998). As Howard Buchbinder (1993) put it:

> academic policy now appears to derive solely from budget conditions, and the university as an institution must rationalize itself in accord with these constraints. The objectives of higher education which are expressed as the production and

> transmission of knowledge as a social good are replaced by emphasis on the production of knowledge as a market good, a saleable commodity (335a).

In this way, the changes bode ominously for the ability of the graduate to comprehend how Nigeria arrived at the present situation and what alternative courses of action are available. Operating the university system as a market circumscribes the production and dissemination of knowledge in its robust and diverse paradigms and perspectives. The ultimate impact of this process is to hamstring the capacity of Nigerians to think for themselves.

Market–oriented syllabi have other implications. Many Nigerian universities had incorporated local materials into the syllabus. As part of this, degree courses are available in the three main languages of Hausa, Ibo and Yoruba, just as literary and anthropological materials from the other nationalities are part of reading materials. These programmes, which no doubt contributed to a better understanding of Nigerian society, are now imperilled because they may be unable to 'pay their way'. It would seem as if local relevance and the advancement of culture, once cardinal goals of education are now in jeopardy.

Whereas we have concentrated here on university education, the situation at the primary and secondary level is not different. Indeed, the level of decay and privation at these levels is more severe. A recent study of primary schools in Nigeria, for example, found that most have blown-off roofs and lack teachers and teaching materials (Francis et al. 1998). In this way, the impact of globalization on education, indeed social services in all, is complete: from primary to tertiary.

While the essay has concentrated on Nigeria, there are obvious lessons for other African countries under the globalized policies and therapy. As in Nigeria, the emphasis has shifted from welfare, and education as social good to market orientation and application of 'efficiency and cost recovery' (Sawyer 1998, Sherman 1990; Mittleman 1994; Nyerere 1996; Mkapa 1999). As Sawyer (1998) has shown, the decay in municipal services is pervasive in all of Africa; shortages of teaching staff have similarly been experienced in Ghana and Tanzania (Sawyer 1998; Nyerere 1996). As in Nigeria, the globalized policy of structural adjustment has placed more emphasis on debt payment and service rather than investing in the people. In some sense, Nigeria's huge oil resources place it in a better position than many African countries; however, as we have seen, the situation has deteriorated progressively and remains grave. Based on the Nigerian experience, one can only say with trepidation that for other African countries, it is a case of *de te fabula narratur*, (of you the story is told). As Africa marches with the rest of the world into the new millennium, its capacity to think, analyse and comprehend might have been mortgaged by the process of globalization and the economic policies it has imposed on the continent.

## Note

* Department of Sociology, University of Jos, Nigeria.

## References

Adekeye, F., 1999, 'A Citadel of Decay', *Newswatch*, May 10, p. 30-31.

Adekeye, F. 1996 b, 'Editorial', *The Gardian*, May 4.

Adelakun, O., 1999, 'Federalism and Socio-Economic Development in Nigeria', paper presented at the International Conference on Federalism in Africa, *African Centre for Democratic Governance*, Sheraton Hotel Abuja, March 14-18.

Adewole, A., 1999, *The Challenge of Tertiary Education in the Next Millenium*, Jos: Lekacs.

Agbese, P. O., 1992, 'Moral Economy and the Expression of Privatization in Nigeria', *Journal of Common Wealth and Comparative Politics*, Vol. 30, No. 3, pp. 335-357.

Ake, C., 1996, *Is Africa Democratizing?*, Port Harcourt, CASS.

Akhaine, S., 1999, 'Govt. Bans Satellite Courses', *The Guardian* October 30.

Alubo, S.O., 1990, 'State Violence and Health in Nigeria', *Social Science and Medicine* Vol. 31, No. 10, pp. 1075-1084.

Alubo, S.O., 1998, *Sexuality and Reproductive Health in Tertiary Educational Institutions in Nigeria*, unpublished research report.

Alubo, S.O., 1999a, 'In Their Image and Likeness: Reflections on Militarization and the University System in Nigeria', paper presented at the Social Science Council of Nigeria General Assembly, Women Development Centre, Abuja, July 5-7.

Alubo, S.O., 1999b, 'Globalization and The Changing Role of Universities in Nigeria', *Newsletter of the Social Science Council of Nigeria* Vol. 2, No. 1, pp. 11-15.

The Guardian, 1994, 'NANS, Group Criticize Reintroduction of Tuition Fees', May 25.

Anyadele, E. 1974, *Educated Elite in Nigeria Society*, University of Ibadan Press.

ASUU, 1986, *ASUU and the 1986 Education Crisis in Nigeria*, Ibadan, ASUU.

ASUU, 1992, ASUU-Federal Government Agreement 1991.

Bako, S., 1994, 'Education and Adjustment in Nigeria: Conditionality and Resistance', in M. Diouf, and M. Mamdani, *Academic Freedom in Africa*, Dakar: CODESRIA, pp. 150-175.

Bangura, Y., 1994, *Intellectuals, Economic Reform and Social Change: Constraints and Opportunities in the Formation of A Nigerian Technocracy*, Geneva: UNRISD.

Banjo, A., 1999, 'The Future of Scholarship in Nigeria', *Newsletter of the Social Science Council of Nigeria* Vol. 2, No. 1, pp. 2-11.

Bello, W., 1994, *Dark Victory:* The United States, Structural Adjustment and Global Poverty Pennang, Third World Network.

Berlinguer, G., 1999, 'Globalization and Global Health', *International Journal of Health Services*, Vol. 29, No. 3, pp. 579-595.

Buchbinder, H., 1993, 'The Market Oriented University and the Changing Role of Knowledge', *Higher Education* Vol. 26, pp. 331-347.

Chizea, C.A., *20 years of University Education in Nigeria*, Lagos, National Universities Commission.

Daniel, A., 2000, 'Govt. Okays tuition fees in Varsities', *The Guardian* May 10.

Fabowale, Y., 1999, 'UI Shut, Students Union Suspended', *The Guardian* May 4, pp. 3.

Fafunwa, A., 1997, 'Pains and Gains in Nigerian Education', *The Guardian* October 1, pp. 20.
Federal Government of Nigeria, 1986, *Structural Adjustment Programnme for Nigeria*, Lagos, Government Printer.
Francis P. et al. 1998, *Hard Lessons: Primary Education and Social Capital in Nigeria*, Washington: The World Bank.
*The Guardian* (Lagos), 1999.
Hountondji, P., 1995, 'Producing Knowledge in Africa Today: The Second Bashorun MKO Abiola Distinguished Lecture', *African Studies Review* Vol. 38 No 3: pp. 1-10.
Ikime, O., 1998, 'Of Academic National and other Honours', *The Post Express,* Sept 23, pp. 9.
Jega, A., 1994, *Nigerian Academic under Military Rule*, Stockholm: University of Stockholm.
Jega, A., 1997, 'Intellectuals and Academics in the Struggle for Democracy', in Jibril Bala ed., *Expanding Democratic Space in Nigeria,* Dakar: CODESRIA, pp. 143-151.
Joint Admissions and Matriculation Board, *JAMB* News, Volume No 2.
Mittelman, J., 'Academic Freedom, The State and Globalization', p. 1541-149, M. Diouf, M. and M. Mandamni, *Academic Freedom in Africa*, Dakar, CODESRIA.
Mkapa, B., 1999, *Development Challenges Facing Tanzania*, Dar-Es-Salam, Government Printer.
Musa, N., 1999, 'Why Govt. Approved Private Varsities, by Jubril', *The Guardian* May 5, pp. 2.
National Universities Commission, 1990, Annual Report, January–December.
National Universities Commission, 1991, Annual Report.
National Universities Commission, 1992, Annual Report.
National Universities Commission, 1992, Statistical Digest on Nigerian Universities, Abuja NUC.
National Universities Commission, 1993, Annual Report.
National Universities Commission, 1994, Annual Report.
National Universities Commission, 1994, Executive Perspectives of the Development of the Nigerian University System, Abuja: NUC.
National Universities Commission, 1995, Annual Report.
National Universities Commission, 1996, Annual Report.
Navarro, V. 1998, 'Whose Globalization', *American Journal of Public Health* Vol. 88, No. 5, pp. 742-744.
Nyerere, J., 1996, 'Address by the Guest of Honour at the Dar Es Salaam University's 25th Anniversary', *The Dar Graduate* Vol. 2, pp. 1-12.
Obiagwu, E., 'UNIBEN Students Clash Over Fees', *The Guardian* January 30, pp. 2.
Ohiorhenuan, J., 1989, *Capital and State in Nigeria*, Westport: Greenwood.
Olaniyan, R. O. and Nwoke, C. N., 1990, *Structural Adjustment in Nigeria*, Lagos, Nigerian Institute for International Affairs.
Olonade, S., 1999, 'Extortionist Fees in University of Ibadan', *The Guardian,* May 5.
Osakue, G., et al., 1995, *Voices: Findings of a Research into Reproductive Rights of Women in Nigeria*, Benin: IRRAG.
Parfitt, T. and S. Riley, 1989, *The African Debt Crisis*, London: Routledge.

Sawyer, A., 1998, 'Does Africa Really Need her Universities?' CODESRIA Bulletin Nos. 3 and 4, pp. 20-25.

Sherman, A., 1990, 'The University in Modern Africa', *Journal of Higher Education* , No. 61940, pp. 363-385.

Soyinka, W., 1998, 'Redesigning a Nation', a public lecture delivered at the Nigerian Law School on October 16 and published in the popular press, October 18, pp. 3, 28.

Wiliams, G., 1980, *State and Society in Nigeria*, Idanre: Afrographica.

# 13

## Globalization, Islam and Social Policy in Kenya

**Edwin A. Gimode***

### Introduction: Conceptualizing Globalization

Globalization is a concept riddled with ambiguities and contradictions. It is not a homogeneous process. It has both negative and positive dimensions, and both economic and humanistic facets to it. It has led to new problems while at the same time provoking a quest for solutions to these problems.

It connotes much more than just the triumph of liberal democracy and neo-liberal policies (Aina 1997: 8). It involves in addition the spread of a universalism of artifacts, issues, ideas, lifestyles and movements (8). Thus conceptualized, the term allows the better study of complex social phenomena like democracy, economy, human rights, inequality, cultural values, religious movements, unevenness in development, etc.

Globalization has redefined the state and its role, marginalizing its sovereignty and depriving it of the functions of regulating market and coordinating social welfare. The outcome has been an inverted state more committed to the protection of foreign investment and less to the protection of the citizen and the country (Shiva 1997: 135).

Islam has always disapproved of exploitative economic systems as evil and predicated on exploitation of man by man and creating social imbalance. In its neoliberal form, capitalist economics of western civilization is viewed in Islamic lenses as extremely materialistic, fanatically secular, immoral and anti-God (*Al-Islam* 1995: 3).

It is viewed as being anti-Islam in its distribution of wealth and control of the means of production by the wealthy, self-centered and cunning ruling class to whom communal welfare is non-existent (3). Islam, with its elaborate belief system on the provision of social welfare, finds itself in opposition to economic globalization. How it has responded to this perceived unfair system in its effects on the society makes interesting reading. The Kenyan Ummah provides an opportunity.

There is also a cultural trajectory to globalization. In fact, globalization as a concept was first conceived of in cultural terms. According to Malcolm Waters, globalization is a Western and westernizing project. It entails the expansion of European culture across the globe, and is tied up to capitalist expansion (Waters 1995: 2).

Robertson (cited in Waters 1995), deemed the greatest popularizer of the concept of globalization, viewed it in cultural, in fact in religious, terms. According to him, there is no denying of particularities of individual religions, but globalization brings their differences into sharp contrast, forcing them to respond to the claims of other religions.

Thus, globalization packaged as a Western agenda spreading a Western value system leads to a dialectic which we can call the localizing dialectic. In other words, the process of globalization simultaneously involves a process of localization (Shiva 1997: 134). In this way, localization takes different forms in different places: self-help, defiance, military action, etc.

These responses interrogate the false universality of Western culture. It is false because it derives from particular European experiences and is arbitrarily being imposed on all cultures as though this form of humanity, economics, rationality and religion is necessarily superior (Gillardo 1997: 68).

This false globalization denies dialogue, highlights differences in a discriminatory manner, establishes homogeneity, prevents growth, and intensifies domination among human beings in different forms—racial, cultural, religious and economic. It is to this multi-layered domination which claims universal validity that the local, poor and dominated respond, refusing to die and stubbornly surviving.

The outcome has been a renewal of historical forces, '…a mass of religious loyalties, ethnic identity, linguistic differences, and other forms of cultural expression' (Mittelman 1994: 432). This is what Huntington has described as a 'clash of civilizations' (1996).

Speaking of Islamic culture, Huntington states that starting in the 1980s, there has been an 'Islamic Resurgence' not just in predominantly Muslim cultures but also in every country where there is a sizeable Muslim minority. This resurgence is a wish to reassert '…an increase in Islamically oriented government, organizations, laws, banks, social welfare services and educational institutions' (Esposito, cited in Huntington 1996: 10).

Aspects of cultural globalization can also be positive. For instance, positive global thought calls for the development of 'a sense of world or global citizenship' (Gallardo 1997: 64). For Gallardo, we should be bold in imagining a globalization that should be countervailing to the neoliberal programme. Its agenda should include democratization of state power; policies alleviating and resolving extreme polarization in society; policies that strengthen roots, autonomy and interchange of different cultures; policies guaranteeing safe natural habitat; and policies that recognize and respect differences in the worldwide society (64) Globalization so conceived should recognize and accept the contribution of the different cultures of the world.

This study takes the Islamic community—the largest single social category in Kenya—as a test case of the changing concept of citizenship and the response of non-state players in countervailing the devastating effects of economic globalization on Third World countries. It demonstrates how '… the forces of global change are seriously affecting local livelihoods and promoting sharp debates about community rights' (UNRISD 1996).

## Muslims in Kenya

Islam has followers among virtually all ethnic groups in rural Kenya, but in small numbers compared to their Christian counterparts. They are found in fairly large numbers in urban centres. The strongholds of Islam in Kenya, however, are three provinces: the Coast Province, which covers the districts of Mombasa, Kwale, Kilifi, Tana River and Lamu; the North Eastern province, which covers the districts of Garissa, Wajir and Mandera; and the Eastern province, where the Islamic districts are Isiolo, Marsabit and part of Kitui. These districts form the locus of our study on the impact of globalization on citizenship and social provisioning. A few reasons make the study necessary.

Firstly, most of these districts form a continuous and expansive but ecologically harsh territory. They form the arid and semi-arid lands of Kenya (ASAL). These are prone to perennial droughts which often decimate livestock and lead to malnourishment for local populations.

Second, as a consequence of the above, the regions have the highest prevalence of absolute poverty in the country: North-Eastern (58 per cent), Eastern (57 per cent), and Coast province (55 per cent) (Republic of Kenya 1998: 4). Third, the infrastructure in these regions is extremely poor. This was compounded by the 1997-98 *El-Nino* related rains which washed away the roads and bridges.

Finally, the regions border Ethiopia and Somalia, countries which have experienced intermittent civil wars. The effects of these have always spilled over into Kenya in the form of an influx of refugees and with them a proliferation of arms and banditry. This makes the region high risk and prohibitive to outsiders. All these factors have immense implications for the logistics involved in welfare provision.

There are no statistics on the number of Muslims in Kenya. Leading Muslim scholars have estimated it to be anywhere between 30 percent and 40 percent of the national population (Bakari 1995: 234; Yahya 1995: 216). This, however, would appear to be on the high side.

## The Kenyan State, Muslim Citizenship and International Islam

Islam is no newcomer to the East African Coast. It was present here as early as the 9th Century A.D. By 1500 A.D., there was a set of some thirty–seven city states along the coast which practiced Islamic religion and culture (Yahya 1995: 20). At the same time, the intermarriage between the local Bantu-speakers on the one hand and the Arabs and Persians on the other, led to the emergence of the Swahili cultural group.

The advent of British colonialism at the beginning of the twentieth century marked the genesis of tension and suspicion between the state and the Islamic community in what came to be called the Kenya Colony. The secular Western education offered by the colonial government, but presided over mainly by the Christian missionaries, was not acceptable to the majority of the Muslims.

The latter, preferred to educate their youths in the Quranic schools which stressed spiritual and moral values. This did not prepare them for the challenges and opportunities that came with political independence in the early 1960s. Senior jobs in government, civil service and parastatals were taken by non-Muslims. For Muslims this was construed to be a deliberate policy of exclusion from state resources.

In 1923, the colonial government had abolished the application of the Shariah law among the Muslims except in matters related to divorce, succession and marriage (Mwangi 1995: 252). This was viewed as an assault on Islam and remained a long standing grievance.

In 1989, the state-Ummah relations worsened when the government adopted a discriminative policy of identifying Somali citizens who live in the North-Eastern Province of Kenya. Because of the influx of Somali refugees as well as armed militias from across war-torn Somalia into Kenya, the government embarked on a policy of thoroughly screening every ethnic Somali to identify genuine Kenyan citizens. Those vetted were to carry a special identification card.

No other Kenyan ethnic group had been subjected to such a humiliation. The Muslim community protested this apparent discrimination which was viewed as not being against Somalis but against all Muslims (*Weekly Review*, 1989).

This aside, the question of the citizenship of Somalis and Arabs, who happen to be overwhelmingly Muslim, has remained thorny for decades. It has always been pegged to the national origins of the parents of an individual. They are the only Kenyans who have to prove their citizenship by providing the birth certificates of both their parents and grandparents before being issued with national identity cards or passports (*Daily Nation*, 1999). These rigorous procedures are not applied to Christians.

It was such 'agelong grievances and frustrations' (Aina 1997: 40) that came to the fore with the dawn of the 1990s. This decade changed the concept of citizenship from merely identifying with a nation state to citizenship with universal rights and obligations that covered all spheres of life—civil, social, political and economic (UNRISD 1996: 7). This worldwide approach to citizenship proved a turning point in the State-Ummah relations in Kenya.

Until then, the only umbrella organ that publicly articulated the Islamic agenda was the Supreme Council of Kenya Muslims (SUPKEM). It had been formed in 1973. This was borrowing a lead from the Uganda Muslim Supreme Council (Wandati 1999). But SUPKEM had not lived up to the expectations of the Ummah. Its leaders were viewed by most Muslims as having been compromised to become an arm of the government.

The 1990s witnessed the rise of several Muslim pressure groups in the wake of expanded social and political space popularly described as 'the second liberation'. In this, Muslim scholars played a leading role in putting the Muslim agenda on the national map. The most vocal of these is the world renowned Professor Ali Mazrui who set the pace by alleging that the Muslim community had been treated as social, political and economic liabilities in the Kenyan body politic (*Society*, 1992). Mazrui asserted that henceforth Muslims were not going to accept the status of '... marginal and peripheral third class citizens' and were ready to fight if need be. To him, Kenya was tottering on the brink of an Islamic uprising—*a black intifadah*—unless the government urgently addressed the unique problems of the Ummah (1992).

At his most extreme, Mazrui argued for the creation of an exclusive Mwambao (Coastal) region governed by the Shariah and not the secular constitution (*Sunday Nation*, 1993). In his own words:

> Some people are losing control of their best land and their richest resources to citizens of other regions. If no answer is found to these tendencies of internal colonization, no democracy should expect to be stable (*Kenya Times*, September 3, 1992).

In subsequent years, the Kenya government handled Muslim affairs with a lot more sensitivity than it had done hitherto. Apart from the above struggle for full citizenship, the 1990s witnessed the Ummah opening a new page of self-reliance in the area of social welfare provision.

## The Kenyan State and International Islam

Part of the tension between the Kenyan Muslim community and the Kenyan state emanated from the latter's relations with the Arab—and by extension Islami—world. The main issue was Kenya's position on the Palestinian struggle against Israeli occupation. In the 1970s and 1980s, Kenya pursued cordial relations with the state of Israel making her support for the Palestinian Liberation Organization (PLO) mere lip service. This was a time when Arab/ Islamic countries and most members of the organization of African Unity (OAU) identified with the Palestinian cause. The struggle was embodied in the activities of the Palestinian Liberation Organization (PLO). The official position of the Government of Kenya in the Middle East Crisis over the past thirty years has made Kenya as a nation vulnerable to attack by anti-Israeli terrorist groups. There have been several examples of this from 1976 with the latest being the 1998 bombing of the United States Embassy building in Nairobi, Kenya, which left over 200 people dead.

## Pre-Structural Adjustment Social Provisioning in the Kenyan Ummah

### *The Canons of Islam on Social Provision: The Zakat and the Wakf*

Islam has a deeply rooted social policy system to cater for the materially disadvantaged in society. This is spelt out in the Qura'n, the Sunnah and the Hadith. The Quran states:

> And righteous is he who gives, for love of Him, to poor kinfolk and orphans and the needy and the wayfarer and those who ask, and set a slave free (Quran 2:177).

This verse is the basis of the institutions of the *Zakat* and the *Wakf* which have an in-built mechanism to cushion the weaker sections of society in the face of harsh socio-economic conditions.

Technically, the *Zakat* is obligatory charity or alms that every rich Muslim should give to those who are poor and in need. This constitutes an act of devotion and piety (Siddiqi 1987: 550). Zakat is one of the five pillars of Islam.

*Zakat* is thus both a way of providing for those deserving charity, and a mechanism that attempts to ensure an equitable distribution of wealth in the society. In fact, it has the potential of being the perfect antidote to the devastating vagaries of neoliberalism in today's society. It abhors the principle of exploitation of man by man inherent in the practice of neoliberal capitalism.

The institution of the *Zakat* in an ideal Muslim society is centrally controlled by the state, which manages and organizes, collects and disburses the fund. In a secular state, however, the Muslim community is called upon to establish a *Bait-ul-Mal* or a public treasury to oversee the collection and expenditure of the *Zakat* funds as needed. Where this central organization is not possible, the individual Muslim is expected on his own 'to spend money for the help of the needy and the indigent, and to carry on struggling by all means at their disposal to bring about an Islamic system' (Kamal 1991: 17).

The individuals who qualify for *Zakat* include the invalid, the aged, the indigent men, the widows and orphans. They can be put on a temporary fund or provided with a permanent subsistence allowance. In addition, the *Zakat* can be spent on establishing and sustaining institutions like hospitals, orphanages, charitable institutions, schools, etc. (17). In an effort to establish self-reliance, there is also a provision for the *Bait-ul-Mal* to advance interest free loans to the needy. *Zakat* also allows for disbursing help to those in distant lands upon whom natural disaster has befallen. It is through this provision that aid is reserved from Islamic agencies abroad and disbursed locally.

Then there is the institution of the *Wakf*. This has well served the economic and social interests of Muslims worldwide for centuries (Yahya 1995: 214). Wakf means an asset, a sort of endowment, which has been set aside from circulation in order that its yield can be used for charitable purposes. It is not directly mentioned in the Quran or the *Hadith*, but its development can be seen as a variant of *Balt-ul-Mal*. As an economic tool, the institution developed fairly late in the Islamic state. But its suitability in philanthropy has withstood the test of time.

The property of the *Wakf* becomes the sole property of God, while the income or usufruct passes to a designated beneficiary such as a school, dervish convent, hospital or mosque (Williams 1987: 238). In addition, *Khayri Wakf* goes towards feeding stray animals, teaching poor children, marrying off orphan girls, and assisting indigent mothers (238).

The two institutions in the history and development of Islam worldwide seem to have anticipated accurately the development of neo-liberal capitalism and the social disorganization that has always accompanied it. They appear to be an effective antidote to neoliberalism and the devastating natural disasters that have characterized the late twentieth century.

The two can be viewed as the antecedents of the different types of welfare programmes that have been developed at different stages in human history to meet hard economic times. They were the forerunners of the local government, the non-governmental organizations, and generally that whole entity described as civil society.

In the case of Kenya, the relevance of the Islamic social provisioning has become exceedingly crucial, especially in the 1990s when the state drastically pulled out of the arena of social service provision. Islamic social policy has been timely at a time when the full import of the devastating neoliberal policies *has taken its toll* on state-provided welfare and have characterized natural disasters different parts of Kenya, predominantly in Muslim-dominated geographical areas.

## *Welfare Provision Among the Sunni Muslims*

The two main schools of Islam in Kenya are the Sunni and the Shia. The latter are a minority and are found almost exclusively in towns. The former are found countrywide both in towns and in the rural areas, but especially in coastal, Eastern and North-Eastern districts. They are by far the majority and cut across races and ethnic groups.

In the course of the 20th century, the *Sunni* utilized the institution of the *Zakat* to provide for the socially and environmentally disadvantaged among them. The main activities they undertook involved donating food to the needy, establishing orphanages, schools and health centres, and the construction of mosques in urban centres and along highways.

To better facilitate these provisions, the *Sunni* set up the Young Muslim Association (YMA). This agency has focused on alleviating hardships experienced in the Arid and Semi-Arid districts of Northern and Coastal Kenya. One of the most successful projects of the YMA is the Garissa Orphanage, which they constructed to cater for victims of the shifta (Somali) banditry, and which the association has supported since the 1970s (Bakari 1995: 63).

Another agency is the Islamic Foundation of Kenya (IFK) which has focused on gathering and transmitting information both on local and international Islam. The publications have been especially effective in identifying the most needy groups and projects, and then soliciting both international and local assistance.

In the same vein as the *zakat,* the *wakf* institution holds a lot of potential in the arena of social welfare. It has been in existence since the colonial period. It has financed the construction of mosques, social meeting halls and burial grounds (Yahya 1995: 216).

Unfortunately, as a result of poor coordination, the *wakf* as an instrument of social welfare has not done as much as it should have. It has not featured prominently in setting up schools, providing medicare, undertaking clean water supply, etc.

On the whole, it would appear that before the implementation of the Structural Adjustment Programme in the 1990s the Sunnis did not fully utilize the Islamic structures of social provisioning. One reason for this was that the Kenyan state was for a long time viewed as the primary provider of welfare to the citizens. With the retreat of the state as a key player in social welfare, and with the unique problems of Islamic strongholds at the start of the 1990s, the Sunni Muslims were to learn to maximize their resources to alleviate the suffering of their adherents.

### *The Shia and Service Provision up to 1990: The Case of the Ismaili Community*

The Shia school of the Kenyan Ummah is a tiny minority, and is mainly, but not exclusively Asian. The three major clusters are the Dawood Tayyibi Bohras, the Ithinasharis and the Ismailis. The Shias have an elaborate social policy towards the welfare not only of their compatriots but also of other Muslims and Kenyans as a whole. The Shias have responded practically to the Quranic injunction to exercise philanthropy and to assist the weak among them.

It can be convincingly argued that the Ismailis are the best exemplars of the implementation of the Islamic welfare scheme. One feature of the Ismalis is that they are an international but closely knit community. They are highly organized, economically stable and educated. Their successful socio-economic policy can be attributed to their two Imams—Sir Sultan Muhammad Shah (Aga Khan III), 1877–1957, and the current leader, Prince Karim Shah (Aga Khan IV). The Kenyan Ismaili community is part of the international Ismaili family.

These two had the great foresight to successfully adapt to the changing economic, social and political circumstances of the twentieth century (Walji 1995: 1). In implementation of the Quranic injunction of philanthropic obligation to their fellow men, these two put in place institutions that apparently anticipated the difficult social conditions of the twentieth century. While other Kenyans have looked to the state for provision of welfare service, the Kenyan state has looked up to his Highness the Aga Khan as a valuable investor and partner in development and welfare.

A few specific examples will suffice. In the 1930s, the Aga Khan III set up new financial institutions to provide capital for members for purposes of self help. He set up in Kenya the Jubilee Insurance Company and the Diamond Jubilee Development Trust. This took place as the world was emerging from the throes of the Great Depression. In 1946, he set up the Ismaili Welfare Society, which was charged with co-ordinating charitable work among the members. Many members followed the example of their spiritual head. In 1952, Aga Khan III called a Conference at Evian in France to discuss problems of the East African Ismailis ( 6-7). The outcome was a thoroughly worked out programme of provision of healthcare, education and the provision of shelter for the members.

The successor to Ike Aga Khan III has not done less. He took over as leader in 1957 and has continued to further the policies and institutions he inherited. All the Ismaili schools in Africa and Asia were brought under the Aga Khan Education Services. In Kenya there are several such educational institutions. Then all hospitals, dispensaries and clinics were brought under the Aga Khan Health Services. The Aga Khan Hospital, Nairobi, with branches in Kisumu and Mombasa, admits patients from all over Eastern and Central Africa.

The Aga Khan Foundation was set up in 1979 as a umbrella philanthropic agency in Geneva, but with branches world wide, including Kenya. This foundation goes far beyond sectarian service, focusing on development priorities in poor countries in Asia and Africa. In Kenya, the foundation has a development network with other international agencies like UNICEF. Consequently, it can be argued fairly and justifiably argued that the vagaries of the neoliberal policies of the 1990s had little impact on the Ismailis.

## The Structural Adjustment Programme and Nature's Assault on Social Provision

The primarily objective of economic development and social advancement is to eradicate poverty. This entails citizens having access to food, shelter, clean water, health care and education. Given the ecologically harsh conditions of the northern, eastern and coastal districts of Kenya, these provisions have remained a dream for a long time. Yet the special conditions that have marked the 1990s, natural and manmade, have had tremendous impact in shifting the trends of welfare delivery in these areas.

The victory of liberal democracy that came in the wake of the end of the Cold War was closely accompanied by the imposition of the neoliberal economic program for the Third World. In fact, the latter took precedence over the demands for democracy. This involved the implementation of Structural Adjustment Programmes. Its instruments were the World Bank and the International Monetary Fund (Ezcurra 1997: 77).

Adjustment involved opening up to transnational capital and emphasizing competition, privatization of basic social services (like health, education), and giving absolute precedence to market economics. It involved redefining the role of the state whereby the latter withdrew from directly regulating economic activities and instead guaranteed the protection of the multinational investor.

In Kenya, as elsewhere in the Third World, the programme caused social dislocation on a large scale. Its implementation began with the dawn of the 1990s. The poor bore the brunt of the effects. These realities involved increased poverty, scarcity of resources and declining purchasing power.

Apart from the World Bank and IMF conditionalities, natural disasters compounded the hardships. Earlier, in 1985-86, sub-Saharan Africa experienced a severe drought. Countries in the Horn of Africa were especially badly affected. The ASAL districts of Kenya were affected equally seriously (Abdallah 1995: 200). They lost most of their livestock.

Then in 1994 and 1995, the East African region as a whole experienced a prolonged drought. For the districts under our study, the drought continued unabated throughout 1996 and into 1997. By this time, the state had already retreated considerably from the arena of social service provision. Nomadic Muslims lost most of their livestock on a large scale, apart from experiencing widespread malnourishment due to starvation.

With the end of the long drought in August 1997, a new form of disaster began in September. The *El-Nino* related rains began all over the country, leading to the worst floods in the country in half a century. Yet, by some strange twist of fate, the most negatively affected areas by the floods were the northern-eastern-coastal districts usually notorious for drought. The floods virtually turned the lives of the inhabitants upside down. The roads were completely destroyed, and the bridges broken (*Daily Nation*, February 6, 1998).

Gradually, the only means of transport remaining, air transport, became ineffective as the floods covered all airstrips. This led to starvation, malnutrition and exposure as 75 per cent of the surviving livestock perished due to floods and diseases, and as floods swept away shelters.

## Relief Activities and Agencies in the 1990s

It is against the background of such special conditions of the 1990s that the shift in operations of Muslim relief agencies has to be studied. Like other independent states in Africa, the Kenyan state was considered by the citizens as the main provider of services: employment, education, healthcare, shelter, water projects, road construction, etc. The annual budget usually involved the financing of these services in the different parts of the country. Indeed, until the neoliberal global approach to development in the late 1980s, Kenya was a typical social service state. This was especially the case for the Arid and Semi-Arid regions under study.

However, with the implementation of the IMF and World Bank policies, the role of the state in welfare provision declined. The suspension of aid and loans by the donor community to Kenya compounded an already complicated socio-economic situation. But it led to a new development. For the first time, the ASAL areas were opened up to non-governmental agencies, both local and international, Islamic and non-Islamic. These became the primary providers of social welfare.

In addition, following a decade of civil wars in Somalia in the 1980s, there was an influx of refugees into north-eastern coastal Kenya. The significance here is that refugees were a category under the auspices of the United Nations, and had to be accessed by the relevant and other civil society agencies. The work of these agencies among refugees assumed a wider scope to incorporate the locals. It became part of the duty of these agencies to highlight to the international community their hard conditions. This transition from state to non-state welfare provision was a turning in the ASAL areas.

It was non-Islamic agencies which first moved into the north-eastern region of Kenya to provide relief to the residents following the worsening economic and ecological conditions. The main ones were Oxfam, World Vision, GTZ, Médicins Sans Frontiers, the International Red Cross and Red Crescent, Action Aid, Kenya World Food Programme, UNICEF, etc.

Their first service had been to the Somali and Ethiopian refugees on Kenyan soil. Their highlighting of the problems of the region to the international community was to pave the way for the coming of Islamic NGOs. The main concern of these organizations was to provide medicines, relief, food and clothes, temporary shelter (tents), to sink boreholes and to maintain shallow wells. With time, these agencies came to work with Islamic relief agencies when the latter began operations. At the close of the twentieth century, most of them were still active in the region.

Before the compelling events of the 1990s, there were no international Islamic organizations allowed in the ASAL areas. The reasons were historical and political. At independence in 1963, when the present North-Eastern province was forcefully incorporated into the Kenyan state, the Somali ethnic group insisted on seceding to join Greater Somalia. The ensuing *Shifta War*, (Somali guerrilla wars) which lasted well into the 1980s, impacted negatively on the local Somali population.

The government had treated all Somalis, who happened to be Muslims, with suspicion as harbouring Somali irredentism. Consequently, any external group that seemed to speak strongly on behalf of the Somali plight was treated with suspicion. It was worse if such a group should be Islamic. Hence no Islamic NGOs had operated there.

However, the inability of the state to cope with the disasters left the government with no option but to allow Islamic Non-Governmental Organizations to operate in the ASAL districts. The service delivery that they were involved in constituted a life line to the residents of the area. Their arrival also linked the Kenyan Ummah with the international Islamic brotherhood. It gave a chance to these agencies to put in practice the injunction of caring for the needy and the disadvantaged on a big scale.

These NGOs, in collaboration with their secular Western counterparts, began a transformation programme of the region of which the state had never conceived. The main ones among these agencies were based in Islamic countries, and came either as agencies of the Islamic states, or agents of groups or individual philanthropic foundations—*Wakf*.

The Africa Muslim Agency (AMA), based in Kuwait, remains the biggest Islamic agency operating in the whole continent. It has many projects in Eastern and Central Africa, especially Malawi. In Kenya, it has widespread projects in the whole ASAL region. In addition, it sponsors several projects elsewhere in the country. A good example is the Eldoret Muslim Academy in the Rift Valley Province.

Other active agencies include the following: The Help Africa People (HAP); the Mercy International Relief Agency (MIRA) based in Ireland; Ibrahim bin Abdul Aziz al Ibrahim Foundation; Habitat Islam Ali Slam; the International Islamic Relief Organization (IIRO); the Muslim World League; the Riyadh-based Al-Harramain, and others.

Throughout the 1990s, these agencies were engaged in service provision activities at several levels. The first level was response to conditions of disaster, whether through drought or floods. They also addressed starvation, sickness, lack of shelter and lack of water. Here, the NGO workers received material supplies like food, tents, medicines, clothes and other necessities and distributed them as an emergency measure to residents. They opened small mobile clinics for distribution of medicine to both humans and livestock (Abdi 1999).

At the second level, the NGOs were engaged in more durable development projects that aimed at long-term welfare provision to the populace. This has simultaneously involved soliciting community participation in a number of ways. These included setting up health units, sinking boreholes, maintaining shallow water pans, initiating livestock rearing projects, sponsoring education of orphaned children from primary up to higher levels, setting up and maintaining children's homes and building and maintaining mosques and Islamic Madrassa schools.

For purposes of convenience, different foundations concentrated their activities in specific areas. This helped in avoiding duplication of effort, while ensuring effective outreach. For instance the African Muslim Agency has been most active in Wajir and Mandera where, together with other Kuwait agencies, it has built children's homes and is catering for whole orphaned families on a quarterly basis (MEDS, 6.4: 2).

Another agency, the Riyadh-based Al-Harramain, before being banned, had many projects in Isiolo, Garissa and even Nairobi. It did a lot of work among orphans in these areas. The Mercy International Relief Agency mainly worked among Somali and Ethiopian refugees in the districts.

## Impact of Islamic Resurgence and International Islamic NGOs

It is no exaggeration to state that the interface of the international and local Islamic NGOs in the 1990s was part of the worldwide Islamic resurgence in the late twentieth century. The movement has sought to reaffirm the identity, meaning, development and legitimacy of the Muslims in the present world (Huntington 1996: 109). The resurgence embodies the acceptance of modernity but also the rejection of Western culture. The movement is intellectual, cultural, social, political and economic, and affects Muslims in all countries.

The presence of the international Islamic relief agencies was an eye opener to the rather disorganized local agencies. With time, the local agencies went through a transformation. There was an awakening, especially among the younger local Muslims. Consequently, throughout the decade these youths have aggressively defended their faith at every possible platform. They have backed this up by giving practical voluntary service to their own in need. The cross-fertilization they have experienced has gone a long way in vigorously shaking off the various negative stereotypes so long ascribed incorrectly to Muslims in Kenya.

The Islamic Foundation of Kenya (IFK) and the Young Muslim Association (YMA)—two national organizations among the Sunni Ummah—have been invigorated and have expanded their scope of operations. They have learnt quickly the art of soliciting funds to run their projects.

In its quarterly publication (*Al-Islam* 1991) the IFK has taken the trouble to exhort readers to be faithful and generous in their charity obligations. The

Foundation is run to cater for the hungry, the needy, and the orphans. The Foundation runs several children's homes: Mombasa (300 children), Isiolo (240 children), Machakos, Nyeri and Garbatullah. The foundation has also set up a bursary scheme to contribute towards the education of intelligent students who have no means of raising school fees.

In an effort to make its operations self-sustaining, the foundation has set up two big farms in Isiolo (Baraka farm) and in Lamu. When fully operational, they are expected to be used to fund children's homes.

The sister organization, the YMA, has been involved in philanthropic work throughout the decade. It participated fully in relief provision at the height of the *El-Nino* floods, especially in the Garissa district (*Daily Nation*, December 2, 1997). The association has set up an orphanage in Tana River District and is in the process of establishing a farm there. It has also been associated with the Garissa Children Home for over two decades.

Apart from these two national Islamic bodies, quite a number of other local organizations were formed in the 1990s in the ASAL areas. These were quick to learn from the international agencies. Today, most are involved in service delivery either in cooperation with the international ones or taking over from them (Bardad 1999).

Some of these agencies include Caravan Relief Development (CRD), Garissa Human Resources Consultancy (GHRC), Pastoral Shelter Organization (PSO), Kenya Muslim Charitable organization (KMCO), Green Earth Program (GEP), and the Mandera Education Development Society (MEDS). The last of these merits more detailed discussion to illustrate the working of the local NGOs in partnership with international funders.

### *Mandera Educational Development Society (MEDS)*

The Mandera Educational Development Society was formed in 1989 following a severe drought (Absiye 1999). It led the Sheikhs in Mandera to suggest the idea of self-help approach in resettling families, in restocking and in educating the children. The events of the 1990s were to vindicate the formation of this agency.

MEDS was conceived as a family crisis intervention program. It sought sponsorship from outside Kenya. The government of the Royal Kingdom of Kuwait responded and decided to sponsor a specific project, namely the education of children from orphaned families by paying full fees and related costs. Currently some 827 orphans are on sponsorship from this programme. The organization disburses about $340,000 per annum. The payments come at the rate of $100 per orphan per quarter. There are two categories of orphans on the programme. The first category stays with their families. The funds due to them are given to the family heads to disburse on their behalf. Some 547 of them fall under this category. What in reality happens is that this stipend is used to cater for the needs of virtually the whole family. Essentials like food are addressed first. A family with more orphaned children on the programme counts itself blessed.

A second category of some 280 orphans live in two boys' boarding schools or homes. Examples are Mandera Boys/Islamic Centre and the Al-Ridhwan Children's Home. Their fees and all costs are paid directly to the school. However, having received the funds from Kuwait, the Board of Trustees disburses only $70 per orphan per quarter. The remaining $30 is retained and re-channelled to pay staff, rent offices, buy stationery and start other projects which are deemed urgently needed by the community.

In other words, the Board of Trustees and the community decided to be innovative by turning MEDS into a wide-ranging problem solving mechanism (Harun 1999). It covers a fairly wide terrain in its intervention for food, shelter construction, restocking of goats, religious and moral awareness campaigns, HIV/AIDS awareness campaigns, getting clean water and conflict resolution among feuding families. In this way, MEDS has attempted to improve the living conditions of those who have no access to financial resources.

The programme has been successful in the face of the adversities of the 1990s. During the El-Nino related floods, MEDS received relief food and other supplies from the Muslim world and was able to cater for a fairly big section of the community (Mohamed 1999). Over the years, the organization has been able to develop some 80 shallow wells which benefit about 30,000 people in the district. In addition, during the prolonged 1994–97 drought in the district, MEDS, in collaboration with Action Aid Kenya, was able to provide an emergency water supply to 1500 families in Takaba area (Ahmed 1999).

MEDS would appear to be a good example of a synthetic relief organization. It has worked, and still does, with Islamic international agencies. It has also developed a close working relationship with Action Aid. The latter has assisted by training the MEDS staff via short term courses. The areas of training include field monitoring, evaluation, book-keeping courses, community organization and coordination with other NGOs. So successful has MEDS been that the people of Wajir and other area districts are making feasibility studies to see how they can initiate similar programmes (Abdullahi 1999).

## Conclusion

This account throws up several questions on the nature and process of globalization and its impact on the state and citizens in the Third World. It combines social policy and the response of non-state agencies in the face of both vagaries of nature and the neo-liberal policies of the World Bank and the IMF.

Globalization is portrayed as having two sides. In its neo-liberal form, it has unleashed on the Third World countries Structural Adjustment Programmes that have elevated the primacy of capitalism at a high cost to welfare. The result for social provision has been devastating, given that states have been reduced to facilitators of investment of international capital.

In its cultural form, globalization has led to a broader view of citizenship which stresses universal human rights and obligations. At the same time, it has led to a reassertion of historical and local forces in a fast-changing world.

Taking the case of the Islamic communities of Kenya, globalization in the 1990s has led to a reexamination and has revitalized the application of the social provisioning enshrined in the canons of Islam - The *Quran*, the *Hadith* and the *Sunnah* of prophet Muhammad. The *Zakat* and the *Wakf* institutions, both at national and international levels, have played a crucial role of social welfare in the face of the difficult conditions of the current times. These institutions have been reorganized to link the efforts of international Islamic agencies with those of the local groups. The training of local manpower in the management and distribution of relief, soliciting for aid from outside, and establishing income generating projects demonstrate a great advance in Islamic social policy in Kenya today.

## Note

* Department of History, Kenyatta University, Nairobi.

## References

Abdallah, Ahmed, 1995, 'Poverty Alleviation and the Muslim Community', in Bakari and Yahya, eds. *Islam in Kenya*, Nairobi: MEWA Publications, pp. 200-213.

Aina, T. A., 1997, *Globalization and Social Policy in Africa: Issues and Social Research Directions,* Working Paper Series, Dakar, CODESRIA, June.

Al-Islam, 1991, *Quarterly Journal of the Islamic Foundation,* Nairobi, Kenya. Vol. 15, No.1.

Al-Islam, 1995, *Quarterly Journal of the Islamic Foundation of Kenya*, Nairobi, Vol. 19, No.1.

Bakari, Mohamed, 1995, 'Asian Muslims in Kenya', in Bakari and Yahya, eds., *Islam in Kenya,* MEWA Publications, pp. 53-68.

Bakari, Mohamed, 1995, 'Muslims and the Politics of Change in Kenya', in Bakari and Yahya, eds., *Islam in Kenya,* Nairobi: MEWA Publications, pp. 234-251.

Central Bank of Kenya, 1991.

*Daily Nation,* September 10, 1997, Nairobi: Nation Media Group.

*Daily Nation,* November 9, 1997, Nairobi: Nation Media Group.

*Daily Nation,* December 2, 1997, Nairobi: Nation Media Group.

*Daily Nation,* February 6, 1998, Nairobi: Nation Media Group.

*Daily Nation,* February 12, 1998, Nairobi: Nation Media Group.

*Daily Nation,* September 9, 1998, Nairobi: Nation Media Group.

*Daily Nation,* September 20, 1998, Nairobi: Nation Media Group.

*Daily Nation,* October 3, 1998, Nairobi: Nation Media Group.

*Daily Nation,* July 20, 199, Nairobi: Nation Media Group.

Ezcurra, A. M. 1997, 'Globalization, Neo-Liberalism and Civil Society: Challenge for the Latin American Social and People's Movements', in Batista, ed., *Social Movements: Challenges and Dilemmas*, Geneva: World Council of Churches, pp. 76-91.

Gallardo, H., 1997, 'Globalization and Social Movements in Latin America: A Conceptual Approach', in Batista (ed.), *Social Movements: Challenges and Dilemmas*. Geneva, World Council of Churches, pp. 63-75.

*Holy Quran*, translation, A. Y. Ali.

Huntington. S. P., 1996, *The Clash of Civilizations and the Remaking of World Order*, New York: Touchstone.

Kamal, A. A., 1991, 'Zakat: The Prescribed Charity', in *Al-Islam*, Vol. 15, No. 1, pp. 16-20.

*Kenya Times*, September 3, 1992, Nairobi: Kenya Times Media Trust.

Mamdani, M. and Wamba-dia-Wamba, E. (eds.), 1995, *African Studies in Social Movements and Democracy*, CODESRIA Book Series, Dakar: CODESRIA.

Mittelman, J. 1994, 'The Globalization Challenge: Surviving at the Margins', *Third World Quartely*, Vol. 15, No. 3.

Mwangi, K. 1995, 'The Application and Development of Sharia in Kenya, 1895–1900', in Bakari and Yahya, eds *Islam in Kenya*, Nairobi: MEWA Publications, pp. 252-9.

Republic of Kenya, 1996, *Statistical Abstract*, Nairobi: Central Bureau of Statistics.

Republic of Kenya, 1998, *Poverty in Kenya*, Vol. II, Nairobi: Central Bureau of Statistics.

Said, A.S. 1995, 'An Outline History of Islam in Nyanza Province', in Bakari and Yahya (eds.). *Islam in Kenya*, Nairobi, MEWA Publications.

Salim, I.A. 1973, *Swahili Speaking People of Kenya Coast, Nairobi*, London: East African Publishing House.

Shiva, V. 1997, 'Democracy in the Age of Gloalisation', in Batista, ed. *Social Movements: Challenges and Dallenges and Dilemmas*, Geneva: World Council of Churches, pp. 134-141.

Siddiqi, M.H., 1987, 'Zakat', in Eliade, ed., *The Encylopedia of Religion*, New York: Macmillan Publishing Co., Vol. 15, pp. 550-551.

*Society*, June 29, 1992 Nairobi: Nyamora Communications Limited, Vol. 2.

*Sunday Nation*, February 14, 1993, Nairobi: Nation Media Group.

*Sunday Nation*, May 7, 2000. Nairobi: Nation Media Group.

UNRISD, 1996-97, *Social Development Research*, Geneva: UNRISD Activities.

Walji, R. S. 1995, 'Ismailis in Kenya: Some Perspectives on Continuity and Change', in Bakari and Yahya, eds. *Islam in Kenya*, Nairobi: MEWA Publications.

Waters, M. 1995, *Globalization*, London and New York: Routledge.

*Weekly Review*, July 12, 1976. Nairobi: Stellascop Ltd.

*Weekly Review*, January 9, 1981. Nairobi: Stellascop Ltd.

*Weekly Review*, November 17, 1989. Nairobi: Stellascop Ltd.

Williams, J.A., 1982, 'Wakf', in Eliade, ed., *The Encyclopedia of Religion*, New York: Macmillan Publishing Co., Vol 15, pp. 337-339.

Yahya, S.S. 1995, 'The Uses and Abuses of Wakf', in Bakari and Yahya, eds., *Islam in Kenya*, Nairobi: MEWA Publications.

## Oral Respondents

Abdi, Maulid Abdi, Teacher – Shuric Secondary School, Garissa.
Abdille, Shalle Ibrahim, Teacher – Mandera Boys town.
Abdullahi, Mohammed Ibrahim, Headmaster – Wajir High School.
Absiye, Mohamed Omar, Teacher – Arabia Secondary School, Mandera.
Ahmed, Mohammed Sheikh, Secretary of MEDS, Mandera
Bardad, Adow Mohammed, Teacher – Mandera Arid Zone Primary School.
Harun, Sheikh Adow, Businessman – Mandera
Hassan, Ibrahim Maalim, Teacher-Arabia Secondary School, Mandera.
Mohamed, Dahanse, District Education Office, Mandera.
Wandati, A., Executive Director, Muslim Consultative Council of Kenya.

# 14

# Harambee Self-Help in Kenya: An Interplay Between the Global and Local

**Pius Kakai Wanyonyi***

## Introduction

This chapter examines the institution and mechanism of 'Harambee' as an interplay between local and global factors affecting the mobilization of community resources for the provision of social services. It also examines the contradictions involved in the use of this approach in the light of Kenya's colonial and post-colonial politics and economic development proven. The study uses the case of Bungoma District in the Western province of Kenya to illustrate this interplay. But before we go on, what do we understand by Harambee? The discussion below provides both the setting and the substance.

## Context of Harambee Self-Help in Kenya

The Harambee self-help approach draws its spirit of commitment, inspiration, continuity and informality from the African indigenous setting (Mbithi 1972: 149). Though the term harambee may not have been in vogue among all indigenous Kenyan communities, the mood of co-operation, community and participation in the self-help projects was present. It was witnessed in marriage negotiations, funeral and initiation rituals, work and sport. This collective social responsibility was not unique to Kenya. As Nyerere's (1969) 'Ujamaa' demonstrates, it operated in many traditional African societies. So while Tanzanians described the spirit as Ujamaa, Kenyans described theirs as harambee. In the initial sense harambee was understood to be a basically voluntary engagement (Muyia 1994: 42) which empowered the society to collectively settle some problems and challenges. The self-help collective form dates from the pre-colonial period and continued throughout colonialism. Even in this post independence period, the self-help initiatives are still carried out. The initiatives in all those periods have not been aimed at connoting attainment of absolute self-sufficiency in production as much as avoiding dependency. What self-help has done is to make members of the community devise mechanisms of settling their problems by mobilizing community resources such as finance and other resources, and where need arises, seeking support from neighbouring communities as well as organizations.

The pre-colonial initiatives gave harambee an entirely indigenous appearance. However, during colonialism, the global element was introduced. This global dimension emanates from certain disruptive features introduced often coercively by the colonial forces. The external global elements were 'linked and shaped by events occurring miles away' (Aina 1996: 11) in the colonial metropole. One such feature was the ushering in of the colonial administration in 1895 under the label of 'British East Africa Protectorate'. Indeed, even before the protectorate was established, European explorers and missionaries as well as Arab traders had long interacted with local indigenous communities. Unlike the pre-colonial voluntary and largely informal engagements, the self-help initiatives which operated in the colonial dispensation were often truncated with colonial officialdom under the ethnically based Local Native Authorities, introduced in Kenya from around 1924.

Hill (1990) argues that through the Native Authorities, the British colonial government in Kenya brought in its brand of *Community Development* policy as a facilitator of 'active co-operation of the people of each community in programmes designed to raise standards of living and to promote development in all its forms' (45-49) . From this extract, one notices the colonial insinuation of the 'backwardness' of the colonized communities. Thus the so-called *community development* policy was hegemonic and aimed at imposing Western values on Africa and other Third World regions (Berger 1994: 260). The model represented the Third World as so underdeveloped that it had to adopt Western values if its problems were to be solved. Amin (1993) underscores the side effect of this capitalist perception of 'development' because it polarizes societies into the rich and the poor. True 'development' should aim at overcoming social polarization since it mobilizes collective effort to attain desired goals.

Assumptions of using the Western European modernization model as a panacea for solving Third World developmental issues was not tenable as later, especially, post-independence scenarios unfolded. However, in the 1950s, the use of community development to mobilize mass participation was not unique. As Hill (1990) asserts, Kenyan District Commissioners' annual reports of the 1950s onwards did not illustrate how different their self-help community development was from the pre-colonial alternative (49). Instead, the projects were largely communal under a new name. The labour was unpaid, organized by chiefs, approved and sometimes contributed to by district or local councils. It was, however, largely coercive.

The self-help work or harambee initiatives under the colonial dispensation centred on building primary schools, earth dams, water catchments, maintaining or extending local roads and soil conservation projects. The foregoing highlights those projects which colonial administrators considered important to the improvement of the colonized standards of living. However, as our discussion on Bungoma below indicates, this was not all. To rely only on the formal records is to exclude the numerous informal self-help projects which formed part and parcel of the indigenous communities' activities in Western Province generally, and Bungoma District, in particular. Whereas the 'self-help' in the precolonial time clearly indicated the communities' determination to work collectively and voluntarily to improve the groups' collective and individual standards of living, the use of the concept during the colonial situation was double-edged. To some extent, it was in these initiatives that colonial regimes benefited at the expense of the indigenous. The subsequent discussion will help to shed more light on the issue.

## Harambee Self-Help Initiatives in Bungoma District in Colonial Times

Bungoma District is one of the districts constituting Western Province. Other districts are Mt. Elgon (which was hived off from Bungoma in 1993), Teso, Busia, Lugari, Kakamega, Butere-Mumias and Vihiga. Apart from Mt. Elgon and Teso, the rest are mainly inhabited by the Abaluyia. Bungoma up to 1956 formed part of North Nyanza District whose size was approximately similar to the current Western Province. However, since 1956, the North Nyanza District was split into two. One section retained the name of 'North Nyanza' and the new one adopted the name, 'Elgon Nyanza' which in 1964 was renamed Bungoma. Bungoma was mainly occupied by Abaluyia (Abatachoni and Babukusu) as well as the Sabaot (Kalenjin). Self-help activities continued while being affected by the colonial situation. For example, initiation rituals, funeral expenses, marriage negotiations as well as other aspects of community life continued operating as in the pre-colonial times. The materially able from within the various clans assisted the less able without necessarily expecting the recipients to pay back. This collective spirit was indeed true of many other parts of Africa. Nyerere (1969) states that because of the Ujamaa spirit, the society in traditional Africa looked after its members whether old, young, widows, widowers or orphans (159). However, as the impact of colonialism entrenched itself, forms of self-help took new turns, often becoming formalised and even exclusionary. The exclusionary trend was in line with the capitalistic Western orientation which created individualistic, exploitative and competitive tendencies among residents of not only Bungoma but also the entire Kenya colony and Protectorate (*The Constitution of Kenya*, 1963; Nasong'o 1999).

Christian missions and Local Native Authorities (LNA) enabled educated inhabitants of Bungoma to form associations through which harambee initiatives were carried out. For instance, in the 1930s, residents of the then Kimilili Location established the 'Kimilili Farmers Association' which mobilized its members into collective activities aimed at improving soil conservation, farming methods as well as identifying good buyers for their maize (Wolf 1977: 50; Wipper 1977: 111; Askwith 1995). Gradually, the farming activities gave rise to certain personalities emerging as beneficiaries while many ordinary people did not. Herein lay the capitalistic acquisitive and exploitative traits. This clinches Hutchful's (1995) view that social movements such as community associations influence decisions that affect ordinary people's lives.

Askwith's quote below aptly illustrates a harambee initiative that absorbed new farming skills into a communal milieu:

> Groups planted maize in lines, two of the team held each end of the spacing line, another scooped holes for the seed, another followed placing a handful of manure in the holes while another followed to plant the seed. …In this way field after field was rapidly and efficiently planted and the resulting yields were most impressive (Askwith 1995: 191).

The quote best illustrates how the harambee self-help efforts were used by colonial administrators to improve farming yields in Bungoma District and beyond. But the initiative was not locally known as harambee. For this Kiswahili concept had not yet spread among members of the region. However, residents of Bungoma had their own version. They include *buambari* or *obulala* (Winser, 1959; Elgon Nyanza Annual District Report). Working was accompanied by traditional rhythmical work songs that boosted the workers' morale and cautioned against laziness. Here it should be noted that the 'traditional' was dynamic and changed with situations and time (Aina 1996). In addition to the planting of maize discussed above, other tasks included ploughing, pasture clearing, spring protection, digging coffee holes and preparing vegetable seed beds. Similarly, during colonialism residents of Bungoma through Local Native Council and the Christian missions raised funds through harambee initiatives and sponsored students for further studies. Products of this early colonial harambee initiative were later on among the leading nationalists in Kenya. For instance Masinde Muliro dominated politics in Western province, especially in Bungoma, from the 1950s to 1992 when he died mysteriously (Wandibba 1996: 2; Chikati 1988: 51).

## Harambee Self-Help Initiative in Post Independence Era

Kenya attained independence in 1963. Soon afterwards, Jomo Kenyatta, Kenya's first President, announced a strategy of harambee self-help as a core policy (Holmquist 1984: 176). This core policy in a way also reflected Kenya's social policy. Kenyatta's quote below succinctly captures the mood of the spirit at the birth of independence. He declared that:

> You and I must work together to develop our country, to get education for our children, to have doctors, to build roads, to improve or provide all the day to day essentials in the spirit of Harambee (Kenyatta 1968: 217).

In essence, Kenyatta was appealing for a sense of community organization, involvement and initiative as well as the community contribution of finance, labour, or both to any project such as the building of schools, health facilities, community centres, roads, bridges, cattle dips and water projects. This idea as the previous sections illustrate, was not new. What appears new was harmonising the nomenclature by popularising the use of a Kiswahili version, harambee, instead of local parallels like *obulala* or *buambani*. In addition, the fact that the initiative was articulated by Kenya's president instilled enthusiasm in the citizens to emphasize the nation state context of the policy. The term harambee was therefore uniformly applied to the policy and movement whose history dates from pre-colonial time.

As Mboya (1970: 98) asserted, the citizens' response was vigorous. Local communities began such projects as schools, clinics, cattle dips, rural roads among others often without having acquired enough resources to complete them (Willis 1994: 133). Especially on the side of education, almost every community struggled to put up schools to meet the increased demand. Many young people who would have otherwise failed to secure learning opportunities seized on the chance to acquire secondary and sometimes technical and vocational education. Some of the learners even reached university level and are important personalities in both public and private sectors in the country. Nonetheless, though learners obtained some useful skills, the majority of them were poorly equipped, hence harambee schools produced lop-sided graduates who could not effectively operate in the more scientific fields. Similarly, due to the upsurge of harambee school leavers, the government was faced with urgent unemployment problems (Mwiria 1987: 2). Consequently, what was perceived as a right step in facilitating development became a source of worry to the government.

In Bungoma district the distribution of harambee projects raised some ethnic suspicions which sometimes exploded into hostilities among Babukusu and their Sabaot neighbours. This fact is well articulated by Chebet (oral interview, 1996) a Sabaot–retired educationist. He asserts that unlike in the other parts of Bungoma, the Mt. Elgon region was not adequately provided with such facilities as schools and health units. Given the region's inability to raise funds to construct enough schools, local members of the Sabaot group often changed their identities in order to impersonate members of the

Babukusu and consequently benefit from facilities initiated in the Babukusu–occupied zones. His sentiments were succinctly captured below.

> At independence, there were few schools in Mt. Elgon. They included Kaptama, Kapsakwony, Kapkateny and Cheptais. Hence, to get admission into schools most Sabaot adopted Luyia names, I was known as Abraham Juma. I chose the name because it sounded like those given to Babukusu. If one could not acquire a Bukusu identification, even if he/she had done well at the common entrance examination, he/she would not be selected into an intermediate class (Chebet, oral interview, 1996).

It was in recognition of the above disadvantage that the Sabaot insisted in 1963 on electing a Sabaot, Daniel Mossi as their Member of Parliament (MP) so that he could mobilize funds through harambee and develop the area. Their collective commitment to see Mossi win degenerated into the 1963 ethnic conflict in which non-Sabaot houses were burnt down and their property destroyed on suspicion that they were anti-Mossi. Yet still, Mossi's effort alone, fruitful though it was, could do little. Harambees conducted in the region and the assistance from government and non-governmental organisations could hardly bring up the area to the level of the rest of Bungoma. This inequality forced the Sabaot to continue agitating for their district, which they received in 1993.

*Bungoma District Development Plan*: *1994–1996* indicates the continued inequality in resource distribution in the district. While noting the importance of agriculture and livestock, the Plan adds that 'cattle dips are evenly distributed except in Mt. Elgon areas including Cheptais and Kapsokwony where dips are fewer than in other areas' (76). The implication of the foregoing is clear. Since all cattle dips were constructed through harambee, it follows that Mt. Elgon people could not raise the funds and labour to construct enough of them. Furthermore, the inadequacy of dips suggests that Sabaot cattle hardly receive sufficient chemical protection against ticks and related pests.

However, having dips was not enough assurance that all local cattle could be dipped. Each cattle owner was required to pay a minimal fee for the chemical pesticide. This responsibility was not organised through harambee. Hence most dips were under-utilized. This problem seems to have affected the entire Bungoma District.

## Harambee Since the 1980s

1980 and beyond are years charactered by President Moi's leadership and political manipulation in employing harambee rallies to ensure his impact in various parts of the country, especially the Rift Valley Province. During the period of one party-rule, the regime harnessed the services of the provincial administration and KANU party officials to extort money and other materials to be donated at the many harambee functions which the president conducted.

This crude approach, whether to raise money for construction of class rooms, as when the government was implementing the controversial 8-4-4 education system, or the construction of what came to be known as Nyayo wards in hospitals and the frequency with which the funding drives were conducted overwhelmed ordinary citizens, causing them untold deprivation and a major dislike for the otherwise noble initiative (Kanyinga 1995).

But this dislike was mainly when the harambee initiatives were associated with political dictation. In the ordinary informal settings however, low keyed harambee functions were continually practised by adults, youth and women with varying results (Bungoma District Development Plan, 1994-1996, Muyia, 1994; Kanyinga 1995). Through these low keyed harambee initiatives, for instance, women groups in Bungoma district operated grain grinding mills, practised livestock keeping and organized frequent cyclical credit schemes—'merry-go-rounds' (Bungoma Development Plan: 1994–1996: 103).

Due to these projects, the communities were boosted financially leading to their significant contributions at educational, commercial and other institutional levels. This study examined one rural–based self-help initiative and another mainly urban initiated but mobilizing contributions territorially, to illustrate the mechanics the various organisers employed to assist in helping particularly needy cases.

Katosia self-help group in rural Bungoma district brought together ordinary peasants who raised money and bought cross breed dairy cattle in the 1980s. The sale of their milk enabled the owners to purchase feeds for the cattle, pay school fees for their children as well as empower them to construct more durable shelters for themselves (Muse, Oral Interview, 1998). Besides, the achievements of the members led organizers of the Bungoma district agricultural show to give the self-help group a stand to display their products. Thus, through the harambee projects, the Katosia self-help group attracted many customers, students and instructors to their farms in the 1980s and 1990s.

Another aspect of the harambee initiative is the initiative the staff at the Nation Media group organized to raise resources towards assisting residents in the famine stricken Turkana district in 1999. This harambee initiative, known as the 'Nation Famine Relief Campaign' was launched on November 1999, and collected several millions of shillings, foodstuff, clothing and medicine from individuals and institutions.

The Fund which ran into early 2000 helped in alleviating starvation and sickness in Turkana. Indeed, one of the victims, six year old Aro Koriang, whose skeleton-like picture appeared in the *Daily Nation* of November 22, 1999, was in January 2000 admitted to Gertrudes Garden Hospital, situated in Nairobi and specializing in treating children. The hospital staff, *Nation Media* team and other well wishers attended to Aro so well that by the time she was discharged in March, 2000, her features had tremendously improved (*Daily Nation*, March 17, 2000).

This latter example demonstrates the dynamism inherent in the operation of harambee initiative. Firstly, unlike in the traditional setting, the plight of those who require help and even the method of collecting donations, are communicated through the print and electronic media. Similarly, the donations were sent both physically by contributors visiting the Nation Centre building in Nairobi as well as by postage.

Besides, donors were both local and international, young and old. Hence the nobleness in giving and sharing transcended ethnic and racial boundaries just as the spread of the news reached many and sundry. Even some NGOs participated in this *Nation Media* group initiative. Consequently it is in this aspect that this paper considers non-governmental organisations' contributions as a form of harambee. Through their collective efforts, famine in Turkana was temporarily minimised. Since some of the NGOs which participated in the funds are international, one can agree with Annan-Yao (1997: 2) that indeed some sectors of the African population benefited from globalization.

Of immediate concern here is how harambee was corrupted to serve parochial political interests not only since the 1980s but even within the first regime of independent Kenya. The sub-section below addresses this aspect.

### *Harambee and Power Politics*

While the initiative of harambee may have been nurtured in the womb of ordinary people in the pre-colonial era, the subsequent events in both colonial and post-independence Kenya ushered in elements of a political nature. Already this has been alluded to when the first president of independence era, Kenyatta (1968), as well as his successor Moi (1986) stressed the need to employ a harambee spirit in sustaining and even improving post-independence rate of development. But since the two leaders' orientation was towards the Western liberal material persuasion, elitism was encapsulated in their articulation of 'harambee'. In this aspect, those people in high offices, or with political aspirations were expected to take the lead in raising huge sums of money.

Furthermore, since politicians in independent Kenya were deprived of their statutory authority or influence in their constituencies, the elected officials turned to community development initiatives, 'harambees', as a strategic base for power outside the central administration (Kanyinga 1995: 72). Even in the areas of self-help, politicians had to contend with provincial administrations which often aimed at frustrating local politicians' efforts in carving a niche among the electorates. As a consequence, tension between politicians and provincial administration emerged. This was especially so when specific politicians were perceived as being diametrically opposed to the views of those in power or their local agents. In this connection, areas with politicians who were thought to be politically correct readily received licences from the provincial administration to conduct harambee functions, whereas those believed to be in disfavour with the regime or their agents were frustrated. This explains why in Kenyatta's days, especially between 1967 and 1973, annual per capita contributions to harambee were 69.6 per cent in Central Province and only 29.8 per cent in the next most generous province, Rift Valley (Gibbon 1995: 20). It is also stated that Kenyatta himself donated hefty amounts in Kenya Shillings (Ksh.) 314,400/- to projects between January 1971 and April 1974 (20). Over half of these donations were for harambee in Central Province –an area which is dominated by the Agikuyu, Kenyatta's kinspeople.

While actual figures have not been documented regarding Moi's donations, it is believed that his were mainly for the harambees organised in the Kalenjin-dominated Rift Valley Province. Murungi (*Daily Nation*, January 28, 1995) contends that most of the harambees which raise millions of shillings were for projects in the Rift Valley, President Moi's home province. Even politicians from hardship areas avoid concentrating on initiating projects in their districts and spend their meagre resources participating in huge harambees in the president's district, Baringo (*Daily Nation*, January 28, 1995). As a consequence, schools in Kalenjin-dominated Rift Valley province are so well furnished that whenever national examination results are announced, the province has always topped the list while less advantaged ones, especially the North Eastern province has appeared last. Therefore, predictably, as harambee has contributed to positive performance in some areas, it has also resulted in disparities in the national distribution of resources. Yet it is also true that both presidents used harambees to establish clientelism in other parts of the country (Morton 1998: 20, 130). For instance, in the 1980s cabinet, ministers Elijah Mwangale, Moses Mudavadi and Peter Okondo were believed to be Moi's close agents. Consequently, they received licences to conduct fundraising activities where huge amounts of money were raised. This aspect led ordinary citizens to associate MPs and especially cabinet ministers with money whose source very few cared to question. Besides, some politicians, after raising such money, ended up not using it for the intended public projects (*Sunday Standard*, May 9, 1999: 9; *Sunday Nation*, May 16, 1999: 7; Personal conversation with informants 1999).

Using their money, irrespective of its source, local power groups also recruited their own agents through whom their wishes were communicated to the voters. In Bungoma District, where Mwangale dominated the political scene between 1969 and 1992, it was mainly those areas which gave him a lot of votes which received most donations for harambee projects while areas perceived to be opposed to his style of politics received hardly any. Even if projects initiated by the electorate in such areas needed little financial support to finish, that was not expected to come easily. Either the reigning politician in the district would not attend the function or he would prevail upon the provincial administration to cancel the license to carry out the function, to refuse to issue the license, or merely disrupt the function (Okondo 1995).

This misuse of political and administrative offices to frustrate harambee projects was a countrywide affair. Murungi (1995) illustrates how his opposition status provoked the provincial administration in Meru district of Eastern Province to deny him clearance to conduct a harambee to set up an 'Education Revolving Fund' for his South Imenti constituency in 1994.

The reintroduction of multipartyism in 1991 led to the fall of previously powerful politicians not only in Bungoma District but also in other parts of the country. Those affected included Mwangale, Burudi Nabwera and Okondo. All of them hailed from Western Province. Their disappearance heralded the end of huge harambee donations from MPs. The new crop of politicians in Bungoma since 1993 belonged to opposition parties such as Forum for Restoration of Democracy-Kenya (Ford-K) and Forum for Restoration of Democracy-Asili (Ford-A). Given that these were young political parties with a lifespan not exceeding ten years, their financial base could not be compared to KANU's. Therefore, whenever these new MPs participated in harambee functions, their contributions were so meagre and disappointing that their voters yearned for past days when the likes of Mwangale could give huge sums ranging from between Ksh. 10,000 to over Ksh. 100,000 at a single event (Wafula Personal Conversation 1998). It became evident that whatever amount was raised by the new breed of politicians could not initiate long-lasting projects. Nor could they raise enough to furnish classes with sufficient equipment and other requirements that could facilitate a good learning milieu.

Yet the voters could not understand the inability of their MPs. The electorate continued inviting their MPs to harambees. This forced some of the MPs to start complaining (Kituyi, Sifuna, Munyasia, in KBC 'Insight', 1998). The legislators want to be left with the task of making legislation instead of being inconvenienced with harambee functions. But since the previous politicians' participation at harambees is still deeply entrenched in the minds of the electorate, it may take some time and intense grassroot mobilization to make the electorate stop associating legislators with huge sums of money.

Indeed, some revelations (*The Weekly Review,* Dec. 4, 1998) intimated that most pro-establishment politicians and others in the opposition who donated huge sums of money at fundraising functions had acquired big loans on which they had defaulted. The failure to pay back led to the collapse of some small banks and even almost led to one of Kenya's leading banks, National Bank of Kenya (NBK) going under. Late in 1998 NBK suffered a massive run on deposits amounting to Ksh. 7 billion, forcing it to liquidate some of its assets (*Sunday Standard,* March 28, 1999: 13). This behaviour tarnished the harambee initiative of pooling resources together so as to improve the peoples' lives.

Okondo (1995: 130, 240-244) identifies other ways in which the harambee initiative was abused. First, civil servants used their positions not only to extort money from their juniors so as to contribute at fundraisings which were presided over by senior politicians, but also these senior officers even diverted money from budget project allocations funds which the officers donated at harambee functions while secretly expecting to be rewarded with promotions. Of course such misallocation adversely affects the originally intended project.

Besides, provincial administration officials often demanded bribes in return for licences in the name of harambee. While this corrupt practice was widespread, no stern measures have been taken to discipline the errant criminals. As a result, whenever members of the provincial administration asked for harambee money, very few people took the officers seriously (Khaikwa, personal conversation, 1999). It becomes more objectionable when some of those administrative agents employ force in seizing people's property in the name of harambee.

## Impact of Globalization on Harambee

The previous section has mentioned areas where globalization has boosted the effectiveness of harambee initiatives. However, globalization has also negatively impacted on the harambee initiative. Both Nzomo (1994) and Aseka (1996) argue that globalization through the Structural Adjustment Programmes (SAPs) have been ruthlessly applied on the African continent. Aseka sees the poor who constitute 90 per cent of Africa's population as the victims of SAPs or a 'chaotic world economy'. In the same vein, Nzomo (1994) holds that Kenya's implementation of SAPs has led to substantial cut-backs in government's social expenditure in critical areas such as health and education (430).

For instance, whereas in the past patients in government hospitals received medical treatment without incurring exorbitant financial charges, from the mid-1980s the situation changed. A policy of cost-sharing was introduced, requiring patients to meet some of the expenditure by either buying the prescribed drugs or bed charges.

To worsen the situation, this cost-sharing has spread to other critical areas like education. Citizens who could not raise enough money to pay ended up not receiving proper medical and educational facilities for their families. As Nzomo points out, women and children were the most affected because they largely depended on the services which were pruned. This scenario equally affected the ordinary folk. Indeed, with the liberalisation of the economy, especially since the 1980s, several issues emerged. First, the government stopped fixing prices for agricultural produce in the entire country. Second, businessmen were allowed to import cheaper products from outside Kenya. And finally, local produce was sold below the cost of production or sometimes remained abandoned in warehouses for long periods without receiving any buyers. This is what Hammouda (1997: 8) describes as growth dynamics directed towards external markets at the expense of the needs of internal markets.

The above fate affected sugar cane, maize and cotton produce planted in Bungoma and other parts of the country. Hence, most ordinary farmers in the district could not easily participate in the harambee project or the cost-sharing process. Accordingly, the standard of living in rural areas such as Bungoma actually declined.

## Conclusion

In concluding, it is necessary to point out that the programme of harambee self-help initiatives was introduced to effectively mobilize people in all parts of the country to implement many desirable projects. Main actors in the harambee activities involved local members assisted by some other groups and institutions. But with the unnecessary lack of transparency, corruption, administrative high-handedness, over-taxation and the introduction of SAPs, harambee initiatives went on the decline. The contributors, who include politicians, business people, professionals, and farmers felt the expectations from their people were too much for them to manage. Besides, the element of corruption that had infected the harambee initiative rendered the primary driving force of fostering self reliance hollow. While individuals and organizations raised money and other forms of materials to help improve the living standards of specific communities, some of these funds were misappropriated by a few corrupt individuals. In this regard, the lives of those in whose name the harambee initiatives were conducted either remain poor or have even worsened.

More corrective measures will need to be applied to resuscitate the harambee initiative. These may include transparency in the organization and distribution of resources raised during harambee functions. This paper proposes that the openness which operated during the pre-colonial and informal obulala or buambani functions may be useful boosters to the morale of those who sacrificed their meagre resources in the hope that the fruits would benefit the broader society.

Also to be addressed is the issue Holmquist (1984: 176) called 'a policy in default'. Money, material and other resources should not be raised without having a long term vision. There should be openness, transparency and accountability to accompany the whole process. Furthermore, the vision should not be tied to political and bureaucratic bottlenecks. The welfare interests of the grassroots should be at the centre of the entire process.

Harambee initiatives can still benefit by having members from other districts and provinces actively help to boost in the welfare of their compatriots in less advantaged regions as the Nation Famine Relief Campaign illustrates. This spirit has worked in the past. It has also enabled NGOs to raise funds aimed at helping residents of the Third World. Thus, globalization, if well managed, can boost the harambee initiative. But if such corrective measures are not undertaken, one fears that the initiative might become a thing of the past.

## Notes

* Department of History, Kenyatta University, Nairobi.

## References


Aina, A., T., 1996, 'Globalization and Social Policy in Africa', *CODESRIA Bulletin*, Dakar: CODESRIA. No. 4.

Aina, A., T., 1997, *Globalization And Social Policy in Africa: Issues and Research Directions*, Dakar, CODESRIA.

Annan-Yao, E., 1997, 'Comments on Globalization and Social Policy', *CODESRIA Bulletin*, Dakar: CODESRIA, No. 3.

Amin, 1993, 'The Challenge of Globalization: Delinking', in *Facing the Challenge*, London and New Jersey: Zed Books.

Aseka, E. M., 1996, *Africa in the 21st Century*, Eldoret: Zapf Chancery.

Askwith, T., 1995, *From Mau Mau to Harambee*, Cambridge: African Studies Centre.

Berger, M., T., 1994, 'The End of the Third World?', *Third World Quarterly*, London, University of London, Vol. 15, No. 2 .

*Bungoma District Development Plan 1994-1996*, Nairobi: Government Press.

Chebet, A., 1996, Interview on November.

Chikati, J., 1988, 'The Biography of Chief Musa Namutala: 1930-1973', B.A. dissertation, History Department, University of Nairobi.

*Daily Nation*, 1999, November 22, Nairobi: Nation Newspapers Ltd.

*Daily Nation*, 1999, December 28, Nairobi: Nation Newspapers Ltd.

*Daily Nation*, 1999, December 30, Nairobi: Nation Newspapers Ltd.

*Daily Nation*, 2000, March 17, Nairobi: Nation Newspapers Ltd.

*Daily Nation*, 2000, May 10, Nairobi: Nation Newspapers Ltd.

Gibbon, P. ed., 1995, *Markets, Civil Society and Democracy in Kenya*, Uppsala: Nordiska Afrikainstitutet.

Hammouda, B. H., 1997, 'Remarks on Globalization and Social Policy in Africa', *CODESRIA Bulletin*, Dakar, CODESRIA, No. 2.

Hill, D.J.M., 1990, 'The Harambee Self-Help Movement in Kenya', Ph.D Thesis, London: University of London.

Holmquist, F., 1984, 'Class Structure, Peasant Participation and Rural Self-Help', in J.D. Barkan, ed. *Politics and Public Policy in Kenya and Tanzania*, New York: Praeger Publishers.

Hutchful, E., 1995, 'The International Dimensions of the Democratisation Process in Africa', in E. Chole and J. Ibrahim, eds., *Democratisation Processes in Africa: Problems and Prospects*, Dakar: CODESRIA.

Kanyinga, K., 1995, 'The Changing Development Space in Kenya: Political Changes and Voluntary Development Activities', in Gibbon, P., ed., *Markets, Civil Society and Democracy in Kenya,* Uppsala, Nordiska Afrikainstitutet.

Kenyatta, J., 1968, *Suffering Without Bitterness*, Nairobi: East African Publishing House.

Khaikwa, V.K., 1999, *Personal Conversation*, April 20.

Kituyi, M. Munyasia, J. and Sifuna L., 1998, KBC INSIGHT PROGRAMME, Nairobi: KBC.

Mamdani, M., 1996, *Citizen and Subject,* Princeton, New Jersey: Princeton University Press.

Mbithi, P.M., 1972, 'Harambee Self-Help: The Kenya Approach', *The African Review*, Nairobi: East African Literature Bureau, Vol. 2, No. 1.

Mboya, Tom, 1970, *The Challenge of Nationhood*, London: Heinemann Educational Books.

Moi, D.T., 1986, *Kenya African Nationalism*, Nairobi: Macmillan Publishers.

Morton, A., 1998, *Moi: The Making of an African Statesman*, London: Michael O'Mara Books Ltd.

Murungi, K., 1995, 'MP's View on Rift Valley Exam Results', *Daily Nation,* January 28, Nairobi: Nation Newspapers Ltd.

Muse, L., 1998, Interview, December 28.

Muyia, N., 1994, 'Education Through Self-Help: The Case of Kenyan University Students with the Introduction of University Fees Payment', in G. S. Were, ed. *Eastern African Research and Development,* Nairobi: Gideon S. Were Press, Vol. 24.

Mwiria, K., 1987, 'Kenya's Harambee Secondary School Movement: A History of Contradictions', Kenyatta University Bureau of Educational Research Seminar paper no. 20172.

Nasong'o, W., 1999, 'Constitution-Making and the Minority Question: Assessment of Mwambao Separatism and Somali Irredentism', in L. Chweya, ed., *Constitutional Politics and The Challenges of Democracy in Kenya,* Nairobi: Sareat.

Nyerere, J.K., 1969, 'Ujamaa - The Basis of African Socialism', in E.K. Svendsen, and Merete T., eds., *Self Reliant Tanzania,* Dar-es-Salaam: Tanzanian Publishing House.

Nzomo, M., 1994, 'External Influence on the Political Economy of Kenya: The Case of MNC', in W. O. Oyugi, ed., *Politics and Administration in East Africa*, Nairobi: East African Educational Publishers.

Okonndo, P.H., 1995, *A Commentary on the Constitution of Kenya*, Nairobi: Phoenix Publishers.

*Sunday Standard*, March 7, 1999, Nairobi: Standard Ltd.

*Sunday Standard,* March 28, 1999, Nairobi: Standard Ltd.

*Sunday Standard,* April 25, 1999, Nairobi: Standard Ltd.

*Sunday Nation,* April 25 1999, Nairobi: Nation Newspapers Ltd.

*Sunday Standard*, May 9, 1999, Nairobi: Standard Ltd.

*Sunday Nation,* May 16, 1999, Nairobi: Nation Newspapers Ltd.

*Sunday Nation*, July 26, 1998, Nairobi: Nation Newspapers Ltd.

The Constitution of Kenya, 1963, Nairobi: Government Press.

*The Weeky Review*, December, 4, 1998, Nairobi, The Weekly Review Ltd.

Wafula, R., 1998, personal conversation, July 20.

Wandibba, S., 1996, *Masinde Muliro: A Biography,* Nairobi: East African Educational Publishers.

Willis, M., 1994, 'Central-Local Relations', in W. O. Oyugi, ed., *Politics and Administration in East Africa*, Nairobi: East African Educational Publishers.

Winsor, 1959, *Elgon Nyanza Annual Report*, Nairobi: KNA/DC/EN/1/4.

Wipper, A., 1977, *The Rural Rebels*, Nairobi: Oxford University Press.

Wolf, J.J., 1977, *Differentiation and Integration in Western Kenya,* The Hague: Morton and Co. B.V.

# 15

## Conclusion – Future Agenda: Beyond Globalization

**Chachage S. L. Chachage* & Elisabeth Annan-Yao****

This project was conceived at a time when the euphoria of the 'globalization' thesis was at its zenith: that is, when it had 'become the stock in trade of journalists, media pundits, policy makers, politicians, corporate elites and many an academician' (Hirst & Thompson 1999: 154). The 'Green Book', *Globalization and Social Policies in Africa: Issues and Research Directions* (Aina 1997), which set out the agenda for the these studies, besides examining the relationship between globalization and social policies, fundamentally did three things. It attempted at clarifying and challenging, as well as identifying, some trends and dynamics in the studies of these aspects. This was in recognition of the fact that the studies that exist were riddled with contradictions, ambiguities and inconsistencies.

The simple reason for this was the fact that while there were those who criticized Structural Adjustment Programmes (SAPs) in Africa and attempted to demystify the realities of the processes which were taking place, there were also other scholars (from outside and inside Africa) who went as far as invoking the past and present 'history' of the continent to present arguments to justify the need for it to be 'globalized'. These more or less laid the ground for the eventual acceptance of what was to be accepted as a matter of fact: the inevitability of globalization and the necessity to cohabitate with it. In a way, one could say that these were attempts at the moral rehabilitation of what was being contested by the critics of SAPs.

These scholars supported the liberalization of economies and the operation of the market forces, rather than use of the state to determine the allocation of resources. Their support was justified ideologically in terms of defence of the welfare of the peasants. Their position was more or less consolidated by studies on the operations of the 'informal sector' or 'second-economy', studies which were conducted to account for the way the poor people coped with the crisis. These came to the conclusion that there were a host of activities outside official circuits in which people were engaged, which provided them with survival mechanisms as entrepreneurs or lowincome earners given the failure of the official economy to provide sufficient commodities and income earning opportunities.

Some of these scholars pushed the view that individual strategies for survival and pressure 'from below through parallel marketing system... laid the basis for many of the liberalization measures that the state adopted later'. The 'informal economy' was a catalyst for change as it forced an involuntary 'redefinition of the boundaries of state control'. Liberalization was simply a process that involved the state's gradual recognition of the 'way people go about procuring their livelihood'. The 'second economy', and its activities were conceptualised in terms of being 'adaptations to social or market forces working towards societal harmony or equilibrium'. In these studies, liberalization measures were viewed positively and the governments were advised to support those 'legal' activities, which supposedly played a supportive role in the private sector (Tripp 1989: 45-6).

Studies such as those of Bates (1982), MacGaffey (1987) and Rothchild and Chazan (1988), among others re-conceptualised the state/market relations in terms of existence of a 'second economy', 'informal sector', 'parallel markets', etc. aimed at demonstrating that policy reforms which could overcome the crisis needed to take into account the entire spectrum of economic activities rather than simply the figures provided by the national accounts, which excluded all non-official activities. The 'second economy' was viewed as an 'initiative from below', as 'autonomous forms of accumulation which provided the means of survival, and accumulation of wealth which was being [re]invested in productive enterprise'. This re-conceptualisation of state/market relations was aimed at demonstrating that the principal policy reforms which could overcome the crisis needed to harness the energy of these activities and to politically rehabilitate them. In MacGaffey's (1991) formulation, studies that included the 'second economy' had 'important implications for international aid donors, for potential investors, both foreign and national, and for government planners' (23). Even the existence of Non-Governmental Organizations was viewed from the same point of view. In this way, the circulation of the concept 'civil society', in terms of activities outside the state structures and individual and private property, gained a momentum.

In the same vein, Goran Hyden, against the Dependency theories, and more or less in support of Bill Warren's (1980) thesis that imperialism had a progressive role to play in the Third World countries, had declared that the assumption that the prevalence of underdevelopment in Africa was a result of capitalist and imperialist global functioning was false (Hyden 1983: 5). What Africa had, in his formulation, was an 'unintegrated peasant society'.

Therefore, it was those countries which made international capital their ally (or a necessary evil), which were able to develop their national economies, and those which rejected it for fear of neo-colonialism and attempted at self reliance did not achieve much by way of development. For Africa to achieve meaningful and sustainable development, according to Hyden, it was necessary to reorient the politics in such a way that it is possible to live with capitalism and learn how to deal with it constructively. Rather than pre-empt it, African countries needed to give more scope to managing it: 'Greater reliance on the market force, for instance, will produce growing social cleavages along class lines. Rather than assuming that some form of classless society is possible, the question arising from the emergence of cleavages must be more effectively addressed' (204).

Thus, in a way, the crisis facing African countries was viewed in terms of the crisis facing the agricultural sector due to its pre-modern nature. As revealed by the Newly Industrializing Countries (NICs) which provided the role model, success was perceived to lie in developing strong manufacturing sectors based on exports - mainly exports of primary goods of which agricultural products were the most important. It came to be believed that developing countries could achieve similar successes as the Asian Tigers (Hong Kong, Taiwan, South Korea and Singapore), provided they were able to stabilize and restructure their economies. This was essentially in support of the concept of globalization. The thesis that was that 'international competitive processes would force the convergence of public expenditures in particular towards the lowest possible norm'. (Hirst & Thompson 1999: 171) They held the notion of a 'one world', in which a single market for goods, capital, services, skills and technology prevailed.

In the same vein, the International Monetary Fund (IMF) and the World Bank spearheaded SAPs, in an attempt to deal with the economic crisis which had been facing Africa from the early 1970s. These institutions attributed the causes to the predominance of welfare-oriented policies pursued by governments and the neglect of pure economic concerns. The perception that states are the driving force of economic growth was replaced by the perception that what was necessary was an increased role for market forces in the allocation of resources and a much-enlarged role for the private sector in production and the management of the economy. SAPs stressed the efficiency of free market allocation of resources and emphasized deregulation and export orientation so as to achieve international competitiveness based on comparative advantage. SAPs, it was alleged, were the pre-condition for growth and implicitly for poverty reduction—since the benefits of growth would trickle down to the poor.

These International Financial Institutions (IFIs), had specifically demanded that the African countries introduce external sector reforms to bring domestic prices into line with world market prices. These would induce international competitiveness, promote exports, liberalize imports, enhance the availability of foreign exchange through liberalization of its allocation, devalue currency, and eliminate tariff barriers. Beyond this, they were supposed to liberalize internal trade markets by the removal of price controls, de-confinement of industrial products, liberalization of interest-rates, etc. They further demanded management reforms so as to bring expenditure into line with real resources, in terms of control of the growth of the money supply, cuts in government spending, cost-sharing measures, elimination of subsidies, etc. Alongside this was the question of public sector restructuring through the removal of protection, subsidies, and support for parastatals; commercialization of public sector enterprises; privatization; closure of certain parastatals; and civil service reform. Finally, they demanded sectoral reform in terms of the restructuring of agriculture (including introduction of individualization, titling and registration as far as the land tenure system was concerned), industrial rehabilitation, etc.

With these notions of globalization, even the very history of processes that sparked the spiral of the international crisis was thrown overboard. This history needs to be retold, if we have to make sense of the status of the current debates around the question of globalization and social policy the world over and in Africa specifically.

## The Myths and Realities of Globalization

In the mid-1990s, the anti-globalization (if it may be called so) road show, which started in Seattle (against the World Trade Organization) moved to Davos (against the Trilateral Commission, the World Economic Forum) and to Washington D.C. (against the World Bank and the International Monetary Fund), and took place at the threshold of the millennium, was not anticipated at all. For those who were celebrating 'globalization', such anticipation amounted to a midsummer's night dream. This road show marked an open revolt against an open international economy in the advanced countries, in favour of protectionism from a broad political spectrum - environmentalists, trade unionists and many others. The trade unionists, for example, opposed the threat of accelerated job losses to low wage countries or those countries that utilize child labour. They considered this a threat to their own survival.

With these events, Third World critics of the phenomenon, who for almost twenty years had been dismissed as champions of autarchic, nationalist and welfarist policies, were finally being vindicated. They could now just as well boldly paraphrase Malcom X's famous remark soon after the death of John F. Kennedy in 1963 that the chicken had finally come home to roost. Critics of the process came out with theoretical and empirical criticisms against SAPs. They pointed out that the neo-classical model of perfect competition and their assumptions were not necessarily valid in many developing countries. Many of these assumptions did not hold water as far as Africa is concerned. This was because these assumptions accepted that the external trade sector operated solely on the basis of international comparative advantage; that the nation state was functioning and recognizable; and that economics, rather than social and environmental factors, were primary determinants of development decisions. They identified a number of other factors as having an important influence. These included increasing vulnerability to external shocks and pressures, institutional reform, physical infrastructure, distributional equity, gender equity, social services and natural environment (Mkandawire & Olukoshi 1995; Reed 1992; Gibbon & Olukoshi 1995).

They further pointed out that SAPs failed to recognize that it was not possible to attain a static equilibrium under conditions whereby there were pervasive market failures arising from dynamic and unpredictable externalities. They further argued that there was a lack of strong empirical evidence to justify the link between export performance and increased productivity. Furthermore, these policies failed to recognize other key factors that influenced efficiency and productivity, especially the role of capabilities in terms of skills and technological endowment (Mkandawire and Olukoshi: 1995; Reed: 1992; Gibbon and Olukoshi: 1995).

Although some of these aspects are being incorporated in the current generation of SAPs in the forms of SAPs with a human face, poverty alleviation programs, etc., they have often been only partially implemented or have been distorted within the political economy of decision-making. In practice, as it is with the studies in this book, critics cited examples of countries, which adjusted intensively for a number of years and yet remained marginal to the world economy and heavily indebted with little prospect of renewed economic vitality. There are those who even questioned the premise that trade liberalization is a necessary component of successful outward-oriented strategies.

What is revealed today is the fact that after the 1997 Asian financial crisis and the consequences of the globalization of finance, even those countries cannot be cited as models of sustainable development. There is ample evidence which shows that the success of the Asian Tigers was mainly due to the active role of government in promoting exports in an environment where imports had not been fully liberalized. The Economic Commission for Africa, for example, accused the World Bank of selectivity and inconsistency, and hence misleading conclusions. As far as the Commission was concerned, the major weakness of SAPs was that they used short-term approaches to solve long-term problems. Such short-term stabilization tended to divert attention from action to attain sustainable longer-term economic growth and development goals. In some countries, according to the Commission, the undifferentiated sudden trade liberalization (e.g. reduction of import tariffs) gave rise to the process of de-industrialization. More serious was the fact that even those reform efforts failed, because of the vested interests of certain groups. For example, the tradeable goods sector opposed devaluation; firms producing import substitutes opposed trade liberalization; farmers resisted the cutting of agricultural subsidies; workers resisted privatization and retrenchment; poor people detested cost-sharing as far as social services and infrastructure was concerned; etc.

Over the years, SAPs have tried to change the role of the state by making it lose some of its powers to control the movement of capital (mainly financial and money capital). State operations have to some degree been reduced to the role of finding ways to promote public subventions to capital, and a favourable business climate. SAPs have become the answer to welfarism, nationalism, socialism, and so on. But then, despite the implementation of all these measures, even the IFIs have finally admitted that there has been no convergence of per capita income levels between the North and the South as it was anticipated as a result of globalization (IMF 1997: 72). They have shown that the number of low-income countries has actually risen from 52 in 1965 to 105 in 1995. As UNCTAD (1997: 2) finally admitted, 'capital has gained in comparison with labour, and profit shares have risen everywhere'.

## Internationalization of Money Markets?

Here, the immediate questions that arise are: How did globalization come about and what is new about it? Don't things identified as globalizing elements amount to mere naming, whereby a new label is used to describe what Daniel Bell (1973) had termed the 'post-industrial society' in the 1970s? Given the debates surrounding the whole question of globalization and its consequences, are there any quantitative or qualitative indicators to measure the degree of this process or lack of it? In which way, for example, can ordinary people realize what globalization is, judging by their own standards? Why is it that some of the basic experiences have to be re-qualified, even if not rationally explained, as globalization? Isn't the uncritical acceptance of globalization an attempt to turn vices into virtues?

As the studies in this book have demonstrated, globalization in one way or another has been responsible for the erosion of people's welfare, job destruction and mass unemployment. It has thrown people into deeper immiseration and resulted in tensions. One aspect which is apparent to all analysts is the fact that what marks the period termed globalization is that the world economy is more open than it was during the inter-war period. With the network of computers the world financial markets have hooked-up around the clock trading, with take-over specialists busy buying and selling off corporations, regardless of what they are producing or the fact that millions of workers will be unemployed.

The developments in communication technology, whereby the world is now more or less linked through computer networks and the Internet by the telephone line, allowing shopping, discussion forums, downloading of information, etc., it is said, has disembodied experience.[1] The media has substituted itself for the rich order that the world once knew, of nature, needs, art, aesthetics, religion. What exists, instead, are theories of chaos and complexity, with chaos being seen as a kind of order without periodicity, while complexity refers to the complex systems in which a host of independent agents act with each other to produce spontaneous self-organization. The theories of everything simply suggest that there are limits, serious ones, to our scientific knowledge. Hence, the demolition of the 'grand narratives', particularly those theories that pose questions of human emancipation.

In sum, what marks this period, unlike the previous stages of capitalism, is the fact that what exists is what has been characterized as 'disorganized capitalism', of a 'consumer society and mass production'. Above all, production is now no longer the determining aspect, but markets and stock exchanges. It is a period when consumer dominance is the new focus of society and not real needs, and individuals are integrated into this consumer society through seduction or repression. The period is marked by the dominance of the 'supermarket ideology' disseminated by the media, which goes as far as defining 'love' in terms of the relationship between a person and his/her car, or 'revolution' as a new brand of soap, a microwave or a washing machine. Therefore, it is possible for the state to withdraw from social provisioning, since the market can fill the vacuum. To the extent that markets can create conditions for development and human welfare, the state in its current form can only confine itself to management of law and order. In this regard, it no longer requires social policies for purposes of legitimation, as it was previously the case before the advent of this stage of capitalism. Rather than the state playing statistics, it is now the upper class doing so, while the middle class play the stock market and the lower classes await fortunes from bingo: the best person wins!

Simply, what we have is the dominance of a universalistic cult (something of an intellectual movement) of a programme of desired ends rather than an empirically supported understanding of more general trends with regard to the various activities internationally. Waters (1995: 158), who admits to making 'sweeping and occasionally offensive claims', predicts the results of globalization:

> In a globalized world there will be single society and culture occupying the planet. This society and culture will probably not be harmoniously integrated although it might conceivably be. Rather it will probably tend towards higher levels of differentiation, multiplicity and chaos. There will be no central organizing government and no tight set of cultural preferences and prescriptions. In so far

> as culture is unified it will be extremely abstract, expressing tolerance for diversity and individual choice. Importantly, territoriality will disappear as an organizing principle for social and cultural life, it will be a society without borders and spatial boundaries (1995: 3).

Thus, the process conceptualised by right wing utopianism. Globalization in these terms can only be grasped as a salvation to the bourgeois image from its critics, and it is in direct continuity with the 'post-industrial theories' of the 1970s.

The theory itself, is an expression of the rise of the 'new capitalist classes' of the 'post-industrial' era in the 1970s, based in the media, finance, advertising, academia, merchandizing and international stock-exchange. They emerged via the new speculative forms of accumulation based on finances and plunder of natural resources, rather than productive investments of the formerly productive 'old capitalist classes'. It is in this respect, for example, that one can understand why oil and tourism are the biggest industries respectively in the world, followed by the communication industry. Through corporate and finance capital which was highly mobile, the whole world was turned into speculative markets, whereby they entered and left at any time regardless of the long-term goals of the particular country. The main preoccupation was to purchase equity and bonds through stock exchange and financial markets. They were mainly involved in the buying and selling of rights—whether investments in liquid assets or existing assets which were being privatized. These new forms of accumulation had no interest in investment and development of new industries, but in commercial real estate and 'mercantilist' forms of profit making.

The 'new middle class' completely recast even the notion of work as the activity that provides individual motivation, social integration and systemic reproduction. Instead, what became central was consumer conduct and freedom in the market as the cognitive and moral focus of life, which had the efficacy to integrate society and manage its system. In this regard, even the 'grand narratives' to legitimate power, which were necessary in the past, had become obsolete. The role of the intellectuals who formerly did this work of legitimation also became obsolete, including the traditional roles of knowledge and its production. Legitimation, in the form of social policies, as an instrument of power had been replaced by the seduction of the consumer by the market, and where this failed, by repression. Thus, the withdrawal of the state from the social sphere, since, if the markets were playing that important role, there was no need to justify the state and its activities as true and moral.

The origin of these new capitalist classes is in the very history of the emergence of the crisis itself in the early 1970s. This aspect has not been examined very much in the studies in this book, since it has been taken for granted. But in order to make sense of the functioning of the modern forms of finance and multilateral capital, it may be necessary to highlight them a bit here. Only in this way can one make sense of what is being suggested below as the way forward.

The beginning of the global economic crisis and the emergence of the new forms of accumulation based on financial speculation coincided with the crisis of the model for accumulation and accelerated development in Africa of the first decade of independence, which was formulated by the World Bank. The model had stressed the need for state intervention as means to achieve industrialization. Within this context, developmentalism (the post-colonial model) was premised on the need for the concentration of powers in the executive arm of the state with promises to bring about social services, industries and infrastructure to the people. In return, people were expected to accept a high degree of economic control and at the same time offer unified political loyalty, therefore, they were politically and socially demobilized in terms of their organizational capacities.

This model seemingly registered reasonable rates of growth in a number of countries. Industry in Africa grew at the rate of 7.5 per cent between 1960 and 1975 and the GDP growth rates between 1965 and 1973 were at 6.1 per cent. The state was the major source of investments, employment and social services (Bangura 1992: 89). The accumulation model resulted in a profound crisis by the late 1970s when most Sub-Saharan African countries began experiencing negative per capita GDP growth. This fell from 6.1 per cent in 1965-73 to -1.3 per cent in 1987. This was accompanied by a drastic decline in the rates of growth in agriculture, industry and services. Exports began to decline to the extent that the total debt of Sub-Saharan African countries increased from USD 21.1 billion in 1976 to USD 137.8 billion in 1987 (91-9).

By early 1970s, the crisis being faced by African countries was a crisis of the states. They had become non-responsive and non-accountable to their subjects, since in the context of Africa, social policies were part and parcel of development policies in general as seen in the trade-offs made between society and the state in the post-colonial period. In the context of Africa, social policy meant guaranteeing some basic social rights. With the attack on social provisioning by IFIs, what became new in social policy was the question of purchasing private insurance and the creation of social security and welfare systems which are dual and stratified within differential market-clearing rates of pay, regardless of the fact that there are people who are poor or unemployed.

The states had become completely dominated by the multilateral and trans-national institutions, increasingly becoming a powerless institution as far as powers to control the movement of financial and money capital was concerned. In reality, the paradox of the SAPs, like the globalization process, is that the tendency of the state to intervene in economic affairs has tended to increase over the years. This is regardless of the political, economic and ideological rhetoric. This tendency has tended to increase when its effectiveness has been on the decline. Part of the reason is that SAPs measures which seek to reduce public expenditure, human development and welfare are incompatible with democracy and human rights. People tend to resist some of the measures. Practically, this has necessitated the expansion of state bureaucracy with a weakening power in the economic sphere.

It is perhaps in this context that one can understand why the IFIs have become obsessed with the question of 'good governance' and capacity building in recent years. They have begun to express the need for strong states that can facilitate the integration of the African countries in the capitalist global economy. That is states that can make effective interventions in terms of adjustments to cope with inflation, trade policies, tax incentives, export subsidies, privatization, sectoral policies (in terms of master plans and integration of activities), research policies, regulations and controls. It is essentially an attempt by the IFIs to make sure that the new type of the state is able to effectively control the rebellious populations and restructure the balance of class forces, so that trans-national and multinational capital is able to operate without any major hindrances.

Under such conditions, it is clear that the state in its current form in Africa cannot guarantee its tasks of welfarism, unless it is reorganized. The problem is that alternatives to the monetarist globalization ideology have not been problematized nor sufficiently elaborated. It is this which is more demanding: to transcend the assumptions so fashionably current that 'There Is No Alternative' (TINA - à la Thatcher). To take 'for granted that maximum growth, and therefore productivity and competitiveness, are the ultimate and sole goals of human action; or that economic forces cannot be resisted'. (Bourdeau 1998: 30) The irresponsibilization of the state as far as welfare issues are concerned and the removal of the notion of the public and public interests, currently taking place more or less mark the defeat of the achievements which had been made by social movements and social sciences in the past. It is essentially submitting us to the 'belief' in the values of the economy—the 'return of individualism' (self-help, self–employment, cost-sharing, etc) and the destruction of all philosophical foundations of welfarism and collective responsibility towards poverty, misery, sickness, misfortunes, education, etc.

## The Way Forward

What the studies in this book have been able to demonstrate unanimously is the fact that globalization is a capitalist process which is emphatically economistic. It has been indexed as one of the main causes of the decline of national economies in Africa. The power of globalization is regarded as manifesting itself through the flows in the financial markets of big capital which 'is able to manipulate and destabilize', as Magubane's study in this book amply demonstrates. It is this process, which has led to the loss of sovereignty of nation-states in Africa, and hence the neglect of the basic social needs of the people. Virtually all the studies have demonstrated the fact that social policy issues in Africa have always been linked to socio-economic development, as a dynamic process with a wide coverage ranging from basic human needs and well-being to industrial processes that can promote economic growth for redistribution and human development. It is for this reason that one can understand why the development models of the post-independence period were premised on the fight against 'poverty, ignorance and disease', and not pure economic considerations.

Analyses of the relationships between globalization and social policy in this book have clearly established that there are enormous consequences as far as the debates on the state are concerned. The multinational firms have gained control over everything to the extent that they can do whatever they please. These studies seem to imply the fact that laissez-faire government policies have taken for granted issues such as skill-biased changes in the world, the reduced bargaining power of the producers. The latter is clearly a result of their being fragmented class–wise and even territorially. Under the current conditions, whereby mass retrenchments have been almost the norm, and the unemployed secretly wish the enterprises would fire those employed so that they would be employed, and the neighbouring country is a competing enemy for capital or higher prices of exports, and the persistence of market ideology, the nation-state in Africa is rendered incapable of delivering social and welfare services.

Thus, gaps that need to be filled in further studies include a proper understanding of the situation of the African poor masses as social actors capable of making interventions and reconstructing other organizational capacities, including states which can effectively deal with the global economy for their mutual survival. Most important in this regard should be the possibilities to deal with the differentials in access to land and natural resources in the context of redressing gender, class, race, age, ethnic, national, and other forms of imbalances, while at the same time problematizing citizenship in the global context, which over the years has contested the very humanity of the African masses as citizens of this world.

All the above points will require closer analysis with regard to ascertaining a way forward, beyond the poverty alleviation measures being undertaken so far. These do not seem to have any positive impact, either on the urban or on the rural poor. What are in demand are measures to eradicate poverty. Access to land and natural resources and their control have become thorny issues causing socio-economic and political unrest all over the continent. Citizenship is being distinguished as being formal or substantive and in this sense creates irregularities in access to political and social rights (Mamdani 1996). And this is the question that is being posed, for example, by the refugee crisis in Africa, the declaration that Kenneth Kaunda is not a citizen of Zambia, xenophobia in South Africa and Côte d'Ivoire.

With the weakening of the power of the nation-states to control capital and deliver social and welfare provisioning in their current form, it would seem that the reconceptualization of these issues can yield some fruits if done so within a pan-territorial/pan-African context. It is necessary to grasp the issues of dealing with poverty and other social and political malaise within social, economic and political organizational forms that transcend the current boundaries, so that the workers of the multinational companies and farmers are able to bargain and negotiate continentally rather than compete, for example. These issues will have to be addressed seriously, and further investigations need to be done to ensure a way forward.

In sum, to stand against this destruction of all those ideals associated with public services, equality of rights, rights to education, health, culture, social justice, citizenship as well as access to land, and in order to rehabilitate human emancipatory tendencies in the context of Africa, it seems it is necessary to reconceptualize the state beyond the 1884 territorial boundaries. 'State building' and 'Nation building', in their current form lead to balkanisation (as witnessed currently in the form of attempts to come with a concept of citizenship which includes or excludes certain categories of people in attempts to please capital). They lead to concerted defeats in attempts to control and govern economies, and hence be in a position to be more responsive to human needs. Salvation lies in the renewal of a militant Pan-Africanist identity (of those who have been enslaved, colonized, dominated and neo-colonized historically), which singles out the collaborators and those who have benefited or still benefit from the current chaos. A United States of Africa may be the answer, even to those refugee problems, problems of exclusion, and an integrated economic system that is responsive to ordinary and poor people's real needs.

## Notes

* Department of Sociology, Univerity of Dar es Salaam.

** IES, University de Cocody, Abidjan, Côte d'Ivoire.

1. Eduardo Galeano's description of this system in the 1970s: '...that the computer program that alarms the banker who alerts the ambassador who dines with the general who summons the president who intimidates the minister who threatens the director general who humiliates the manager who yells at the boss who insults the employee who scorns the worker who mistreats his wife who beats the child who kicks the dog' (1983: 30).

## References

Bangura, Y., 1992, 'Authoritarian Rule and Democracy in Africa: A Theoretical Discourse', in L. Rudebeck (ed.) *When Democracy Makes Sense*, Uppsala: AKUT.

Bates, R.H., 1982, *Markets and States in Tropical Africa: The Political Basis of Agricultural Politics*, Berkeley: University of California Press.

Bell, D., 1973, *The Coming of Post-Industrial Society: A Venture into Forecasting*, London: Heinemann.

Bourdeau, B., 1998, *Acts of Resistance: Against the New Myths of our Time*, Cambridge: Polity Press.

Chachage, C.S.L., 1995, 'The Meek shall Inherit the Earth but not the Mining Rights: the Mining Industry and Accumulation in Tanzania', in P. Gibbon, ed., *Liberalized Development in Tanzania: Studies on Accumulation Processes and Local Institutions*, Uppsala: SIAS.

Gibbon, P. & Olukoshi, A.O., 1995, *Structural Adjustment and Socio-Economic Change in Sub-Saharan Africa*, (Report No.102), Uppsala: Nordiska Afrikainstitutet.

Giddens, A., 1990, *The Consequences of Modernity*, Cambridge: Polity.

Harvey, D., 1995, 'Globalization in Question', *Rethinking Marxism*, Vol .8, No. 4.

Hirst, P. & Thomson, G., 1999, 'The Tyranny of Globalization: Myth or Reality?', in F. Buelens ed., *Globalization and the Nation-State*, Cheltenham, UK: Edward Elgar.

Hyden, G., 1983, *No Shortcuts to Progress: African Development Management Perspective*, University of California Press, Berkeley.

MacGaffey, J., 1987, *Entrepreneurs and Parasites: The Struggle for Indigenous Capitalism in Zaire*, Cambridge: Cambridge University Press.

MacGaffey, J., 1991, 'Initiatives from Below: Zaire's "Other Path" of Social and Economic Restructuring', in G. Hyden and M. Bratton eds., *Governance and Politics in Africa: Perestroika without Glasnost*, Boulder: Lynne Rienner.

Mamdani, M., 1996, *Citizen and Subject: Contemporary Africa and the Legacy of Late Colonialism*, Kampala: Fountain Publishers.

Reed, D., 1992, *Structural Adjustment and the Environment*, London: Earthscan Publications.

IMF, 1997, *Globalization: Opportunities and Challenges*, Washington D.C.: World Economic Outlook.

Rothchild, D. & Chazan, N., eds., 1988, *The Precarious Balance: The State and Society in Africa*, Boulder: Westview.

UNCTAD, 1997, *Trade and Development Report: Globalization*, Distribution and Growth, New York: United Nations.

Warren, B., 1980, *Imperialism: Pioneer of Capitalism*, London: Verso.

Waters, M., 1996, *Globalization*, London: Routledge.

World Bank, 1989, *Sub-Saharan Africa: From Crisis to Sustainable Growth*, Washington D.C.: World Bank.

World Bank, 1991, *Restructuring Economies in Distress*, Washington D.C.: World Bank.

# THE PUBLISHER

The Council for the Development of Social Science Research in Africa (CODESRIA) is an independent organisation whose principal objectives are facilitating research, promoting research-based publishing and creating multiple forums geared towards the exchange of views and information among African researchers. It challenges the fragmentation of research through the creation of thematic research networks that cut across linguistic and regional boundaries.

CODESRIA publishes a quarterly journal, *Africa Development*, the longest standing Africa-based social science journal; *Afrika Zamani*, a journal of history; the *African Sociological Review; African Journal of International Affairs (AJIA); Identity, Culture and Politics: An Afro-Asian Dialogue;* and the *Journal of Higher Education in Africa.* Research results and other activities of the institution are disseminated through 'Working Papers', 'Monograph Series', 'CODESRIA Book Series', and the *CODESRIA Bulletin.*

www.ingramcontent.com/pod-product-compliance
Ingram Content Group UK Ltd.
Pitfield, Milton Keynes, MK11 3LW, UK
UKHW040228290926
15471UKWH00001B/68